Paradox at Play

Paradox at Play

METAPHOR IN MEISTER ECKHART'S SERMONS

WITH PREVIOUSLY UNPUBLISHED SERMONS

CLINT JOHNSON

The Catholic University Press
Washington, D.C.

Copyright © 2023
The Catholic University of America Press

All rights reserved.

Library of Congress Cataloging-in-Publication Data
NAMES
Johnson, Clint (Daniel Clinton). Paradox at play.
Eckhart, Meister, –1327. Sermons. | Selections. English.
TITLE
Paradox at Play: Metaphor in Meister Eckhart's Sermons:
with Previously Unpublished Sermons / Clint Johnson.
DESCRIPTION
Washington, D.C.: The Catholic University of America Press, [2022] | Includes bibliographical references and index. | Summary: "Fresh translations of Meister Eckhart's sermons are made available in this volume: three for the first time in English and sixteen others for the first time since C. de B. Evans translated them in 1924 and 1931, long before the critical editions of the manuscripts were published in 2003. Other important sermons are included in the translations as well. They are meant to improve upon previous translations through sensitivity to Eckhart's metaphorical repertoire and his subtle word choice and phrasing. The monograph portion of the volume describes Eckhart's metaphors and how they work together to form a cohesive whole. All of his homiletic choices are argued to be in service of the greater goal: catalyzing transformative change in his audience by insisting on his paradoxes and jarring people out of their customary way of relating to God and themselves"—Provided by publisherIDENTIFIERS
LCCN 2022059029 (print) | LCCN 2022059030 (ebook)
ISBN 9780813235288 | ISBN 9780813235295 (ebook)
SUBJECTS
LCSH: Eckhart, Meister, –1327. | Metaphor—Religious aspects—Christianity.
CLASSIFICATION
LCC B765.E34 P37 2022 (print) | LCC B765.E34 (ebook)
DDC 189/.5—dc23/eng/20230309

Book design by Burt&Burt
Interior set using Warnock Pro, Minion Pro, & Meta Pro

FOR MY FAMILY,
WHOSE LOVE
IS A REFLECTION
OF THE DIVINE

Introduction   1

PART I

1. Situating Eckhart in History   9
2. The Problem with Interpreting Eckhart   61
3. Metaphor, Paradox, and the Spirit of Play   71
4. Eckhart's Metaphorical Repertoire: 87
   Rhetorical Details and Metaphorological Dynamics
5. Eckhart's Metaphorical Repertoire: 115
   Metaphors of Desire and Personal Experience
6. Eckhart's Metaphorical Repertoire: 127
   Passivity, Activity, and the Individual
7. Metaphors and the Development of Modern Thought   171
8. The Relevance of Eckhart Today   189

Abbreviations of Frequently Cited Works   207
Bibliography   209

PART II

Eckhart's Sermons: Translator's Note   225
Sermon 52: *Beati pauperes spiritu*   226
Sermon 2: *Intravit Iesus in quoddam castellum*   233
Sermon 24: *Induimini dominum Iesum Christum*   239
Sermon 40: *Manete in me*   243
Sermon 54a: *Unser herre underhuop*   247
Sermon 64: *Die sele die wirt ain mit gotte vnd nit veraint*   251
Sermon 87: *Ecce, dies veniunt, dicit dominus*   253
Sermon 88: *Post dies octo vocatum est nomen eius Iesus*   257
Sermon 89: *Angelus domini apparuit*   260

Sermon 90a: *Sedebat Iesus docens in templo*	263
Sermon 90b: *Sedebat Iesus docens in templo*	267
Sermon 91: *Voca operarios, et redde illis mercedem suam*	271
Sermon 92: *Cum sero factum esset*	277
Sermon 93: *Quae est ista, quae ascendit quasi aurora*	280
Sermon 94: *Non sunt condignae passiones huius temporis*	286
Sermon 95a: *Os suum aperuit sapientiae*	291
Sermon 95b: *Os suum aperuit sapientiae*	296
Sermon 96: *Elisabeth pariet tibi filium*	303
Sermon 97: *Qui manet in me*	307
Sermon 98: *Nisi granum frumenti*	311
Sermon 100: *Et quaerebat videre Iesum, quis esset*	315
Sermon 106a: *Aemulor enim vos Dei aemulatione*	319
Sermon 106b: *Aemulor enim vos Dei aemulatione*	323
Sermon 106c: *Aemulor enim vos Dei aemulatione*	326
Sermon 106d: *Aemulor enim vos Dei aemulatione*	329
Sermon 107: *Qui vult venire post me*	332
Sermon 108: *Si non lavero te, non habebis partem mecum*	336
Sermon XXIV.2: *Domus mea domus orationis est*	340
Concordance	345
Index	361

Introduction

By nature, surprises inspire curiosity. We enjoy being stirred to movement, and surprises set our minds in motion. A surprise indicates that expectation does not match experience. It is a reaction to encountering the unfamiliar when we expect the familiar. Eckhart's rhetoric is surprising, but it is not necessarily *shocking* in the sense of being offensive. In fact, to many of his modern readers, the surprise felt in reading Eckhart is tinged with *hope*. We will return to explain that hope with the help of Huston Smith at the very end. For now, let us try to understand surprise. A surprise catalyzes interest in proportion to the importance of the things it touches. Surprises invite us to think further, to devote energy to making the unfamiliar familiar. We cannot help being surprised when we hear a fourteenth century master of theology say this: "It would be a small thing to me that 'the Word was made flesh' for man in Christ as a person distinct from me unless he was also made flesh in me personally so that I too might be the Son of God."[1] Is he actually saying that the historical birth of Christ does not matter? No, but our attention is sparked by the idea that God become flesh in Christ is anything other than the highest importance. So what is he doing here? The meaning and purpose of the Incarnation are at stake. Eckhart does not doubt or deny the historical Christ. He merely points to the spiritual importance of the Incarnation in and to the individual as paramount. Why? Because whatever is God is of the highest importance and everything else has what

---

[1] LW III, 101:14–102. Meister Eckhart, *In Ioh.* n.117, trans. Bernard McGinn in *Meister Eckhart: The Essential Sermons, Commentaries, Treatises and Defense* (Mahwah, NJ: Paulist Press, 1981), 167. Translation modified.

importance it has from God, including both Christ and the divinity of each individual insofar as we refer to God within.[2]

Consider what Eckhart says in speaking of Christ's birth in the beginning of a Christmas sermon: "What does it help me if this birth is always happening and yet it does not happen in me? All that matters is that it happens in me."[3] Likewise, "He gives birth to me, his Son, the same Son. I say more: he gives birth to me not only as his Son, but rather, he gives birth to me and me to him, and to me as his being and his nature."[4] Are we to understand not only that we are sons of God but also that we are the Son of God, Christ himself? This is the doorway to understanding what Eckhart is doing: he compels us to direct attention and energy to understanding what we are as individuals and how individuality relates to God, just as Christ was both God and man.

It is no coincidence that the locus of our surprise in Eckhart's rhetoric is the nature of the individual. Though it is not often given enough attention when telling the story of Western intellectual history, we can explain why many philosophical and intellectual movements arose when they did if we look at changes in our conception of what an individual is in relation to other individuals, to nature, and to the divine. We will see that the changes occurring in Eckhart's time prefigure the intellectual and cultural developments of the Renaissance. While Eckhart looks medieval in certain aspects of his thought, the novelty in his theological ideas and even the subtle novelty in the way he expressed his ideas may be usefully[5] traced to a single source: the changing conception of the individual that would ultimately give birth to the modern world.

Eckhart's words about Christ may leave us with a peculiar feeling. There is something theologically commonplace but beautiful about contemplating

---

[2] This introduction's rhetoric is a microcosm of both the argument of this book and the sense of Eckhart's thought—the terms chosen (motion, surprise, et cetera), the verbs, little connecting words ("in," "at," and others), the contention that we as individuals can become the only-begotten Son of God, the book's conclusion about the relevance of Eckhart today and the phenomenology of our reaction to reading him, and even the fact that this ostensibly wild idea traces back to both Augustine and Origen.

[3] Eckhart, Sermon 101, DW IV, 1:336.4–5. Eckhart cites Augustine. He may have been referring to *Sermo 189 in Nat. Dom.*, 6c.3 or to *Confessions*, IX.12.19. We also find a similar passage in Origen's *Homilies on Jeremiah IX*, *Homilies on Luke XXII*, and *Homilies on Judges II*.

[4] Eckhart, Sermon 6, DW I, 109.8–10.

[5] Though it appears that I am making a hardline philosophical claim here about history, this one word should serve as a reminder that the ultimate goal of this historical narrative is to aid the reader in coming to see the world more like Eckhart did and to enable more sympathetic readings thereby. In other words, it is useful for us to consider the possibility that this one undercurrent *caused* all of the conceptual and rhetorical novelty we see in Eckhart.

divinity flowing through even the smallest bit of nature in the ground of its being (God is "He Who Is" and is "to be" itself, as we read in Exodus 3:14). Yet we struggle to square our usual way of thinking about who "I" am with Eckhart's linking of our being to God himself (I am his Son and I likewise give birth to God). Am I my individual being, someone with a name and a history, full of will and desire? Yes, but I could not be at all without my very existence. If this is God, then we have an intuitive but difficult paradox. This paradoxical feeling is just that: a *feeling* that complements the intellectual recognition of the conceptual dissonance that paradoxes contain. That feeling is what compels us to look further. The topic is both clearly surprising and important in what it implies. It invites us to comprehend how we can be both God and man as Christ was.

This may point us in the direction of understanding how Eckhart provokes interest. Does this explain his surge in popularity in the twentieth and twenty-first centuries? In the past century, there has been a surge of interest in his works in spheres ranging from Western Buddhism to his own intellectual orbit in orthodox Catholicism. To answer *why* we are drawn to Eckhart, we will need to understand why his rhetoric seems shocking today and why it was not *more* shocking during his time. Doing this implies several distinct goals. First, we must recognize the possibility that Eckhart's rhetoric arose from changes in the intellectual undercurrents with the nature of the individual. Next, we must understand what metaphor is, as well as why and how it affects us. Only then will we be in a position to fully appreciate Eckhart's metaphorics and to undertake a detailed exploration of his metaphorical repertoire. With all the pieces in place, we can then more confidently propose an answer to the question of what draws us to him today. This will also cast light on the direction of religion in the Western world in the twenty-first century.

Despite his unusual rhetoric, Eckhart's mysticism is essentially traditional, heir of a lineage that includes Augustine and Dionysius. In its ground, all mysticism points to divine oneness. If oneness could be different for different theological or practical approaches, it would not be oneness.[6] Eckhart's mysticism is "traditional" in this way. Beyond this, Eckhart's use of Christian ideas, stories, and practices is traditional insofar as it continues the orthodox traditions of Augustinian theology and Dionysian negative theology. Though certainly orthodox, the elements from these theologies are less familiar to mainstream thought today. Likewise, some of Eckhart's exegetical practices were more common in his time than they are in ours.

6 See Eckhart, *In Sap.* n.146.

These factors, compounded by his self-conscious choice of rhetoric that was meant to shock, cause him to appear more radical than he actually was.

Though we commonly hear of the mystery of the Trinity and the Incarnation, we move on to other topics and don't often hear more than that. Eckhart, by contrast, focuses on the mysteries and little else. Part of what is so important for us to hear today is the voice of apophatic theologians like Eckhart who tell us not to be satisfied with merely recognizing the mysteries as paradoxes. He exhorts us to go deeper and make spiritual progress that is otherwise stalled by resignation.

Eckhart's own rhetoric persistently orbited around a nonconceptual core, moving out into the conceptual divisions necessary for theological speculation only to quickly snap back to God. At all times, he designed this motion to push his audience to think in a way that conduced to their own return to God. Similarly, the discussion here is intended to establish a trajectory of thought that will move us closer to Eckhart's own imaginative horizon, enabling us to see the world more clearly through his eyes. As Hans Blumenberg said about his own speculative narrative of what he calls a "protohistory of theory," perhaps the best we can hope for is a story that "fits" our needs. The notion of "fit" is a part of the overall *fitness* of a story, measured by how well it fits like a piece of a jigsaw puzzle with our cognitive needs. Such a story is useful to us insofar as it continues to fit with our needs and helps to produce coherent understanding. Consequently, though we will make use of the particular philosophical systems and ideas of Blumenberg, William James, Lakoff and Johnson, and Erazim Kohàk, their projects do not need to be embraced in order for their ideas to be usefully appropriated toward this project's eminently pragmatic end.

In detail then, our approach will be as follows. After introducing Eckhart, we will draw a historical arc through the changes in the notion of the individual over time. This will suggest that Eckhart's rhetoric was a natural byproduct of the underlying intellectual causes that would ultimately lead to the development of the modern world. We will also see that the treatment of paradox matters, particularly with the question of whether his paradoxes can be explained away or otherwise domesticated without requiring us to change the way that we think and see the world. We will see that Eckhart insists upon his paradoxes. This creates a stubbornly persistent novelty that pushes us away from habitual, conceptual thought and toward immediate experience. Having done the work of understanding how metaphors work and why Eckhart's techniques with them are effective, we can then explore Eckhart's metaphorical repertoire in detail. Though his use of language appears wild, it is not loose. His metaphors all fit tightly together. This will become evident after looking closely at each piece of his metaphorics and the complementary rhetorical techniques. We will then be in a good position to look at some broader theological themes for Eckhart and his times that were important in the transition from medieval to Renaissance thought: cosmology, natural knowledge, and curiosity. With each, Eckhart at first looks medieval. Once we peer beneath the surface, however, we find that his account of the individual, insofar as he or she is divine, undermines the otherwise traditional-looking structure. His account of "living without a why" exemplifies this trend. His view of the cosmos is Aristotelian and consequently embraces teleology, especially with respect to creation existing for man's benefit and all aspects of the world benevolently designed to lure us back to God. Nevertheless, this teleology unravels as Eckhart describes what it is to live without a why. Having arrived at a point where we can describe why Eckhart appeals to us today, we will conclude with a reflection on what the recent interest in Eckhart tells us about the direction for religion more generally in the West.

As an ancillary philosophical goal in presenting a strategy like this to understand Eckhart, I hope to accomplish a push in the direction of reorienting philosophical tendencies, away from leveling cultural differences in order to translate ideas into comparable forms. Instead, by emphasizing continuity and demonstrating subtle changes in what is most metaphysically fundamental, more sympathetic readings become possible. This is done by analyzing rhetorical devices in order to gain insight into the tendencies for thought that produced such writing and made it intelligible to others. Blumenberg was right to push for a metaphorology of this kind. Instead of doing typical textual analysis, analyzing concepts, and thinking in terms of definitions in order to translate the argument into a form that is acceptable to our own conception of what an argument is, we should look beneath the concepts and attempt to understand the way in which the modes of expression reflect the needs of the cultural milieu. For Eckhart in particular, once we see that his unusual expressions fit the needs of his time, we can look past his "new and unusual" style and see more clearly that his message itself is not so new and unusual.[7] If this project succeeds, it will not simply show Eckhart to be a forerunner of modernity. Rather, it will hint at the possibility that the germ of the modern worldview was already present in a substantial way in thinkers who are often considered distinctly medieval. My aim is

---

7 *nova et rara*, LW I, 149.

to provide a subtle and sympathetic reading of Eckhart, while suggesting that Blumenberg's tools provide an effective means for describing how the unusual rhetorical techniques that he uses in his mystical speech suitably addressed the needs of his time.

Finally, my motivation to translate the texts in this volume arose from the study of Eckhart's metaphors. That left me peculiarly situated to understand why Eckhart used certain words and phrases consistently in his vernacular works. As I attempt to lay plain in the notes to the translations, this led to conscientious choices of words in English that would enable Eckhart's spirit to shine through. After all, if the translator does not recognize an instance of a metaphor and why it likely appears where it does, the resulting translation may obfuscate the metaphor and deny the reader the opportunity to recognize it. My hope is that the understanding of his rhetoric that I gained over the years of studying Eckhart has enabled me to create readable translations that are true to Eckhart's own spirit and of value to the community of scholars and readers who are interested in his works today.

PART I

1

Situating Eckhart in History

Eckhart von Hochheim was probably born into a family of feudal knights near Erfurt in Thuringia in Germany around 1260 and died on January 28, 1328.[1] We know very little about his personal life and nothing of his formative years. Nevertheless, he became one of the most influential theologians of his time. His work influenced Johannes Tauler, Henry Suso, Nicholas of Cusa, and the writing of the *Theologia Germanica* (also called the *Theologia Deutsch*), which in turn influenced Martin Luther. In many cases, Eckhart's ideas were carried forward without his name. For example, in one dialogue, Suso as a "disciple" speaks with Eckhart as the "nameless Wild One."[2]

Eckhart first appears in the historical record on April 18, 1294, when he preached as a *lector Sententiarum* (Reader of the Sentences), also called the *baccalaureus formatus*, on Easter.[3] Since we know the characteristic steps that preceded someone becoming a baccalaureus as a Dominican, the latest date for Eckhart's birth is around 1260, with some likelihood that it was a few years before that. This timing is important because it places Eckhart in the Dominican order and perhaps even in Paris when several important events occurred. In 1277, the bishop of Paris, Étienne (Stephen) Tempier, issued an

---

[1] Walter Senner, "Meister Eckhart's Life, Training, Career, and Trial," in *A Companion to Meister Eckhart*, edited by Jeremiah M. Hackett (Boston: Brill, 2013), 77. In this piece, Senner provides a careful, detailed summary of research and evidence we have to that point on Eckhart's life.

[2] See Colledge and McGinn, *Essential Eckhart*, 16 and 16n33. Notably, he also describes a vision he had where the "blessed [*selig*] Master Eckhart" was "divinized in God" (Colledge and McGinn, *Essential Eckhart*, 18). Colledge explains this and tells us that "there were in Suso's lifetime two German Dominicans known as 'Meister Eckhart,' and it was the tradition of their order that it was not the friar condemned for heresy who had appeared to Suso in this vision, but the other of the same name" (*Essential Eckhart*, 19).

[3] LW V, 157

expanded version of his formal condemnation of radical Aristotelianism from 1270, this time including 219 doctrines, some of which were held by Thomas Aquinas. Aquinas worked to make Aristotelianism palatable, and while he ultimately succeeded, was canonized in 1323, and has since been named a doctor of the Church, the debate over his legacy raged throughout Eckhart's life, from 1274 (when Eckhart was very young) until Thomas's canonization a few years before Eckhart's death in 1328. Prior to Aquinas's canonization, Eckhart saw Tempier's successor reverse the condemnation of 1277, which may have encouraged his thinking that "better theologians than those then prosecuting him in Cologne had been forced to eat their words."[4]

We should notice that while Eckhart was the only medieval master to be investigated for heresy, many of the great theologians of this time were subject to other investigations and censored. In Eckhart's defense, he speaks of "our times" (*nostris temporibus*) in referring to his fellow Dominicans Thomas Aquinas and Albert the Great, a statement that has led to speculation that Eckhart was in Paris in 1286.[5] He may have even been the student of Albert the Great (d. 1280) if he was in Paris around 1277, as Joseph Koch speculated.[6]

Since he rose to prominence in the Dominican order, we do know something of Eckhart's travels since we have documents that place him in different cities for important events and appointments within the order. A *baccalaureus* was a necessary stepping-stone to becoming a *magister*, a master of theology, the highest academic title. We know from his *Councils on Discernment* around the time that he was a baccalaureus that Eckhart was elected the prior of Erfurt by the local community and was appointed as the vicar of Thuringia by his provincial, who may have been Dietrich of Freiberg. Not long after, Eckhart obtained his licentiate and became a master in 1302, which is why we today call him "Meister" Eckhart. Most of Eckhart's Latin commentaries and the *Parisian Questions* probably date from this time. Eckhart spent the academic year 1302–3 teaching in Paris. He was elected prior provincial of Saxony in 1303 and general vicar in Bohemia in 1307. It is likely that he began

---

4 Edmund Colledge, "Historical Data" in *Essential Eckhart*, 7.

5 Senner, "Meister Eckhart's Life, Training, Career, and Trial," 12.

6 Senner, "Meister Eckhart's Life, Training, Career, and Trial," 12. We might also notice that another Dominican, William of Moerbeke, made a translation of Proclus's *Elements* in 1268. As a result of this translation, the assumed apostolic origin of Dionysius's works that had been largely unchallenged since Maximus the Confessor came to be doubted. Though Eckhart does not comment on Dionysius's authenticity, since he was a Neoplatonic thinker it is evident that such ideas were in the air in the same circles in which he moved.

his *Opus Tripartitum* (Three-Part Work), a work that was never finished, at this time. Many of the sermons translated in this volume also date from his time as provincial from 1303–1311.[7] They were included in the *Paradisus anime intelligentis,* a collection of Dominican sermons collected probably around 1340 in Erfurt, many of which were attributed directly to Eckhart. Elected prior of Speyer in 1310, he was not confirmed at the general chapter the next year but instead sent back to Paris to teach in 1311. Eckhart shared only with Aquinas the honor of having been sent twice to Paris for this purpose though he may have also been sent to ameliorate a problem with the way the order was perceived in Paris at that time. He appears next in Strasbourg in 1313, possibly because it was a center for female piety and mysticism and flashpoint for the debates surrounding that at the time. Though there is clear affinity between Eckhart's ideas and the well-known female mystics of the time like Mechthild of Magdeburg and Marguerite Porete, recent work examining the connection between them has failed to provide convincing evidence that Eckhart was influenced directly by their ideas.[8] Eckhart also took pains to avoid being confused with the heresy of the Free Spirit in his sermons. Many of the vernacular sermons we have from him may have been given during this time. From 1323 on, Eckhart lived in Cologne, likely teaching advanced students at the *Studium Generale* there.

Though there has been speculation on the dates and places where Eckhart wrote his works, we should perhaps notice that Eckhart's major themes are present throughout his writings. It does not appear as though Eckhart underwent any pronounced changes or development in his ideas over time, a continuity that has frustrated attempts to date his works.[9] Even in the earliest writings we see him as a foil to Aquinas's twofold theology (separating philosophy and revelation), instead insisting upon the unity of philosophy and theology and making use of most of his major themes and metaphors. Since the trial for heresy consumed the last several years of Eckhart's life, we will return to this story when we address the question of Eckhart and the Inquisition in the next chapter.

---

[7] Bernard McGinn, *The Mystical Thought of Meister Eckhart: The Man from Whom God Hid Nothing* (New York: Crossroad, 2001), 5.

[8] Bernard McGinn, ed., *Meister Eckhart and the Beguine Mystics: Hadewijch of Brabant, Mechthild of Magdeburg, and Marguerite Porete* (New York: Bloomsbury, 1997).

[9] See Senner, "Meister Eckhart's Life, Training, Career, and Trial," 32n172, 36n195.

SITUATING ECKHART IN HISTORY

Our first step will be to trace a historical arc through Western intellectual history that describes the emergence of the increasing metaphysical significance of the individual. Too often, we assume that we can read ancient and medieval philosophy through the lens of the modern conception of the individual, not adequately appreciating how this fundamental component of our worldview was substantially different for ostensibly familiar thinkers like Plato and Aristotle. By showing how the conception of the individual changed over time, we will more clearly distinguish elements that are genuinely new in Eckhart's thought. These innovations and novel forms of expression can be largely understood as responses to the changing needs of his time, necessary to effectively reach his audience.

In that same spirit, we will call Eckhart a *mystic* and refer to an individual who *experiences*, since these conventions best fit the needs of people who think with the modern notion of the individual and have that as their starting point. The term "mystic" is used here as a rhetorical expedient, not as a claim about the truth of the application of some theological category. We might say that the words *mystic* and *experience* in this book conspire to create a likely story for a modern reader insofar as they carry the scent of truth and enable the modern reader to rush ahead, catalyzing useful motion.[10]

To understand how the novelty in Eckhart's speech is a natural consequence of casting traditional mysticism in a form that is appropriate to changing historical conditions, we must first describe the salient aspects of those changing conditions and situate his thought within them. This will be done by tracing an arc through intellectual history that shows how the notion of the individual has become ontologically inflated over time. Questioning the nature of the individual can be awkward for us as moderns because contemporary philosophy does not often question what it means to be human, preferring instead to assume that everything in mental experience is fully the province of the individual. Instead of emphasizing difference by cataloguing theological and philosophical positions, historical trends are more easily seen by emphasizing continuity in the changes to the underlying ground of thought that enables the disagreements to occur at all. When properly situated, it will be easier to see that Eckhart was part of the process of the ontological inflation of the individual and that he anticipated future developments. Ultimately, we will see that while much of what Eckhart

---

10 The same spirit informs Buddhist discussions of *anatman* ("no-self").

does is traditional (even the parts that are unfamiliar to us), the "new and unusual" (*nova et rara*) residua are specific to changes in the conception of self. This is more than a philosophical change or metaphysical proposition that can be assented to or denied. It is a part of the "subterranean stratum of thought" that is constitutive of self- and world-understanding.[11] When expressed, it resulted in statements that carried enough of the scent of heresy to arouse suspicion. To see that the audience was more of a problem than the metaphysics, we need only notice that the propositions censored by the bull *In agro dominico* drew primarily from Eckhart's *vernacular* works, where his rhetoric and audience differed from his Latin works while the content remained the same.

A useful way of thinking about intellectual history, starting at least with the Ancient Greeks, is to conceive of a continuum between unity and multiplicity, much like Plato's divided-line metaphor in the *Republic*. On one side is the world of things, finite in time and space, ephemeral, and changing. On the other is the divine, not bound by time and space, eternal, and unchanging. Of particular interest for understanding Eckhart is the way in which the conception of the individual comes to inhabit more and more of the space along the continuum, participating more in the divine unity without ceasing to be spoken of as an individual that also inhabits the realm of multiplicity. Many of the changes in this history can be drawn out by asking the question: at what point should we stop speaking of the individual as individual?

Ontologically expanding the individual has many implications that are not obvious. For example, the capacity for spontaneous action is a natural consequence of individuation. When we read about the life of action (*vita activa*), we most often and naturally connect this with the question of the *vita activa* and *vita contemplativa* rather than the notion of the individual. In fact, however, spontaneous action is enabled by the individual's capacity for creativity. As the individual is less subject to the influence or "possession" of outside forces (as will be described shortly) and consequently loses his or her individual control, the ability of the individual to contain and therefore be responsible for spontaneous action increases. In other words, the individual no longer ceases to be individual in those situations. Therefore, when we see Eckhart ennobling the active life of Martha over the contemplative life of Mary, we may understand this as a direct consequence of the inflated

---

11 Hans Blumenberg, *Paradigms for a Metaphorology*, trans. Robert Savage (Ithaca, N.Y.: Cornell University Press, 2010), 1.

individual capacity for self-created impulse to action without ceasing to be individual. By Eckhart's time, Mary's humble effacing of her individuality in contemplation is no longer a prerequisite for approaching the divine. With the ontologically inflated individual who is capable of spontaneous action, the divine may be approached by remaining within oneself and exercising one's own creative power for spontaneous action as divine. The individual does not have to be left behind if the conception of the individual is inflated to include more than the ephemeral world of change.

Whether this "inflation" was good or bad depends on one's view of what an individual should be. From the standpoint of the modern individual, the inflation was good, a necessary part of the progress toward the modern scientific mind. By contrast, most human societies, especially traditional societies, and to a lesser extent the Ancient Greeks and Christianity before the Renaissance, would have regarded this kind of individual as hubristic and attempting to usurp abilities that properly belong to the divine realm of the eternal. From that standpoint, an individual cannot be temporal and eternal. We too easily think of the shortcomings of previous ages, accustomed as we are to hearing Baconian rhetoric about how their way of seeing the world delayed the inevitable awakening of the modern individual and its capacity for scientific thinking. What may surprise us is that the previous way of viewing the world may in fact be more *salutary*. For our purposes, the negative connotation of "inflation" has purposeful disharmony with modern values, encouraging us to make the effort to understand how previous people saw the world and how it might not just be an embryonic form of our own.[12]

Claude Lévi-Strauss advanced the idea that traditional societies had a "total" understanding of the world, one that admitted of no gaps and made everything familiar: "Its aim is to reach by the shortest possible means a general understanding of the universe—and not only a general but a *total* understanding. That is, it is a way of thinking which must imply that if you don't understand everything, you don't explain anything. This is entirely in contradiction with what scientific thinking does."[13] While he qualifies these statements and says that a total understanding is ultimately an illusion and that his description should not imply that it is the equal of scientific thinking, none of that matters for our purposes. We should instead see that the impulse to close gaps in understanding as quickly as possible grows from the

---

[12] We should notice that this rhetorical direction is for the sake of the modern reader, not for Eckhart. The inflation of the individual was not problem for Eckhart because he had a solution for it.

[13] Claude Lévi-Strauss, *Myth and Meaning: Cracking the Code of Culture* (New York: Schoken Books, 1995), 17.

disharmony and discomfort that we feel with what is unknown and unfamiliar. Though meaning is not obviously at stake here, it is the root of the anxiety in our response. If we understand the world as a whole overflowing with meaning, gaps threaten the harmony of the whole and the efficacy of its function to stave off anxiety. Lévi-Strauss's *bricoleur* works within this framework, doing *bricolage* (using only materials available at the time) by using only existing pieces and the tightly interwoven network of meaning, resulting in explanations that recycle existing understandings in the interest of reinforcing the integrity of the whole rather than taking the scientific path which carries a twofold threat of admitting a genuine gap and looking for a novel explanation. So when Blumenberg said of Nicholas of Cusa, one of the last recognizably medieval figures in his account of the transition to the modern world, that "everything" about his ideas "seems to be designed to prevent the crisis," we should respond: of course it does.[14] The crisis fundamentally threatened the total medieval way of seeing the world. My account of the history of the change in the individual should also be understood as a response to Blumenberg's own account of the change from the medieval to modern world. Blumenberg's thesis in the *Legitimacy of the Modern Age* is that modern thought is legitimate because it is a reoccupation of *function* rather than a mere transposition of substance (as is claimed by those like Karl Löwith who called it a mere secularization). In making this claim, Blumenberg chose two figures to historically bookend the transition from medieval to modern thought: Nicholas of Cusa (1401–64) as medieval and Giordano Bruno (1548–1600) as modern. In part, I am suggesting here that we can turn Blumenberg's own metaphorological analysis to Eckhart and see that a recognizably and arguably "modern" conception of the individual was substantially present more than a century before Nicholas Cusa.

Even if a total understanding is an illusion, our minds rest content with certainty and incur stress without it. While approximate knowledge opened the doors wide for technological advancement, the cost came from its permanent uncertainty, which created existential anxiety that came to full flower in the nineteenth and twentieth centuries.[15] Instead of drawing from the

14 Hans Blumenberg, *The Legitimacy of the Modern Age*, trans. Robert M. Wallace. (Cambridge, Mass.: MIT Press, 1985), 502.
15 Blumenberg dedicated an entire book, *Shipwreck with Spectator*, to tracing changes in the way a single metaphor was used before and after this transition. By the nineteenth century, we start seeing descriptions of being adrift at sea without any land, forced to make new ships out of old shipwrecks, a reference to approximate knowledge's progress without ever achieving certainty that would quell anxiety. Hans Blumenberg, *Shipwreck with Spectator: Paradigm of a Metaphor for Existence*, trans. Robert M. Wallace (Cambridge, Mass.: MIT Press, 1997).

existing storehouse of eternal meaning and purpose that lies beyond the province of each individual, the modern individual creates explanations that are ever better approximations. Such approximate knowledge must also *guess* at meaning and create it, rather than taking it from the safety of eternal knowledge that is beyond our ability to change. After all, looking closely at boundaries between ideas strains teleology. The modern world could only be born in a vacuum of meaning. Writers like Eckhart who understood what was at stake in compressing the Platonic ontological hierarchy saw this coming. Long before Nietzsche responded to the threat of nihilism and advocated for the restoration of meaning in creating our own values, Eckhart's *living without a why* provided a solution to the problem, one that increasingly resonates with readers today who inherit this legacy of existential anxiety. The primary challenge for Eckhart, as true in his time as it is in our own, is that mysticism is difficult, and we have an impulse to quickly close gaps by using whatever conceptual hardware we have that allows us to rest comfortably in familiarity.

While the negative connotation of "inflation," the use of "mysticism" and "experience" serve practical rhetorical purposes, we should also notice a *coincidentia oppositorum* (meeting of opposites) here in the continuum between unity and multiplicity. We can approach mysticism by either eliminating all difference and returning to divine oneness by dissolving all difference into unity (as Parmenides recommended), which annihilates the individual; or, we can approach mysticism from the Heraclitean side, by emphasizing difference and making any abstraction beyond the infinite richness of individuals untenable, which inflates the individual to divine proportions. Whether we reach oneness by annihilating the individual so that it to takes up no ontological space or by inflating it to consume everything, oneness is oneness. Which one is better is merely a practical question.

HISTORICAL ARC
Pre-Homeric Times

In traditional societies, the individual is not at all in a place of privilege. What is individual is transitory, part of the world of change. In a cyclical conception of time, individual life has meaning insofar as it reenacts or participates in what is archetypal and beyond the profane world of change.[16] Lévy-Bruhl

---

[16] One might object that the Greek gods and the deities of traditional societies had more individuality than what we see later. Gods took the forms of people, and some people (especially heroes and emperors) became gods. However, to say that a hero or king is divine is to speak of

recounts an example of this: "'A man told me that when he went fish shooting (with bow and arrow) he pretended to be Kivavia himself.' He did not implore Kivavia's favor and help; he identified himself with the mythical hero."[17] We should notice, of course, that the qualifying word "pretends" is a modern insertion in attempt to preserve our notion of what an individual can be when speaking of divine possession. As he says in recounting another story, "when a man goes to court a woman, if he knows the name of Maraï … he does not whisper, 'Maraï, help me.' … Instead he thinks without even a whisper, 'I am Maraï in person, and I will have her.'"[18] Interestingly, he begins the section by saying, "It is difficult—and perhaps better not to succeed too much—to draw from it an account of participation that is completely clear."[19] He is right, of course, precisely because the participation is itself paradoxical, blending the time-bound world of particulars with the timeless world of myth (for Eliade, *in illo tempore*, in mythical time—that is, outside of time). Insofar as an individual participates in what is archetypal, he or she *ceases* to be individual. By this way of thinking, how could one be both universal and individual[20]?

Classical Greece

The alteration of the conception of the individual from Homer to Plato can be seen through the changes in the use of the word *psyche* (soul). This point is more clearly seen by going into more detail on the variety of words that are involved in this transition, building from David Claus's work. It is clear in looking at the collection of words that describe various feelings, thoughts,

---

them in terms of inhabiting the sacred qua archetypal rather than the profane qua particular. As Joseph Campbell remarks in describing the relation of the kings of traditional societies to the stars, "the king and his court are the heavens themselves on earth." *Masks of God: Primitive Mythology* (New York: Penguin, 1991), 404. In this way, the king qua king is not wholly individual insofar as he fulfills his archetypal role. The gods similarly are archetypes themselves. If we translate the names, it is easy to notice that Jupiter (*zeus* + *piter*, god the father), Cupid (desire) and Pluto (wealth) are thinly veiled archetypes, though they must appear as individuals in their stories insofar as they are characters.

17 Mircea Eliade, *The Myth of the Eternal Return* (Princeton, N.J.: Princeton University Press, 2012), 33. The quoted passage is from F. E. Williams, originally cited by Lucian Lévy-Bruhl in *La Mythologie Primitive* (New York: AMS Press, 1978). Chapter 5 of Lévy-Bruhl's book describes many instances of this kind.

18 Lévy-Bruhl, *La Mythologie Primitive*, 164, my translation.

19 Lévy-Bruhl, *La Mythologie Primitive*, 161, my translation.

20 Though this may be clear, I am trying with this rhetoric to describe preclassical times and also to foreshadow later developments. The idea of Christ as man and God was objected to on similar bases during the Arian controversy.

vitality, and mental strength that what we think of as a "person" was to them a loose, decentralized collection of many forces and actions. The words also referred, in large part, to tangible, temporal events and states rather than abstract, universal ideas. For Homer, the soul was a kind of life-force, something that could be lost. If the soul leaves the body, the person dies. It was more of a motive force than an individual soul. Things with souls move on their own and with apparent purpose (they are *anima*ted, recalling that *anima* is Latin for "soul"). In the sixth century BC, "soul" was used to describe anything self-moving, including plants and animals (and, for Thales, even magnets). By the end of the fifth century BC, it was common to speak of the soul with reference to sensual pleasures like food and drink. During the fifth century, the soul came to be thought of as the source or bearer of moral qualities. This period of time also included the Pythagoreans and their talk of the immortality of the soul, a significant contrast to the Homeric shades which roamed the underworld after death.

As with religion in traditional societies, the Greek gods were archetypes of a kind, forces in the world that could possess the ephemeral individual and move it in a particular direction. Consider the Greek story of Arachne and Athena: Though Athena was the goddess of spinning and weaving, Arachne, a proud girl, took credit for the beautiful tapestries she wove. Since the Greeks knew Arachne owed her skill to Athena, they considered Arachne hubristic for taking credit for what was not rightfully hers. Even in prosaic circumstances, the gods were perpetually involved in what we might call the individual's mental life.

Gorgias appeals to something like *enthousiasmos* (divine possession, literally *en* + *theos*, a god within) in his *Encomium of Helen*. Gods possess the individual in a way that makes certain thoughts, feelings, and actions not wholly individual. "If then the eye of Helen ... gave to her soul an eagerness and response in love, what wonder? If love, a god, prevails over the divine power of the gods, how could a lesser one be able to reject and refuse it?"[21] This is one of Gorgias's arguments for the moral exculpation of Helen, a line of reasoning that is only coherent if Helen temporarily loses her identity as a moral agent when a god overpowers her.

Plato conceived of significance and value just as it always had been conceived of in traditional societies with similarly cyclical conceptions of time.

---

[21] P. P. Matsen, P. B. Rollinson, and Marion Sousa, *Readings from Classical Rhetoric* (Carbondale, Ill.: SIU Press, 1990), 34.

The individual was at the lowest point in the ontology, limited to the world of change. The individual had significance insofar as he or she could be taken up into (participate in, be possessed by) the archetypes. Where we see a change with both Plato and the emerging monotheism of the Egyptians and Hebrews is in the inflated importance that the most fundamental and overarching principles have. In terms of Greek ritual life, Ouranos and Gaea did not figure as prominently as many of the "lesser" deities that were more clearly relevant to daily life. With Plato, however, the Form of the Good occupied the place of privilege. Additionally, the philosopher's goal was not merely to participate in the Forms as Eliade's hunter did with Kivavia. It was also to contemplate and break through with one's "knowledge" (a term that meant far more for Plato than it typically does for us). Plato describes this as a sudden flash of insight into the Form of Beauty in the *Symposium*, as insight that comes through contemplation in the *Phaedrus*, and as a spark of insight that feeds upon itself and grows in the seventh letter.[22] Of course, we should not expect Plato to talk of *union* with the Good; he spoke of *theoria* instead.[23] Plato's conception of the individual was one that inhabited the world of change (even if it was a winged soul, as we read in the *Phaedrus*, which ascends to communion with what is higher). Naturally then, the identity of the individual is lost in some way as we ascend the ontological hierarchy. Going down the hierarchy instead of up, we can also say that the lower levels are *more individuated* and that individuation is their defining characteristic. Given that schema, if the defining characteristic of the individual was to lack the being that characterizes the higher and more universal parts of the great chain of being, it is a contradiction to say that individual ascends the chain while maintaining individuality.

The polytheist equivalent of mysticism was to be in archetypal *participation mystique*,[24] infused with the divine all the time. The same was true for Plato. The difference lies in the fact that, for the polytheist, what was individual fell away during participation. For Plato, the individual participates in and gains "knowledge" of the Forms, enigmatically (and paradoxically)

22 *Symposium*, 210E and 211B; *Phaedrus*, 243E–257B; *Seventh Letter*, 341C.
23 McGinn mentions this with the implication that there is a distinct difference between Platonic mysticism and later Christian mysticism, though he does recognize that Plato is a mystic. However, it is not so clear that this is a difference in mysticism so much as it is a difference in the *manifestation* of mysticism when it finds expression in a particular worldview. As stated in the introduction, if ineffable oneness differed from one mystic to the next, it would not be oneness.
24 The term was initially Lévy-Bruhl's, though it was co-opted by Carl Jung. It refers to a relationship where identity between subject and object is not clearly able to be distinguished.

being at once both individual and not individual. The West inherited this part of Plato's legacy. As we will see, though we arguably moved further away from Plato as time wore on, with an apex in the Enlightenment, more recent history indicates movement back toward Plato and polytheism.

Another barometer for change in the conception of the individual is the notion of love or desire. Since, for Plato, eros always involved a lack, it could not be attributed to the gods. By the time of Plotinus, however, erotic love became something more transcendental.[25] Instead of eros being based on need, it became for Plotinus a means for lover and beloved to become wholly one.[26] The modern conception of individual "will" could not have arisen with Plato since he regarded eros as belonging to the contingent world of manifestations. Additionally, Plato's highest Form could be Good or Beauty (or Justice, perhaps, if the transcendentals were convertible for Plato as they were for the medievals), but it could not be Love, as we hear so poignantly several centuries later in the Gospel of John.

In Book IV of the *Republic*, Plato describes justice in the ideal city as analogous to justice in the individual soul. The rulers, guardians, and people correspond to the rational, spirited, and appetitive parts of the tripartite soul. His analogy is revealing since it tells us that in the soul that is not fully just, the parts of the soul are relatively autonomous and constantly competing. For Plato, unlike for later philosophers, there was no faculty of will or any other overarching faculty that subsumed the others. The rational part of the individual soul participates in divine reason by coming to know the Forms, rather than entirely ceasing to be individual. In other words, the soul can now be thought of as at least partly divine. Indeed, in the *Theaetetus*, Plato defines the destiny of person as likeness to the divine as far as possible, which clearly anticipates the Christian idea of the *imago dei*.[27] In his description of the winged soul in the *Phaedrus*, Socrates says, "the mind of the philosopher only has wings, for he is always, so far as he is able, in communion through memory with those things the communion with which causes God to be divine."[28] This discussion takes place during Socrates's discussion of madness

---

[25] Bernard McGinn, *The Foundations of Mysticism: Origins to the Fifth Century* (New York: Crossroad, 1992), 47.

[26] McGinn, *Foundations of Mysticism*, 48.

[27] Rowan Allen Greer, *Origen: An Exhortation to Martyrdom, Prayer, and Selected Works*, Classics of Western Spirituality (New York: Paulist Press, 1979), 25.

[28] *Phaedrus*, 249C. In *Euthyphro, Apology, Crito, Phaedo, Phaedrus*, trans. Harold North Fowler, Loeb Classical Library 36 (Cambridge, Mass.: Harvard University Press, 1914). We can see some

(*mania*). The philosopher has the highest kind of madness, which, he tells us, is the highest of all "inspirations," *enthousiaseon* (*entheos*, possessed by a god). The use of these terms is significant since "divine madness" (*theia mania*) is how Plato, and the Greeks generally, understood the actions of seers like the Pythia, who spoke from something higher than themselves as individuals because they were possessed by gods.[29] In Plato, since the individual is in some sense still individual while also participating in what is beyond the level of individuality, there is a tension, well known to Christianity: how can someone be both individual and divine?

For Plato, the individual was thought to be the kind of thing that could—and should—engage in philosophy, which involved personal understanding and insight into the *logos* (ordering principle) of the created world with the vision of the Good. Plato's treatment of knowledge and love in the ascent to the Good set the stage for much of Christian mysticism. The similarity is that much stronger when we notice that the differences in expression are largely due to the different conceptions of the individual. The recognition of this underlying similarity may have been what led later Christian thinkers like Augustine to declare that he had found all of Christianity in the Neoplatonists except for the Incarnation.[30] Eckhart mentions this passage from the *Confessions* and extends it by saying that we see the glory of the incarnate Word wherever a Form is manifested.[31] This is part of Eckhart's overall view on extra-Christian sources, as exemplified by his statement, "Moses, Christ and the Philosopher [Aristotle] teach the same thing, differing only in the way they teach."[32]

We should also notice the role of verisimilitude in Plato. In the *Phaedrus*, Plato coins the term "truthlikeness."[33] In the *Timaeus*, we hear that things which only appear to be true have a way of disorienting us and causing

---

foreshadowing of Eckhart in the line that follows: "Now a man who employs such memories rightly is always being initiated into perfect mysteries and he alone becomes truly perfect."

29 Descriptions of this kind occur in both the *Phaedrus* and the *Ion*. Plato does not use the term ἔκστασις ("ecstasy"—literally, "to stand outside of oneself"), but the connection with the Pythia implies something quite similar.

30 *Confessions*, VII.9.13; Cf. James O'Donnell, *Augustine: Confessions, Volume 2: Commentary, Books 1–7* (Oxford: Oxford University Press, 2012), 416.

31 *Commentary on John*, n.125, LW III, 108.9–13.

32 *Commentary on John*, n.185, LW III, 154–5; *Essential Eckhart*, 27. Here, Eckhart makes a much stronger statement than Augustine since his observation is tantamount to recognizing a complete continuity between Platonic philosophy and Christian revelation. This is rendered more coherent, I believe, in terms of the notion of "connoisseurship" that I will take up in a later chapter.

33 *Phaedrus*, 273D.

confusion.[34] "Likelihood," by contrast, is deemed a "representative" of the truth and it can at least lead us to the truth if we "stay the course."[35] Thus, Plato's "likely story" in the *Timaeus* which ostensibly justifies his use of myth is understood to be like truth and lead us to it. This means that truthlikeness has a moral utility for Plato, leading us to the Good. This harmonizes with his overall conception of knowledge as ethically salutary. Using the word *eikôs, which* is a form of *eikôn* (image), makes Plato's "likely story" an "image story," where the "story" is presumably on the order of true knowledge of the Forms and of the Good. This makes Plato's claim apophatic: we cannot give a true account in words, so the next best thing is to give an incomplete and imperfect reflection or image (manifestation) of it. Timaeus declares, "the accounts we give of things [should] have the same character as the subjects they set forth."[36] The question of truth and truthlikeness gets at the heart of what metaphor is. Metaphor is a likeness to truth that leads us to it.

Aristotle divides the soul into intellective (rational) and desiring (non-rational) parts. For Aristotle, it is possible to have an action that is voluntary (*hekousion*) but not chosen (*prohairesis*, determining the means to achieve a rational end that is set by *boulesis*, desire). This points to a lack of an overarching faculty of choice. Translating from Greek to Latin, we get *voluntarium* from *hekousion* and *voluntas* from *boulesis*. Though *hekousion* and *boulesis* are unrelated in Greek and their connection is rejected by Aristotle, later Latin authors like Aquinas were led to connect *voluntarium* and *voluntas*.[37]

With the Stoics, instead of an array of competing desires, there is the *hegemonikon*, the "commanding faculty." The faculties are abilities of the mind rather than relatively autonomous desires that compete with one another. Further, *synkatathesis* ("assent" or "consent") plays an important role in Stoicism since this is the final gatekeeper to action, making it a forerunner of the concept of an individual *will*. As Aquinas says, "acts are called voluntary because we consent to them," and also, "consent belongs to the will."[38]

---

34 *Timaeus*, 48D.

35 *Timaeus*, 56A.

36 *Timaeus*, 29B3–5.

37 *Eudemian Ethics*, 2.7.1223b29; *Summa Theologiae*, Ia.IIae.6.5; as cited by Charles H. Kahn, "Discovering Will from Aristotle to Augustine," in *The Question of "Eclecticism": Studies in Later Greek Philosophy*, ed. John M. Dillon and A. A. Long (Berkeley: University of California Press, 1988), 241.

38 *Summa Theologiae*, Ia.IIae.15.4, as cited by Kahn, "Discovering Will from Aristotle to Augustine," 247.

As the concept of the individual continues to change from this point forward, the development in the concept of will is useful for tracing the inflation of the individual. The first turning point is evident in Epictetus's formulation of Stoicism. Epictetus took Aristotle's notion of *prohairesis* that was previously not central to Stoicism and spoke of it as though "we *are* our *prohairesis*."[39] This is accompanied by another shift in emphasis. The divine logos for Epictetus is described as a "personal 'will of Nature' (*boulema te phuseos*) or 'will of Zeus'; and his own *prohairesis* is described as 'a part of God which he has given to us'" and one that should be made like the divine will.[40] This anticipates later Christian theological writers who wrote that we are made in the image of God insofar as we have will and intellect.[41]

The Emergence of Christianity

As the scope of the individual expanded and it became increasingly possible to speak of the individual as being divine, it also became possible to speak of the divine as being individual. The idea of the Incarnation and the idea that man is created in the image of God are only feasible if the scope of the individual and the divine are not wholly exclusive. In fact, early arguments in the ancient world against Christ's dual nature stemmed from the older worldview's inability to think of the individual as being divine without losing its individuality.

Further, we can see differences that evidence a shift in the conception of the individual in the practice of early Christianity. We find exegesis throughout the history of Christian mysticism.[42] This is important since the tradition of regarding exegesis as a religious activity was not more than a few centuries old. This practice evolved for the Hebrews in parallel with the evolution of the notion of the individual in Ancient Greece. Not only were the texts

---

39 Christopher Gill, "The Ancient Self: Issues and Approaches," in *Ancient Philosophy of the Self*, ed. Paulina Remes and Juha Sihvola (New York: Springer, 2008), 46. Gill, Kahn, and Sorabji all refer to Epictetus's *Discourses*, 1.1.23. The tyrant says, "'I will put you in chains.' 'What did you say, man? Put *me* in chains? My leg you will put in chains, but my will (*prohairesis*) not even God can conquer,'" as cited in Gill, "The Ancient Self: Issues and Approaches," 46.

40 Kahn, "Discovering Will from Aristotle to Augustine," 254, citing Epictetus *Diss.* 1.1.27; cf. *Diss.* 4.7.20.

41 For example, in the *Summa Theologiae*, the discussion of the human will (Ia.82) follows that of divine will (Ia.19) and the will of angels (Ia.59.1). His notion of human will is built from the model of divine will. Cf. Kahn, "Discovering Will from Aristotle to Augustine," 245.

42 McGinn, *Foundations of Mysticism*, 3.

themselves seen as important, but the act of interpreting them was a kind of meditation. This marks a point of significant departure from the polytheistic systems and older religious systems where the rites and rituals themselves were the religious activities. More intellectual activities like textual interpretation depend on the perspective of the interpreter, meaning that the individual reading the text plays a more central role. In the ancient mystery religions that flourished alongside Christianity in the ancient world, we see a focus on individual experience and transformation rather than mere archetypal reenactment. It is in this way that Christianity inherited the mysticism of the ancient mystery religions. The mystery religions provide a midpoint between the older polytheistic systems exemplified by Homeric Greece and the burgeoning, more philosophical monotheism of Plato.

Apocalyptic writing in general, and Jewish apocalyptic writing in particular, was a natural outgrowth of the increasingly linear conception of history that developed during the few centuries immediately before Christ. Jewish exegetical practices (corresponding at least in part to Platonic *theoria*) increasingly emphasized the inner life of the individual as individual. Ancient Greek religion and Judaism are case studies (or perhaps better, two inflections of a larger cultural complex which is itself a case study) in the transition from cyclical to linear history, in other words. While Jewish and Greek factions were evident politically and socially, the worldview of the two and how well they understood one another demonstrates much greater commonality. The closer the worldview, the more potential for fighting and influence. There is a limit, after all, to how much and how strongly you can disagree with someone if you have no idea what they are saying.

The apocalyptic writings were stories about people who were seekers, having a decidedly more individual context than older First Temple Jewish stories.[43] During this time, revelation also changed from a living oral tradition to a fixed written one. From this point on, from around 200 BC, we see a rise in exegesis as a religious practice, which hinges upon individual insight, not revelation whereby the individual is temporarily put aside. With the emphasis on individual insight, we might notice that it is natural for allegorical and other "deeper" meanings to be sought insofar as depth is a quality of individual understanding. These meanings are deeper insofar as they move beyond the level of interpretation necessary for the practice of participatory rites. In such rites, the details of practice are what is described,

---

[43] McGinn, *Foundations of Mysticism*, 11.

not the inner mental life of the individual. By contrast, Jewish exegesis of this time did not focus only upon practice, but also upon individual insight. The idea of the resurrection of an individual's body that appeared during this time also points to the changing trend. The role of the individual in religion had changed fundamentally.

Along with this came a notion of authorship that is fits with the newly inflated significance of the individual. If the individual steps aside when receiving revelation and participating in the archetypal, then no substantive debate about authorship or pseudonymity can arise, only questions about the authenticity of revelation. Alongside the fact that sacred books are not as easily modified as an oral religious tradition, we see crystallization of the canon in a way that would have been unnecessary in a cyclical history. We will have occasion to return to the question of pseudonymity later on.

Philo of Alexandria, a contemporary of Christ, is perhaps the most recognizable Jewish example of someone who advocated the search for deeper meanings in scripture. Philo's attempt to harmonize the differences between Jewish and Greek philosophical practices testifies to their commonality in geral as much as it does to their differences in detail. In the century that followed, we also see the more clearly individual-centered Song of Solomon. Erotic imagery implies individual disposition and feeling, categories that were not prominent in previous generations' more ritually oriented sacred texts. It implies inner experience and the search for insight and union with God. It does not imply rite and ritual.

Origen

It is not traditionally spoken of in this way, but because writers like Rowan Greer recognize Origen alongside Plotinus as "one of the founders of Neoplatonism," we may sensibly describe the development of Neoplatonic thought as happening *within* and as *part of* Christianity rather than being a wholly separate philosophical development that is added to Christian history as an alien influence.[44] With Origen, we have an author whom Eckhart may have read in the original and by whom he was much influenced. Consequently, for our purposes, it is useful to see that Eckhart's appeals to authority for some of his rash-sounding ideas were justified. This allows us to see that what was new and unusual in Eckhart's thought was *not* what he had in common

---

44 Greer, *Origen*, 5.

theologically with Origen. We must, therefore, look in greater detail at Origen so as to properly characterize his similarities with Eckhart.

Before looking at the parallels, a few concepts from Origen's metaphysics will provide a backdrop for understanding the necessary aspects of his thought. Origen's theology is Platonic. For him, things are material in proportion to their distance from God.[45] Thus, the ephemeral body weighs down and is ultimately unnecessary for the rational soul, which understands (a divine activity since it is incorporeal) and is closer to God. He goes so far as to assert that the particular body we have now will not be resurrected. Indeed, so long as we are tied to the body, perfection is impossible and temptation to move further from God is ubiquitous. By moving toward the understanding and away from the material world, including the body, man begins to return to God both by grace and by his own doing. This foreshadows future issues with Pelagianism, though Origen himself probably had nothing of the sort in mind.

Origen understands the Word as a mediator that unifies God and creation. He sees God the Father as the primary One, the Son or Word as subordinate as the image of the Father (the Father is the archetype for the Son), and rational souls are the image of the Son (the Son is the archetype for souls, the Neoplatonic "mind," and Platonic demiurge). Origen argues that "production," understood as the generation of animals, cannot apply to the Son being produced from the Father. He tells us:

> The Son is not generated by a production from Him, as some think. For if the Son is a production of the Father and *production* is defined as the sort of generation by which the offspring of animals or of men are accustomed to come into existence, then necessarily both He who produces and He who is produced will be bodies. For we do not say, as the heretics suppose, that any part of God's substance has been turned into the Son or that the Son has been generated from the Father from no substance at all, that is, outside His own substance, so that there would be a time when He was not. But we remove all notion of corporeality and say that the Word and Wisdom is generated from the invisible and incorporeal God apart from any corporeal passion.[46]

Production creates separate beings (where matter is the distinguishing principle, as in Aristotle, and the notion of existence applies to beings alone, as

---

45 Origen, *On First Principles*, IV.4.6, in Greer, *Origen*, 210–11.
46 Origen, *On First Principles*, IV.4.1, in Greer, *Origen*, 205. Emphasis original.

Eckhart would later say). Though Eckhart opposed Aquinas in these matters, his metaphysics was closer to Origen's than to anything new.

We see a Neoplatonic hierarchy of being in Origen. Though his subordination of the Son is compatible with his Platonism, it came to be rejected by many of the later church fathers, and decisively at the Fifth Ecumenical Council of 553 even though Origen's "image of" dynamic was like Eckhart's insofar as it did not imply any corruption or difference. That is, the Son was subordinate to the Father, but not different than or a corruption of the Father in the sense that Platonic manifestations were imperfect copies of their archetypes. Origen tells us that image and likeness do not imply corruption (citing Col 1:15, 2 Cor 4:4, where Christ is called the "image of God"), or else Christ himself would be less than God.[47] Thus, our being made in the image of God does not imply corruption in and of itself. As with Eckhart, though there is a hierarchy, God is present at all times in all things, a setup that flows into Origen's notion of the *apokatastasis*, the eventual return of all things to God (the *reditus* which is the opposite of the Neoplatonic emanation, *exitus*, of creation). This parallels and may have been the authoritative support Eckhart had in mind for his contention that there is no distance between spiritual things and the understanding of them (since God himself is understanding), as we hear in his wood and eye example in Sermon 48. Eckhart tells us that when his eye sees a piece of wood, they are united in the act of seeing, but they are not united in essence. It is different for spiritual things, he tells us, as understanding and essence are one since spiritual things are immaterial.

For Origen, our love for God comes from his creative love. The individual's love is still appetitive, but there is something nonindividual about the love for God, just as we see later in Augustine.[48] This is true for understanding as well, since Origen tells us it is noncorporeal and thus universal. Souls that turn away from God are immediately given bodies because, for Origen, turning away from God implies corporeality.[49] This is sensible, since division is a falling away from unity and is only coherent if there is a substrate in which the division can take place, as with Aristotle's matter being the differentiating principle. This was a problem for medievals as well, who wanted to maintain that angels were different beings even though they were incorporeal. This

---

[47] Origen, *On First Principles*, IV.4.10, in Greer, *Origen*, 215.
[48] Greer, *Origen*, 26.
[49] Greer, *Origen*, 12.

led to some curious solutions around Aquinas's time. For Origen, as it would be later for Eckhart, the celestial hierarchy had levels defined in proportion to something other than being since God's being was still God's and not the creature's.

The esteem with which Origen regards Hellenistic philosophy is easily seen in his claim that the truth found by the philosophers is the same truth to be found in Scripture.[50] When Eckhart echoes the same sentiment, his account is a return to Origen. While this may seem outlandishly different than received Christian teaching, if as Origen and Eckhart both assert, understanding is divine, then the philosophers were merely pursuing what was most purely divine in searching for insight into the universal (Origen parallels what is "first" and "last" in Isaiah with first principles in philosophy). Since Plato refers to a rather mysterious process by which flashes of insight occur (see the previous description of *theia mania* and the spark), by relabeling this as "grace," we may not be far at all from orthodoxy.

For Origen, God informs creation but He is not contained by it. In other words, as Greer puts it, "God's transcendence implies His immanence; and the very fact that He is not limited by the creation enables Him to fill all things with His presence and power."[51] Once again, we see Eckhart's ideas presaged in Origen. Though the individuals themselves would later be reconceived as intensively infinite and would occupy a different portion of the ontological space between God and creation, the dynamic by which God was immanent in all things even with the presence of a recognizable celestial hierarchy was already present in Origen. As we will see later in this chapter, modifications to the hierarchy of being were part of the tumultuous changes in theology for Eckhart and Ockham in the early part of the fourteenth century.

Origen viewed the contemplation of God as the end of the Christian path. He thought of activity as purgative preparation for contemplation and contemplation as providing clarity which enables activity.[52] Although Origen's pragmatic focus tends toward favoring activity (a form of the *vita activa*, perhaps), this is not the same endorsement of the superiority of the active life that we hear from Eckhart. Nevertheless, it is significant that Origen's (and the later Cappadocians') vision of the Christian life did not depict

---

50 Greer, *Origen*, 6. See the above discussion of Plato for similar passages in Augustine and Eckhart.
51 Greer, *Origen*, 8.
52 Greer, *Origen*, 27.

the active life as inferior to the contemplative in the way that we began to hear from Evagrius Ponticus and Dionysius in the fifth century.[53]

Origen's notion of the inner and outer man is of particular interest since it points directly to his understanding of the interior life of the individual and thus to his understanding of what an individual is. The very idea that God could be aware of our inner life implies that the inner psychic life of the individual had become a matter of some import.[54] Origen's inner man is the soul that is the *imago dei* while the outer man is the corporeal portion of his being.[55] Further, like Eckhart, Origen does not separate philosophical contemplation from lived experience. That is, pragmatic considerations are never far from his mind. Rowan Greer tells us that "Origen is not concerned with mere abstraction but with a truth embodied in a living community."[56] Action, for Origen, is a natural byproduct of desire (love). This love is the vehicle by which one returns to the Father. It is unmistakably experiential. It is also how Origen understands the divine love in the Song of Songs:

> If anyone has been able to hold in the breadth of his mind and to consider the glory and splendor of all those things created in Him, he will be struck by their very beauty and transfixed by the magnificence of their brilliance or, as the prophet says, "by the chosen arrow" (Is 49:2). And he will receive from Him the saving wound and will burn with the blessed fire of His love.[57]

Recall that for Plato, *eros* could not be divine since it properly belonged to the ephemeral world of manifestations. In Origen, however, we witness an expansion of this notion when he says that God could be equally well called *eros* as John calls him *agape*, even though the term *eros* is peculiarly scarce in the New Testament.[58] This signals a change in the notion of the individual since his *eros*, which previously was not suitable for the divine since it had a lower ontological status, now appears in Origen as a perfectly good substitute for *agape* (*caritas*) as a transcendental which may be thought of as God.

Since individual *eros* is now appropriate for God, we should not be surprised that the notion of individual perfection in Origen is likewise

---

53 Greer, *Origen*, 27.
54 Cf. Origen, *On First Principles*, IV.4.10, in Greer, *Origen*, 216.
55 Greer, *Origen*, 19; cf. Origen's *Prologue to the Commentary on the Song of Songs* and Rom. 7:22.
56 Greer, *Origen*, 6.
57 Origen, *Comm. Song of Songs*, prologue, in Greer, *Origen*, 223.
58 Origen, *Comm. Song of Songs*, prologue, in Greer, *Origen*, 228.

expanded. Origen describes the possibility of revelation that is beyond Saint Paul's experience:

> You will know as friends.[59] ... For friends learn not by enigmas, but by a form that is seen or by wisdom bare of words, symbols, and types; this will be possible when they attain to the nature of intelligible things and to the beauty of truth. If, then, you believe that Paul was caught up to the third heaven and was caught up into Paradise and heard things cannot be told, which man may not utter (2 Cor. 12:2, 4), you will consequently realize that you will presently know more and greater things than the unspeakable words then revealed to Paul.... For in God there are treasured up much greater visions than these, which no bodily nature can comprehend, if it is not first delivered from everything corporeal.[60]

Here, Origen describes exactly where he differs from the earlier tradition: "There are realities that are so great that they find a rank superior to humanity and our mortal nature; they are impossible for our rational and mortal race to understand. Yet by the grace of God poured forth ... these realities have become possible for us."[61] We find similar passages in other places where he describes the deepest level of meaning in Scripture for "those who are perfect" is the "secret and hidden wisdom of God" as described in 1 Corinthians 2:6–7.[62] Nevertheless, for Origen our corporeality holds us back as individuals. This is quite natural since his conception of individuation implies differentiation, which is a fall away from God and thereby implies matter. As with Plato, the two are simply exclusive, even if Origen does describe how man participates in God's wisdom by his adopted sonship. The missing link is Origen's conception of unending progress. As he says:

> No matter how far a person advances in his investigation and makes progress by a keener zeal, even if the grace of God is within him and enlightens his mind (cf. Eph 1:18), he cannot arrive at the perfect end of the truths he seeks. No mind that is created has the ability to understand completely by any manner of means, but as it finds some small part of the answers that are sought, it sees other questions to be asked. And if it arrives at those

---

59 Eckhart describes this same scriptural passage and idea in a very similar way especially in Sermon 10, but also in Sermon 29 and *In Sap.*, LW II, 561.8–10, *In Ioh.*, LW III, 313.13, 568.8.
60 Origen, *An Exhortation to Martyrdom*, §XIII, in Greer, *Origen*, 50.
61 Origen, *On Prayer*, in Greer, *Origen*, 81.
62 Origen, *On First Principles*, IV.2.4, in Greer, *Origen*, 182.

answers, it will again see beyond them to many more questions that they imply must be asked.[63]

This is similar to the perpetual striving toward God described by Gregory of Nyssa's *epektasis* and by Gregory Nazianzus.

Still, Origen leaves doors open for further mystical speculation. If we participate in God's wisdom as adopted sons and God's wisdom is unitary (i.e., as it is God, it cannot have parts), then mortal or not, our participation in this wisdom seems to imply more than a foretaste. Similarly, when Origen cites Galatians 2:20, which says, "it is no longer I who live, but Christ who lives in me," he does not connect this to the discussion immediately preceding this one on the impossibility of created intellects having divine wisdom.[64] As with Augustine's similar rhetoric, a reader who is familiar with Eckhart may expect to hear the *in quantum* principle in the very next breath.

In addition to those ideas just mentioned which foreshadow Eckhart, we should also sense a kindred spirit in spiritual or anagogical interpretation of Scripture between Origen and Eckhart. Not only was Origen famously willing to interpret Scripture in novel ways, the direction he took was in many ways the same as Eckhart's. As Greer describes Origen's approach, "Origen's allegorical interpretation does not so much dissolve temporal sequence as catch it up into eternity."[65] In other words, the historical side becomes entirely secondary to the underlying spiritual message, which needs to be relevant for the individual in the present moment. As Origen says in a passage that recalls Eckhart's ostensibly novel and radical formulation in Sermon 101, "Who would dare to say that what is written 'by the Word of God' is of no use and makes no contribution to salvation, but is merely a narrative of what happened and was over and done a long time ago, but pertains in no way to us when it is told."[66] Throughout his works, Origen makes plain that the spiritual interpretation is the highest level of exegesis. In many cases, the Holy Spirit intentionally included contradictions and impossibilities to prod us into seeking out the spiritual meaning.[67] As he plainly says, "since what first appears cannot be true or useful, we might be called back to examine the truth to be sought more deeply and to be investigated more diligently, and

---

63 Origen, *On First Principles*, IV.3.14–15, in Greer, *Origen*, 202–4.
64 Origen, *On First Principles*, IV.4.2, in. Greer, *Origen*, 206.
65 Greer, *Origen*, 32.
66 Origen, *Homily XXVII on Numbers*, in Greer, *Origen*, 248.
67 Origen, *On First Principles*, IV.2.9, in Greer, *Origen*, 187–88.

might seek a meaning worthy of God in the Scriptures."⁶⁸ Further, the ostensibly prosaic meanings like those we find in the legal texts are merely a "veil" for spiritual meanings in which "certain ineffable mysteries are revealed to those who know how to examine accounts of this kind."⁶⁹ Finally, there is symmetry between Origen's unsystematic approach and his view on the utility of such things in pursuing the highest spiritual matters:

> Everyone who is concerned with truth should be little concerned with names and words (cf. 1 Tm. 1:4), because different nations have different customs about words. And he should pay more attention to what is meant than to how it is expressed in words, especially in the case of great and difficult matters ... there are some things the meaning of which cannot in any way rightly be explained by any words of a human language (cf. 1 Cor 2:4), but they are made plain by a purer intellectual apprehension rather than by any properties words have. As well, the understanding of divine letters must be kept to that rule by which what is said is judged not according to the common character of the word but according to the divinity of the Holy Spirit, who inspired their writing.⁷⁰

Such a sentiment could have easily been included in Eckhart's defense and seems to inform the spirit of his writing.

Augustine

The question of the divine and human in Christ (Christology) was one of the most important issues for Christian orthodoxy between 400 and 700.⁷¹ The conception of the self was central: how are we to understand how Christ is both human and God? With any of the distinctions Augustine draws in his theology, we must bear in mind that doctrine is a means to an end, not an authoritative end in itself.⁷² Augustine's conception of the self is most evident by looking at his account of the conversion of the will in the *Confessions* and his notion of the *imago dei* in *On the Trinity*.

For Augustine, occurrent desires are the product of a perverted and fractured will, first corrupted by Adam's original sin. This is how desires arise

---

68 Origen, *On First Principles*, IV.2.8, in Greer, *Origen*, 188.
69 Origen, *On First Principles*, IV.2.8, in Greer, *Origen*, 184.
70 Origen, *On First Principles*, IV.3.15, in Greer, *Origen*, 204–5.
71 Bernard McGinn, *The Growth of Mysticism: Gregory the Great through the 12th Century* (New York: Crossroad, 1994), 12.
72 Augustine, *On the Trinity*, VIII.iii.7.

in us for things that harm us—that is, things that move us further from God (absolute goodness) and toward evil (the absence of being). Action follows when all parts of the will align. Repeatedly willing to pursue sinful desire strengthens such pathological habits that hold us in bondage (like prisoners chained in a cave). When the reasoning part of the soul sees the destructive nature of sin and resolves to fight it, a war of will ensues and creates the possibility for a situation where the conscious will is entirely confident in what it believes but struggles in vain against ingrained habits. From here, all movement away from corrosive, worldly desire is movement toward God and comes only by the grace of God. As one approaches being able to will wholeheartedly against carnal desire, one's will aligns with God's will. Experiences here are not such that "I see God" but that God sees himself.[73] And so, through the Son and with the Holy Spirit, one sees how God became man so that man may become God—by extinguishing one's worldly, personal will and by becoming transparent to God's will. Since this progression is both argumentative and chronological, it proceeds roughly in order, beginning in Book VII and continuing through Book VIII of the *Confessions*. The turning point for Augustine's wrestling with the problem of evil was his realization that he had a will and that the will was the source of sin.[74] Augustine says, "the consequence of a distorted will is passion. By servitude to passion, habit [*consuetudo*] is formed, and habit to which there is no resistance becomes necessity."[75] So he tells us, it was "not I" that brought this about "but sin which dwells in me."[76]

Augustine's use of *consuetudo*, "customary action" or "habit," is similar to our use of "habit," though more broadly construed. Augustine shares the modern view that repeated actions become habitual. At a certain point, they cease to require the assent of the will, for as the habit grows stronger the action becomes easier to begin and harder to resist once begun. As we read in the *Confessions*, "in large part I was passive and unwilling rather than active and willing."[77] Augustine saw the desires as arising independently of the individual's will on a momentary basis.

---

73 Augustine, *Confessions*, XIII.31.46.
74 *Confessions*, VII.iii.5.
75 *Confessions*, VIII.v.10.
76 Rom 7:17, 20.
77 *Confessions*, VIII.v.11.

As with many of Augustine's seemingly firm theological stances, the expression of his philosophy of will is at all times rhetorically situated in opposition to the Manicheans. To avoid a Manichaean conclusion, Augustine cannot say that man has one bad will and one good will, as if they were two natures within.[78] Instead, Augustine suggests that one's soul can be pulled in different directions by opposing portions (*voluntates*) of the will within it.[79] Ultimately, Augustine will say that if something is "wholeheartedly" willed (*toto vult*),[80] then it is acted upon: "For as soon as I had the will, I would have had a wholehearted will. At this point the power to act is identical with the will. The willing itself was performative of the action."[81]

Augustine's conversion is a chronicle of his aligning his will with God's will. This process is only necessary since the human will is naturally fragmented, being drawn both in spiritual and worldly directions. Augustine marveled that although he willed to move away from carnal habits, he found himself unable to do so.[82] This naturally sinful state is fallen and cannot be from God. Thus, Augustine posits *original sin*, which enables him to say that naturally sinful dispositions (habits) are still "of my own choice"[83] "because I was a son of Adam."[84] Note that the idea of original sin becomes necessary for Augustine after thinking through the notion of the fallen will to the end.

Since he allies with Saint Paul in thinking that moral prohibitions only water the desires,[85] Augustine chose not to oppose reason to desire and make it a test of will. Rather, he preferred to recognize the desire for God as the

---

78 *Confessions*, VIII.x.22.

79 *Confessions*, VIII.v.10.

80 *Confessions*, VIII.ix.21.

81 *Confessions*, VIII.viii.20.

82 *Confessions*, VIII.i.2.

83 *Confessions*, VIII.v.10, VIII.v.11.

84 *Confessions*, VIII.x.22. If we are overly concerned with the individual soul qua individual, then his argument seems strange. It makes sense in light of the Platonists and Plotinus in particular. After all, Augustine tells us, "In all the Platonic books, God and his Word keep slipping in" (VIII.ii.1). In Platonist terms, the fallen world is the world of multiplicity where individuals matter less than the return to the divine One. Augustine is careful, however, to maintain separation between creature and creator and insist that it is not the soul that is divine. Instead, according to his notion of grace, the closer one gets to God, the more the will becomes God's will and God "sees" himself. It is significant that Augustine uses the Plotinian three-stage model—*corporis, sensibus, anabasis*—separation from the corporeal world, movement within the soul, and passage to the divine.

85 Rom 7:7–8: "I would not have known what coveting really was if the law had not said, 'You shall not covet.' But sin, seizing the opportunity afforded by the commandment, produced in me every kind of coveting."

deepest desire. Desires arise outside our control (i.e., there are no habits of desire), thus we need intellectual activity to open up possibilities for desire, and we need faith (as we read in *De Trinitate*) since it provides motivation where knowledge is lacking (as with Eckhart's "rushing ahead" that we will encounter later). Loving God is possible because, although we cannot love what we do not know, we are told to "first love by faith" because "something can be loved which is unknown if it is believed."[86] As he says, people can become what they see "by cleaving to that same form which they behold, in order to be formed by it."[87] In other words, habit via repetition is necessary because the initial experience of understanding and simply willing at a particular moment are not sufficient. This limits the scope of knowledge in a manner that would have been foreign to Plato. Will reoccupies the space created by that limit.

Turning now to *De Trinitate*, God for Augustine is more present to us than other minds are (as he established in *Conf.* X) since we cannot completely know other minds: "There now, he can already have God better known to him than his brother, certainly better known because more present, better known because more inward to him, better known because more sure."[88] We can be "more sure" of our knowledge of God because we find God by looking within our minds and, as established in *De Trinitate* VIII.4, nothing is better known to us than our minds.

Will, however, not only characterizes conversion; God's will is also God himself. For Augustine, we come to understand God by moving inward and understanding ourselves, since "The God within is the God above."[89] As this process culminates, our "seeing" of God is God seeing himself,[90] just as Augustine's will became "wholehearted" and aligned with God's will. Since "the will and power of God is God's very self,"[91] speaking of a union of wills between creature and creator allows us to approach what Augustine describes in a letter to Paulina around the year 413: "The person who is able to see God invisibly can adhere to God incorporeally." The same idea can be

---

86 Augustine, *On the Trinity*, VIII.iii.6.

87 *On the Trinity*, VIII.iv.9.

88 *On the Trinity*, VIII.v.12.

89 Augustine, *Homily on Psalms*, 130.12.

90 "When people see these things with the help of your Spirit, it is you who are seeing in them" (*Confessions*, XIII.31.46).

91 *On the Trinity*, VII.iv.6. Cf. Plotinus, *Enneads* 6.8.13.

heard in 1 Corinthians 6:17, "whoever adheres to the Lord is one spirit [with him]."[92] Turning toward God (*conversio*) with the will is implicitly divinizing.

Further, as we may love an object of faith and thus God may love himself through us, Augustine observes that we know love in the moment that we love. It requires no further reflection to say that we love or that we love loving. To love is to desire unity with the beloved. Still, this implies a separation between lover and beloved. It is this separation, though, that Augustine finds to be a shortcoming of the trinity of love.[93]

In the end, Augustine simply says, "There you are, God is love," referring to 1 John 4:8. He sums up his discussion, "Why should we go running round the heights of the heavens and the depths of the earth looking for him who is with us if only we should wish to be with him?"[94] In other words, why should we search the classical heavens and hells (given the contemporary conception of the earth in the middle, heavens above and hells below) if the answer lies within us? Augustine's dramatic characterization thereby serves to exhort his audience to refocus desire from without to within.

In Augustine, we see movement toward interiority and development of the concepts of the individual will and divine will, including the theological innovation of original sin. Still, the individual will progresses by grace alone and yields to God's will not only by aligning the competing human wills with God's will, but also by allowing God to love and know himself through the individual. This yielding to God's will echoes Plato's characterization of the refocusing on understanding and the climbing of the ontological hierarchy as one approaches knowledge of the Good, while cultivating virtues which involve the governing of the competing appetites by reason. Still, what Augustine does with the will would have been foreign to Plato, which demarcates it as the point at which Augustine clearly inhabits a different cultural climate—one that includes different notions of the self and the life of the mind. Augustine, unlike Plato, conceived of an overarching faculty of will.

Neoplatonism

By Plotinus's time, we see a milestone in the ontological inflation of the individual: Plotinus identified Forms for individuals.[95] This made Platonism

---

[92] Letter 147, as cited by McGinn, *Foundations of Mysticism*.
[93] *On the Trinity*, VIII.x.14.
[94] *On the Trinity*, VIII.v.11.
[95] Plotinus, *Enneads*, V.7.

even more compatible with Christianity and its emphasis on the individual soul.[96] Thus, Boethius said, in picking up on this idea, that Plato has the Form of *Platonitas* because Plato has a property of being the individual that he is above and beyond the peculiar combination of attributes that he possesses.[97] For Plotinus and Porphyry, as for Origen, the material world (including the body) comprised an obstacle to attaining to the superior, immaterial heights of the contemplation of universals. Only with later Neoplatonists like Iamblichus and Proclus do we see the movement toward "theurgy," which was the Neoplatonic appropriation of pagan rites to put the individual in contact with the divine through worldly things. The highest kind of theurgy in Proclus is characterized by negative theology, mystic silence, and faith (*pistis*, which goes beyond "knowledge," *gnôstikôs*, because knowledge is not enough). The culmination of negative theology for Proclus is the negation of negation, just as it is for Dionysius[98] and Eckhart.

The account of causality and emanation in Neoplatonic philosophy directly affected the ontological status of the individual. As Proclus describes the most important aspect of this, "Every effect remains in its cause, proceeds from it, and reverts upon it."[99] Created individuals, therefore, instead of being separate from the One and mere manifestations, remain in the One and return to it. Rather than being an imitation or shadow that evanesces and returns to the nothingness from which it came, the individual instead returns to the One, just as Origen described in his notion of *apokatastasis*. This points to an increased valuation of the individual. Further, as emanations from the One, individual beings owe their being to Being, so to speak. Divine unity is still present in the individuals since those individuals are emanations of the divine. This divinization of creation makes the realm of multiplicity itself into something divine, insofar as its being derives from divine Being.

96 David Yount tells us that although Plato's "one-over-many" rule (one Form for many manifestations) from *Parmenides* and *Republic* Bk. X seems to exclude the possibility of there being individual Forms, in fact Plotinus specifically endorses this aspect of Plato's thought. *Plotinus the Platonist: A Comparative Account of Plato and Plotinus' Metaphysics* (London: Bloomsbury, 2014), 126. Even if Yount is right that Plato does not explicitly exclude the possibility of Forms of individuals, it seems unlikely that he would have shared Plotinus's view on this.

97 "Since 'Platonicity' is referred to Plato only, when we hear the word 'Plato,' we are led with our thoughts to a single person and to a single particular substance." Claudio Moreschini, *A Christian in a Toga, Boethius: Interpreter of Antiquity and Christian Theologian* (Göttingen: Vandenhoeck and Ruprecht, 2014), 57. Cf. *Commentariorem in librum Aristotelis Perihermeneias*, edition secunda II, c.7.

98 Dionysius, *Mystical Theology*, chap. 5.

99 Proclus, *The Elements of Theology: A Revised Text with Translation, Introduction, and Commentary*, trans. E. R. Dodds (Oxford: Oxford University Press, 1992), §35.

Clearly, if individuals remain in the divine, are reflections of it, and seek to return to it, little distance must be crossed to say that an individual can be both man and God. In Christianizing Neoplatonism and making the Neoplatonic One into the Christian God, Dionysius could declare that all of creation was a "theophany,"—that is, God revealing himself.[100] Similarly, if moving from creature to creator is a matter of effacing the constraints (the *contraction*, as Nicholas of Cusa would later say) of self upon Being, then the method of apophatic theology is employed not only to describe or "name" God (as Dionysius might say) but to thereby effect a return to Him. As with Dionysius, one attempts to *name* God in order to come to "know" Him, which implies approaching Him and moving away from multiplicity.

Some Neoplatonists extended the meaning of *eros* to refer to the desire to produce beauty rather than just to possess it. At that point, *eros* could sensibly be applied to the gods or even to the first principle. Unlike Plato's conception of *eros* as a mediating force, Dionysius saw *eros* as the force that made us want to be like God. Bernard McGinn goes as far as saying that Dionysius's conception of *eros* as more than a merely mediating force was his greatest contribution to Christian theology.[101]

Overall, like Proclus, Dionysius is remarkable more for his influence than for his innovations. Both Proclus and Dionysius are significant figures though, since their influence extended by historical chance to have enormous impact on the medieval world. Proclus's work was transmitted in part by way of the *Liber de Causis* (Book of Causes), which enjoyed success partly due to the misattribution of its authorship to Aristotle—a mistake that persisted until Thomas Aquinas noticed the similarity after reading William of Moerbeke's translation of Proclus's *Elements of Theology* in 1268.

John Scotus Eriugena

Eriugena's anthropology shows us that the notion of the individual has evolved further. Dionysius and the other Neoplatonic thinkers described a celestial hierarchy where lower forms had only mediated access to those that were higher. Augustine talks about the "mid-rank" (*medietas animae*) of the soul: "The tree of life planted in the middle of paradise signifies the wisdom by which the soul should understand that it is ordered in a certain middle

---

100 See Donald Duclow, *Masters of Learned Ignorance: Eriugena, Eckhart, Cusanus* (Burlington, Vt.: Ashgate, 2006), 7.

101 McGinn, *Foundations of Mysticism*, 166.

range of things."¹⁰² At the same time, Augustine says that "between our mind, by which we know the Father, and the Truth, that is to say, the inward light through which we know Him, no creature intervenes."¹⁰³ Eriugena echoes this in saying that "between our mind and Him no nature intervenes" and that we contemplate God in perpetual circular motion "with no intervening creature."¹⁰⁴ Though Eriugena sounds like Augustine, his anthropology goes further. He says that Christ not only raised human nature "to a parity [*aequalitas*] with the angelic nature, . . . but also exalted it above all angels and heavenly powers, and in short, above all things that are and all things that are not."¹⁰⁵ Eriugena appears to be inconsistent on this point, though. On the one hand, he ostensibly limits humanity to the level of the angels: "The human intellects of the holiest theologians ascend to the height of [the angels'] contemplation, as Paul was taken up, but they neither exceed their excellence, nor are they more deiform than they."¹⁰⁶ On the other hand, he makes an exception for John the Evangelist, saying that he "passes beyond every created heaven and every created paradise, that is, every human and angelic nature."¹⁰⁷ Further, Eriugena remains Platonic about the body, saying that in the end, "the whole of human nature will be poured back into intellect alone, so that nothing in them will remain except the intellect alone by which it will contemplate its Creator."¹⁰⁸

In contrast to Origen's account of creation *ex nihilo*, Eriugena's account is closer to creation *ex Deo*, something we could equally say for Eckhart. For Origen, all living things are theophanies, appearances of God that can be contemplated to effect a return to the divine source of all things. There are

---

102 *Against the Manichees*, 2.9.12. As cited in Duclow, *Masters of Learned Ignorance*, 91. Cf. Plotinus, *Enneads*, IV.8.

103 *nulla interposita creatura*. Augustine, *On the True Religion*, 55.113. As cited in Duclow, *Masters of Learned Ignorance*, 77.

104 Eriugena, *Periphyseon*, 531B–C; *Commentary on John*, SC180. As cited in Duclow, *Masters of Learned Ignorance*, 77.

105 Eriugena, *Periphyseon*, 895B. As cited in Duclow, *Masters of Learned Ignorance*, 81.

106 Eriugena, *Expositiones in Ierarchiam Coelestem* 6, 146–51. As cited in Duclow, *Masters of Learned Ignorance*, 82.

107 Eriugena, *Homily*, 225C, SC 151:218–20. As cited in Duclow, *Masters of Learned Ignorance*, 82.

108 Eriugena, *Periphyseon* 874B. Cf. 872B–875B. This is part of Eriugena's account of the general return by which corporeal things return to the incorporeal and all matter reverts to incorporeality in a solely intellectual existence. This is where humanity achieves its originally planned-for status as a perfect image of God, without the division of the sexes and all materiality. Further, Eriugena describes a special return by which the elect are deified and become entirely one with God.

two important aspects of God's presence in created things that will surface again in Eckhart: the paradox of being both created as creatures and uncreated as God, and the way that God is wholly present in each individual while He is also beyond being. His account of physical nature as theophany elevates the natural world. His account of the human mind as *imago dei* insofar as it empties itself of worldly knowledge and thus acquires learned ignorance (making itself as formless as God is) elevates man.

The paradox of created and uncreated paradox is present in the fourfold division with which Eriugena frames the *Periphyseon*. He enumerates the four possibilities of created and uncreated things that create or do not create. God is uncreated, he tells us, and He both creates (as efficient cause) and does not create (as final cause). Eriugena explains that the distinction between creating and not creating is an artifact of the "double direction [*intentio*] of our contemplation."[109] All four possibilities come back together in unity by the metaphor of divine self-creation.[110] In addition to the similarity between divine self-creation and Eckhart's birth of the Word, Eriugena even takes time to describe the disciple's shock at hearing such a thing and says that, "like almost everyone else, I was unfamiliar with this view before and had not even heard of it. If it is true, anyone would immediately shout and proclaim: 'And so God is all things and all things are God.' Such a judgment will be regarded as monstrous."[111] Eckhart described similarly his own teaching: "At first glance some things from the following propositions, questions, and expositions will appear monstrous, doubtful, or false."[112]

Eriugena uses a metaphor which describes a parallel between the hierarchy of the liberal arts and the cosmological hierarchy: earth and history, water and ethics, air and physics, fire and theology.[113] He tells us that dialectic works because it comes from the actual ordering of the universe (the logos of the cosmos), not because it is a human creation.[114] The ordering principle of the universe provides the universe with structure and informs the content of the lower Forms. By associating human cognition with this overarching logos, Eriugena's metaphors show us how human thought is effectively the

---

109 *Periphyseon*, 527B.

110 *Periphyseon*, 516C, 452A–B. As cited in Duclow, *Masters of Learned Ignorance*, 31.

111 *Periphyseon*, 650C–D. As cited in Duclow, *Masters of Learned Ignorance*, 31.

112 LW I, 152.3–5. Eckhart goes on to describe how such things are actually found in the highest authorities, including Scripture itself, just as I attempt to show in this chapter.

113 Duclow, *Masters of Learned Ignorance*, 46.

114 *Periphyseon* 748D–749A. As cited in Duclow, *Masters of Learned Ignorance*, 47.

creative speaking of the Word by God, just as increasing abstraction for Plato implies the ascension of the ontological continuum toward the Good. For Eriugena, there is something divine about the work that symbol does, just as Marie-Dominique Chenu claims of Dionysius.[115] Thus, Mary Brennan and John O'Meara say that Eriugena sometimes speaks *in divinis*, from God's point of view, just as C. F. Kelley said of Eckhart.[116]

Eckhart's Contemporaries

As we approach Eckhart's time, we see many similarities between his thought and that of his immediate predecessors and contemporaries. This is especially true with Albert the Great, who was Thomas Aquinas's teacher and perhaps Eckhart's as well during his time at the *Studium Generale* at Cologne. Albert accepted a rational approach to natural phenomena and also used Maimonides's distinction between faith and reason.[117] The increasing separation between faith and reason was characteristic of the overall trend we see in the thirteenth century. For Albert, the practice of theology should orient one toward loving and enjoying God. Beatitude is only available in the afterlife. We perceive things through the representation that we receive upon seeing it (like Roger Bacon but *contra* Peter Olivi, who said that we cannot describe vision in this way else we would not see the thing itself, but only the representation). However, in seeing God, there is no representation or intermediary. With all of this, we see Albert drawing a line between our knowledge of the physical world (he famously says when investigating the natural world that God's miracles are nothing to him) and the knowledge of God through theology. This provides a clue as to the status of inquiry into the natural world. If knowledge is *adequatio intellectus ad rem*, which means that the intellect is well matched to things, then knowing things means having intellectual representations that are equivalent to the things themselves (like Plato's Forms) and not just creating approximate conceptions of them. However, if the physical world is not an immediate given, this creates space for the possibility of a lesser form of knowledge that is the province of the individual.

---

115 Duclow, *Masters of Learned Ignorance*, 62.
116 Duclow, *Masters of Learned Ignorance*, 123; Carl Franklin Kelley, *Meister Eckhart on Divine Knowledge* (New Haven, Conn.: Yale University Press, 1977), xxii.
117 Gordon Leff, *Medieval Thought: St. Augustine to Ockham* (Atlantic Highlands, N.J.: Humanities Press, 1958), 208.

Albert's treatment of being also foreshadows important themes in Eckhart. Albert saw creatures as nonbeing in themselves, something that followed directly from the notion of all things flowing from God, an idea that Eckhart adopted.[118] This is what Armand Maurer had in mind when he said that, regarding the condemned proposition that creatures are nothing (have no existence) in themselves, Eckhart works from Albert's model of soul.[119] Albert says that there are two ways of considering the soul: as it is in itself as a pure formal reality, and as the soul is the form of the body. As the form of the body, the soul is diffused throughout the body. The soul is in the body just as any form is in its manifestations without itself being material.

For Aquinas and Albert, God willed individuals as well as universals, a crucial move away from Ancient Greek metaphysics and toward the elevation of the individual.[120] Individuals were part of the perfection of creation. Like Albert, Thomas Aquinas saw individual difference as adding to the world's beauty and as manifesting the fullest expression of God's will.[121] Albert described God as a divine font which was "overflowing" (*ebullitio*) into the world, an image that Eckhart also used.[122]

The early thirteenth century saw an expansion in thought about our mental life and how we know ourselves. For Thomas Aquinas, the mind is only manifest to itself when it interacts with the outside world in experience (i.e., any embodied act). Even our knowledge of ourselves, *contra* Albert, is not preexisting or above the level of individual experience. It is a product of it. Thus, for Aquinas, human nature is essentially embodied. This makes inquiry into the physical world a positive thing since such inquiry makes self-knowing possible. Further, Aquinas envisions each person having a single Form (the soul) rather than being a mixture or multiplicity of Forms. For the sake of the unity of the individual, he said that the single Form manifests many powers.

For Aquinas, the agent intellect (active intellect) is particular to each individual. We come to knowledge by a power that was given to us by God

---

118 Bernard McGinn, *The Harvest of Mysticism in Medieval Germany (1300–1500)* (New York: Crossroad, 2005), 17.

119 Meister Eckhart, *Parisian Questions and Prologues*, trans. Armand A. Maurer. (Toronto: Pontifical Institute of Mediaeval Studies, 1974), 37. For example, see Sermon 80, where Eckhart repeatedly refers to Saint Albert while talking about the union of the soul with God.

120 Heinz Heimsoeth, *The Six Great Themes of Western Metaphysics and the End of the Middle Ages*, trans. Ramon Betanzos (Detroit: Wayne State University Press, 1994), 207.

121 Heimsoeth, *Six Great Themes*, 201.

122 For more on this, see McGinn, *Harvest of Mysticism*, 16.

but is nonetheless individual. A number of thinkers around Eckhart's time reacted against Aquinas and reasserted that the uncreated light in the soul could clearly and directly come to know things. In other words, they reasserted Platonism by putting the knowledge of things and their forms and outside of their material manifestations. Aquinas and other contemporary Aristotelian thinkers pushed to place the source of knowledge in the material, with all its concomitant limits.[123]

By equating the form of an individual with his soul, Aquinas places the ontological status of the individual on the same level as material reality. The individual's being is wrapped up in material reality, and it knows only the material world by way of concepts abstracted from the material world. This is in contrast to the Augustinian approach, which sees the intellect as superior to the body ontologically. Thus, we see Aquinas saying that we abstract the concept of God from the material world while Henry of Ghent argues that we can abstract the concept of God from the concept of being itself.

Duns Scotus criticized them both on this point by saying that this inappropriately draws the analogy between the created world and God.[124] Thus, *contra* Aquinas's attempt at synthesizing faith and reason, Duns Scotus emphasized their difference, going as far as insisting that a theologian and philosopher can never be the same.[125] By making so much of faith inaccessible to reason, he effectively cut reason loose and gave it free reign over natural phenomena. Since he left the physical world for reason and claimed the rest for faith, he implied that faith played no role in thinking about natural phenomena.

Returning to the Forms of individuals, we see a similar elevation of individuals in Richard of Middleton, who claimed not only that there were forms of individuals but also that individuals were the goal of creation. After all, God grants eternal life to *individuals*. Richard contended that the individual is individual because it is deprived of divisibility (it is literally *in* + *dividual*). Duns Scotus disagreed, claiming that the individual must have something positive about it rather than being merely a privation of divisibility. He tells us that God wills individual differences as much as he does species and genera. Individuals crown his work and are higher than other things. As

---

[123] A clearer example of this and one from Eckhart's own lifetime was William of Ware (d. 1300). He described knowledge through intellectual abstraction (natural light of the intellect) rather than through divine illumination.

[124] Leff, *Medieval Thought*, 265.

[125] Leff, *Medieval Thought*, 264.

well, *contra* Aristotle, the individual cannot be only the result of a mixture of form with matter—that is, matter cannot be the individuating principle. Individuals must be positive forms in themselves. Duns Scotus describes individual difference as formal, his well-known notion of *haecceitas*, "this-ness," which is the indivisible unity that makes an individual an individual. Instead of individuals being particular manifestations of Forms that happen to inhabit a particular position in time and space, he argues that individuals are not intelligible by merely appealing to their parts or manifestations of humanity. Socrates is more than a particular manifestation of humanity—he is Socrates. We recognize such an individual differently than we recognize a commodity like a pear, which is arguably important to us for the kind of thing that it is rather than the individual that it is. By contrast, we recognize in Socrates a personality and individuality that is not reducible to any combination of features.

Like Bonaventure, the Augustinians generally described the ascent of knowledge from particular things to God himself. This involved a moving up the divided line and climbing the ontological ladder to the form of the Good itself. Eckhart, by contrast, was more concerned (just as Eriugena was) with the divinity inherent in being itself. He compressed the hierarchy of essences that one had to climb and thereby enabled one to go directly to God without intermediaries. Eckhart was not the only one to compress the ontological hierarchy. William of Ockham is representative of the push to prune the ontological tree down to almost nothing for theology *and* the physical world. Ockham trimmed the ontological tree of real entities by eliminating universals (collapsing it vertically) and by recognizing only substance and quality (collapsing it horizontally), leaving only individuals and their qualities.

Once individuals were fully enriched with significance, the scales could tip in the other direction and the individual could come to the foreground while God retreated to the background. This is when God became the *deus absconditus*, the "hidden god." Once the verisimilar forfeits its commensurability with absolute truth (when human understanding is no longer equal to what it tries to understand), it separates from it and can be considered a new kind of knowledge. When probability gained a firm foothold and the "truth" of mathematical knowledge was empirically demonstrable, truths of the natural world gained a means of standing on their own.

William of Ockham can easily be made to look more modern than he is if we endue his thought with the significance of ushering in the transition to the modern world. For our purposes, his infamous "razor" is not as significant as his near-elimination of the gradations of being. Ockham's razor is methodological, not metaphysical.[126] In fact, Ockham rejected metaphysical razors entirely.[127] It tells us how to reason well in metaphysics, but it does not tell us anything about metaphysical reality. Ockham also allowed for self-evident experiences to count as knowledge and register in his ontology.[128] In other words, his nominalism did not imply skepticism like that of Descartes or Quine. Further, Ockham maintained that God makes things with more than he needs to, but these are not subject to the principle of parsimony: God willed it, so it is worthwhile. In light of these aspects of his thinking, we can perhaps understand why Duns Scotus objected that we cannot do without the universal to the extent that Ockham claims since that would make knowledge impossible and we would fall into skepticism.

Eckhart's generation saw an increased questioning of the way we come to know things and how we should understand what knowledge is. For Peter Aureole, like William of Ockham, only the individual was real. Our concepts deal with how things appear to us, not with the things themselves. In this way, concepts are the province of the individual; they do not require divine intervention or something supra-individual like the active intellect to create understanding. This puts more of what we recognize as an individual's mental life in the domain of the individual and leaves it less clearly affected or intermixed with the divine. This makes the thing known separate from the process for knowing—that is, the intellect is not *aedequatio* to the thing known.[129]

The question of secondary causes also demonstrates a change in the notion of the individual. For Aquinas, every secondary cause was from itself and equally from God. Ockham and Bradwardine took the opposing extremes. For Ockham, it was from itself. For Bradwardine, it was from God, almost to the exclusion of its own impetus. So, after God acts as a primary cause, some questioned whether the secondary causes were the province of the individual rather than God. This possibility is only rendered coherent by a changed conception of the individual and a departure from received tradition, which emphasizes the persistent role of God even in the free actions of rational individuals. For example, Paul tells us "he be not far from every

---

[126] Rondo Keele, *Ockham Explained: From Razor to Rebellion* (Chicago: Open Court, 2010), 96.
[127] Keele, *Ockham Explained*, 104.
[128] Keele, *Ockham Explained*, 103.
[129] Leff, *Medieval Thought*, 282.

one of us: For in him we live, and move, and have our being."[130] It is against this backdrop that we may most readily understand where the differences are between Eckhart and his predecessors and contemporaries.

ECKHART'S THEOLOGY IN HISTORICAL CONTEXT

As Eckhart said in his defense, he drew many of his seemingly radical ideas from standard church authorities. However, Eckhart's inquisitors were more concerned with the idea of God being within us than they were with his lack of concern with the role of the historical Crucifixion in salvation.[131] In other words, his inquisitors homed in on Eckhart's rhetoric of the individual, especially insofar as it was a part of sermons that were given to uneducated people. We will look briefly here at some of the links that Eckhart rightly pointed to between his ideas and those of his predecessors. If Eckhart points to an authority as saying the same thing, it is worth taking note of any significant differences between Eckhart and that authority, since the differences will likely exemplify changes in culture and rhetoric. For now, we will describe Eckhart's theology in its historical context and leave aside questions of rhetoric. First, however, a bit of the history of Eckhart's time will fill out the details of the social backdrop.

Gordon Leff says that mysticism became a veritable movement at the end of the thirteenth century and its center was Cologne.[132] Bernard McGinn likewise tells us that mysticism of unity really came to the fore in the thirteenth century.[133] Finally, Kurt Ruh is known for calling Eckhart's era the *kairos* of German vernacular mysticism.[134] This is all to say that Eckhart was hardly alone in the direction of his thought. Albert the Great, who was active in Cologne and may have been Eckhart's teacher in the *Studium Generale* there, developed a Neoplatonic theology that recalled Eriugena's. During

---

130 Acts 17:27–28. Cf. 1 Cor 12:6, 2 Cor 3:5, Is 26:12; see Alfred J. Freddoso, "Medieval Aristotelianism and the Case against Secondary Causation in Nature," in *Divine and Human Action: Essays in the Metaphysics of Theism*, ed. Thomas V. Morris (Ithaca, N.Y.: Cornell University Press, 1988), 74–118.

131 John Connolly, *Living without Why: Meister Eckhart's Critique of the Medieval Concept of Will* (New York: Oxford University Press, 2014).

132 Leff, *Medieval Thought*, 299.

133 McGinn, *Harvest of Mysticism*, 120.

134 McGinn tells us that Ruh does not use the word *kairos*, but Köbele says that he suggested it to her. Bernard McGinn, "Mystical Language in Meister Eckhart and His Disciples," *Medieval Mystical Theology* 21, no. 2 (2012): 214n1.

Eckhart's formative years, his fellow Dominican, William of Moerbeke (d. ca. 1286) produced translations of some of Proclus's important works. Eckhart may have been in his twenties when William translated three of Proclus's short treatises and his voluminous *Commentary on Plato's Parmenides*. In 1270 and again in 1277, Étienne Tempier, the bishop of Paris, issued condemnations of Averroist and Aristotelian doctrines, some of which ostensibly targeted Aquinas. Though Proclus's star waned a bit after the condemnation of 1277, he was still, as Loris Sturlese put it, "a privileged discussion partner" for the German Dominicans.[135] In short, Neoplatonic thought remained a live topic of conversation during Eckhart's formative years.

After Eckhart's first stint as a Master in Paris in 1302-3, he was made provincial of the new province of Saxony from 1303-11. Pope Clement summoned a general council from Avignon in 1308, which met in Vienne from October 1311 to May 1312, to deal with the Free Spirit problem and other issues. The heresy of the Free Spirit refers to a collection of ideas, perhaps never sufficiently organized to warrant being called a "movement," that includes the beliefs that: the perfected soul was entirely one with God; the Church's intercession was not necessary; and the perfected person was above sin and was above the moral prescriptions of the church. The Beguines (lay religious women who lived communally, but outside the official monastic orders) enjoyed sanction for a century despite their tension with the Fourth Lateran Council (1215) and Second Council of Lyons (1274), which prohibited new forms of religious life. They came under fire only after the publishing of the Clementine Constitutions by Pope John XXII in 1317. The Beguines and Beghards who resisted institutionalization and wandered as mendicants received the greatest suspicion. It was also during this era that Marguerite Porete, the writer of *The Mirror of Simple Souls*, was burned at the stake (1310). Eckhart may have stayed at the house of her inquisitor in the following year when he returned to Paris for his second appointment. Given Eckhart's proximity to key figures and prominence in theological circles, surely we must conclude that his nearly two decades of teaching by this time could not have been generally regarded as problematic, even less as heretical. Finally, he was in contact with spiritual women in convents in Germany in the years following. This created the possibility that Eckhart's thought was influenced by them, something that has been much pursued. However, Bernard McGinn's assessment seems most reasonable: we have no

---

135 McGinn, *Harvest of Mysticism*, 46.

compelling evidence for influence from that direction.[136] Throughout his life, in Paris, Cologne, and Avignon, Eckhart was in the heart of the theological and mystical thought of his time.

We see Eckhart pushing the mystical thought of his time further with his use of "boiling" (*bullitio*) and "boiling over" (*ebullitio*). He describes the intradivine generation of the persons of the Trinity as *bullitio*, "boiling."[137] Likewise, he describes how God's superabundant goodness "boils over" (*ebullitio*) as creation. While Augustine, Aquinas and Bonaventure saw echoes of the Trinity in creation, Eckhart is perhaps closest to Eriugena, who saw that God was present in all creation and that this presence was the pathway back to God.[138]

All activity is trinitarian because *bullitio* is the "cause and exemplar of creation," of *ebullitio*.[139] The key to understanding this is in his idea that a form and what is informed share an essence: "Note that an image properly speaking is a simple formal emanation that transmits the whole pure naked essence."[140] Consequently, "a form and what it informs make up no number."[141] That is, the informed is formed by an *internal* principle, not as a result of an *external* cause. For Eckhart, since efficient and final causes require multiplicity and action from outside, they are external. For the act of creation itself, referring to the *logos* of John 1:1, Eckhart says, "the reason of things is a principle in such a way that it does not have or look to an exterior cause, but looks within to the essence alone. Therefore, the metaphysician who considers the entity of things proves nothing through exterior causes, that is, efficient and final causes."[142]

---

136 However, Eckhart's use of *viriditas* (greenness) is intriguing. He uses this term in much the same way that Hildegard of Bingen did. Oliver Davies, "Hildegard of Bingen, Mechthild of Magdeburg and the young Meister Eckhart," *Mediävistik* 4 (1991): 57. See especially the section on the spark of the soul in chapter 6.

137 As will be discussed at length in the analysis chapter, it is important that boiling is an *activity* rather than something passive. As our return to God through the birth of the Word in the soul mimics this *bullitio* and *ebullitio* pair, it is accomplished in an active fashion within the multiplicitous world, not merely through world-renouncing contemplation.

138 In explaining *ebullitio*, Anne Hunt says, "While Augustine of Hippo and Thomas Aquinas had recognized Trinitarian vestiges in everything in creation, and Bonaventure the trinitarian structure in everything in creation, Eckhart presses further and articulates an understanding of all activity as essentially trinitarian in its structure and dynamism." Anne Hunt, *The Trinity: Insights from the Mystics* (Collegeville, Minn.: The Liturgical Press, 2010), 84.

139 Meister Eckhart, Sermon XXV, LW IV, 236.7–8, trans. Bernard McGinn in *Meister Eckhart: Teacher and Preacher* (New York: Paulist Press, 1986), 218.

140 Eckhart, Sermon XLIX, trans. McGinn in *Teacher and Preacher*, 236.

141 Eckhart, Sermon IV, trans. McGinn in *Teacher and Preacher*, 210.

142 Eckhart, *Commentary on Genesis* B.4, trans. McGinn in *Essential Eckhart*, 83.

As we read some of Eckhart's ostensibly unusual exegeses of Scripture, we also do well to bear in mind his place in the tradition of allegorical interpretation. Eckhart follows Augustine in saying that "every true sense is a literal sense."[143] Further, "the literal sense is that which the author of a writing intends, and God is the author of holy scripture."[144]

Eckhart's notion of detachment by turning away from our desires for worldly things and the activity of discursive reason recalls the work of Bernard of Clairvaux, William of Saint Thierry, and others.[145] As vernacular preaching came into its own in the thirteenth century, the term *religion* came to be applied to the lay population as well, bringing with it a different language, one which Eckhart both used and helped to form.[146] We see similar language and mystical elements in other thinkers around the same time and place as Eckhart.[147] Most of the terms which we think of as distinctively Eckhartian were appropriated from previous thinkers and given their own meaning in Eckhart's work.[148] Conceptually, Eckhart's listeners may have been familiar with quite similar ideas in the work of Dietrich of Freiburg.[149] Even the birth of the Word in the soul, the concept that drew the most attention at his trial, was a used by early Christians to describe baptism and is found in Gregory of Nyssa and the Greek Fathers.[150] Similarly, the desert

---

143 Eckhart, *Book of the Parables of Genesis*, LW 1.1, 449.7–8; cf. *Essential Eckhart*, 93; cf. Thomas Aquinas, *Summa Theologiae*, Ia.1.10; Augustine, *Confessions*, 12.31.42. Duclow puts it nicely: "Eckhart blurs all distinction between literal and parabolical meanings." *Masters of Learned Ignorance*, 171.

144 *Book of the Parables of Genesis*, LW I.1, 449.6–7, quoting Aquinas, *Summa Theologiae*, I.q1. a10.

145 Saskia Murk-Jansen, "Hadewijch and Eckhart, Amor intellegere est," in *Meister Eckhart and the Beguine Mystics*, ed. Bernard McGinn (New York: Continuum, 1994), 25.

146 Lynn White, "Medieval Engineering and the Society of Knowledge," *Pacific Historical Review* 44, no. 1 (1975): 7–8. For example, although Eckhart uses the language of the Minnesingers, which was in the German vernacular, he "never leaves us in doubt that this secular love vocabulary has now been restored to a theological purpose, but has, at the same time, lost none of the meanings that had accrued to it during its secular use" (Kenneth Northcott, "Preface" in *Teacher and Preacher*, xiv).

147 Oliver Davies, *Meister Eckhart: Mystical Theologian* (London: SPCK, 1991), 93.

148 Eckhart, *Book of Divine Consolation*, 3.11.27. For example, Boethius refers to a "spark," which may have influenced Eckhart's use of the term.

149 "There are many echoes in particular of Dietrich of Freiberg in Eckhart's thought: the primacy of knowing over being, the wholly dynamic and transcendent character of our intellectual substance and, not least, the belief that we are at our core linked in an immediacy to God through the principle of participation in his divine knowledge." Davies, *Mystical Theologian*, 92.

150 Elizabeth Brient, *The Immanence of the Infinite: Hans Blumenberg and the Threshold to Modernity* (Washington, D.C.: The Catholic University of America Press, 2002), 172; Bernard McGinn, "Love, Knowledge, and Unio Mystica in the Western Christian Tradition," in *Mystical*

(*einöde*) and wilderness (*wüste*) were used by others in the late medieval Rhineland school of mystics in apophatic contexts.[151]

Physics and Being, Compressing the Hierarchy, and the *In Quantum* Principle

Eckhart saw all creatures as having their being directly from God and belonging only to God. This means that God is present in his entirety in the smallest part of even the lowest of creatures. By the fifteenth century, individual things would come to be seen as infinitely rich. By endowing each created thing with the richness of God's infinity in even the smallest part of its being, Eckhart helps to lay the groundwork necessary for this development.[152]

In a rare passage where Eckhart addresses physics,[153] he says, "To be set in motion denotes an imperfection. Accordingly, the more perfect something is, the less it participates in motion and place ... whatever has existence fully is immutable, for example God. But whatever has only a part of existence is mutable."[154] Eckhart says very little of cosmology. By this nearly complete omission of what is otherwise a staple in medieval theology, we should understand that his references to cosmology and physics are subsidiary to his concern for the overall Neoplatonic metaphysics of flow, whereby the created world flows from God and ultimately returns to God. Even on the rare occasions when he mentions physical or cosmological principles, they are primarily examples and alternative approaches to his usual themes. For example, Eckhart tells us, "in every superior being there exists [every inferior] as such; and insofar as the former exists, to that extent does the latter. So there must be an order in nature, which consists in nothing else other than the relation of superior to inferior. Water, for example, moves downward

---

Union and Monotheistic Faith: An Ecumenical Dialogue, ed. Moshe Idel and Bernard McGinn (New York: Macmillan, 1989), 75.

151 Paul Dietrich, "The Wilderness of God in Hadewijch II and Meister Eckhart and His Circle," in *Meister Eckhart and the Beguine Mystics*, ed. Bernard McGinn (New York: Continuum, 1994), 31.

152 Brient, *Immanence of the Infinite*, 184.

153 As Maurer observed, "The fourth Question raises a problem in the philosophy of nature: Can there be motion without a terminus or end? This is an unusual topic for Eckhart. To judge from his literary remains, he seems to have almost completely ignored this branch of philosophy." Maurer, *Parisian Questions and Prologues*, 24.

154 q.4; Maurer, *Parisian Questions and Prologues*, 68–69.

and upward through the motion of the moon, and that motion is swifter and more delightful."[155]

Esse est deus: Eckhart's Ontology

We are never far from God with Eckhart. We must remember that although he refers to greater and lesser degrees of existence which might seem to imply an ontological hierarchy, the connection between the individual beings and God for Eckhart is without intermediaries. Eckhart cites Augustine and says that God is immediately present in his entirety to each thing.[156] It is on this point that we see a divergence in rhetoric between Eckhart and Augustine. Eckhart goes further and tells us that it works this way with substantial forms as well, "The soul with its whole self, without an intermediary, is immediately present to, and informs, the whole living body."[157] This recalls the common maxim, used by Eriugena and known also to Augustine and Boethius: *omne quod in deo est deus est*—all that is in God is God.[158] Eckhart's extension of Augustine traces directly to the notion of the individual.

Eckhart's description also recalls Eriugena. As Eriugena says, "all things in the Word are not only eternal, but are actually the very Word Itself."[159] An individual thing is a being insofar as we may speak of limits to its existence which differentiate it and thereby put it further from God while at the same time it is never apart from God in its being. In the *Book of Causes* XXIII §180, we read that things receive the first cause in proportion to their capacity to receive it: "by 'being' I mean only 'knowledge,' for to the extent that the thing knows the First Creative Cause to that extent it receives of it and takes delight in it."[160] This defines the hierarchy and makes existence the differentiating principle by the proportion to which things are receptive to the God.[161]

---

155 q.5; Maurer, *Parisian Questions and Prologues*, 74. Eckhart makes the same point in a similarly offhanded manner in referring to Ptolemy. Eckhart, *Commentary on Exodus* n.152, trans. McGinn in *Teacher and Preacher*, 92.

156 q.5; Maurer, *Parisian Questions and Prologues*, 98. Eckhart refers us to *Conf.* I.3.

157 q.5; Maurer, *Parisian Questions and Prologues*, 99.

158 Duclow, *Masters of Learned Ignorance*, 122.

159 Eriugena, *Periphyseon*, 641. As cited by Duclow, *Masters of Learned Ignorance*, 57.

160 *The Book of Causes*, trans. Dennis J. Brand (Milwaukee, Wis.: Marquette University Press, 2012), 39.

161 Maurer, *Parisian Questions and Prologues*, 100.

For Eckhart, however, the being that God gives does not become the creature's exclusive property. God does not depart from it or separate from it. Yet it is also part of what the creature is. This makes the individual both created and divine. Eckhart straddles this difficulty with his *in quantum* principle: insofar as (*in quantum*) man is created, he is ephemeral and imperfect; insofar as he has understanding, justice, and goodness, there is no separation between him and the divine. Eckhart thus preserves the rhetoric of Platonic ontology while simultaneously raising individual beings to God by way of their being, which is God's Being. Individual existences, as imperfections, become rather like the traditional Platonic theodicy: their imperfection has no existence, just as there is no Platonic Form of evil. This is a natural consequence of Eckhart's compression of the hierarchy: all Forms less than God himself obtain a kind of phantasmal quality and do not have their own existence apart from the oneness of Being. Individual things are thereby "created nothings."[162] Even though Eckhart preserves a hierarchy, insofar as created things are considered as particular things, individual things are simply not unqualifiedly individual. This is less a matter of theological reasoning than of rhetorical implication. In effect, he blurs the boundary between the individual and God.

Eckhart is at pains to limit *being* to refer only to individual beings of the created world.[163] Thus, being is not convertible with God in the same way that justice and goodness are. Existence is God (*esse est deus*) insofar as all beings have their being from God. God, however, is not existence (*deus est esse*) insofar as God is not the existence of any created thing qua created. God is created things qua Being (existence in general) but God is not created things qua created things (existence in particular).[164] As Eckhart says, "existence is through itself and by itself the principle of distinction [between things]."[165]

---

162 Maurer describes the situation like this: if God alone is existence, how do creatures exist? "Creatures exist within existence, that is to say within God and through the divine existence. Eckhart's justification of this bold stand engages him in some of his most abstruse metaphysical speculation." Maurer, *Parisian Questions and Prologues*, 33–34.

163 q.2; Maurer, *Parisian Questions and Prologues*, 52.

164 This point does not have widespread agreement since Eckhart's *esse est deus* thesis appears to be in tension with his contention that the being of all things is God. I believe the tension can be resolved by appealing to the difference between the kind of existence that differentiates things (being) and existence in general (Being). To exist as a particular thing (being) implies a falling away from God and thus not being God. However, to exist at all is to participate in existence in general (Being). The idea of Being adds nothing to God while the idea of being would add something and thus cannot be God.

Even though this is the case, individual things still look rather like phantasms since inferior things (as effects) owe everything to the superior things from which lesser things flow. This is the order of the world.

Albertus Magnus says that something exists when it stands outside of its cause.[166] So, existing things are caused things. God is not caused, so he cannot be defined by existence. In other words, Eckhart has Saint Albert and Henry of Ghent as allies in opposing Aquinas on being. Eckhart takes the further step and reverses Aquinas by saying that "existence is God" (*esse est deus*) instead of Aquinas's "God is existence" (*deus est esse*), a move that is not so radical and new when considering contemporaries other than Aquinas.

It is a quintessentially mystical move. Mysticism can be thought of as the progressive erasure of our assumptions and conceptual distinctions by un-thinking and methodically challenging the foundations of our worldview and way of being in the world. I would add color to this idea by way of another metaphor: the assumptions and concepts that previously looked real and substantial to us are progressively shown in mystical writing to *evanesce* by losing their ultimately illusory reification. The thing that we previously thought to be so certain and so real still remains, but only as a kind of phantasm that no longer has existence in itself, from itself, and through itself (as Eckhart might say).[167] This evanescence is the mechanism by which we may understand Eckhart's notion of *detachment* as well. Our attachment to "images" has strength that derives from our assessment of the substantial and meaningful reality of the images. As the images ontologically deflate and become phantasmal, the habit of attachment naturally atrophies. At the same time (and in a way of juxtaposition of opposing metaphors), we might prefer to characterize this as having assumptions, concepts, and all distinct (individual) things flow back into their source. This is the Neoplatonic "metaphysics of flow," a metaphor that captures the way that created individuals depart from their source without departing and without their source departing from them, facilitating our realization that they may flow backwards into their source and lose their distinctions. In this way of speaking, the distinctions are illusory, but their being is not.

---

165 Maurer, *Parisian Questions and Prologues*, 100.

166 In doing this, he breaks apart existence into *ex* + *sistere*, meaning "to stand out"—as in, to stand outside of its cause, in the same way that Richard of St. Victor did. Maurer, *Parisian Questions and Prologues*, 17.

167 This trope is one that will be explored in greater detail when we discuss Eckhart's metaphors.

With Duns Scotus's treatment of *haecceitas* in mind, we can see Eckhart commenting on contemporary issues in his *Parisian Questions* while also extending the discussion in his characteristic fashion:

> Existence belongs to the whole and only to the whole. And because the whole is one, so also is existence one.... The part does not have existence, for there are many parts, and all are one, for existence is one. Hence the part as such has no existence; but it has existence only through the relation it bears to the whole as to existence. The part, lacking the whole, is non-being, but as related to the whole it has existence.[168]

Just as parts have their existence only in the whole, individual beings have their existence only in God. Things that are parts, accidents, or effects owe their existence to their cause, which in the end is God. Eckhart tells us that "in each mixed body there is only one substantial form."[169] We might interpret this to mean that there is a single form of the individual, which is not incorrect provided we also maintain the paradox of God's presence in his entirety in the smallest part. If the soul is the Form of the body and the soul is the image of God who is its exemplar, we once again see no distance between individual rational souls and God considered in their essence (i.e., as rational). For Aquinas, being is the perfection of all things, even the forms.[170] For Eckhart, God is beyond being. Rational souls are divine insofar as they understand. We know this since understanding is indeterminate and is not a being,[171] since it "is a sort of conformity to God or deification, for God is understanding itself and not existence," and since it is uncreatable.[172] Understanding is superior, given the principle that one thing is better than another if it "is the exact reason why we are pleasing to God. This is understanding: one is pleasing to God precisely because he understands, for if knowledge is taken away absolutely nothing is left."[173] This is Eckhart's understanding of the *imago dei* and the way in which mankind straddles the divide between the creaturely and the divine with understanding. In this way, he appears thoroughly Dominican.

---

168 q.5; Maurer, *Parisian Questions and Prologues*, 72–73.

169 q.5; Maurer, *Parisian Questions and Prologues*, 71.

170 Maurer, *Parisian Questions and Prologues*, 35.

171 q.3; Maurer, *Parisian Questions and Prologues*, 54.

172 q.3; Maurer, *Parisian Questions and Prologues*, 59.

173 q.3; Maurer, *Parisian Questions and Prologues*, 59.

It is worth observing that by pushing toward a compression of the celestial hierarchy by emphasizing God's presence without mediation, Eckhart is part of the mounting opposition to what was traditional teaching at that time. Dionysius and Proclus (by way of the *Book of Causes* if the ideas ultimately trace back to him) both conceived of the world in terms of an ontological hierarchy. Eckhart says, pointing to the standard authorities, that he does as well, though his continued emphasis on the lack of intermediaries and creatures as created nothings is a characteristically scholastic, clever middle ground between the Neoplatonic celestial hierarchy and Ockham's radical pruning of the ontological tree.

The Active Life: Man as Creator

Eckhart's emphasis on individual action, even with total humility and obedience, is perhaps the clearest evidence of how his rhetoric prepares for and presages later developments in the conception of the individual. Spontaneous activity can happen in proportion to an individual's ability to self-generate action. At the extreme, such an individual would be completely individuated, completely isolated from other individuals (as with Leibniz's monads and Valentin Weigel's account of spontaneous individual action).[174] We can only say that a thing *acts* rather than being *acted upon* when that thing is sufficiently individuated. Recall Aristotle's conception (since many of Eckhart's contemporaries would have had Aristotle in mind) of motion: when potential becomes action. Turning potential to action is one way of speaking of God's act of creation since it is self-moving, not influenced from the outside. Similarly, man's free will is self-moving. His reason can be as well, for Eckhart, if he strips himself of all the created nothings that prevent his will from becoming God's will. His is a new theology of action, made possible by man sharing God's divinity. That the individual is still spoken of as individual throughout gives us reason to think that Eckhart thinks about man as a *creator*. Indeed, this is the way that Eckhart speaks about man in Sermon 52: "For in God's own being where God is above being and above distinction, there I myself was, there I willed myself and knew my own self to create this man. Therefore I am my own cause with respect to my being, which is eternal, and not with respect to my becoming, which is temporal."[175]

---

174 Heimsoeth, *Six Great Themes*, 208.
175 Eckhart, Sermon 52, DW II, 502.7–503.2.

This represents a *maximum* of creative capacity since it is God's own creative capacity. In other words, we should not be disappointed that Eckhart did not speak of our ability to create mundane things like spoons (to recall one of Cusanus's examples) since he spoke of man as being a creator in the highest sense. That may be too simple, however, because Eckhart did not consider anything less than God to be a creator, "nothing that is this or that is the first and universal cause of everything, nor does it create."[176] Cusanus was, after all, working with an epistemology that evolved in the century after Eckhart.

Up to the late medieval period, any knowledge that went beyond sense perception was assumed to be knowledge of the universal. Since our minds are well matched to what we perceive, there is no need for approximate knowledge. As Blumenberg tells the story in the *Legitimacy*, the idea of the *deus absconditus* resulted in the legitimation of theoretical curiosity and the unknowability of the material world (which can be "known" only through approximation). Eckhart again represents a preparatory stage for this. Although he did not go so far as to speculate on knowledge by approximation, his anthropology of man as divine and as creator facilitated such thinking. Approximate knowledge became a possibility with the fading of the pre-givenness of the natural world. This transition did not occur without resistance, of course, though the defenses ironically (as is often the case) ended up hurting their cause.[177] This is not actually all that surprising. If the change is already in the air, the expressions of defenses will necessarily include the change in their thinking, thus appearing to and in fact contributing to the opposite of their intentions. In Eckhart's case, we have less of a defense than a deemphasizing by omission. The medieval views of man and knowledge constituted part of the inertia that had to be overcome to enable the emergence of the modern age. Eckhart participated in this transition in two subtle ways. First, he omitted or downplayed elements of the medieval worldview that were later to be overcome. Second, his anthropology pushed in a direction that was compatible with the changes that were happening.

The transition from adequate to approximate knowledge happened at least in part due to the change in the conception of the individual. If the soul can take any form and knowing is being like the known (Aristotle), then adequate knowledge is implied. However, knowing is limited to mere approximation when the soul itself cannot be all things. Eckhart stands squarely on

---

176 Maurer, *Parisian Questions and Prologues*, 101.
177 Cf. Blumenberg, *Legitimacy of the Modern Age*, 346–47.

the medieval side of this so far. However, once the particulars of the natural world are enriched, the soul is no longer assumed to be able to become them through knowledge, as it was for Aristotle. Thus, the move toward the intensive infinitization of particulars also enables modern conceptions of approximate knowledge. Since Eckhart's rhetoric of the individual enables him to speak of the individual as individual even with God's Being, we may recognize Eckhart as an intermediate step between the medieval and modern notions of self, with the concomitant consequences for epistemology.

Eckhart helped clear one of the most significant roadblocks to the modern conception of creativity: the idea that man cannot produce anything since God is the only rightful possessor of active intellect. Eckhart himself would not have been interested in exploring the consequences of this for worldly creation of things (like Cusanus's spoon maker) because, he thought all worldly preoccupation of that kind was simply a species of attachment. Eckhart enabled thinking about man as creator because of his metaphorics, not because of his explicit theological arguments—as we see with the intensive infinitization of particulars. His mysticism was fundamentally traditional, while his metaphorics contained important elements that facilitated the transition to a new era of thinking about what humanity is. Although Eckhart did not argue for the legitimacy of curiosity and approximate knowledge of the natural world, he spoke in a way that cleared the way for more modern developments.

Eckhart does not say much at all about knowledge of the natural world, practically eschewing this application of the topic of knowledge altogether. This may be a distant echo of Roger Bacon's important separation of moral knowledge, which is reserved for God, from natural knowledge.[178] In those terms, Eckhart only concerns himself with moral knowledge. Though he does not reassert this division (which surely would have been a topic of conversation in his university education), by addressing only the divine, moral knowledge Eckhart downplays the significance of knowledge of the physical world. This indirectly helped Bacon's cause and furthered the development toward modern thought. Blumenberg tells this story in terms of God's truth receding from view as his absolute transcendence was overemphasized, which resulted in humanity reverting to pursuing its own truth about the natural world. *Contra* Blumenberg, we can describe the situation in the late medieval world as Socrates was described by Cicero: "Socrates was

---

178 Cf. Blumenberg, *Legitimacy of the Modern Age*, 387.

the first who called philosophy down from the heavens."[179] As the ontological hierarchy was compressed in different ways by Eckhart and Ockham,[180] the sphere was compressed to a circle and the poles became the center, to borrow an image from Eckhart's Sermon XXIV.2. Man "rises" as the hierarchy compresses.

Pseudonymity and *Auctoritas*

To round out the history of the individual and bring into focus the way in which medieval authors thought of originality and creative work, we must address the question of pseudonymity. First and foremost, pseudonymous writing was an entirely different phenomenon in the ancient world than it is today. When we think about the use of a pseudonym, the most obvious things that we can say are a result of our valuation of the individual as a meaningful entity. Being possessed by a god (or by the Holy Spirit, in Augustine's Christianity, so as to let the Father speak through you) so effaced the identity of the person doing the speaking as to render his or her identity relatively unimportant and entirely transparent to the deity. In other words, people in ancient times did not assume, as we often do, that a person claiming to speak in the name of a god could only be *merely* a person claiming to speak in the name of a god. Instead, the divine was understood in a way that allowed for personal identity to be effaced. This idea in particular is one that people today struggle to relate to and understand.

So when we hear McGinn say that "the apocalypses are written texts claiming to be both inspired and ancient, claims based on the use of pseudonymity, that is, ascribing a piece to a seer or holy man of the past. Thus, an apocalypse is a new book pretending to be an old one," we may be too easily inclined to sympathize with his flippant use of the term "pretending" and its concomitant connotations.[181] Given my description above, my divergence from McGinn on this passage may be plain: "Pseudonymity, common in both Jewish and non-Jewish literature of the time, indicates a belief that revelation was in the distant past and is fixed in written texts, and it also implies that those who sought to identify themselves with the heroes of Israel's past felt

---

179 Cicero, *Tusculanae Disputationes*, V.10.

180 Eckhart worked to compress the Neoplatonic hierarchy while Ockham pruned the Aristotelian hierarchy. Though both worked to modify scholastic ontologies, they worked against the two different major branches of scholastic thought at the time.

181 McGinn, *Foundations of Mysticism*, 12.

that they could claim an equally inspired authority for writings issued in the seer's name."[182] I would say instead that it is not merely a matter of a people seeking to "identify" with past heroes. Rather, their inspiration was *on par* with and thereby *identical to* the past figures. As with divine possession, we describe it in a hopelessly reductive manner if we do not take seriously the claim that the individual's identity can be lost or taken over. Questions of identity are moot since the function and significance are identical. In other words, if one speaks from the same spiritual place as a famous figure, then it makes sense to do away with pretenses and say that your words are not your own—the words are theirs. Rhetorically, we intuitively understand part of the significance of this. If you believe, for example, that the *Divine Names* was written by Dionysius the Areopagite, then your reception of it will be colored by your esteem for that figure and reverence for words that derive from that source. In ministry, Augustine, the former professor of rhetoric, would have been in the best position to recognize and understand that the way in which speech is received is significantly altered by the use of pseudonymity. The problem with the modern intuition is that we tend to think of pseudonymity as a kind of lie. Rhetorically, there is an important sense in which the objective truth of what is said (I use this phrase only to emphasize the absurdity) is secondary to the effect that the words have on the listener. In other words, if a sermon causes you to realize as Aquinas did that "all is straw" compared to the experience that was had, then what difference does it make if the statements made are "literally" true? If the experience is what counts, then the means are merely tools. In fact, Eckhart made use of this sort of rhetorical tool by his (amusing) trope of saying "A master once said" when he was referring to himself. There is also a sense in which philosophical dialogues (those of Plato and Kierkegaard in particular) usurp some of this power and leverage the same phenomenon. Theatrical performances also involve a setting aside of identity and temporary assumption of another persona for the purposes of a particular rhetorical and dramatic end. This is easily underestimated and misunderstood now. Our difficulty derives from the all-too-facile assumption that personal identity is something fixed and permanent, incapable of being any more than figuratively superseded for a time.

---

182 McGinn, *Foundations of Mysticism*, 13.

CONCLUSION

The historical narrative should lay plain two things. First, the idea of what the self is ontologically and where the boundaries between it and the divine lie was changing during Eckhart's time. Second, although he cited authorities who did indeed express the same ideas in their theology, the rhetorical differences between Eckhart and those authorities may be explained in large part by the changes in the notion of the individual.

If we do not allow for something other than the individual to have primacy, then mysticism can appear as merely one theological option among many and its rhetoric must be conformed to a system of categories that facilitates comparison, a system that is foreign and inimical to it. By looking at some of the interpretive issues with Eckhart and how certain approaches miss the mark and steer our understanding in the wrong direction, we will be in a better position to understand how to avoid such pitfalls.

2

The Problem with Interpreting Eckhart

Philosophy has difficulty coming to terms with mysticism. That is because it attempts to put terms to it. Those who treat mysticism as a philosophical or theological phenomenon often attempt to domesticate it and fit it into a larger narrative: as one path among many in Christian spirituality or one option among others in philosophical practice.[1] In both cases, it is *compared* to other practices or arguments. Comparison requires a minimum of similarity. This cannot help but to miss the point of mysticism. Mystical oneness is not similar to anything. If it were, it would not be oneness. Concepts have only a limited utility in describing the stripping away of all concepts and the thinking that arises from them. As soon as we dualistically divide the world up into A and not-A, we move away from mysticism. Ironically, however, no understanding of mysticism can begin without concepts because we must begin from wherever we are. Our starting place is likely in conceptual thought. So we begin there and use rhetoric to inspire action in the most useful direction—namely, toward a stripping away of concepts and conceptual thinking. This is why Eckhart's focus is pragmatic and hortatory.[2]

---

[1] Robert Forman echoes this sentiment in *Meister Eckhart: The Mystic as Theologian: An Experiment in Methodology* (Rockport, Mass.: Element, 1991), x.

[2] Forman says that Echkart's "theory passages are all hortative in intent," which goes too far only if we understand them as merely hortatory. See *Mystic as Theologian*, 160. We find a similarly paradoxical situation with Socratic irony: Socrates knows the ultimate end lies outside of dialectic, but the practice of it and the statements he makes are still *honest and genuine*. We do not have to think of mystics as *lying* when using concepts to push others closer to seeing for themselves.

INTERPRETING ECKHART

Eckhart's theory as theory is still useful to those who think in philosophical terms and have these terms as their starting point—a description that fits his Latin readership. The trouble is that some recent scholars, typified by Kurt Flasch, attempt to exclude mystical experience and characterize Eckhart as only a philosopher. Their motivation for doing so is not entirely clear, though it may relate to a perception that excess in ecstatic forms of mysticism is somehow illegitimate.[3] Eckhart lived at a time when experiential mysticism was popular in the same circles in which he moved. If he had a problem with it, surely he would have said so. He spoke against overly somatic mysticism, any practice which stops with love or knowledge, and unnecessarily ascetic practices, but never against mystical union. If you see Eckhart as a philosopher, you might think that union with God is a state of mind for an individual and, ultimately, an illusion created by a certain oceanic feeling. If you are a mystic, the situation flips: self is the illusion, and the progressive stripping away of all concepts and possibility for concepts eventually results in the decomposition, dissolution, and "annihilation of self" (*vernihten sîn selbes*).[4] The difficulty for us today is that this attempt to separate Eckhart from mysticism not only does violence to his thinking, but also it discourages his modern readers from sympathetically identifying their own experiences and ways of seeing with Eckhart. These scholars' position is characteristically difficult to argue against, however, precisely because one must *argue* against it to do so. Ineffable experiences that lie beyond intellectual understanding cannot be formulated or even referred to by traditional speech, since they are not *like* anything we have experienced and know. The best Eckhart can do is to point in the directions we must move to see for ourselves, embody what it is like to live in them, and not allow others to rest comfortably with their existing understanding. This is why I will argue that Eckhart *insists* upon his paradoxes. It is perfectly obvious to anyone who has had mystical experience that Eckhart speaks as one who knows and perpetually points back to it. It is my hope that my argument for connoisseurship in the next chapter will

---

[3] Though Mojsisch tacks on general, negative comments about mysticism to the end of various arguments, at the very end of one of his books he comes close to telling us what he thinks mysticism is: "Knowledge as action, however, is not action as an end in itself; it is not a contemplative fall into a self-related egoism or a trusting in God eliminative of all consciousness; it is not a dissolution into mysticism." *Meister Eckhart: Analogy, Univocity and Unity*, trans. Orrin F. Summerell (Amsterdam: Grüner, 2001) 170.

[4] Eckhart, *Councils on Discernment*, §23, DW V, 292.7.

be understood in part as an answer to those who would interpret Eckhart merely as a philosopher.

Interpreters of Eckhart walk a fine line between attempting to stay faithful to what he says and describing him in the context of their larger intellectual enterprises. On one extreme, we have Steven Katz's work, which claims there are no unmediated experiences, placing him squarely in the camp of those who insist in a characteristically modern way on the ineradicability of the individual. It is hard not to notice how well this fits with the intellectual fashion of the mid-twentieth century in emphasizing difference. Bernard McGinn does better than this, of course, in his multivolume history of Christian mysticism. He recognizes Eckhart as a mystic and is careful to represent his thought accurately. Still, he says that "indistinct union can be described as a continuous state of non-absorptive and transformative awareness."[5] It is hard to imagine Eckhart agreeing with this, since it amounts to saying that the individual only has the illusion of unity as part of a mental *state* while remaining individual. This separates the "human subject" from God and makes union merely rhetorical. McGinn makes this more explicit elsewhere when he speaks of "responses of the human subject to the divine presence" and says that "mysticism of union is just one of the species of a wider and more diverse genus or group" since it is "one of" the "ideals of Christian perfection."[6] By saying that mysticism is "one of" the ideals of Christian perfection, McGinn implies that it is a member of a group of like things, able to be compared with other members of that group.

Many of Eckhart's modern commentators proceed with due scholarly diligence in representing his thought. Still, many of his most careful interpreters cannot follow him all the way, unable to let go of their own understanding of what an individual is. Blumenberg showed remarkable scholarly care, being true to the thought of a great many historical figures, including Eckhart, which makes reading him wonderfully useful. Nevertheless, we still find at bottom a minimal backdrop of individual subjectivity.[7] For any writer who does not directly identify with the mystics, the task of describing them well is difficult indeed since mystical speech resists any attempt at description that does not also demand a transformation of the way that

---

5 McGinn, *Harvest of Mysticism*, 183.
6 McGinn, "Love, Knowledge, and Unio Mystica in the Western Christian Tradition," 59–60.
7 Franz Josef Wetz, "The Phenomenological Anthropology of Hans Blumenberg," *Iris: European Journal of Philosophy & Public Debate* 1, no. 2 (2009): 389.

you see yourself and the world. As with Augustine's self-effacing, humble language, McGinn likens his history to Plato's "likely story" in the *Timaeus*, and Blumenberg qualifies his own account by saying that he only hopes for a Husserlian fitness that stubbornly resists being set aside.[8] Such rhetorical devices naturally deemphasize argumentative claims to truth and instead cast light on the effect the writing has on the reader. This makes the text pragmatic and perhaps implicitly hortatory by encouraging a similar way of seeing. Indeed, my own project here reflects similar ambitions to be an image of Eckhart, though without recourse to a minimal backdrop of individuality except where such rhetoric is kairotic.

Fundamentally, posing the question, "What do we get out of reading Eckhart?" has more depth than asking "What does he say?" Eckhart poses an acute interpretative challenge because his aims are inextricably wrapped up with ineffable religious experience. The question of interpreting Eckhart implies the question of what experience can and should mean to philosophy and theology. Instead of simply arguing for abstract truth, Eckhart shows us what it is like to live in the awareness of God's being in all things.[9] The tie to experience militates against facile distillation of traditional philosophical claims from his work. Consequently, interpreting Eckhart is like trying to capture the living, breathing, what-it's-like experience of listening to a sermon. Though it may be convenient to talk of individual pieces abstracted from the whole, ultimately the lived experience of understanding Eckhart is itself nonconceptual and dynamic. It is natural then to have recourse to metaphor in describing it, something that is true whenever we can "get in the head" of a particular author.

Eckhart's words are important because of what they *do* rather than what they *say*. His speech loses its primary function when lifted from its context. Recognizing this will shed light on how the inquisitorial process against him was destined to miss his meaning, focused as it was on distilling particular claims by considering statements in isolation. Once we see that the modes of thinking are mismatched, Eckhart's defense, often thought to be strangely inadequate, will look more like a natural response to these ways of misunderstanding him.

8 McGinn, *Foundations of Mysticism*, 6. Hans Blumenberg, *Laughter of the Thracian Woman: A Protohistory of Theory*, trans. Spencer Hawkins (New York: Bloomsbury, 2015), vii.

9 Cf. McGinn, *Harvest of Mysticism*, 165. McGinn uses the term "presence" instead of "being." This is part of his overall talk of "God's presence" that a "human subject" experiences ("Love, Knowledge, and Unio Mystica in the Western Christian Tradition," 59). I believe my formulation is more Eckhartian.

ECKHART AND THE INQUISITION

An inquisitorial process was opened against Eckhart in 1326. The circumstances leading up to the trial are strange, as are many of the events therein. Pope John XXII was embroiled in conflict with Louis of Bavaria, the king (from 1314; later emperor, 1328–47) of the region in which Eckhart lived. Louis wanted to be, and subsequently was, declared emperor without the pope, though not without first being excommunicated in March 1324. In this, the Dominicans sided with the pope. An important ally for the pope was the archbishop of Cologne, Henry II of Virneburg, who had a reputation for combatting heresy.

When the Dominican General Chapter met in 1325, they sent Gervasius, the prior of Angers, to investigate friars delivering sermons to uneducated people that might easily lead them into error and to punish those who had not published a papal bull against Louis of Bavaria.[10] This same language and concern with an audience of unlearned people appears again in the condemnatory bull against Eckhart in 1329. The trial itself only got started after two attempts by two friars with problematic reputations, Hermann of Summo and William of Niddegen. Hermann achieved some notoriety for distributing pamphlets to spread rumors about certain friars, including Eckhart. Both were under investigation for their conduct by the Dominicans. Hermann had made enough enemies that a movement was afoot to appeal to Nicholas of Strasbourg, the general vicar of the province, to expel him.[11] When Hermann and William were accused, they in turn accused Eckhart of heresy. Eckhart sent a written response and Nicholas cleared him of the charge.

Though much research has been done on Eckhart's trial and the circumstances leading up to it, we could perhaps be forgiven for thinking that we are still missing some essential detail that might explain why the powers at the time were so intent on pursuing an investigation for heresy when it was clearly inappropriate and why a curiously written condemnation was issued even though Eckhart had died. One such detail may be *why* Hermann and William were motivated to start the case against Eckhart. Even at the time, the Dominican procurator recognized their ulterior motive of avoiding punishment. Nevertheless, the archbishop set up a special commission to look at Eckhart's case.[12] For charges of heresy, the accused must obstinately

---

10 Walter Senner, "Meister Eckhart's Life, Training, Career, and Trial," 46. Cf. McGinn, *Mystical Thought of Meister Eckhart*, 14.
11 Senner, "Meister Eckhart's Life, Training, Career, and Trial," 51.
12 Senner, "Meister Eckhart's Life, Training, Career, and Trial," 54.

(*pertinaciter*) maintain his or her errors. Eckhart protested the charge on such grounds, but the case was still not changed to one of censorship. If it had been, Eckhart could have used his privilege as a Dominican not to stand trial outside of the University of Paris or the papal curia, something he tried to do. Winfried Trusen, the first legal scholar to undertake a detailed examination of Eckhart's trial, saw the continuation of a trial for heresy as decisive evidence that the proceedings were unlawful, something that Eckhart observed.[13] It seems there was an interest in keeping the trial at the court of the Archbishop of Cologne. Eckhart complained of being unjustly treated for all of the reasons mentioned and because the trial took an abnormally long time. Finally, he appealed to the Holy See, which sent the case to the papal curia.

Eckhart went to Avignon, the seat of the papacy during its "Babylonian exile" from Rome (1309–1377), to appear before Cardinal Jacques Fournier, who presided over the proceedings and succeeded Pope John XXII as Pope Benedict XII in 1334. The process culminated in a set of Eckhart's propositions being condemned in the bull *In agro dominico* in 1329. Fournier expressed reservation about the method of lifting passages out of context. As a master of theology and high-ranking Dominican official, it was unusual for someone of Eckhart's stature to undergo this process. It was also unusual for the condemnation to be issued even though Eckhart had died the previous year. As recently as 1980, Ursula Fleming led a movement to have Eckhart officially rehabilitated. In 1992, Timothy Radcliffe, the Master of the Dominican Order, wrote the chairman of the Eckhart Society and said, "I wonder whether you know that we tried to have the censure lifted on Eckhart and were told that there was really no need since he had never been condemned by name, just some propositions which he was supposed to have held, and so we are perfectly free to say that he is a good and orthodox theologian."[14]

Eckhart argued that he could not be convicted of heresy, saying "I can be in error, but I cannot be a heretic, because the first belongs to the intellect, the second to the will."[15] In the bull, a total of fifteen passages from his works were condemned as heretical and another eleven as *male sonantes*, "evil-sounding," with an additional two that he denied having said. Calling them "evil-sounding" may indicate that the inquisitors were not always sure

---

13 Senner, "Meister Eckhart's Life, Training, Career, and Trial," 62, 65.

14 "Eckhart: The Man," Eckhart, The Eckhart Society, December 14, 2015, http://eckhartsociety.org/eckhart/eckhart-man.

15 "Selections from Eckhart's Defense," trans. McGinn in *Essential Eckhart*, 72.

they understood him.[16] While this is certainly possible given Eckhart's shifty rhetoric, a more plausible explanation may be that medieval judges in the inquisition made decisions based on what sounded like heresy rather than what was intended.[17] Instead of drawing the too-obvious conclusion that the inquisitorial process was misapplied, we should instead notice the effect that this practice has: to oppose what *sounds* like heresy is to attempt to cut off undesirable *influence* on others, regardless of the intention of the accused. Furthermore, the trial proceeded even though Eckhart had died before its conclusion. Normally, cases were dropped when the accused died. This has led many to suspect with good reason that there were political motives behind the bull's propagation.[18] Further, Eckhart's own protestations appear to have won him a small battle, as evident in the "insofar as" language that appears in the bull itself: "Eckhart ... professed the Catholic faith at the end of his life and revoked and also deplored the twenty-six articles, which he admitted that he had preached, and also any others, written and taught by him, whether in the schools or in sermons, insofar as they could generate in the minds of the faithful a heretical opinion, or one erroneous and hostile to the true faith."[19] In speaking of the first thirty-three of the original forty-nine articles, he insists that "I hold that they are all true, although many are uncommon and subtle."[20] Evidently, the commission found Eckhart's conditional revocation—"insofar as" what he preached could arouse heretical thoughts in the simple—to be sufficient. In other words, Eckhart did not say he was wrong and the bull itself does not say that he was wrong. Toward the beginning of the bull, after some rhetoric that is typical of pronouncements on heresy, we read, "He presented many things as dogma that were designed to cloud the true faith in the hearts of many, things which he put forth especially before the uneducated crowd in his sermons and that he also admitted into his writings."[21] Thus, we understand why the writings should be condemned: "lest articles of this sort and their contents further infect the

---

16 Bruce Milem, *The Unspoken Word: Negative Theology in Meister Eckhart's German Sermons* (Washington, D.C.: The Catholic University of America Press, 2002), 3.

17 McGinn, *Harvest of Mysticism*, 57.

18 Cf. Senner, "Meister Eckhart's Life, Training, Career, and Trial," 7–84. See Senner also for detail on the political situation involving the questionable character and motives of Eckhart's accusers, the archbishop's agenda and the pope's reasons for giving the archbishop what he wanted.

19 "In Agro Dominico," trans. McGinn in *Essential Eckhart*, 81.

20 "Selections from Eckhart's Defense," trans. McGinn in *Essential Eckhart*, 72.

21 "In Agro Dominico," trans. McGinn in *Essential Eckhart*, 77.

hearts of the simple among whom they were preached, and lest in any way whatsoever they should gain currency among them or others."[22]

To the credit of the inquisitorial commission, the bull makes clear that they did not presume to know what Eckhart was trying to say. It says that Eckhart "presented" the statements "as dogma" and that they "were designed to cloud the true faith," which emphasizes how they were likely to be *received* rather than what they actually *meant*. The works containing any of the twenty-six articles were condemned, even if they only contained articles from the second list of eleven that were not heretical, but merely "quite evil sounding and very rash and suspect of heresy, though with many explanations and additions they might take on or possess a Catholic meaning."[23] Clearly, the principal concern of the bull was to avoid arousing heretical thoughts in simple, uneducated people.

Though the original list of forty-nine articles was trimmed substantially into the final form of the twenty-eight used in the bull, it is significant that two passages that Eckhart denied having said were included in the final document. This, along with the unusual fact that the bull was promulgated despite Eckhart's death, should provide us with an indication that Eckhart was not the only and probably not even the primary target of the bull. Indeed, we find one copy of the bull in the collection of documents of a Mainz inquisitor, likely assembled for use in the 1390s.[24] The list of offenses in the bull addresses many of the church's concerns with mysticism and fringe religious groups of that time. It may have been intended as a kind of official statement on how to distinguish a particular kind of heresy that was then growing in popularity. We should also recall that Archbishop Henry of Virneburg had a reputation for hunting heretics[25] and that the pope wished to preserve Henry's favor since he was a valuable ally in the papal struggle against Louis of Bavaria. We have records that the pope ordered the dissemination of the bull in Cologne, and it was likely published in Mainz as well, and probably posted on the door of the cathedral in Avignon since this was customary for such constitutions.[26] Its circulation must have been limited,

---

22 "In Agro Dominico," trans. McGinn in *Essential Eckhart*, 80.
23 "In Agro Dominico," trans. McGinn in *Essential Eckhart*, 80.
24 Robert Lerner, "New Evidence for the Condemnation of Meister Eckhart," *Speculum* 72, no. 2 (1997): 352–54.
25 Bernard McGinn, "Eckhart's Condemnation Reconsidered," *The Thomist* 44, no. 3 (1980): 393.
26 Lerner, "New Evidence for the Condemnation of Meister Eckhart," 348–49.

however, since William of Ockham wrote two treatises in Munich between 1337 and 1341 and complained that Eckhart had never been condemned.[27]

Eckhart scholars are nearly unified in saying that the bull's condemnation was not entirely sound. For example, although the bull ties proposition fourteen ("Since God in some way wills for me to have sinned, I should not will that I had not committed sins") in the list of heretical statements to the *Book of Divine Consolation*, Eckhart rightly cites both Saint Paul and Saint Augustine in his *Councils on Discernment* when making this same point, providing a pedigree for the idea that the commission should have taken into account.[28]

The process of the inquisitorial inquiry itself was inherently incompatible with a proper understanding of Eckhart. Though there was long precedent for conducting the trial in the manner it was done, the commissioners did not read the author's works, relying instead upon the research of their subordinates and themselves considering only statements in isolation.[29] We have a document from Cardinal Jacques Fournier, who presided over Eckhart's trial, which describes how inadequate he thought this process was.[30] When Durandus of Saint-Pourçain was on trial, Fournier "protested that he could not with justice [pass judgment on the case] until he had seen the contexts from which the propositions had been taken."[31]

In reading Eckhart's own response to the articles, it is clear that he did not entirely take the accusations seriously and had little patience for the way that he was being misunderstood. It is reasonable to assume that Eckhart would have been familiar with the usual thinking that guided inquisitorial hearings. He would have likewise known that a hearing of that kind was unprecedented for someone of his stature. Further, the counsel he received from his fellow Dominicans would have been well informed with respect to the inquisitorial process. Consequently, perhaps Eckhart would have been *surprised* if he had known that some of his statements and the works containing those statements would ultimately be condemned after he died. As Edmund Colledge put it, Eckhart "does not seem to have admitted the

---

27 Lerner, "New Evidence for the Condemnation of Meister Eckhart," 349.

28 Colledge, "Historical Data," in *Essential Eckhart*, 13–14.

29 Colledge, "Historical Data," in *Essential Eckhart*, 11.

30 Colledge, "Historical Data," in *Essential Eckhart*, 11; see also Edmund Colledge, "Meister Eckhart: His Times and His Writings," *The Thomist* 42, no. 2 (1978): 240–58.

31 Colledge, "Historical Data," in *Essential Eckhart*, 11–12.

possibility that the verdict could go against him."[32] Eckhart probably did not fully appreciate the political situation in which the pope was issuing the bull. Thus, we may interpret this surprise as an indication that the ultimate reasons for the result of the trial were not foreseeable to Eckhart insofar as he considered the matter of the case only as it applied to him.

---

32 Colledge, "Historical Data," in *Essential Eckhart*, 11.

3

Metaphor, Paradox, and the Spirit of Play

We can understand large-scale cultural changes over time by noticing that the stories people tell and the metaphors they choose appear sensible to them as answers to the rhetorical exigency of their circumstances. Hans Blumenberg was right about this. Philosophy often behaves as though we are consciously aware of why we think the things that we do and that, by dint of the irresistible force of reason, we are in control of what we believe. We know this is not true: it relegates rhetoric to mere decoration for ideas that are already effective via pure reason. This sentiment is a leftover of the Enlightenment-era philosophical project of using the natural light of reason alone to achieve objective truth. In such circles, reason compels belief and personal experience is left entirely aside as untrustworthy. We might respond that any philosophy that casts aside feeling, intuition, and the rich, complex phenomenology of immediate experience is missing most of what it means to be human. Beginning with Kant and running through Nietzsche and Husserl, the groundwork was laid for Blumenberg to continue this trend and apply it to historical investigations of the history of thought by noticing that the metaphors we choose are expressions of the metaphysical foundations of our worldviews. Readers of Eckhart have come to see that *what* he says is not as important as *how* he says it, though I would modify this to claim that what he says and how he says it are both secondary to any means of catalyzing spiritual motion in his audience. What we should notice about Eckhart is that the surprising and ostensibly novel aspects of his rhetoric trace back to the changes in the conception of the individual. When we set aside the portions of his theology and rhetoric that are shared with Origen, Augustine, Dionysius, Aquinas, and others, what remains is a series of images and shades of meaning that reflect the change in the metaphysics of the individual which lies at the most foundational level of our worldview.

Hans Blumenberg is a privileged discussion partner not because of the way he handles mysticism,[1] but because his work on metaphor initially pushes us in the same direction that Eckhart does. He insists that the ground of conceptual thought is not itself conceptual, meaning that our attempts to answer fundamental philosophical questions have not been frustrated because we lack the appropriate conceptual apparatus, but because the questions themselves point to the nonconceptual ground of thinking that makes conceptual thought possible. Historical shifts in this ground of thought cause superficial changes and eventually manifest as wholly different philosophical and theological movements. Before we see these surface changes however, the changes in the use of metaphors provide the first indications that a shift is underway. Thus, Blumenberg's tools for approaching metaphor and his metaphorology more broadly enable us to detect fundamental metaphysical shifts that point to the creation of the modern world in figures that appear prima facie medieval, like Eckhart. Metaphors allow us to enter more deeply into a thinker's imaginative horizon than concepts do because they operate at an aesthetic, preconscious level that springs from the most fundamental metaphysical building blocks of the way we see ourselves and the world. We are attracted to metaphors in the same way that we are attracted to music and art. They simply feel like they fit because their relationships are already implied by our way of seeing the world.[2] Metaphors function by manifesting a particular part of a lived experience of being in the world. This invites the mind to play in their space and experience firsthand the "what-it's-like" and see the insights that follow. In this way, they guide thought.

The exercise of understanding Blumenberg requires a reorientation of the way we are accustomed to thinking about philosophy and history, which makes him outstandingly useful for entering into an orbit around Eckhart's own mode of thought. Still, when studying mysticism, we must eventually leave Blumenberg behind. When thinking about how Eckhart's metaphors work at the level of the individual's psychological reception of those ideas, it is not necessary to make use of Blumenberg's own metaphysical commitments with respect to what actually constitutes an individual. As Franz Josef

---

[1] Cf. Blumenberg, *Legitimacy of the Modern Age*, 515.

[2] Blumenberg, *Shipwreck with Spectator*, 84. While this notion of the connections already being implied is Blumenberg's idea, I mention it here because it orients thinking in a useful direction, not because it is a hardened psychological truth.

Wetz put it, with Blumenberg, "the hard rock where our spade is turned, because we are unable to dig down any deeper . . . is the finite character of the human being."[3] We might echo Robert Forman's criticism of Steven Katz's seminal work on the "constructivist" interpretation of mysticism. Katz holds that "there are NO pure (i.e., unmediated) experiences" and uses this claim to attack the "perennialists," like Aldous Huxley, who claim that mysticism is the same across religions and throughout time.[4] Forman points out that this assumption is built upon the phenomenological account of intentionality.[5] Katz's claim that there are no unmediated experiences implies the primacy of the individual and denies the possibility of insight into anything that is unsullied by individual experience. Since Blumenberg builds from this kind of phenomenological base, we might extend this same criticism to him and, with Forman, insist that "insofar as any account of mysticism is grounded on these doctrines, it is profoundly flawed."[6] Since an individual is an individual insofar as it is differentiated from other individuals and breaks oneness into number, the current fashion of claiming that the mysticism of oneness is conditioned by individual experience is puzzling. Perhaps we should imagine Plato looking askance at the suggestion that knowledge of the truths of mathematics might be similarly conditioned by individual experience.

METAPHOR AND PARADOX

Metaphors connect disparate domains, borrowing experience from one to help elucidate an experience in another. For ordinary experiences that we share in common (Kant's "intuitions"), communicating understanding by way of words often suffices. When the content cannot be communicated straightforwardly (Kant's "symbols"), we often resort to metaphors that push us in the direction of change that will enable understanding.[7] Metaphor

---

[3] Franz Josef Wetz, "The Phenomenological Anthropology of Hans Blumenberg," *Iris: European Journal of Philosophy & Public Debate* 1, no. 2 (2009): 389.

[4] Steven Katz, "Language, Epistemology, and Mysticism," in *Mysticism and Philosophical Analysis*, ed. Steven Katz (London: Sheldon Press, 1978), 26.

[5] Robert K. C. Forman, *Mysticism, Mind and Consciousness* (New York: SUNY Press, 1999), 56. We should note that "intentionality" specifically refers to Husserl and Brentano's use of the term. This is particularly salient in a discussion of Blumenberg since Husserl always lies in the background of his writing, though he is rarely mentioned by name.

[6] Forman, *Mysticism, Mind and Consciousness*, 53.

[7] Note that this is an Eckhartian modification to Kant and Blumenberg's discussion of him. Kant tells us that the symbols must be communicated through representations that have the "'form

carries the richness of particular experiences, while concepts prune away particularity to arrive at abstract notions that many things can share in common. For example, when I say that my children are rays of sunshine, I am appealing to the quiet happiness that comes with the way that bright light from a clear sky makes all things appear crisp and colorful and then transferring that experience and suggesting that being around them is like that. If a metaphor suggests a link that seems viable but incompatible with an element of our worldview, it destabilizes our normal coherence and harmony just as paradoxes do. Paradoxes' incompatibilities are simply more explicit than the dissimilarities between a metaphor's domains.

The stories people tell and metaphors they choose are often the first indications of changes in the cultural undercurrents that determine how we feel about our place in the world, how we think of what we are as individuals, and what life means to us. The metaphors we use point beyond all concepts to the nonconceptual ground of thinking that makes mental motion and conceptual thought possible. They point to that *in which* we live, as Kierkegaard might say, rather than particular truths about things. Using the term "truth" here can lead to cognitive dissonance since we do not normally think of truths as salutary and therapeutic in the way the ancients did. Though we customarily equate intellectual understanding with internalization, Kierkegaard recognized that something was missing. That *something* is the difference between a cold and naked fact that we understand as an external object and a truth that breathes purpose into life.[8] This is the fundamental challenge with Nietzsche's recommending that we create such values: we cannot simply will to change, nor can others' wills force us to change the fundamental metaphysical components of how we see the world. Augustine's *Confessions* illustrates this because it tells a story that fits with our lived experience, not because it offers an argument for how this works.

It is hard to create a metaphor for an experience you have not had. We choose metaphors because they fit with our own way of seeing and understanding the world and ourselves. Eckhart's metaphors show us what it is like to be imageless and live without a why since that is the worldview he

---

of the reflection' in common with the intended referent" (Blumenberg, *Paradigms for a Metaphorology*, 4). Though *Paradigms* spoke of metaphor as a preparation for concept-formation, Blumenberg expanded this in the decade that followed, saying instead that metaphors not only facilitate conceptual thinking but also guide thought and provide orientation to the lifeworld, looking for the *gestalt* of things rather than only their Kantian "form" of reflection. Blumenberg, *Shipwreck with Spectator*, 88, 96–97.

8 Cf. Blumenberg, *Paradigms for a Metaphorology*, 50–51.

inhabited. Eckhart's rhetoric, carefully tailored to his audience's spiritual needs, responded to and gave expression to this fundamental ground. Since they target the nonconceptual ground of thought from which conceptual thought arises, his metaphors become more impressive, paradoxical, and surprising as we approach increasingly fundamental aspects of self- and world- understanding. Blumenberg called this class of metaphors *absolute metaphors*. We might notice that as fundamentality increases, the metaphors themselves likewise become subtle and hidden in the rhetoric, as with Eckhart's shifty use of pronouns, little words (in, through, with), specific verb tenses (was/*erat*), or even omissions. A metaphor might even attempt to refer to what is nonconceptual, miss the mark, and become an effective metaphor for the nonconceptual by also being a kind of apophatic metaphor for its failure to reach the nonconceptual.

Since the content a metaphor targets cannot be communicated conceptually, it must suggest connections that catalyze productive change, inciting a kind of thought that is similar insofar as it leads to the desired understanding. In this way, metaphor is "like" truth in the same way that we should understand Plato's "likely story" in the *Timaeus*. A metaphor may be understood to be sufficiently "like" truth insofar as it catalyzes experience that ultimately incites insight into and experience of what is fundamentally nonconceptual. A poignant example of this is what Blumenberg called *explosive metaphor* (*Sprengmetapher*).[9] An explosive metaphor is a type of paradox where one idea is beyond the normal horizon of meaning for the other and thus thought is implicitly directed toward the horizon. Instead of containing an explicit contradiction, explosive metaphors have an inherent air of reasonableness that compels the reader to pursue thought in a particular direction. At the horizon, discursive thought is inadequate to resolve the tension and the metaphor explodes, breaking through to a new way of thinking. Though Eckhart's mathematical metaphors are the clearest examples of this, others like the "hinge" metaphor do the same.[10] While individual paradoxical expressions may not be explosive, they are essential to the rhetorical trajectory which, taken as a whole, is explosive. Explosive metaphors perform a Socratic function in that they show the incoherence of existing concepts without the ironic pretense of searching for conceptual truth.

---

9 Bernard McGinn argued that *grunt* ("ground") was an explosive metaphor for Eckhart. *Harvest of Mysticism*, 85; cf. 121.
10 Eckhart, *On Detachment*, DW V, 422.7-11.

Just as we should expand the idea of metaphor to include instances of rhetoric that function like metaphors, so too should we broaden the notion of paradox. It is not clear that all paradoxes that result from opposites meeting (as with the *coincidentia oppositorum*, the coincidence of opposites) function as explosive metaphors. In addition to guiding thought toward its limits so as to burst through to a new way of seeing, it is equally possible to strain concepts with the eventual consequence of *deflating* them and robbing them of significance. For example, if the love and hatred of worldly things can be shown to meet, the result may be an atrophying of attachment, just as when one learns how to attenuate a bad habit by first becoming aware of how it works. Of course, this is closely related to explosive metaphorics. It is in this way that Eckhart's sermons themselves have the dynamic of explosive metaphors. Just as Plato did, Eckhart often lists ideas beginning with the most common and moving quickly into paradoxical, mystical territory. For example, in Sermon 30: "Speak the word, speak it aloud, speak it forth, bring it forth, give birth to the Word!"[11] This progression occurs over the time of the entire sermon in Eckhart's different versions of the "little castle" in Sermon 2 and in his notions of poverty in Sermon 52.

Eckhart's paradoxes are not illusions that mask ideas that could be more clearly stated. In fact, Eckhart *insists* on his paradoxes, resisting our attempts to disarm them, explain them away, and rest comfortably within our familiar mode of thinking. In so doing, he preserves tension long enough to push concepts to the breaking point.[12] If his paradoxes were able to be tamed and solved like logical puzzles, they would be little more than parlor tricks, perhaps meant to maintain interest. There is a significant danger in thinking that we can solve the paradoxes like a puzzle. Robert Forman tells us that "the critical factor standing at the heart of Eckhart's solution to this paradox can be summed up in the word *perspective*. From one perspective God is unitary, beyond attributes. From this perspective there is no naming, and thus no

---

[11] Eckhart, Sermon 30, DW II, 93.2–3.

[12] After speaking of the mathematical metaphors as explosive, something Blumenberg would have no doubt agreed with, two more crucial steps were taken to expand and then implicitly critique any rigid conception of a metaphorological category like "explosive metaphor." First, with Eckhart we see how an explosive dynamic can actually serve a deflationary function for concepts. Second, the explosivity was tied to Eckhart's sermons as a whole and his insistence upon paradoxes within and across sermons. The overarching metaphorological point here is that the "explosive metaphor" should instead be thought of as part of a larger rhetorical dynamic that can be localized with a particular linguistic metaphor like an infinite sphere, but need not be limited to specific artifacts of language.

problem of how to name the *nomen innominabile*. From another perspective, God has attributes; in fact, He is the name which every true attribute names, the *nomen omninominabile*."[13] To say that the paradox can be resolved by appealing to different modes of "perspective" amounts to taming the paradox by rendering it intelligible in terms that we already understand and making it merely an *apparent* paradox. In other words, if the two sides were merely "perspectives," then that tells us that they are comparable to other perspectives we have, able to be filed away under an existing concept without having to change the way we see the world in the presence of something genuinely new. The way that we see the world changes because the paradox renders progressively more fundamental assumptions—which constitute the way we see the world and understand ourselves—unstable. If we feel that what Eckhart says is true but simultaneously incompatible with our existing assumptions, this disharmony disrupts the stability of our worldview.[14] In a manner similar to the erosion of habits, changes in metaphors and assumptions that are the building blocks of worldviews occur slowly through disruptions. Provided that we have the tools to "rush ahead" and give motion toward building new foundations (one is tempted to align this with the tables of values that Nietzsche's "child" of the third metamorphosis creates), nihilism and confusion can be avoided, and salutary spiritual progress can result. In other words, making Eckhart's paradoxes into apparent paradoxes renders them ineffective, incapable of performing their primary function.

Eckhart's paradoxes force the mystery to remain. Fundamentally, the ideas of the human soul as the image of God and the simultaneous divinity and humanity of Christ are paradoxes that are at the heart of Christianity. When Eckhart spoke on these topics, if he allowed the paradoxes to be resolved, he

---

13 Forman, *Mystic as Theologian*, 203. Eckhart also uses this language in his Latin works. Though Forman has a lot of things to say that are helpful in understanding mysticism, his rhetoric of "pure consciousness" and his psychoanalytic vocabulary are couched too much in the language of atomic individual identity. This encourages us to think in terms of the "I" that we are used to, rather than questioning it in the comprehensive manner that Eckhart and other mystics would have us do.

14 An alternative (to Husserl and Blumenberg) but equally useful account of this would be to consider our worldview as an unstable illusion of coherent threads running through the welter of competing and conflicting thoughts about the world. Metaphor might then serve to propose new viable streams of connections that are felt to be incompatible with the dominant streams, thereby destabilizing the whole. In other words, we might also consider consciousness to be a tension between opposites and competition between possible connections, hearkening back to Plato's tripartite soul and the charioteer metaphor. The correctness of the model of mind is not as important as the way in which Eckhart's rhetoric catalyzes recognizable, useful motion.

would have implicitly advocated thinking about these paradoxes by using concepts that are already familiar to us. If instead Eckhart understood that the mystery of Christ and the mystery of the soul as the image of God could not be grasped without a transformational change in self- and world-understanding, then it was clearly in his best interest to insist upon the contradictory nature of the mysteries and maintain the paradoxes, even heightening the tension that they create to further motivate his audience to move away from their present mode of thinking and being. That is precisely what he did.

As an example of such paradoxes and a chain of paradoxes that have their own palpable metaphorical trajectory, Eckhart describes a progression of paradoxes: God's creation of the temporal world in eternity, the Incarnation of Christ as both divine and human, the human soul as the image of God, and finally, the actions of the individual soul with a why and without a why, which exemplifies the return of the soul to God by reversing this progression (Neoplatonic *exitus* and *reditus*). Encapsulating and collapsing the entire progression, Eckhart says in Sermon 52, "I am the cause of myself on account of my being."

Discursive reason and its concomitant images, as Eckhart calls them, constitute an obstacle to spontaneous action that does not have a why. A similar situation can be found with "immediate" experiences, which are experiences that do not have conceptually driven content (what Eckhart Platonically calls "images"). Eckhart uses rhetorical strategies that aim to redirect our focus from the conceptual bricolage of philosophy and theology to the here-and-now quality of momentary human experience. Immediate experiences do not propose arguments that take place within a particular dialectical sphere of discussion. Even Thomas Aquinas did something similar: although he constructed an ostensibly systematic theology through argumentation, each argument concluded with an appeal to the experience of our sentiment of certainty—"and this all men know to be God."[15]

Of all of Eckhart's commentators, Cyprian Smith comes closest to what I am attempting to express about Eckhart's use of paradox: for Eckhart, God "can be grasped only within the tension in clash of opposites ... and this involves *paradox*."[16] I could do little to improve upon his characterization of Eckhart's use of paradox:

---

15 Erazim Kohàk, *Embers and the Stars: A Philosophical Inquiry into the Moral Sense of Nature* (Chicago: University of Chicago Press, 1984), 190.
16 Cyprian Smith, *The Way of Paradox: Spiritual Life as Taught by Meister Eckhart* (London: Dartman, Longman and Todd, 1987), 24.

> I cannot attain [union with God] by remaining what I am now; I have to die somehow to the life I am living, so as to find the new life in God. This death and rebirth must involve my *whole* self, not only my daily life, but also my thought and speech. No part of me, not even my mind and tongue, can get through to God without passing through the clash of contraries. That is why Eckhart talks constantly in antithesis and paradoxes. . . . Eckhart keeps us perpetually swinging from one pole to the other; he will not let us rest in either. To rest in one and forget the other is to lose hold of the truth, which is essentially paradoxical.[17]

Smith's "Way of Paradox" for Eckhart extends to one's overall disposition. In his words, speaking in a tone very much as Eckhart does with the self, to approach the "Permanent Self" which resides in the Ground of the Soul (this "self" is the only one that is capable of Eckhartian *activity*) is to live in a fundamentally paradoxical way. Every move that one makes in stripping away the self as normally conceived is fraught with paradox, since the very possibility of logical cohesion and an observer-observed worldview is being unraveled. We find paradoxes at every turn with Eckhart. We must eventually realize that we cannot and should not resolve them. Resolving the tension of a stubborn, irreconcilable paradox can only happen, ironically, by dismantling the foundation that enables the paradox to be a paradox in the first place.

Presaging much of what I say about why Eckhart appeals to us today in the last chapter, Smith says that ages that try to resolve the paradox of Christ's dual nature (by overemphasizing his humanity) lose sight of the divinity and vice versa. This reflects a similarly one-sided view of what humanity is and what we are as individuals.[18] It is only when we do not try to *resolve* the paradox of Christ's nature that we also can see the paradoxical truth of our *own* nature. A truth which is not paradoxical risks losing its life-giving mystery, the mystery that enables spiritual progress. We might also notice that mystery is ironically missing from our scientific worldview as well. Though our rhetoric commonly embraces what we do not yet understand, we tend to think that we know what form the answer will take. This falls under the general heading of there being no more *frontiers* or *horizons*. Even for places on the map, in the unexplored depths of both the sea and space, we either think we know very well what to expect or we know the form that any novelty

---

17 C. Smith, *Way of Paradox*, 27.
18 C. Smith, *Way of Paradox*, 74–75.

can take with all but the rarest of exceptions. This is outstanding and unusual in human history. When we encounter some theory or aspect of our world that reinforces the prevailing paradigm of incremental progress of conceptual and mathematical truths that we inherited from the Enlightenment, we have a nagging feeling in the background that this cannot be the whole story. It is as if we know that we are not done. Eckhart would tell us that this hollow incompleteness is characteristic of all things that fall short of God and that we cannot find rest and are ultimately not satisfied with anything less than God.

Immediate experience of the Word is like a direct experience of music or hearing natural sounds. Natural sounds inhabit a world that is outside of civilization and bear no marks of human design, just as, for the Ancient Greeks, the sea was a region that was unconquerable by civilization and thus remained linked with the chaos that antecedes order. When we design an object or space for a particular use, that stamp of intentionality is felt in the way that it is *limited*. Since it grows out of a conceptual scheme, the intention of accomplishing particular ends is experienced by us as we enter the space or interact with the thing. Indeed, our worldview is reaffirmed by interacting with objects and concepts which exude that same mode of thinking.[19]

We can always look away with our eyes. We cannot look away with our ears. Sound is also more ambient. What we see always occurs in a particular place and has a particular size. Sound, by contrast, is less spatially specific and can thereby more easily appear to be everywhere. What appears to be everywhere can similarly be experienced as all-consuming and be felt predominantly as inside rather than occurring in a space outside. In other words, sound is more easily felt as something universal, while vision more naturally gives us particulars.[20] As Eckhart himself tells us, "I am passive in hearing. I am active in seeing. Still, our bliss does not lie in our activity, but rather in that we undergo God."[21] Likewise, Eckhart's paradoxes and the rhetoric surrounding them are stubbornly nonconceptual in the same way

---

19 See Kohàk, *Embers and the Stars*, 22–23.

20 I suspect this was behind Schopenhauer's elevating music over visual art for its heightened ability to give us a temporary reprieve from the pain of willing. Interestingly, an exception to this is Nicholas of Cusa's painting that accompanied *De Visione Dei*. The eyes of the figure in the painting appear to be looking at the viewer regardless of where one stands in viewing it, a most unusual feeling for a visual thing since it is an experience of the universal.

21 Eckhart, Sermon 102, DW IV.1, 421.143–422.145. One could also say, as Matthew Fox does, that "I undergo hearing." For more on the active and passive metaphorics in Eckhart, see chapter four of this volume.

that natural sounds are. Paradox has ambience that fills the environment of his sermons in the same way because it resists being tied down to a single place by conceptual resolution.

The fact that Eckhart's paradoxes work for modern readers may be in no small part due to their ability to confound our otherwise-familiar habits of conceptual thought that maintain a world of lifeless, inert things, devoid of meaning. Mystery may at least crack the door, leaving open the possibility for things to be meaningful. As in meditation, if one experiences just a touch of the bliss that naturally flows from single-pointed concentration, one immediately appreciates it as something different and at odds with our expectations, paving the way for confidence that there is more unexpected beauty waiting for us to discover if we can let go of what is individual about us.

CONNOISSEURSHIP

At this point, I want to attempt to shed light on how we may enter into Eckhart's world by appealing to what I call *connoisseurship*,[22] which is the ability of people who have some understanding or experience to intuitively recognize an equal or lesser level of that same understanding or experience in others. When we hear someone profess to speak from the standpoint of expertise on something, if we do not share that expertise, then we mostly infer the extent of their expertise based on how confident they seem. Much could be said about politics and managers in business here. If we share the person's expertise, however, we quickly see through the words and enter into their imaginative horizon.

Cyprian Smith uses a metaphor for silence that subtly builds on the apophatic tradition of silence and is worth quoting at length. In real communication between people:

> Words are few, but telling and to the point. They arise out of the depths, and they express silence rather than obliterate it.... It is also characteristic of natural sounds that they seem to heighten rather than destroy silence. Anyone who listens to wind stirring the leaves of the trees, to waves breaking on the sand, even to thunder splitting the sky, will have no difficulty in grasping this. It is not simply that silence precedes and follows these

---

[22] I first introduced this term in my essay on Eckhart and Zen, "How Mysticism Can Point the Way to Tolerance: Recognizing a Common Ground of Nonconceptual Experience in Meister Eckhart and Zen," in *Atone: Religion, Conflict, and Reconciliation*, ed. A. Adebayo, S. Hayes, B. Lundy (Lanham, Md.: Lexington Books, 2018), 135–51.

sounds; it remains as a background to them, and even expresses itself in them. They, in their turn, point back to it. We cannot claim, therefore, not to know what a true 'word' is. It is something we come across frequently in our own experience.[23]

The aesthetic experience of natural beauty is immediate and, at best, wholly nonconceptual. Nature readily does this for us since its sounds are not words and they provide an ambience instead of forming arguments. Speech can be boring when banal because the rich complexity of individual sounds and experiences is pruned away in favor of the simplistic conceptual content that is the expression of an equally simple intention. The communication that Smith describes does not occur because of the precise referents of the words or some notion of shared definitions. Instead, real communication is a matter of entering sympathetically into another's imaginative horizon and gaining an intuitive feel for how the other thinks. Words "express silence" because the words are signposts to the underlying shared understanding that is mutually recognized and enables fluid communication.

If Blumenberg, Lakoff, and Johnson are correct in pointing to the central place of metaphor in our lived experience and thought, then we may sensibly point to a different way of 'knowing' that is similar in kind to their conception of understanding that is based on metaphor. For them, understanding is a matter of intuitively feeling that a particular metaphor "fits" with the experiential gestalts of the source and target domains. This fit cannot itself be something that is objectively knowable or reducible to conceptual understanding. Though neither explicitly treats the topic, can we recognize when another shares some measure of our own nonconceptual understanding? I suggest that we can and that we do this whenever questions of expertise arise. We also do this when making friends. Of course, we do not and cannot

---

23 C. Smith, *Way of Paradox*, 60. Smith expresses a similar thought in his other book: "Very different is the silence of wild, remote places, far from any human habitation. This has a quality all its own. It is by no means simply the absence of noise. On the contrary, wild places are full of sound: wind stirring the leaves; the cries of birds; waves breaking upon the sand. Yet behind all this there is a background of silence, which the sounds punctuate but do not efface; indeed, they seem to intensify it. It is a silence which is deep and calm yet pulsating with energy and life. It makes prayer easy and natural; and that is not surprising, since it is a kind of icon of creation. As sounds emerge from the silence and fall back into it, we can see there an image of the universe spoken forth by God, and then breathed back into him again" (*The Path of Life* [York: Ampleforth Abbey Press, 1995], 66). A few pages later he continues, "Real communication happens when words are like the sounds of wild nature, emerging from silence, returning to it, but never obliterating it. They do not negate it but rather articulate and express it. That is what real communication is: it is articulated silence" (*Path of Life*, 68).

fully know what another person's understanding is like. William James dedicated an entire essay to expounding on how significant this lacuna is in our lives.[24] Nevertheless, it is equally clear that experts can quickly recognize one another simply through observation and conversation. We learn much more about another person's personality and level of understanding through experience than we can frame with concepts for objective consumption.[25] The idea of connoisseurship that I forward is an extension of the recognition of the richness of the individuality of another person. It also answers the question of how mystics recognize other mystics and, consequently, whether mysticism has a core of unity.

In Zen, the process of dharma transmission works by connoisseurship. Masters recognize new masters by *feel*. Though speech can help to communicate, Zen is perpetually focused on creating the kind of genuine communication that Smith describes. This may happen with words, yes, but it happens outside of ordinary conceptual experience. In the West, we see a similarly institutionalized form of this with doctoral committees that control the conferring of Ph.Ds. The final dissertation defense amounts to a recognition of whether the candidate has reached a similar level of expertise and can be identified as a peer.

This is why we should take Daisetz Suzuki seriously when he recognizes Eckhart as a peer in Zen. Though academics can and have looked at the theological and rhetorical similarities, these are all superficial details.[26] Suzuki recognized a core *experiential* commonality and identified Eckhart as another expert. Especially when we have more than a little contact with another expert, we are not often mistaken in our intuition that they share our mind in common expertise. In other words, conceptual and methodological

---

24 William James, *On Some of Life's Ideals* (New York: Henry Holt, 1929).

25 C. Smith, *Way of Paradox*, 74–75.

26 The word "superficial" does significant work here to establish a contrast with those who would treat Eckhart only as a philosopher and not as a mystic. The more someone sympathizes with that position, the less likely they are to be favorably disposed toward comparisons to Buddhism of the sort that Daisetz Suzuki and I have made. This is partly because any notion of substantive differences between mystics depends very much upon what someone believes to be most fundamental. For those who are inclined to think of Eckhart as a philosopher, he will be judged by the common standards of philosophical analysis as though those standards and the truths they are meant to reveal could somehow be prior to oneness. I do not oppose this school of thought because it is in any way conceptually or logically incoherent. After all, philosophical analysis can enrich one's understanding of a mystical author just as studying religious and philosophical history can. Nevertheless, in the end, it is not a matter of philosophical speculation, since no amount of intellectual study can match the worldview-shattering experience of seeing for yourself.

similarities are visible on the outside and are amenable to objective scrutiny. Intuitively recognizing a likeminded expert happens beneath language on the inside where it is not open to objective verification and consensus. The consensus in Zen and in academia is based on *trust* in the expert who recognizes another expert, not objective measures. With this in mind, we should notice a commonality between Suzuki's rhetoric about Eckhart and Eckhart's words in his defense. Both appealed to experience and meaning, things that were lost on readers who were looking to cling to evidence they could see for themselves.

Suzuki describes Eckhart as being "richly equipped with experiences" and having views that were "based on his own experiences."[27] He goes as far as saying, "I am sure that Eckhart had a satori."[28] If you have not shared the core of these experiences and you do not trust Suzuki as a master, such statements may fall flat. They cannot be translated into conceptual speech that will be familiar to those who do not have the experience because the experiences *are not like* anything. Though it could not be more obvious from connoisseurship to those who share his experiences, there is no general scholarly consensus that Eckhart spoke from a position of experience, perhaps especially among those who prefer to think of Eckhart as a philosopher rather than as a mystic.[29] Eckhart says:

> Therefore one writing, a gloss,[30] says very well that no one can understand or teach Saint Paul's writing unless he possesses the spirit in which Saint Paul spoke and wrote. And this is what I always lament, that crude people, empty of God's spirit and not possessing it, want to judge on account of their crude human understanding what they hear and read in Scripture, which is spoken and written from and in the Holy Spirit.[31]

How this could refer to anything other than personal experience is hard to imagine. The thrust of this is common among Dominicans in their tradition of *contemplata aliis tradere*, or giving over to others what one has learned

---

27 Daisetz T. Suzuki, *Mysticism: Christian and Buddhist* (New York: Harper, 1957), 7, 27.

28 Suzuki, *Mysticism*, 79. In Zen, *satori* is generally described as a flash of insight or sudden enlightenment experience. We might enter into some understanding of this by taking Suzuki to mean that Eckhart had an *experience* of enlightenment. This is to distinguish it from a merely intellectual understanding of enlightenment.

29 Davies, *Mystical Theologian*, 3.

30 McGinn refers us to the *Glossa Ordinaria*.

31 Eckhart, *Book of Divine Consolation*, DW V, 43.5–11.

through meditation.³² Perhaps even more clearly stated, "If a man were in a house that was beautifully decorated, another man who had never been inside it may well speak of it: but he who was inside would know."³³ Similarly, we read that "those who have never been familiar with inward things do not know what God is. Like a man who has wine in his cellar but has never tasted it, he does not know that it is good."³⁴ And among the most well-known passages of this kind, "Whoever does not understand what I say, let him not burden his heart with it. For as long as a man is not like this truth, he will not understand what I say. For this is a truth beyond thought that comes immediately from the heart of God."³⁵

NOVELTY AND THE SPIRIT OF PLAY

Eckhart's metaphors effectively catalyze change because they exhibit *stubbornly persistent novelty*. We are naturally excited by novelty, meaning that we are motivated to dedicate conscious resources to understand what appears new. An unthreatening environment can be relaxing, but it can also be boring. If it is beautiful, it is relaxing. If it is sterile, it is boring. Though it requires effort and we tend to economize our expenditure of the energy that is needed to become consciously aware of something, deliberate upon it, and make it familiar, we nevertheless do not enjoy our conscious resources lying fallow. In animals and humans alike, there is a drive to *play* with new things, to see what can be done with them.³⁶ The spirit of play is the action implied by mostly harmless novelty. Something new becomes increasingly threatening in proportion to the perceived risk it poses to what we *value*.³⁷ A

---

32 Davies, *Mystical Theologian*, 3. Cf. McGinn, *Mystical Thought of Meister Eckhart*, 10.
33 Eckhart, Sermon 68, DW III, 150.6–9.
34 Eckhart, Sermon 10, DW I, 164.5–8.
35 Eckhart, Sermon 52, DW II, 506.1–3. Note that "immediately" in English should be understood to literally mean "without an intermediary." It is also notable that Eckhart subscribes to the Aristotelian notion that likeness to truth is a prerequisite for understanding. According to this thinking, being like the truth implies understanding and also has a salutary moral implication.
36 Here we might profitably recall Edmund Burke's treatment of how we take pleasure in grief and are otherwise allured by stimuli for unpleasant emotions. We have a penchant for perseveration, perhaps commonly called "worry," which responds to whatever threatens our values and what we value.
37 I proposed a similar conception of stress, noting that positively and negatively appraised stressors elicit the same physiological response. See Daniel Clinton Johnson and Lisa Barbanell Johnson, "Reinventing the Stress Concept," *Ethical Human Psychiatry and Psychology* 12, no. 3 (2010): 218–31.

physical threat endangers the body or other things in the world that we value. Ideas and metaphors are threatening insofar as they threaten the values that underwrite the constitutive elements of our self- and world-understanding.

Novelty first threatens habits of thinking and feeling. Our concepts and habits provide a kind of horizon of thinking, beyond which we cannot see that certain avenues of thought and experience are closed off for us. Since our concepts work principally in terms of family resemblances and our thinking is relatively loose, we only refine the boundaries of our concepts once we are forced to look at them. In other words, our habits and abstractions serve to separate us from immediate experience. Changing a metaphor that someone feels to be true is difficult in proportion to the amount of action that the metaphor implies. We become susceptible to new metaphors depending on how well they are nonconceptually felt to fit and what new experiences we have had. Once we feel a metaphor fits, then it acquires force which is not entirely within our control.

4

Eckhart's Metaphorical Repertoire
Rhetorical Details and Metaphorological Dynamics

Philosophy and theology are ineluctably metaphorical. This is especially true when lived experience and a transformation[1] in being and worldview are goals. If what is sought is ultimately ineffable and defies all conceptions of agency, then all possible statements of subjects, objects, actions, properties and things are inevitably metaphorical. As Augustine said and Eckhart runs with, Scripture and any statements about the divine are clothed in a worldly mode of thinking, which includes but is not limited to worldly concepts. In other words, we necessarily think in terms of worldly things and events because our thought arises in concert with our experience. As it is for Eckhart, the details as to *why* that is and *how* it happens are often not as important as the fact *that* it happens and what *practical* steps we can take to overcome it. Thus, in a way that is perhaps shocking to lovers of contemporary philosophical thinking, such thorny issues from philosophy of mind may be blithely set aside in favor of addressing the pragmatic concern of how we deal with the matter at hand. As with much of Eckhart's approach to theology and living, this theme is familiar to Buddhists and may bring to mind the parable of the poison arrow: when shot with a poison arrow, should I ask who made the arrow, who shot it, and what path it took? No—I should pull it out and address the practical concern that presses upon me

---

[1] Deciding what is the best metaphor to describe this "change" that defies our normal logic of change is not a trivial task. Throughout, I have adopted Eckhart's practice of speaking of "transformation" as part of advocating that it is a good tool to think with.

with immediacy. As Eckhart puts it, "If one has a foot in the fire, one does not reflect but immediately pulls it out. And so, a prisoner does not consult a guard about his escape but flees without delay when he has the chance."[2]

This is all to say that Eckhart's ultimate concern is always with the divine. All terms, concepts, and reasoning thus clothe themselves ineluctably in metaphors that are judged and understood in terms of their *practical utility* in transporting us first in intellect (since intellect "rushes ahead," motivates us, and enables experience) and then in being. Also ironically implied here, just as it is throughout Eckhart's work, is the idea that the starting point is knowable and intelligible in the traditional sense, using our current modes of thinking and being in the world. The end point, which is no point at all, allows none of these. As Eckhart says, "Therefore, as man nakedly yields to God with love, so will he un-form, inform, and transform in the divine uniformity where he is one with God."[3] We cannot possibly use our existing mode of thinking and concepts to logically sort out what it means to unform, inform, and transform, especially in divine oneness that admits of no change. As we wrestle with it and feel the confusion that flows from the interplay of juxtaposed concepts, memories, and feelings, we may not even notice that our thought has taken on motion, something that happens so consistently that rhetoric can be designed to capitalize on this motion, guiding thought and directing it toward new understanding that transforms our current understanding by way of unforming, informing, and transforming it into the divine.

When I began scrutinizing the details of Eckhart's writing, I expected to find many aspects of his work that were metaphorical and indicative of his thought but at the same time were likely used without his awareness of their implications. What I discovered instead was that Eckhart demonstrates an intense awareness of rhetorical minutiae, the kind that one would expect from a professor of rhetoric like Augustine. This became apparent in several different ways.

First and most transparently, Eckhart talks openly about the detailed choices that he made in his exegesis, often interpreting Scripture in ways that depend upon grammatical subtlety. It became clear that Eckhart was willing to employ any detail or interpretation he could find, no matter how small and counterintuitive, to accomplish his rhetorical aims. Eckhart's project, I

---

[2] Eckhart, *Commentary on John*, n.234, LW III, 196.6–8.
[3] Eckhart, Sermon 40, DW II, 278.4–6.

contend, revolves in a tight orbit[4] around a center point that is the oneness with God. Speaking of an individual soul attaining this straightforwardly implies a paradox, since the soul is created and (in part) temporal. This contention will be treated at length since it is central to understanding Eckhart's rhetoric. The experience of achieving oneness with God is fundamentally ineffable, though the *practical* steps that one can take to get there and prepare the mind for getting there are amenable to endless description. For Eckhart, speech about lower things takes place using abstractions which are higher things, just as Platonic forms are higher than their manifestations. The distinction is that the forms would be used to describe the manifestations, but "one cannot properly speak of God, for nothing is higher than God."[5] As Eckhart approvingly quotes from Augustine regarding God's ineffability, "When you hear that he is truth, do not ask, what is truth? Remain if you can then in that very first flash when you touched upon its dazzling light, when you first heard someone say 'truth.'"[6] The point of this passage is not limited to the suggestion that we actually remain in that moment. It is effective because it functions like a haiku that paints a picture of what that moment was like and thereby enables us to partially revive and reexperience that moment. Here, we have the first of many hints that truth is posterior to the divine and is in fact less than God.[7] Eckhart speaks of the "veil of truth" for God, just as he does of the "veil of goodness" and the "veil of being itself."[8] All that was commonly spoken of as "convertible" (used interchangeably) with God in the late medieval world Eckhart makes less than God, perhaps indicating that it

---

4 Cf. Eckhart, Sermon 9; Venus's close and stable orbit makes it analogous to the *bîwort*, "adverb." Just as Venus orbits as closely as it can to the sun, so should man endeavor to stay as close to God at all times. Venus is Eckhart's analogy to the famous "adverb" passage of Sermon 9, as is evident from his scriptural choice for the sermon in mentioning the morning star: *quasi stella matutina*.

5 Eckhart, Sermon 20b, DW I, 346.7–8.

6 Augustine, *On the Trinity*, VIII.2, as cited in Eckhart, *Prologue to the Book of Propositions*, LW I.1, 170 n.7 lines 1–3; cf. *In Ex.* n.18. Eckhart adds to this, "And Augustine meant that this is God."

7 For example, Eckhart tells us in Sermon 13 that "wisdom and goodness and truth add something. One adds nothing other than the ground (*grunt*) of being" (DW I, 219.4). Mojsisch mentions this in the context of the *negatio negationis*, citing a parallel passage from Eckhart's Latin works ("One adds nothing to being, not by reason anyway, but by negation alone; it is not so with the true and the good" (*Commentary on Wisdom*, n.148 as cited by Burkhardt Mojsisch, *Meister Eckhart: Analogy, Univocity and Unity*, 98–99. My translations). He even says that for Eckhart, "negativity appears as a determinative moment of the unum furnishing it a certain priority before the verum and bonum." Burkhardt Mojsisch, *Meister Eckhart*, 98).

8 "Veil of goodness" (*velamen veri*), "veil of truth" (*velamen boni*), and the "veil of being itself" (*velamen ipsius esse*). Eckhart, Sermon XI.2, LW IV, 114.4–6.

still retains enough vestigial conceptual content to preclude it from identity with the divine ground. In the same way, he recasts detachment as the highest virtue. If truth is not the highest, then the highest that is above truth must be ineffable and reached only through practical action. Interestingly, Eckhart elsewhere uses the word "truth" in a contrary way: "He has spread truth on creatures, but they are not truth itself as God is. However, in some ways truth does pertain to creatures."[9] His rhetoric here is qualified. Creatures are not the truth as God is. This tells us that he is here using "truth" to mean the truth just as God is truth itself and not the truths of things in the world. Eckhart does not always include such qualifications, which make plain his intention to use a word in a particular fashion as a kind of aside. Similarly, "For I tell you in eternal truth, if you are not equal to this truth of which we want to speak now, then you cannot understand me."[10] Again, by "eternal truth" we must be "equal to" (as in *adaequatio*) the truth. With characteristic irony, we must have had the proper *experience* of being raised up to be equal to this *truth* in order to understand it. To be equal to the truth is for a person to be "true"; as Eckhart says, "each thing is said to be true on two grounds: first, if it attains the substantial form of its nature; and second, if it has nothing foreign mixed in with it."[11] For man, this means having attained pure *humanity* with nothing foreign to the form (i.e., none of the imperfections and falling away of a particular manifestation). Combine this with Eckhart's statement that "when Christ became man, he did not take on a particular man. He took on human nature. Go out of all things in this way so there remains only what Christ took on. Then you will have put on Christ."[12] To be equal to the truth is to put the soul in Christ's position and deify her. In other words, this strains the normal concept of truth to a breaking point (but not the thought that "God is truth"), as will be discussed in the section on explosive metaphors.[13]

Second, Eckhart uses his metaphors so consistently that they obtain a character of their own through repetition. His metaphorical repertoire is actually quite limited, which enables certain rhetorical effects that require repetition. For example, since he always uses fire in the same way, all previous

---

9 Eckhart, Sermon 93, DW IV.1, 127.33–34.
10 Eckhart, Sermon 52, DW II, 506.1–2.
11 Eckhart, *Commentary on John*, n.87, trans. McGinn in *Essential Eckhart*, 155.
12 Eckhart, *On Detachment*, DW V, 430.8–11.
13 Even in making a simple point about God being above truth, we see the dialectical spiral in action, leading us into a variety of topics and implications to attempt to plumb the depth of what Eckhart is saying. This complexity is usual rather than unusual in Eckhart's speech.

experience that the reader has with Eckhart's use of fire informs the way that he uses it in a new context. Thus, as with common interpretations of Scripture, we come to expect Eckhart to do something in a certain way. When he deviates from this, or more commonly when he omits certain important details (a rhetorical technique that actually extends his point in productive and perhaps provocative ways) the reader is led to see even greater depth in a sermon that otherwise does not contain some particular bit of content on its own. Just as Eckhart recommends his listeners work toward an orbit of ever-smaller radius around God (like a figure skater who brings in his or her arms, decreases the overall radius, and gains speed), my analysis of Eckhart's rhetoric will necessarily follow a similar trajectory. Eckhart's rhetoric never goes far from God, and it never leaves him for long. This does not mean, as C. F. Kelley argued, that Eckhart speaks *in divinis*. Further, he repeats himself so often, both theologically and metaphorically, that his rhetoric often features many different metaphors at the same time, which mutually encourage one another's rhetorical effects and create a tight orbit around God. Thus, although we move from one to the next in the course of this analysis, the trajectory described is more like a collection of eccentric orbits rather than a straight line.

Lakoff and Johnson make much of metaphors that people use without being aware of their significance. They describe metaphors of space (where nonspatial things have fronts and backs), position (where ideas are far away or close to us in terms of understanding), and so on. Eckhart however, scrutinized his metaphors to such a degree that it is difficult to tenably claim that he was unaware of the rhetorical details of how some things are "higher" than others, for example. As will be addressed in the sections below that treat his cosmology and theory of knowledge, Eckhart was quite aware of when he used "high" and "low." He explains, "whenever I say, 'the innermost,' I mean the highest. And whenever I say 'the highest,' I mean the innermost of the soul. In the innermost and in the highest of the soul – they are both the same."[14] Regarding spatial metaphors, Eckhart quotes Augustine: "Nothing in the universe's body is really 'below.' Those who conceive of before and behind, right and left, above and below in the universe are deceived, because it is hard to oppose custom and the senses."[15] Yet it can be done, and "After

---

14 Eckhart, Sermon 30, DW II, 95.3–5.
15 Eckhart, *Commentary on Exodus*, n.127, trans. McGinn in *Teacher and Preacher*, 85.

we abolish these words, we have to make a real mental effort in order to see the point."[16] Eckhart explains:

> If we consider heaven as far as its parts in the whole are concerned, since heaven is a simple body, there will be no place in it for above and below and the other four. But if heaven and its parts are compared with the whole universe (of which heaven is a part) as far as its place there is concerned, then we can talk about right, left, before, behind, up, and down in it. For example, in man the head is above, the feet below, the face before, the back behind, one hand is right, the other left. These do not vary among themselves insofar as they are related to man. Whatever direction a person turns, his face will always be above and his feet below if we refer these parts to the whole person, but if the parts are referred to some exterior location, then the upside-down man is said to have his feet above and his head below. … This is why Avicenna well says that heaven exists and is moved in a "where," because "where" takes its meaning from place without any consideration of the order of parts in the place.[17]

Clearly, Eckhart is aware to a remarkable degree of the metaphorical considerations that Lakoff and Johnson study.

An analysis of his metaphors cannot merely be a lexicon of Eckhartian terminology. His images and words often do not have single objects and single functions. Instead of providing an illusion of conceptual cohesion and logical consistency as a lexicon may, we will be sensitive to the undercurrent of Eckhart's thought that pervades his speech and informs word choice. This is the reverse of a terminological lexicon, which begins with words and backs into thought. Instead, we will see that Eckhart's rhetoric is Robert Forman's approach in action: many different ways of describing the process and experience of stripping away this-worldly "images."

RHETORIC ABOUT RHETORIC

At all times, I would like to claim, Eckhart's emphasis is remarkably *practical* for someone so deeply embedded in scholastic theology. This is a consequence of his mysticism and perhaps also of his order's focus on preaching. For Eckhart, the soul needs words just as it needs all worldly things: "If she could know God without the world, the world would not have been created

---

[16] Eckhart, *Commentary on Exodus*, n.127, trans. McGinn in *Teacher and Preacher*, 85.
[17] Eckhart, *Commentary on Exodus*, n.128, trans. McGinn in *Teacher and Preacher*, 85.

for her. And so the world was created for her to train and strengthen the soul's eye to suffer the divine light."[18] Eckhart continues, telling us that parables and matter enable the soul to undergo God, letting the divine light flow into the soul and uniting the soul with God.[19] It is salient that the Middle High German (and modern German similarly) for "parable" is *glichnisse*, which also means "likeness." A parable is thus a story that is similar to or reflects its intended object. Through likeness, the mind can rush ahead to facilitate motion, which is necessary for progress[20] As Eckhart says, "if a painter considered every stroke of his brush when he made his first stroke, he would paint nothing. If someone was to go to a city and thought beforehand how he was to take the first step, nothing would come out of it. This is why we should follow the first suggestion and go forward."[21] Similarly:

> Plato himself and all the ancient theologians and poets generally used to teach about God, nature and ethics by means of parables. The poets did not speak in an empty and fabulous way, but they intentionally and very attractively and properly taught about the natures of things divine, natural and ethical by metaphors and allegories.... As the poet Horace himself says in his *Art of Poetry*: "Poets want either to be useful or to entertain." And later: "He who mingles the useful and the entertaining wins all the applause."[22]

The "attractive" way of teaching is the "proper" one, which results in motion. Our desires follow what we recognize to be beautiful and good, though the soul that is far from God mistakes worldly things as being good. Therefore, divine teaching must be clothed in worldly images so that the preacher may guide someone far from God, connecting the dots that describe a path between worldly "images" that are thought to be good and the authentic good that is the nakedness of the divine essence. It is a sophisticated pedagogical approach, one that recognizes the necessity of maximally exciting motivation by capitalizing on the good that people can understand at various stages

---

18 Eckhart, Sermon 32, DW II, 134.5–135.1. Note that *liden* here means to "undergo" or "suffer" which is an important metaphor for Eckhart that describes the soul's passivity in receiving God, as will be discussed. Also, *gewenet* can mean both "habituated" and "familiarized," which goes beyond simply becoming strong enough to endure the divine light.

19 Eckhart, Sermon 32, DW II, 135.4–5, 142.2–3.

20 In Sermon 3, Eckhart says, "knowledge runs ahead, surpassing and breaking through" (DW I, 49.1–2). Cf. Sermon 19, where Eckhart likewise says the intellect "runs ahead," and Sermon 111.

21 Eckhart, Sermon 62, DW III, 515.68.5–69.2.

22 Eckhart, *Book on the Parables of Genesis*, n.2, trans. McGinn in *Essential Eckhart*, 93.

of the process. It appeals to all, as Eckhart says recalling Augustine: "In the beginning, Scripture laughs at young children and attracts a child to it" and thus "there is no one so simple-minded that he cannot find what suits him."[23] Similarly, "Moses only wrote like that: he knew better, but he did it for people who could not grasp it otherwise."[24]

Using the analogy of baking, Eckhart tells us, "If someone heats a baker's oven, ... the single temperature of the oven does not work the same way in different doughs.... In the same way then, God does not work alike in all hearts; he works as he finds readiness and receptivity."[25] This accords with the more general claim that "He gives to each according to what is best and most fitting for him."[26] Putting the pieces together: while each person finds what suits him, God works in each person in whatever way is most suitable and *useful* to that person. Eckhart's keenness for "baking the right bread" for the tastes of his listeners may explain statements like "Those who do not understand this should not worry about it"[27] and "Whoever does not understand these words, let them not trouble their hearts over it. For as long as someone is not like this truth, they will not understand these words."[28] It is an indication that his sermons are layered like Scripture and contain different elements that are useful depending on where we are on the path.[29]

At various times, we see evidence that Eckhart wants his audience to maintain confidence that they can achieve what he is describing. For example, he admonishes his hearers, "No one should think that they cannot get here."[30] Moreover, he develops this further by (perhaps ironically) insisting that what he describes is *easy* and quickly attainable. "Nothing is so easy

---

23 Eckhart, Sermon 51, DW II, 467.

24 Eckhart, Sermon 101, DW IV.1, 358.141–42.

25 Eckhart, *On Detachment*, DW V, 424.4–11. Cusanus used a similar image, telling us that "hunger" is met by the preacher who, like a baker who cooks different bread to suit different tastes, tailors the content of his sermons to best reach his audience such that each can take what is important for him. Wolfgang Lentzen-Deis, "Les prédicateurs sont comme des boulangers," in *La Prédication et l'Eglise chez Maître Eckhart et Nicolas de Cues*, ed. Marie-Anne Vannier (Paris: Cerf, 2008), 115.

26 Eckhart, *Counsels on Discernment*, §23, DW V, 302.1.

27 Eckhart, Sermon 16a, DW I, 259.30–32.

28 Eckhart, Sermon 52, DW II, 506.1–3.

29 As I would object to Milem's handling of Sermon 2 (the little castle), the progression of the sermon cannot be collapsed to the endpoint without losing material that would be useful to those who are still on the path (cf. Milem, *Unspoken Word*, chap. 3, especially pp. 77–78).

30 Eckhart, Sermon 38, DW II, 245.1–2.

and so worthwhile as renouncing what is foreign and rejecting what is from without, whose nature is external, foreign, adverse."[31] Elsewhere, we get an additional clue about what this renunciation will do for us: "There are many people, and we can readily do what they do if we wish, who are not hindered by things they deal with."[32] In another passage that describes this movement to God as easy, he tells us *how* to do it: "No one here is so coarse, so ignorant, or so inept that he that he could not, with the grace of God, wholly unite his will with God's will. He then he only needs to say with desire, 'Lord show me your dearest will and strengthen me to do it!'"[33] The caveat here as with the other passages is that "desire" is not a matter of will. Desire follows what we know to be beautiful. Implicit in this statement is an acquaintance with the divine through experience. This may color his understanding of Augustine as well. If Augustine had wrestled with his will without having experience of God, he might not have succeeded. Eckhart continues in that sermon, explaining that the Virgin Mary's "joy is not far from you, if you will only seek it wisely."[34] "Wisely" and "by the grace of God" are also significant qualifications. If we recall Augustine's herculean struggle to give his will over to God in the *Confessions*, we know that actually accomplishing such a *conversio* of will is harldly easy. Contrast this with Eckhart's Origenist statement elsewhere that "this does not happen all at once, but slowly as a result of the growth of the soul. For if a man were to burn up all at once, that would not be a good thing."[35] Yet with irony in play, Eckhart saw utility in insisting upon ease, perhaps because ease also implies closeness.

Since God is closer to the soul than it is to itself,[36] rhetoric that inspires progress toward understanding this intimacy is valuable, even if it takes the ironic form of saying that conversion of the will is easy.[37] This may be related to Eckhart's tendency to describe God as hurrying to give himself to the humble person: "When God sees that we are his only begotten Son, God hurries so quickly and rushes to us and acts at once, as if his divine

---

31 Eckhart, *Commentary on Exodus*, n.108, trans. McGinn in *Teacher and Preacher*, 80.
32 Eckhart, *Counsels on Discernment*, §7, DW V, 209.7–8.
33 Eckhart, Sermon 66, DW III, 118.13–119.
34 Eckhart, Sermon 66, DW III, 119.5–6.
35 Eckhart, Sermon 82, DW III, 247.6–8.
36 Eckhart, *Counsels on Discernment*, §20.
37 Eric Mangin recently made much of this rhetoric of intimacy in his recent book, *Maître Eckhart ou le profondeur de l'intime* (Paris: Seuil, 2015). The rhetoric of closeness will appear throughout the remainder of the discussion here.

being was about to break apart and become nothing in itself.... God has this lust and joy in his abundance."[38] Elsewhere, Eckhart remarks, "He needs our blessedness so much that he lures us to him by any means, whether pleasant or unpleasant. God forbid that he ever permit anything that does not lure us to him."[39] Although desire is the province of created things and God is above desire,[40] Eckhart may sensibly have decided to describe God's desire hyperbolically, since we approach God with love that increases infinitely.[41] Already we see the emphasis that Eckhart places on factors that motivate and compel the soul to move toward God. This is true even of God's hiddenness in the depth of the soul, in the manner of making such stirring enticingly unfamiliar:

> [God's hiddenness] is most useful for her [the soul]. This unknowing guides her in wonder and makes her pursue it. She indeed judges that it is, but does not know how or what it is. When a man knows the reason of things, he immediately tires of them and seeks to know something else, always in a sorrowful longing to know more without any constancy. Therefore, this unknowing knowing keeps her still and makes her pursue it.[42]

On this crucial point, Eckhart takes influence from Augustine. As mentioned earlier, Eckhart understands the value of the surprising and unfamiliar (or what is "strange, doubtful or false"[43]) in exciting attention and motivation "because new and unusual things more pleasantly provoke the mind than everyday ones."[44]

Eckhart catalyzes transformative change in his listeners by using a particular kind of novelty: he turns familiar material into something unfamiliar. Eckhart uses familiar images and ideas which are read as meaningful by his audience to provide viable pathways on which his listeners may be carried from their habitual torpor into a new way of thinking. The resonance with existing values produces a shock and perception of worldview proximity that is necessary for movement, while the unfamiliar material must produce

---

38 Eckhart, Sermon 12, DW I, 194.2–7.
39 Eckhart, Sermon 73, DW III, 269.2–3.
40 Eckhart, Sermon 44.
41 Eckhart, Sermon 82; cf. God's working "joyfully" (*lustlîche*) in the soul in Sermon 92, DW IV.1, 102.8.
42 Eckhart, Sermon 101, DW IV.1, 361.155–160.
43 *monstruosa dubia aut falsa*, LW I.1, 152.4.
44 Eckhart, *General Prologue*, LW I.1, 148.14–149.1.

enough dissonance not to be serviceable by existing habits, but not so much that it is read as incomprehensibly foreign or as antagonistic.[45]

Eckhart also made the familiar unfamiliar by subverting common exegetical themes. This was accomplished both by directly addressing themes by name (e.g., "'Wife' is the noblest word that one can say of a soul, much nobler than 'virgin'"[46]) and also by omitting ostensibly obvious interpretations (e.g., avoiding the usual Christological interpretation of John 1:43).[47] Further, Eckhart seems to specifically avoid certain staples of medieval preaching almost altogether, a practice that we must conclude constitutes an implicit criticism of the preaching of his day.[48] For example, though it was common to provide practical moral advice, Eckhart's advice in the *Book of Divine Consolation* is hardly common. Likewise, speaking on fear of God and damnation was commonplace. Eckhart dismisses fear of God as counterproductive and only mentions hell to say that even the damned still want God.[49]

Eckhart begins Sermon 30 (*Praedica verbum*, "Speak the Word") by telling his listeners that the Latin passage from 2 Timothy 4:2 means the following in the vernacular, "Speak the word, speak it aloud, speak it forth, bring it forth, give birth to the Word!"[50] Eckhart paraphrases *praedica verbum* (speak the Word) repeatedly until he arrived at the formulation he wanted: "give birth to the Word."[51] Each successive formulation drifts further from the wording of the text, further from what is familiar, and closer to the desired idea of the birth of the Word in the soul, a perennial Eckhartian theme that is decidedly unfamiliar. At the same time, those in his audience who were acquainted with his favorite themes would have waited with anticipation

---

45 Davies argued that Eckhart sought to "awaken his listeners" and to "shake [them] free from their assumptions, in order to deliver a 'metaphysical shock'" (*Mystical Theologian*, 126). He contends that Eckhart's rhetorical devices are there to turn his listeners' minds away from the created and point them to transcendence (*Mystical Theologian*, 200). I generally agree with Davies, but not with his claim that Eckhart was being hyperbolic in his idealization of the union of God in *Beati pauperes spiritu* (Sermon 52) to shake them from spiritual complacency with the tantalizing possibility of what can be (*Mystical Theologian*, 201). Similarly, Cyprian Smith says, "Constantly in his sermons he talks about God in such a way as to shock us into an awareness of how shallow and inadequate our habitual notions of God are" (*Way of Paradox*, 38).

46 Eckhart, Sermon 2, DW I, 27.3–4.

47 McGinn, *Mystical Thought of Meister Eckhart*, 116.

48 McGinn, *Mystical Thought of Meister Eckhart*, 131.

49 Eckhart, Sermon 22, DW I, 385.15–16; cf. Sermon 95, DW IV.1; *Prol. Par. Gen.* n.163.

50 Eckhart, Sermon 30, DW II, 93.2–3. The only portion of what Eckhart says that is in the original verse is *praedica verbum*, "speak the Word."

51 Tobin, *Teacher and Preacher*, 295n2.

to see what strange and novel way he would enter into that territory. He continues, "It is a wonderful thing that something flows out and yet stays within."[52] He emphasizes the incomprehensibility of the statement, validating his audience's feeling that they do not clearly understand it. With the space created for the unfamiliar, he uses the opportunity to introduce more of his unusual-sounding ideas in the following order: God in all things, God's continuous creation of the world in eternity, the birth of the Word in the soul, identity with the Son, and total detachment. Donald Duclow has a memorable way of describing this process in the *Book of Divine Consolation*: "As Eckhart moves into divine knowledge, the perspectival shifts become increasingly radical and their healing power progressively stronger; chicken soup then gives way to veritable psychosurgery."[53]

His talk of the diminution of the personal will in favor of becoming divine is another example of the same tactic. He begins by saying most comfortably and concretely, "I was sitting somewhere yesterday when I spoke a little word from the *Pater Noster*: 'Your will be done!' But what's more, it would be better as: 'May will become yours!'"[54] The wordplay's reversal is more evident in the original: *dîn wille der werde* becomes *werde wille dîn*. Here, we clearly see Eckhart taking a common and familiar idea and making it his own through wordplay, allowing the new formulation to ostensibly inherit some of the familiarity of the original.

In his exegesis of "work in all things" (*omnibus labora*), he repeats the same strategy of proceeding from most familiar to least familiar, from most easily understood to least easily understood. He says there are three ways we should understand "work in all things": 1) to see God in all things, 2) to love all equally, and 3) to love God equally in all things. Just as his earlier discussion of God as eternal leans on Augustine, Eckhart goes as far as citing Augustine to quickly argue for seeing God in all things.[55] His discussion of the second point is particularly interesting. He begins with the well-known injunction in Luke 10:27 to love your neighbor as yourself. In the process of discussing this, however, he makes the unsettling statement "If you have love for one person more than another, this is wrong. If you have love for

---

52 Eckhart, Sermon 30, DW II, 94.1.
53 Donald Duclow, "'My Suffering Is God': Meister Eckhart's Book of Divine Consolation," *Theological Studies* 44, no. 44 (1983): 574.
54 Eckhart, Sermon 30, DW II, 99.1–2.
55 Eckhart cites Augustine, *Confessions*, 4.12.18.

your father, your mother, and yourself more than another, this is wrong."⁵⁶ Though this is implied by Luke 10:27 (as his listeners may have been aware) it is almost a direct reference to the even more unsettling phrasing of Luke 14:26, "If any man come to me, and hate not his father, and mother, and wife, and children, and brethren, and sisters, yea, and his own life also, he cannot be my disciple."

Eckhart, I believe, depended on a form of the *pratfall effect* in soliciting a positive response from his audience. In psychology, the pratfall effect works as follows. If I already have a positive opinion of someone, seeing them make a mistake only causes me to like them more. Of course, the reverse is true as well. If I am already negatively disposed toward an individual, then seeing them make a mistake causes me to like them even less. Eckhart was able to sermonize with an established ethos which probably allowed his audience to give him more than the usual benefit of the doubt when he made outrageous sounding claims. In those situations, because there was a certain amount of trust (or at least curiosity), they would be likely to sustain attention in listening to him. Since some of Eckhart's rash-sounding claims read like mistakes and abuses of the texts (twisting the wax nose of authority too much perhaps), those who were positively disposed toward him may have been all the more likely to keep listening with increased attention.

Since Eckhart's audience came to respect him, when they heard a shocking statement that had the ring of blasphemy they may have been *even more* inclined to seek out the subtle thinking which would instead show the statement to be surprisingly orthodox. Offensive speech, whether it be shocking, indecent, or ostensibly blasphemous, can be a vehicle for breaking away from habitually enforced normative thinking.⁵⁷ Using ordinary words may imply activating ordinary habits. The extraordinary irrupts ordinary thinking and creates space for new understanding and experiences.

In talking about whether the depth of Scripture is suprising, Eckhart answers "yes" for man insofar as he is created and "no" for man insofar as he is

---

56 Eckhart, Sermon 30, DW II, 102.4–6.

57 William Franke, "Varieties and Valences of Unsayability," *Philosophy and Literature* 29, no. 2 (2005): 493. William James makes a likeminded assertion: "Where mendacity, treachery, obscenity, and malignity find hampered expression, talk can be brilliant indeed. But its flame waxes dim where the mind is stitched all over with conscientious fear of violating the moral and social proprieties." *Talks to Teachers on Psychology: And to Students on Some of Life's Ideals* (New York: Henry Holt, 1899), 181.

divine.[58] Wonder is the province of creatures.[59] As a created intellect begins to leave the familiar confines of thinking that is focused on the material world, its eyes open to God in wonder. It is continually *surprised* because surprise is what happens when our expectations are not met as we experience something unfamiliar. When God is unfamiliar and "foreign" (*vremde*) to us, we are surprised. Once the created individual is effaced and the soul returns to union with God and he is thus familiar, we are no longer surprised.

Rhetoric contains great power, as Eckhart says, "Words also have great power: we can perform miracles with words. All words have power from the first Word."[60] As he says, human speech flows forth and remains within, just as divine speech does.[61] Further, Eckhart is willing to identify the speaker with the truth, making for a stronger statement: "If you could look upon this with my heart, you would understand well what I say, for it is true and the truth itself speaks it."[62] This sounds radical, but it flows from his general principle that "What proceeds is in its source; it is in it as a seed is in its principle, as a word is in one who speaks."[63] Thus, the speech of one who speaks the truth is a production or manifestation of the truth itself. Instead of conceiving of speech as necessarily sullying and of truth as mediated by the individual's imperfect understanding, Eckhart asserts that truth shines through fully as truth in such situations and not merely as an imperfect resemblance. This is because the light of grace, and not just the light of the intellect, may shine

---

58 Eckhart, Sermon 22, DW I, 381.3–382.2.

59 In Plato we read, "Wonder is the feeling of the philosopher, and philosophy begins in wonder" (*Theaetetus* 155d, in *The Dialogues of Plato*, vol. 2, ed. and trans. Benjamin Jowett [New York, N.Y.: Random House, 1937]). In Aristotle, "It was their wonder [*thaumazein*], astonishment, that first led men to philosophize and still leads them" (*Metaphysics* 982b12, in *Aristotle's Metaphysics*, trans. W. David Ross, 2 vols. [Oxford: Clarendon Press, 1924]). Since Plato says that the *arche* of philosophy is *thaumazein* and that Iris (the messenger of Heaven) is the child of Thauma (Wonder), it may not be too much of a stretch to think of this in concert with the *arche* (Latin *Principium*) of John 1:1. At the very least, for Eckhart, wonder, like Christ, leads us back to God. It is not clear that Eckhart would have known this portion of Plato, though he would have read the idea in Aristotle.

60 Eckhart, Sermon 18, DW I, 306.5–7.

61 Eckhart, Sermon 9, DW I, 157.3–8, cf. Sermon 30, DW II, 94.1–2. Some readers may object that I am ignoring some of Eckhart's most famous and discussed metaphors, such as "flow," of which McGinn in particular makes much. These have not been ignored, of course. Instead, we should notice that it is not the imaginative portions of those metaphors that contribute the content that is relevant to my project of drawing out the metaphysics of the individual. Flow is an inflection of Neoplatonic emanation. Eckhart's metaphysics of flow is not peculiar to him insofar as it is flow. In the other details of what flows and how it flows, we see metaphors that are more clearly useful for this project.

62 Eckhart, Sermon 2, DW I, 40.5–7.

63 Eckhart, *Commentary on John*, n.4, trans. McGinn in *Essential Eckhart*, 124.

in the enlightened soul.⁶⁴ This is possible because of the "divine light, which shines through the soul like the sun through glass."⁶⁵ So we see that Eckhart understands the individual soul as having the capacity to speak the truth as truth itself because the divine light shines in the highest part of it. Thus, Eckhart does not need to speak from the standpoint of divinity, as C. F. Kelley contends, as if divinity were something external. For the soul that has been purified of images and made receptive to God, the soul as the only-begotten Son speaks the truth as the truth itself, with no distinction between them. That God can shine through at any time and not just when speaking from a particular standpoint energizes Eckhart's rhetoric with possibility. Words are not merely aspiring, nominalist approximations that hope to have the appearance of truth. The soul can do away with its limitations by cleansing itself of images and speak the Word as the truth itself.

All of this is possible because Eckhart's philosophy of language is not based upon a simple understanding of a true statement as being a likeness to what it describes. He touches upon truth in the natural world and indeed has a well-developed cosmology, as we will see. Yet, his discussions of these truths always feel like a side issue, something that is always secondary to his ultimate purpose of getting at the divine itself. Consequently, if we get sidetracked by his particular statements and begin to construct a philosophically coherent system, we lose the rhythm his rhetoric establishes. We will see this most clearly by looking at the dialetical motion that his rhetoric builds in an effort to guide thought toward God. Many of these are explosive metaphors, of course. In preparation for this discussion, let us now consider the little words and use of grammar that give those metaphors a consistent and characteristically Eckhartian tone.

DIALECTIC OF PARTICLES: IN, BY, FOR, WITH, THROUGH

One of the most consistent rhetorical tropes in Eckhart is his parroting of the Scriptural tendency to string together words that express relation: in, by, for, with, through. For example, we read of "One God and Father of all,

---

64 Eckhart, Sermon 73, DW III, 262.1–9.

65 Eckhart, Sermon 95b, DW IV.1, 199.296–98; cf. Sermon 73. Note that the lower powers cannot house the divine light, though they may be made receptive to it (Sermon 10). As he explains, "if God is to divinely shine in you, your natural light will not help you at all. It must become a pure nothing and entirely go out of itself" (Sermon 103, DW IV.1, 476.27–477.28). Note that the "natural light" is the lower intellect.

who is above all, and through all, and in you all" (Eph 4:6) and "For of him, and through him, and to him, are all things" (Rom 11:36). Fundamentally, applying multiple relations like this creates a kind of paradox since they can be mutually exclusive. A God who is "above all, and through all, and in you all" is at once paradoxically above and within. A similar paradox begins the Gospel according to John: "The Word was with God, and the Word was God." I contend that such a structure emphasizes the maximal intimacy and complete oneness of God.[66] A word like "with" establishes a certain relation between two parts, as when we say "x with y." This relation has meaning because it *excludes* other possibilities. We would not say that two things are *with* one another if they are in fact univocally the same thing.[67] So, for things to be *from* God and also *in* God can only be sensible if the relations antagonize one another and revert to oneness. Stringing together such particles, in other words, guides our thought to try to work out the meaning in the combination of relations. In that process, we experience firsthand the futility of applying the exclusions implied by each particle. We are left only with oneness. Eckhart, of course, uses this same structure to refer to God, "whatever exists is from God himself, through him and in him."[68] This is perhaps more surprising where Eckhart uses this same structure with the individual soul, as in "We live with the Son and in the Son and through the Son."[69]

This is part of a more general trend where Eckhart takes rhetorical figures and words which normally apply to Christ or God and then applies them to the individual soul, spark, or intellect.[70] In image language, the Son

---

[66] The effect and language are reminiscent of the infinite sphere metaphor.

[67] This is precisely the issue with Eckhart's comment, "An indwelling, an adhering and a oneness with God—that is grace, and there 'God is with'" (Sermon 38, DW II, 244.7–8). The word *mit* in German indicates a closeness of relation, much like *apud* does in Latin (this is the word used in the passage "The word was with God," *Verbum erat apud Deum*). Though there are subtle shades of difference between *mit*, *apud*, and *with*, they all indicate a close relation rather than straightforward equality, which is what matters most for interpreting what Eckhart is doing with these words.

[68] Eckhart, *Commentary on* Exodus, n.40, trans. McGinn in *Teacher and Preacher*, 55.

[69] Eckhart, Sermon 5b, DW I, 85.2–3. As Matthew Fox describes in one passage, we live in and with and though the inner man just as we do with Christ. *Breakthrough: Meister Eckhart's Creation Spirituality in New Translation* (New York: Doubleday, 1991), 474.

[70] "Eckhart [applies] to the human 'intellect' (or sometimes to what he calls the 'something' in the soul) the terms which are normally reserved for God in the tradition of apophatic theology and of which he himself makes abundant use in his discussion of the divinity. As in the Aristotelian and Neoplatonic traditions generally, the 'intellect' is accordingly free of specific being in the 'here' and 'now', it has nothing in common with anything else, it is entirely united within itself and it reflects upon itself inwardly. These are all precisely the terms which Eckhart has applied to God in his Latin works and which he is now using with reference to the human 'intellect'. And in a

is the true image (*imago*)⁷¹ while man is made in the image of (*ad imaginem*). Eckhart uses both forms to describe the human intellect.⁷² In keeping with this, Eckhart uses *ad imaginem* to describe the human intellect insofar as it has *esse formale*. In Scripture, Paul uses "in Christ" consistently to refer to the relation between the believer and Christ in this life. While he seems to reserve "with Christ" (*syn Christō* or *Kyriō*) for the life to come, in Galatians 2:19–20, he says "I have been crucified with Christ, and I live now not with my own life but with the life of Christ who lives in me."⁷³ We frequently hear this verse quoted, but we are only likely to notice the pattern of usage in the otherwise innocuous-sounding particles if we consider the Pauline writings as a whole. A similar strategy suggests itself with Eckhart. For example, in describing Christ's soul, Eckhart says, "its life was with the body, yet above the body immediately in God without any hindrance."⁷⁴ Eckhart consistently describes Christ's soul in the same way that he describes individual souls. The full significance of this will be explored after we have more fully articulated Eckhart's notion of the individual.

All things stand in an analogous relationship with God insofar as any being has its being analogously from the divine being. God is within them insofar as God is one, God has no parts, God is being, and everything that is has being. In addition to each person standing in this relation as an existing thing, the human soul is also related univocally to God insofar as reason is the ground of the soul. Unlike analogy, univocity is not a descending relation. Insofar as we have the faculty of reason which has yet to break through to the divine ground, we are *ad imaginem dei*, made after the image of God. Insofar as we have reason in the ground of our souls that is univocally God's reason which grounds being itself, we are *imago dei*, the image of God just as Christ is with no possible distinction. This is how we should understand the rhetorical subtlety of Eckhart's example of the fly in Sermon 52. He tells us that God became "God in creatures when creatures came to be" and that "great riches" (i.e., being) are "possessed by even the lowliest creature in God."

---

further passage we find additional imagery which Eckhart has applied to God and which he is now using to describe the 'intellect'. These are chiefly uncreatedness, unnameability, and the concept of the divine ground and desert" (Davies, *Mystical Theologian*, 137; cf. Eckhart, Sermon 28).

71 2 Cor 4:4, Col 1:15.

72 The theological details can be found in Mojsisch, *Meister Eckhart: Analogy, Univocity and Unity*, especially chaps. 3–4, p. 92.

73 McGinn, *Foundations of Mysticism*, 73.

74 Eckhart, Sermon 49, DW II, 442.6–7.

His next statement shows the difference described above: "If it were the case that a fly possessed *reason* and *through reason* could seek the eternal abyss of divine being [the ground] out of which it comes, then we say that God with all that he is as God would not be enough to fulfill or satisfy the fly." The fly would be unsatisfied if it stood in univocal relation to God through reason. Therefore, Eckhart continues, if this is "God in creatures," then "we pray to God that we may become free of God" (i.e., God only insofar as he is being and not in the divine ground of the Godhead).

The situation is somewhat different with "substantive" pronouns. These are words that refer to things that are substantial and have existence in their own right. For Eckhart, the proper referent of substantial pronouns can only be God, since all existence is in God and from God and does not belong to the individual thing, "'Ego', the [Latin] word for 'I', is proper to no one other than God alone in his oneness."[75] Further, "these three words 'I', 'am', and 'who' belong to God in the most proper sense.... A distinguishing pronoun signifies the pure substance—pure, I say, without any accident, without anything foreign, the substance without quality.... These things belong to God alone."[76] Sermon 77 contains the longest exposition on substantive pronouns. In it, Eckhart tells us that "'[I]' means a kind of perfection of the designation 'I', for it is not a proper name: we use it for a name and for the perfection of that name and it denotes immovability and immobility. It means that God is immovable, immobile, and eternal constancy."[77] This same treatment of the substantive informs Eckhart's use of the otherwise-insignificant word "something" (*etwaȝ*): "This pure, bare being is called by Aristotle a 'something.' That is the highest thing that Aristotle ever said about natural knowledge. No master can ever say anything higher that is beyond this unless he were speaking in the Holy Spirit."[78] Despite such substantives belonging only to God, Eckhart uses them for the soul and thinks of the soul qua divine as properly being able to use the same substantive "I."

Eckhart does something similar with "am" and "was" and the difference in tenses: "The word 'erat' most properly belongs to God. In the Latin tongue

---

[75] Eckhart, Sermon 28, DW II, 68.4–5. The same holds for the other transcendentals that are convertible with being like goodness, truth, and justice: "[All good comes] in him and with him and through him" (*In Sap.* n.96, trans. McGinn in *Teacher and Preacher*, 156).

[76] Eckhart, *Commentary on Exodus*, n.14, trans. McGinn in *Teacher and Preacher*, 45; cf. Sermon XXII.

[77] Eckhart, Sermon 77, DW III, 340.10–341.1.

[78] Eckhart, Sermon 15, DW I, 251.10–13.

no word is as proper to God as 'erat.'... All things add something, but it adds nothing other than thought."[79] This notion of adding in thought but not substantively is how Eckhart allows for difference in the divine Persons without disturbing divine oneness. Regarding the tenses Eckhart says that "*erat* signifies a birth, a perfect becoming. I have come now, I was coming[80] today. If time were taken away from 'I come' and 'I have come', then the coming and have-come would be united and would be one."[81] Since the different tenses refer to aspects of temporality, if *erat* compresses them together in birth (since such generation occurs ceaselessly in eternity), then this tense points beyond time and thereby collapses the meaning of the various past tenses together. Such attention to fine grammatical detail characterizes Eckhart's rhetoric generally. Even where he does not explicitly call out grammatical subtlety, this thought lies in the background.

Since the string of particles also refers to divine oneness, Eckhart can conclude that "these three terms (from, through, and in) seem to be not only appropriated, but proper to the divine Persons" and that "universally, even in creatures, that 'from which' any single thing is, is the same as that 'through' and 'in' which it is."[82] This is because "from," "through," and "in" point to being, which only properly belongs to God. However, when they point to existence (which involves alteration and production) rather than being itself (which involves creation), these words can be applied to artists and artisans. The same holds for the relation between parts and wholes, moving from particular to universal: "The parts of any whole... receive existence from, through, and in the whole."[83]

The difference in particles is one of intimacy. As William James commented, "Philosophy has always turned on grammatical particles. With, near, next, like, from, towards, against, because, for, through, my—these words designate types of conjunctive relation arranged in a roughly ascending order of intimacy and inclusiveness."[84] Lakoff and Johnson say that "with" indicates

---

79 Eckhart, Sermon 44, DW II, 347.7–8, 348.1.

80 As Maurice O'Connell Walshe explains, *was komende* straightforwardly means "was coming" in both Middle High German and English, but this grammatical construction does not straightforwardly translate to modern German. *The Complete Mystical Works of Meister Eckhart* (New York: Crossroad, 2010), 147n7.

81 Eckhart, Sermon 44, DW II, 348.4–349.1.

82 Eckhart, Sermon IV.1 n.21; McGinn, Tobin, and Borgstädt, *Meister Eckhart: Teacher and Preacher*, 207.

83 Eckhart, *Commentary on Wisdom*, n.40, trans. McGinn in *Teacher and Preacher*, 155.

84 William James, *Radical Empiricism* (New York: Longmans, Green, 1912), 45.

accompaniment (as a companion) and instrumentality.[85] Little words like "in" and "at" indicate metaphorical relationships. It is in this context that we should understand Michael Sells's contention that Eckhart uses "in" to refer to things that have no place.[86] I would like to extend this and argue that Eckhart uses the personal pronouns "I" and "you" to refer to more than the individual self as commonly conceived, as part of his explosive metaphorics of the self. He also uses "part" to refer to things that have no parts. The particle "in" indicates great intimacy. The case of spiritual things illustrates the significance of the notion of "in": "A master says: if all intermediaries were removed between me and the wall, I would be at the wall but not in it. This is not the case with spiritual things, where one thing is always *in* the other. What receives is the same as what is received, for it receives nothing other than itself."[87] To emphasize the centrality of this point, Eckhart continues by including one of his characteristic statements: "This is subtle. Whoever understands this has been preached to enough."[88] Such statements tell us more than just to be attentive. They signal that the ultimate point of Eckhart's preaching lies not in conceptual understanding of a theological system, but in an experience of "understanding" that strains the very idea of understanding.

Though Eckhart's use of "in" indeed *reflects* the structure of his thought, it would be difficult to argue that it has primacy and actively *structures* his thought in the manner Lakoff and Johnson argue. Instead, Eckhart harnesses this quality in his listeners and plays off of their existing concept of "in" and enriches it by pushing it in new directions. Thus, on Augustine's saying "The image [of God] is in the mind," Eckhart comments, "it says: *in* the mind and not *from*. This is because the soul should be solid and closed all around so that it can produce the image of God like a mountain which produces an echo."[89] This passage in particular demonstrates the difference between an explicit simile (the echo) and a more subtle metaphor (being "in" rather than "from"). Eckhart would have us take our existing intuition about what

---

85 George Lakoff and Mark Johnson, *Metaphors We Live By* (Chicago: University of Chicago Press, 1980), 133–35.

86 Michael Sells, *Mystical Languages of Unsaying* (Chicago: University of Chicago Press, 1994), 163–64. For example, "he himself is the place where he wants to work" (Eckhart, Sermon 52, DW II, 501.1). This is clearly a place that is no place.

87 Eckhart, Sermon 16a, DW I, 258.1–8.

88 Eckhart, Sermon 16a, DW I, 258.9–10.

89 Eckhart, Sermon XL.3, LW IV, 345.6–9; cf. Augustine, *On the Trinity*, XIV.8.11.

interiority and embeddedness "in" imply and apply that *feeling* to what it means for us to be images of God. This is distinctly different from arguing for the conceptual coherence and philosophical rightness of a position. We should understand Eckhart's metaphors as intentional appeals to experience. This is the same strategy Augustine adopts in pointing us to the moment when we first heard "truth," as mentioned above.

Another inflection of note in Eckhart's dialectic of particles is his use of chiasmus. For example, he writes, "There is a something in the soul in which God lives, and there is a something in the soul in which the soul lives in God."[90] Similarly, the human spirit "will be broken through by God. As he breaks through me, I break through him in return!"[91] This is a kind of chiasmus that emphasizes unity by reciprocity. If I cause something and that something causes me, then, when I think the two statements together, I come to see that they must be the same thing. This is a form of guiding thought toward a conclusion, rhetorically much more effective than simply stating that "the two are one." Such flat statements are not only rhetorically less effective in fomenting interest and motivation, but they also have a logical air to them, appearing as claims and statements that must be intellectualized. Eckhart's rhetoric, by contrast, guides us down a prescribed path of thought in an effort to recreate an experience of seeing and experiencing firsthand. Eckhart offers one example of this in the form of riddle: "To find God, there is no better advice than to look for him where you left him."[92] This is a loaded statement. We "left" him where we began to have distance from God. It is a truism, ultimately, but a *guiding* and *useful* riddle that appeals to the personal experience of each listener. Using chiasmus allows Eckhart to describe reflexive relations where they are not normally possible. The effect of the paradox is the dissolution of the relation. This manner of guiding thought by straining concepts until they break is characteristic of explosive metaphors. It is to this kind of dynamic that we now turn.

---

90 Eckhart, Sermon 42, DW II, 301.5–6.
91 Eckhart, Sermon 29, DW II, 76.3–1.
92 Eckhart, *Counsels on Discernment*, §11, DW V, 225.3.

EXPLOSIVITY AND ECKHART'S MATHEMATICAL METAPHORS

Eckhart's rhetoric has motion, often a topsy-turvy, dizzying back and forth that elicits a confusion that provokes us to look carefully at what he says. This confusion is educative and guides us in the right "direction," so to speak, since the proper "direction" is to unravel the very idea of direction. We may understand Eckhart's dialectical yo-yo motion as "explosive" in its dynamics, even where his metaphors are not "explosive" according to the Blumenbergian typology. For example, "The gist of all that one can learn about or be advised of is this: a man should allow himself to be advised by God and see nothing other than him, although this can be articulated using many splendid ways."[93] This seems self-contradictory, since Eckhart is advising his hearers not to take advice from anyone but God. Should we understand the contradiction to destroy his assertion? Or is his speech also from God?

Just as Blumenberg identified Cusanus's mathematical metaphors as explosive, we find similarly explosive mathematical metaphors in Eckhart. Explosive mathematical metaphorics is an underlying theme throughout Eckhart's work. It appears in passages that are not otherwise ostensibly mathematical.[94] This is perhaps less an indication of cleverly designed subtlety than it is merely an indication of the terms in which Eckhart was naturally predisposed to think. For example, Eckhart conceives of the relation between forms and manifestations according to a mathematical metaphor: "The principle of anything is never the thing itself but is outside and above the genus of the thing of which it is the principle. For example, a point has no quantity of magnitude and does not lengthen the line of which it is the principle."[95] Points are infinitesimally small and are parts of a line without adding any length to the line.

Explosive metaphors can function by including the entire territory in which a particular idea can work. In other words, if we think about the

---

93 Eckhart, Sermon 62, DW III, 65.6–66.1.

94 Elsewhere in Eckhart's thought, we find examples that are not explicitly mathematical, but seem to draw from the same manner of thinking. In Sermon 68, we read, "Heaven is in all directions equally distant from the earth. Likewise, should the soul be equally distant from all earthly things, not nearer to one than to the others" (DW III, 147.1–2). For the mind, all physical places are similarly equidistant from my present location, as we read in Sermon 42, "Jerusalem is as close to my soul as this place is" (DW II, 305.3).

95 Eckhart, *Book of the Parables of Genesis*. n.20, trans. McGinn in *Essential Eckhart*, 100; cf. Sermon 19.

possible uses for a given idea as a range of values, one way of getting us to abandon the idea is to address all possible values and show their insufficiency. For example, "If one takes time, and takes it in its smallest part, the now, it is still time and is a point in time itself."[96] If time is a line, then Now is a point that has no length. Even in this limit case, making the slice of time as small as possible, it is still time. In other words, simply by focusing on the present moment, we are still in the field of time and have not gone beyond it. At the other extreme lies the following hyperbole, which is perhaps an easier form of this kind for us to recognize. Eckhart says that if someone who was about to starve to death "was offered the best food, they would starve before ever biting or tasting it if God's likeness was not in it. And if someone was freezing to death, whatever clothing they were offered, they could never accept it or put it on if God's likeness were not in it."[97] That there is no overlap between God and the finest worldly taste tells us that the material and spiritual are utterly incomparable. The spiritual is beyond the material in every possible way.

Following Augustine, Eckhart conceives of one and two as outside of number.[98] Things that are further from God have more multiplicity and thus correspond to higher numbers, which are further from God since "number always comes from imperfection."[99] Thus, in approaching a minimum, one moves closer to God and prepares for crossing over from multiplicity to oneness. Strictly speaking, number belongs to matter and the corporeal world while multitude[100] and negation without privation belongs to spiritual things.[101]

In effort to help us to think beyond number for spiritual things, Eckhart often calls upon the example of the innumerability of angels.[102] He writes in

---

96 Eckhart, Sermon 10, DW I, 169.8–10.

97 Eckhart, Sermon 58, DW II, 612.12–15.

98 Eckhart, *Commentary on Exodus*, n.130.

99 Eckhart, *Commentary on Wisdom*, n.111, trans. McGinn in *Teacher and Preacher*, 162. See also: "Number and division always belong to imperfect things and come from imperfection. In itself number is an imperfection, because it is a falling away or lapse outside the One." (Eckhart, *Book of the Parables of Genesis*, n.17, trans. McGinn in *Essential Eckhart*, 99).

100 Multitude results from a formal distinction while multiplicity results from a material distinction. McGinn tells us that this is not Scotist and instead refers us to Aquinas (*Teacher and Preacher*, 162n115).

101 Eckhart, *Commentary on Wisdom*, n.112.

102 E.g., Eckhart, Sermon 40; Sermon 63; Sermon 74; Sermon 84; Sermon 91; *Commentary on Wisdom*, n.113.

one instance, "The angels are innumerable. They do not make up any particular number, for they are without number because of their great simplicity."[103] The idea of number not applying to angels guides thought as a kind of riddle or thought experiment: Can you think of innumerable angels that make up no number? What is it like to think of distinction without number? To emphasize the difference, Eckhart compares the angels to other things that do have number: "there are more angels than grains of sand, blades of grass, or leaves."[104] Eckhart explains this idea more fully: "I was asked the other day how it could be that there were more angels than the number of all corporeal things.... So I say: those things are great in number when God is properly in them himself and when they possess God and they are near God."[105] A "place" where God "abides" amounts to saying that it is divine. The angels have more or less of God according to their receptivity, like powers of the soul. Therefore, the continuum of spiritual things are ordered according the receptivity for the divine, but all are beyond number.

Mathematical metaphors fit naturally with Eckhart's thought. As Plato assigned mathematics a special place in the Academy, Eckhart may have chosen mathematical metaphors because they have special advantages. If I am considering a new mathematical proof for a particular theorem, my habitual approach to mathematics dictates that I will more conscientiously reevaluate each step for accuracy *even if I already understand it*. Let us consider some explicitly mathematical examples. The following passage is from Latin Sermon XXIV.2:

> Take note: when we hear and read, God speaks to us. When we pray, we speak to God. Take note: the masters say that the lower angels want to speak to the higher angels, not to illuminate them. But if we properly consider it, all who speak are of that higher and primary order. Therefore, it is clear how much the soul must be elevated if it wants to speak to God. According to [what was said of] how this is, elevation becomes only the low and humble. When projecting a sphere onto a plane, the pole and the center are the same.[106] Say how to pray "in spirit and mind" (1 Cor 14:15) according to the Apostle, as you with the weakness of the whole world cast before

---

103 Eckhart, Sermon 40, DW II, 274.8–9. Also, Eckhart conceives of each angel as having its own species, following Aquinas (Sermon 38, DW II, 235.1–2).
104 Eckhart, Sermon 84, DW III, 457.2; cf. Sermon 74.
105 Eckhart, Sermon 74, DW III, 276.9–277.2.
106 This is one of the clearest cases where Eckhart's use of paradox parallels Cusanus's coincidence of opposites.

the feet of God, and secondly, you offer to God the merit and light of the mother of God and all the saints, and thirdly, in what way in the Word itself, in that purity, present to and representing the Father for in that alone are all things pleasing. Luke: "in you I am very pleased."[107]

We find a similar passage in Sermon XXIV.1:

> In Augustine's *Confessions* XI.6, "I have given you today," then he says [of God], "one day of your year and a day for you is not a daily thing. Rather, it is today, because your today is not followed by tomorrow nor does it follow yesterday. Your today is eternity." For this, however, humility is the depth or sublimity of this house. Augustine [said] to the Sabines, "you all who are at home, speak," and further, "ask them with great humility before God," "because humility is the sublime virtue." Hence, if we imagine the center of a circle rises in a sphere, it becomes the pole. Conversely, if the sphere is projected onto a plane, the pole becomes the center.[108]

And another in and Sermon XXXVIII:

> Humility draws its name from "to bury in the earth." Earth truly has its fixity and stability as its own from its form. As with the Psalmist and in Hebrews 1, "in the beginning, Lord, you created the earth." "In the beginning." The first in everything is the cause of all else. Because of which, the commentator himself locates and founds heaven by the earth or the center. Psalmist: "you have founded the earth on its own basis" etc.
>
> Necessarily, however, nature, mathematics, and scripture teach both the stability and the benefit of humility in the ascent of the spirit. Nature, because although for the earth there is the greatest difference between all corporeality and heaven, so the situation is with nature which is as if it were another that is opposed and inimical to itself. So, because the earth humbles itself and almost subjects itself in its entirety to heaven, the innermost heaven, so to speak, reconciles itself entirely with the earth, infused with all the stars and the planets. So it is that diversity of multiplicitous things which are born and live upon the earth is made manifest. Psalmist: "you [Christ] visited the earth" etc. For mathematics, first, as follows: a vessel holds more as [its bottom] is lower. Second, as the circle rises in a cone, the pole becomes the center.[109]

---

[107] Eckhart, Sermon XXIV.2, LW IV, 225, n.245.
[108] Eckhart, Sermon XXIV.1, LW IV, 219, n.235.
[109] Eckhart, Sermon XXXVIII, LW IV, 327–28, n.382.

In the passage from Sermon XXXVIII, the vessel is not only deeper. Its bottom is "lower," *inferius*, a word recalling the idea of humbling. Christ visited the earth and "reconciled" heaven and earth by bringing them together. So, Christ's becoming man brought divinity and creation together, just as the center of a circle may rise in a cone and become the tip of the cone. When this happens, of course, it is no longer a proper cone at all, just as Eckhart's sphere projected onto a plane is no longer a sphere. The mathematical projection of a cone on a plane removes the third dimension and makes the cone a two-dimensional object, a circle. Eckhart describes the desirability of this way of thinking: "The thought came to me last night that God's highness depends on my lowliness; by my lowering myself, God will be raised.... What's more, I thought last night that God should be brought down, not in all but in me. I liked this 'God brought down' so much that I wrote it in my book."[110] That God should be "brought down" corresponds to the leveling of any difference between God and the soul. Importantly, instead of the usual metaphor of the soul's ascent to God, here God is brought down to the soul. This implies that the soul is divine from the onset and perhaps, as he implies here and elsewhere, God needs the soul for his majesty and even for God to be God, "God can do as little without us as we can without him."[111] As the humble person is one with God, "If God's loving us was taken away, his being and divinity would be taken away, for his being flows from his loving us."[112] That is, his love for us *is* his being. Instead of seeing a complete leveling of the hierarchy of being, in fact what we see is that man and God are outside of the hierarchy, "He is as high above being as the highest angel is above a gnat.... God is not a being and is above being, I have not denied being to God; rather, I have elevated it in him."[113] The metaphor of "elevated" or "rising" here is an instance of the same mathematical thinking that results in Eckhart's sphere and cone metaphors. Eckhart wants us to see both directions in his metaphors, where the soul rises to God and God is brought down to the soul.

Eckhart's account of the eternal Forms and material manifestations implies the idea of an *intensive infinity* of forms in their manifestations, meaning that the whole form is contained in the smallest part of a manifestation:

---

110 Eckhart, Sermon 14, DW I, 237.3–5, 6–8.
111 Eckhart, Sermon 26, DW II, 35.1–2.
112 Eckhart, Sermon 41, DW II, 287.3–4.
113 Eckhart, Sermon 9, trans. Tobin in *Teacher and Preacher*, 256.

"*With his whole being God is present whole and entire as much in the least thing as in the greatest.*"[114] This enables a chiastic formulation as well: "All things are in him in equal fashion, and he is equally all things."[115] Moving down from God, Eckhart applies this to all forms and manifestation, observing, "There is an example of this in the sacrament of the Lord's Body which is entire in the smallest part of the consecrated host, and also in every substantial form." Likewise, he asserts that "the whole soul is found in the smallest part of the body it gives life to."[116] This whole-in-part relation confounds our usual notion of spatial position and leads to another quasi-mathematical metaphor: "If a man's head is imagined to be at the north pole and feet at the south pole, his foot will be no further from his head than from itself." As Eckhart says quite plainly, "In unity, then, there is no distance, nothing below another, utterly no distinction of shape, order or act."[117] This is a revealing example of how Eckhart approaches rhetoric. The point he sets out to make is simple: the soul, existence, living, and life cannot be divided into parts like the parts of the body. They do not occupy any space or place in particular, but rather relate to the whole. Given that these things cannot be split into pieces in space, Eckhart tends to take the most extreme spatial examples to make his point. Instead of just saying that they are nonspatial, he gives us a paradox of spatiality, saying that the "foot will not be father from his head than from itself," which confounds our usual way of thinking about feet and heads, and excites a pleasant confusion. This guides thought in a straightforward way: if a spatial paradox applies to the soul, living, existence, and life, then I must reject any and all spatial thinking with respect to them. If Eckhart simply stated that soul, living, existence, and life were beyond spatial thinking, this would not guide thought and provoke the use of mental resources to try and understand something new. Such simple statements are effective primarily

---

114 Eckhart, *Commentary on Exodus*, n.91, trans. McGinn in *Teacher and Preacher*, 75. Though Eckhart does not often use the metaphor of nature as a book, when he does, it relates to this topic: "Every creature is full of God and is a book" (Sermon 9, DW I, 156.9). The idea is that we can and "we must take him equally in all things" (Sermon 5a, DW I, 81.8–9). This is more than an intellectual comprehension; it is an experience of the world as full of God in the least part. Also connected to experience is Eckhart's contention that this applies to moral things as well: "Virtue or moral integrity in like fashion is totally equal in one as in a thousand acts as far as number goes, and in the least act as well as the greatest as far as size goes" (*Commentary on Wisdom*, no. 119; TP 165).

115 Eckhart, *Commentary on Wisdom*, n.96, trans. McGinn in *Teacher and Preacher*, 156.

116 Eckhart, *Commentary on Exodus*, n.92, trans. McGinn in *Teacher and Preacher*, 75; cf. Sermon 20a, Sermon 35.

117 Eckhart, *General Prologue*, LW I.1, 155.8–156.3.

when we *already* understand something. For example, he tells us that God is "totally within and totally without," which appears paradoxical.[118] This sort of rhetorical approach and awareness is rarely seen in contemporary philosophical circles. Instead, it is too often implicitly assumed that readers should have inexhaustible motivation that, if they apply their reasoning faculties rightly, then they can work through the subtleties of the logical argumentation because the argumentation is supposed to play by existing, familiar rules of thought. Even in his Latin works Eckhart does not do this.

---

118 Eckhart, *In Ex.* n.163, trans. McGinn in *Teacher and Preacher*, 95; cf. *In Ioh.* n.12.

5

Eckhart's Metaphorical Repertoire
Metaphors of Desire and Personal Experience

DESIRE

For Eckhart, love inheres in all created things. In his commentary on the book of Wisdom, he writes, "every action of nature, morality, and art in its wholeness possesses three things: something generating, something generated, and the love of what generates for what is generated and vice versa."[1] This applies even on the largest scale, in "every part of the heavenly sphere, because it has a power and hence a thirst and desire in relation to each and every other position.... This is the one true cause of the perpetual motion that is naturally in that body."[2] This quotation points to Eckhart's general principle that desire puts things in motion. Our impulse to love comes only from the Holy Spirit, with the most detached form of that love being God itself.[3] Inanimate things also "love" insofar as they are moved, as a stone is moved to fall to the ground.[4] The stone, however, does not love anything higher because it has no power to recognize any other good: "If a stone were a reasoning thing, it would have to pursue God with love. If one asked a tree why it bore its fruit, if it were a reasoning thing, it would say, 'I renew myself through the fruit in order to approach my origin in the renewal.'"[5] All things

---

1 LW II, 348.9–12. Eckhart, *Commentary on Wisdom*, n.28, trans. McGinn in *Teacher and Preacher*, 150; cf. *Commentary on John*, n.82.

2 LW II, 271.12–272.3. Eckhart, *Sermons and Lectures on Ecclesiasticus,* n.42, trans. McGinn in *Teacher and Preacher*, 174.

3 Eckhart, Sermon 27, DW II, 41.4–43.1.

4 Eckhart, Sermon 19, DW I, 315.1–2.

5 Eckhart, Sermon 63, DW III, 76.1–3.

are stimulated to motion by what they *recognize* to be good: "We love all things according to goodness."[6] The recognition of goodness comprises our anticipation or expectation whereupon we desire to move toward what we love, up to and including the birth of the Word in the soul.[7] This makes the proper work of the soul to desire God, while God's proper work is to give birth to the Word in the soul. Will, as manifested in love, is not itself worldly for Eckhart, though it may be wrongly directed at worldly things if we are not acquainted with spiritual things. One of Eckhart's most provocative statements concerns this: "those who have never been familiar with inward things do not know what God is. Like a man who has wine in his cellar but has never tasted it, he does not know that it is good."[8] This points clearly to experience, something that will be more apparent when we discuss the "taste" metaphor.

For Eckhart, desire implies a principle of ascent: things desire what is the same or better than themselves. That is why everything must seek God whether it wants to or not.[9] God's being lovable derives solely from his goodness, as goodness is the foundation love: "If God lost the name 'goodness,' no more love would arise. Love takes God under a cloak, under a garment."[10] Detachment furthers the end of the ascent by cutting away desires for things less than God. Eckhart traces detachment to Matthew 10:34–36 (and perhaps Luke 14:26 as well[11]) which speaks of cutting away all things and separating a person from all those who are close to him.[12] Those things which are opposed to our ascent become foes of our desires as the desires become more closely attuned to and capable of receiving God.

Everything, from God down to the lowest creature, strives to create what is like itself. This is the structuring principle for Eckhart's traditional Platonic hierarchy of beings. The generating and the generated both love because of likeness, for "the greatest delight in heaven and earth lies in likeness."[13] Thus, as love is based on what is perceived to be good, and that appearance of

---

6 Eckhart, Sermon 81, DW III, 404.8–10.
7 Eckhart, Sermon 44, DW II, 342.4–10, 343.7–8.
8 Eckhart, Sermon 10, DW I, 164.5–8.
9 Eckhart, Sermon 65, DW III, 95.5–6.
10 Eckhart, Sermon 7, DW I, 122.123.1.
11 Cf. discussion of Matthew 19:29 and Mark 10:29–30 in the Book of Divine Consolation, §2.
12 Eckhart, Sermon 102, DW IV.1, 418.113–7.
13 Eckhart, Sermon 81, DW III, 401.13–402.1. This may also link the Christian emphasis on love to the Platonic demiurge's attempt to create what is most like himself.

goodness is based on likeness, we therefore love what we recognize of ourselves in others.[14] The closer we get to our desire, the faster we travel and the more we enjoy the pursuit.[15] With worldly things, however, getting what we desire results in an attentuation of that desire. Familiarity likewise attenuates desire: "There was never a creature so beautiful or noble that one could look at it for a long time without it becoming annoying to do so."[16] This follows for creatures, but it does not follow for God. Since God is beyond finitude, love for God must be without bound.[17] Likewise, he says of those who desire worldly things, "Having gained the goal, they eat and drink and no longer hunger and thirst at all.... It is the opposite in things whose goal is infinite, for such things always hunger and thirst, and hunger more ardently and more avidly the more they eat."[18] Naturally then, our thirst for God only increases with familiarity. This is part of the general desire of everything for existence. Eckhart envisions a continuum of goodness and being, akin to Plato's divided line matephor in the *Republic*. Lower things desire higher things because they desire to have more being: "Every being, in that it is empty in and of itself, thirsts for and desires existence."[19]

Conversely, we fear what threatens to take what measure of being we have.[20] This is why Eckhart proscribes fearing God: "A man should not fear God, for who fears him flees from him."[21] This is sensible, since "man must not be afraid of God" so that "he can boldly go toward God with all that is his."[22] While this fits neatly with his take on love, Eckhart has something more general in mind with this proscription of fear: "man must fear neither the devil, nor the world, nor his own flesh, nor our Lord God."[23] Eckhart appears to see something counterproductive in any fear that does not properly look to God as a positive goal of striving.

---

14 Cf. Eckhart, Sermon 6, DW I, 107.12–108.1; Sermon 63, DW III, 77.5–7.

15 Eckhart, *Book of Divine Consolation*, §2, DW V, 24.3–15.

16 Eckhart, Sermon 91, DW IV.1, 91.49–50.

17 Eckhart, Sermon 82, DW III, 426.7–427.1.

18 LW II, 271.1–6. Eckhart, *Sermons and Lectures on Ecclesiasticus*, n.42, trans. McGinn in *Teacher and Preacher*, 174.

19 LW III, 274.12–3. Eckhart, *Sermons and Lectures on Ecclesiasticus*, n.45, trans. McGinn in *Teacher and Preacher*, 175.

20 "There is no thing that does not flee from what could destroy it." Sermon 15, DW I, 248.1–2.

21 Eckhart, Sermon 22, DW I, 385.15–16.

22 Eckhart, Sermon 87, DW IV.1, 24.37–38.

23 Eckhart, Sermon 87, DW IV.1, 23.28–29.

As for what love actually does to the lover, Eckhart follows Augustine in asserting that we become what we love:

> Saint Augustine says: "The soul becomes like whatever it loves. If it loves earthly things, then it becomes earthly. If it loves God," we might ask, "does it then become God?" If I said that, it would cry out as something unbelievable to those of unsound mind who cannot grasp it. Augustine says further, "I do not say it, but rather I point you to Scripture, where it says: 'I have said that you are gods!'" (Ps 82:6)[24]

This is a rare passage where Eckhart explicitly acknowledges that an idea sounds dangerously radical. In this as well he follows Augustine, since Augustine also recognized the idea as dangerous-sounding. To love something, one must be capable of loving it and must be able to know it. Once a good is recognized as good, desire ineluctably flows.[25] Though all things are naturally drawn to God and the human soul has an innate sense that things do not exist of themselves,[26] we begin by loving creatures—which, by this principle, makes us nothing, since creatures are nothing in themselves.[27] To rise beyond this, we must recognize higher things as good in a quasi-Epicurean fashion, by becoming more acquainted with higher goods which enables us to desire them. In the end, Eckhart tells us, if a person "steps with understanding in his heart"[28] (a perfectly rational person, with reason thus ordering desire) then that person will love "nothing but perfect good."[29]

If we become what we love, how does this process happen? Eckhart says the following of the relationship between the lover and the object of apprehension: "If it is pleasing, then he will adhere to it, and it will stick to him, inhere in him, and so be conceived."[30] With the lover's impulse to

---

24 Eckhart, Sermon 38, DW II, 238.10–239.3; cf. Augustine, *On the Epistle of John to the Parthians*, 2.14. Eckhart refers to this idea, frequently naming Augustine in association with it (e.g., Sermon 44, DW II, 343.3–4).

25 In the *Parisian Questions*, Eckhart says that knowledge prepares the way for love and makes love possible, which enables him to assert the supremacy of knowledge, a typically Dominican position. It is not clear that Eckhart maintained this stance in his other works, however, which view love and knowledge as on par with one another. For Eckhart, God is beyond both love and knowledge.

26 Eckhart, Sermon 115a, DW IV.2, 978.22–34; Sermon 115b, DW IV.2, 978.22–34; Sermon 115d, DW IV.2, 979.22–34.

27 Eckhart, *Commentary on Wisdom*, n.34, trans. McGinn in *Teacher and Preacher*, 153.

28 Eckhart, Sermon 93, DW IV.1, 129.43.

29 Eckhart, Sermon 93, DW IV.1, 129.43–44.

30 Eckhart, *Commentary on Exodus*, n.206, trans. McGinn in *Teacher and Preacher*, 108.

unite with the beloved, we first attempt to reach the beloved and stick to it. Then it inheres in us. Finally, it is conceived and the two are born into one another (as we will see with his metaphor of birth that describes this moment between the soul and God).[31] When this process completes, Eckhart uses the metaphor of property and ownership: "Make God your own so that God will be your own as he is his own himself. He will be God for you as he is God for himself, nothing less. Whatever is mine, I received from no one."[32] As usual, Eckhart pushes the limits with this metaphor. Not only is the beloved mine, but I received it from no one since it was always a part of me. As he says, "Love does not unite in any way. It stitches together things that are already united and ties them together."[33] Thus, to love another is to love what is already one's own and like oneself in the other. Taken to the extreme, with God, who is all in all, the soul loves God and makes God its own through love, which amounts to saying that the soul comes to recognize and, through desire, be united to what it had in itself all along, only it did not know it.[34]

The dynamics described here also explain why God does not love creatures as creatures, but as himself in creatures.[35] At one point, Eckhart emphasizes the greatness of this love, saying that "God loves the soul so powerfully, which is a wonder."[36] This is sensible, since he elsewhere says that God is infinitely lovable and thereby he loves the soul with this selfsame infinite love. The statement provides a characteristically Eckhartian riddle, though. How can we understand infinite love? The trouble is, the infinite is not simply something of great magnitude, which means that Eckhart does not simply recommend understanding God's love by analogy with our lesser love that

---

31 See also Eckhart's Sermon 84 for a description of the stages of this ascent, whereby one begins in hope and fear, then forgets temporal things, and finally strides into God permanently.

32 Eckhart, Sermon 30, DW II, 108.1–3; cf. Sermon 65. Interestingly, Eckhart disparages ownership elsewhere, saying that people who taste of God in one way but not another are tolerable, but still wrong (Sermon 5a). Looking only at this passage, it is not obvious that Eckhart does not object to applying the idea of ownership to God, he merely objects to doing so through an intermediary.

33 Eckhart, Sermon 7, DW I, 122.3–4; cf. Sermon 21, Sermon XXIX. Both verbs in the second clause, *zesameneheften* (*zusammenheften* in modern German) and *zuobinden* (*zusammenbinden* in modern German), refer to sewing and tying things together. Modern translations obscure this fact—Tobin translates "fastens together and binds"; Fox renders them "sticks together and binds"; and Walshe has "fastens together and binds close." This image of stitching together is part of the dialectic of detaching and attaching that runs throughout this sermon.

34 Eckhart emphasizes this point of having the beloved in oneself in Sermon 27: "'Love one another!' That is: in one another. Scripture says this very clearly. Saint John says, 'God is love, and whoever is in love is in God and God is in him.'" DW II, 49.3–5; 1 Jn 4:16.

35 Eckhart, Sermon 109, DW IV.2, 765.24–25; cf. Sermon VI.1, n.55.

36 Eckhart, Sermon 69, DW III, 163.6; cf. Sermon 82.

is of the same kind. Eckhart connects this question with the question of the innumerability of angels and observes, "It exceeds the number in that it is without number and above number, and not, as many wrongly say, 'exceeding the number of corporeal things' because it is greater in number (this is properly not to exceed number, but to be subject to it)."[37] Given that Eckhart's mathematical thinking applies to both topics equally well, we may reasonably conclude that the argument also applies to love and any of the other divine attributes or transcendental that God properly transcends.

Eckhart uses the rather unusual analogy of loving a picture that hangs on a wall without the wall to describe the transition from loving things that are beneath God to loving God himself:

> When an image is painted on a wall, the wall is the support of the image. If anyone loves the image on the wall, he thereby loves the wall. If the wall is removed so that the image remains, then the image is its own support. Whoever then loves the image, loves only the image. When you love all that is lovable and not those things on account of which they appear lovable, you love nothing but God.[38]

When we love anything less than God, we love the goodness that we recognize in that thing. This particular goodness is the "support" that props up our love. Thus, if we seek to love that which has no support, the only choice is the good itself, since love is always based on what we recognize as good. The good then points us to God.

The idea Eckhart expresses with this metaphor is not mysterious, but the metaphor itself is strange. If we step back and look at his rhetorical tendencies more broadly, we will see this same sort of train of thought in other places. Eckhart often begins with an ostensibly mundane example, like the picture on the wall. He then transforms the image into something unusual, which makes us scratch our heads and pause. The unusual metaphor, like the picture in midair, is representative of the kind of image that Eckhart uses generally when he crosses over from the temporal and familiar to the eternal and unfamiliar. The abruptness of the transition is part of what seems so strange about this metaphor. It is not any more unusual than the wood and eye example of Sermon 48:

---

37 Eckhart, *Commentary on Wisdom*, n.113, trans. McGinn in *Teacher and Preacher*, 163.
38 Eckhart, Sermon 63, DW III, 78.6–177.

> As I was coming here today, I was thinking of how I might so intelligently preach to you that you would understand me well. Then I thought of an analogy. If you can understand it well, you will understand both my sense and the ground of all my ideas that I have ever preached. The analogy was about my eye and a piece of wood. When my eye opens, it is an eye. When it is closed, it is still the same eye. . . . If it happens that my eye, which is one and simple in itself, opens and looks upon the piece of wood with the power of sight, each remains what it is and yet becomes one in the act of sight that we can truly say the wood is my eye and call this "eye-wood." If the wood was without matter and it was entirely spiritual like my eye's power of sight then we could truly say that the piece of wood and my eye share a single being in the act of sight.[39]

The example is entirely intelligible until the very last sentence. There, an abrupt transition is introduced as we cross over from familiar to unfamiliar, from worldly to spiritual things. Generally, Eckhart capitalizes on the shock value of these sudden discontinuities. He lulls the mind to rest in a comfortable place with familiarity, only to introduce a new element that shatters the comfort and cannot be squared with the same mode of thinking. This dynamic is a different form of the mechanics of explosive metaphors.

TASTE

One of the principle metaphors that Eckhart uses for desire is taste. In doing so, he builds on a tradition going back to Scripture that describes God's "sweetness" (e.g., Ps 33:9, Sir 24:27). In Latin, the key term is *sapire*, "to taste," just as in Middle High German the word is *smecken*, "to taste." In Middle High German, the word connotes both *taste* and *smell*. The Latin *sapire* has the further connotation of being wise or discerning, recalling the related term *sapientia*, wisdom, which fits nicely for Eckhart.

Taste is a decidedly personal experience that is difficult if not impossible to convey to another person in all its richness. The idea of taste feels intuitively wrong when it is applied to something that cannot also have a personality, at least metaphorically. Dogs can taste things. With plants, it feels like a stretch. With inanimate things, it just seems wrong even though we routinely apply metaphors like love and desire to them.

---

39 Eckhart, Sermon 48, DW II, 416.1–12.

How far does taste go? It goes beyond truth and intelligibility. The soul "tastes God before he is shrouded in intelligibility or truth."[40] The intellect is not limited to intelligible things, which include all forms since the intellect can assume any form.[41] This is why the intellect can still taste.[42] Further, God tastes himself in the soul of one who is "stripped of time and all creaturely flavor."[43] This tells us that the taste dynamic goes all the way to God. The soul's ground is excluded from this, however, in the same way that God is somehow beyond desire: "She indeed receives light, sweetness and grace in her powers, but may only receive God naked in the soul's ground."[44]

Fundamentally, taste describes the expereince of having limited contact with something that is desirable—that is, something of equal or higher station. For less significant experiences, the taste metaphor yields to smell, which is much less common for Eckhart. Smells can linger after an object leaves in a way that taste cannot. Eckhart tells us that Mary went to Christ's tomb because she hoped "something of God remained in the grave. As if I held an apple in my hand for a while, when I put it down, something of the smell would remain."[45] Similarly, God does not even have "the scent or flavor of time—just as a smell remains where an apple was lying."[46]

As the soul ascends, it loses its taste for worldly things and finally has a taste only for God, as "what was sweet to her [the soul] becomes bitter."[47] This dynamic is quite simple. It attains useful rhetorical complexity because it excites in us the full richness of experience. We may think about intellectual connections in terms of love and desire (though they become more personal by doing so), but hearing of *savoring* something brings rich experience to mind.

Eckhart even applies the taste metaphor to his own words, which emphasizes the experience he intended for his audience. He says, "Whoever has let go of all of their will, will savor my teaching and hear my words."[48] That

---

40 Eckhart, Sermon 3, DW I, 56.2–3.

41 As Eckhart often says when this subject arises: just as the eye is without color and so it can see color. This idea traces back to Aristotle.

42 Eckhart, Sermon 69, DW III, 169.1–2.

43 Eckhart, Sermon 73, DW III, 266.1–2. Cf. Sermon 109, DW IV.2, 766.27–31.

44 Eckhart, Sermon 72, DW III, 252.3–4.

45 Eckhart, Sermon 55, DW II, 579.3–5.

46 Eckhart, Sermon 50, DW II, 456.2–3.

47 Eckhart, Sermon 56, DW II, 589.10–11; cf. Sermon 73, DW III, 263.2–6; Sermon 81, DW III, 401.1–2.

48 Eckhart, Sermon 10, DW I, 170.4–5.

his words should taste good implies that he may either exhibit something recognizably good with them or—even better—bring his audience to a new understanding of something as good. As he explains, "an angel pours out his life and his power into heaven and drives it around without stopping. With heaven, he gives motion to the life and power of creatures. In the same way, I intend what I have understood in my heart, words pour out from my hand as I write letters with my pen."[49]

When one desires a taste after becoming acquainted with it being good, we call this hunger. In fact, hunger is necessary for something to be tasty.[50] Hunger can only occur in the absence of what is desired. Thus, "all things feed on him, because he is totally within; they hunger for him, because he is totally without."[51] Just as we are not hungry for a particular taste all the time but can desire it after being reminded of it, "so it is then with a man who has seen God and caught his scent. He keeps up the chase and will not let up."[52] Importantly, the hunger that we have for worldly things follows the usual dynamics of eating: it is pleasant when one is hungry, but disgusting if one is quite full. Thus, the concomitant image of "satiety" corresponds with the hunger for worldly things. Eckhart makes a quick move into unfamiliar territory by telling us that we only hunger perpetually and without satiety for God, because he is infinite.[53] In sum, "in corporeal things eating ultimately brings on disgust, but in divine things as such eating causes hunger."[54]

Finally, Eckhart explains that those who do not know to desire God are akin to the sick. He observes, "if a sick man drinks sweet wine ... the wine loses all its sweetness on the bitterness that is on the outside of the tongue, before it can come inside where the soul identifies and judges its flavor."[55] Similarly: "However pure and noble a drink is, if drunk from a dirty vessel,

---

49 Eckhart, Sermon 81, DW III, 403.12–16.

50 Eckhart, *Sermons and Lectures on Ecclesiasticus*, n.54, trans. McGinn in *Teacher and Preacher*, 179.

51 Eckhart, *Sermons and Lectures on Ecclesiasticus*, n.54, trans. McGinn in *Teacher and Preacher*, 179.

52 Eckhart, Sermon 59, DW II, 633.6–8.

53 This idea occasions one of the most interesting and amusing uses of repetition in Eckhart's Latin works: "he consumes hunger; the more he eats, the more hungry he gets. . . . By eating he gets hungry and by getting hungry he eats, and he hungers to get hungry for hunger" (Eckhart, *Sermons and Lectures on Ecclesiasticus*, n.58, trans. McGinn in *Teacher and Preacher*, 180).

54 Eckhart, *Sermons and Lectures on* Ecclesiasticus, n.57, McGinn in *Teacher and Preacher*, 180.

55 Eckhart, *Book of Divine Consolation*, §2, DW V, 52.11–14; cf. Sermon 11, DW I, 187.7–15, *Commentary on Exodus*, n.12, Sermon 22, DW I, 387.4–12.

it will have an ignoble taste."[56] However, for one who has a taste for God, "everything takes its flavor from God and becomes divine."[57]

JOY

Eckhart has a theology of joy, not fear. He speaks of joy because being stripped of all images and attachments naturally produces "spiritual joy, coming from pure awareness and that makes a man light to all things and raises him above himself."[58] Though he calls it an "outcome," he never considers joy a philosophical *consequence*. Joy does not follow logically from anything. Eckhart is observing and describing the quality of religious experience in order to prime the minds of his listeners, just as Augustine describes the effect of hearing about the life of Antony in the *Confessions*.

Aside from the experiential reference that lies in the background, joy also fits nicely into Eckhart's theology in two ways: first as delight that accompanies being in contact with what one desires; and second as a side effect of being detached from worldly things. Though we might rightly recognize joy as an excitation of the soul, Eckhart warns us against thinking that the saints and perfected people cannot be stirred from rest: "There was never a saint so great that he could not be moved.... Do you think that as long as words can move you to joy or sorrow, you are imperfect? It is not so. Christ was not like that."[59] Of course, Eckhart cannot be thinking of movement away from God in sin. He clarifies, "Great pleasure is not excluded from a sober virtuous person, but burning desire and disturbance of soul and disordered passion."[60] How high does joy go? Eckhart tells us that our eternal joy is more important than existing itself.[61] He explains this more completely in another sermon. Heavenly joy overflows, he remarks, "first, because it has no end; second, because it surpasses merit; third, because it surpasses hope; fourth, because it surpasses desire; fifth, because it surpasses understanding and all apprehension."[62] So, we hear of God feeling joy, Christ being moved, and

---

56 Eckhart, Sermon 91, DW IV.1, 92.58–60.
57 Eckhart, *Counsels on Discernment*, §11, DW V, 229.10–230.1.
58 Eckhart, Sermon 92, DW IV.1, 104.21–23.
59 Eckhart, Sermon 86, DW III, 490.9–12; cf. *Book of Divine Consolation*, §2, DW V, 25.10–13.
60 Eckhart, *Book of the Parables of Genesis*, n.155, trans. McGinn in *Essential Eckhart*, 117.
61 Eckhart, Sermon 87, DW IV.2, 22.16–18.
62 Eckhart, Sermon XII, LW IV, 135.1–3.

joy "overflowing." The last is reminiscent of *ebullitio*, "boiling over," whereby God's inner boiling spills over and creates the world. In short, Eckhart uses the joy metaphor in the same way he speaks of God generally.

As joy is intimately linked with the eternal, it has a loftier place than existence itself. Thus, Eckhart describes God as being joyous: "God has pure amusement and laughter over a good deed."[63] Elsewhere, he asks, "what is the joy of the Lord? A marvelous thing to talk about! How can anyone determine or speak of what no one can understand or know! Still, here is something about it. The joy of the Lord is the Lord himself and no other."[64] Here, we come to a general principle: joy is divine.

The joy metaphor is not simply identified with the divine, nor does Eckhart only apply it to being in general, which is present in every created thing. He applies it specifically to the rational creature, saying that God is in man "in another way which makes him blessed and good, for he is in him joyously, living in and with him blissfully and rationally as in himself and with himself."[65] Thus, God dwells in the rational person, making him blessed and joyous. The difference is one of *awareness*. As rational creatures, we have the capacity to be aware of God—that is, we can come to know God as good and thereby pursue him. Eckhart emphasizes that only this awareness separates nonrational things from higher joy: "If a piece of wood knew God and recognized how near he is to him, as the highest angel knows, it would be as happy as the highest angel."[66]

---

[63] Eckhart, Sermon 79, DW III, 364.8; applied to justice and the just person, cf. Sermon 39; applied to God joyfully working in the soul, cf. Sermon 82. Similarly, "One should give joy to the angels and saints" (Sermon 6, DW I, 101.1).

[64] Eckhart, Sermon 66, DW III, 123.11–124.2.

[65] Eckhart, Sermon 66, DW III, 111.1–3.

[66] Eckhart, Sermon 68, DW III, 142.4–5.

6

Eckhart's Metaphorical Repertoire
Passivity, Activity, and the Individual

Eckhart advocates an active participation in the world, not a detached contemplation that entirely denigrates the value of the body and lived experience. To say that embodied existence has value is to say that it is not devoid of goodness. As the notion of the individual expands and individual human life waxes in worth around Eckhart's time, it is only natural that so too does human *activity*. This is crucial because "human activity" here refers to life as a particular individual and not just life as an instantiation of an archetype. This should call to mind a certain tension in Eckhart's works: the lowliness of matter and created things in tension with the value of embodied human activity. Recall that for Aristotle, matter is the principle of individuation. As we approach the level of the individual, then, we would expect to see a concomitant increase in imperfection. The exception to this rule is the individual soul. The world of created things is infused with God's being, which thereby prevents the hierarchy of things from being a simple scale of value. Even though the lowliest creature is far from God and participates only a little in being, nevertheless, because God in his entirety is present in the smallest part, the hierarchy compresses: everything is divine insofar as it has being.

The case is different with the individual rational soul. This soul is endowed with the spark of divinity, meaning that it shares in God qua intellect in addition to sharing in God qua being. The difference between intellect and being is most significant for Eckhart. He sees intellect as prior to being in God, as we read in his first thesis in the *Prologue to the Book of Propositions*:

Esse est deus (existence is God), a reversal of Aquinas' formula *Deus est esse* (God is existence).[1] As with being, we share in God's divinity as it is in God, not in a merely analogous fashion. Recall that for Eckhart, an image receives its entire being from what it images while being remains in God.[2] Thus, to borrow from Luke 17:21, the kingdom of God is in you—truly *in you* in its essence and all that it is, not just in an analogous way or as a mere reflection. Eckhart is being more emphatic than hyperbolic when he speaks of the sameness of the divinity within the soul and God. Further, as we have already seen and will continue to see throughout this analysis, the individual soul is not the same as the individual self, which is imperfect in its particularity and its worldly cares. Eckhart tells us that Christ took on human nature, not the particularity of an imperfect individual. Indeed, the soul ascends by denying and annihilating its "self" (*vernihten sîn selbes*).[3] Yet this "self" is not the individuality of the soul. As Eckhart says, "a man must be killed and wholly dead and nothing to himself, wholly unlike anyone and being like no one. Then he is truly like God."[4] The soul is not less for losing this worldly attachment. In fact, the worldly attachment in the form of desire for worldly things makes the soul *nothing*. So, to rise to God is to rise in being, to move away from nothing, and to shed "self," including individual will. By detaching ourselves from what is worldly and particular about us, we are left with bare human nature, which is divine.

If the world itself is replete with divinity even in its smallest part, and if mankind has divinity as its own in the innermost reaches of the soul, the stage is set for Eckhart to likewise ennoble *activity* over contemplation. As alluded to earlier, the seed for this is found in the idea of the Incarnation itself. God can come into the world as an individual person only if the human individual shares in divinity. The connection enables us to think that human activity likewise is divine. This brings us to a conclusion that Eckhart would have probably appreciated: his notion of the individual, which gives his work so much of its distinctive chararacter, builds upon a theme that is at the very heart of Christianity.

---

1 Eckhart, LW I.1, 38. For detail on the theological antecedents to this idea, its situation within the thought of Eckhart's contemporaries, and its philosophical significance, see Burkhardt Mojsisch's *Meister Eckhart: Analogy, Univocity and Unity*.

2 Cf. Mojsisch, *Meister Eckhart: Analogy, Univocity and Unity*, 91. Specifically, the archetype is univocally in the image as The Word is in the Father.

3 "Annihilation of self," Eckhart, *On Detachment*, §23.

4 Eckhart, Sermon 29, DW II, 89.4–6.

THE CONTEMPLATIVE LIFE AND THE ACTIVE LIFE

Eckhart argues that the contemplative ideal is simply not possible. As living things, we cannot avoid activity altogether. The saints and even Christ were moved and continued to be moved in their perfection.[5] As he says piquantly, "I will never arrive at the point where an excruciating racket is as delightful to my ears as a sweet piece of string music."[6] Importantly, as he goes on to say, though being moved is inevitable, suffering is not. Once one moves beyond the "sensible will" (*sinnelîcher wille*), which is in need of instruction, and attains to a "rational will" (*redelîcher wille*) that draws closer to God, one approaches the "eternal will" (*ewiger wille*), which assents to all things.[7] With such a will, pleasure and pain are still ineluctably felt, but suffering is not. Eckhart clarifies that to reach God, "One of two things must always happen: either we will take God and learn to hold him in all activity, or we must give up action altogether. Now since man in this life cannot be without activity, which is so plentiful and is part of being human, we must learn to hold God in all things and everywhere remain unhindered in all activity."[8] Though the contemplative ideal is impossible, Eckhart describes what our activity should be: We must "possess God in all things." Once again, he uses the language of ownership and property, which emphasizes the role of individuality in activity. Contemplation at its highest levels tends to imply losing individuality. Here again, Eckhart's notion of activity (even in contemplation) maintains the rhetoric of the individual although the activity itself is properly God's. That is, the activity that is one with contemplation properly belongs to God just as God belongs to such an individual. The chiasmus here emphasizes oneness, just as it does in Eckhart's own rhetoric.

Eckhart's exaltion of the *vita activa* (the active life) is ostensibly in opposition to the *vita contemplativa* (the contemplative life). By Eckhart's time, there was a long tradition of holding up the contemplative ideal, which effectively advocated a world-denying approach, one that put down all things material as less worthy than the contemplative. At times, Eckhart seems to speak in this rather Platonic way. He often tells us, "Every capacity for change, privation, defect, and evil in things comes from matter."[9] Further, temporality

---

[5] Cf. Eckhart, Sermon 86, DW III, 490.9–12., *Book of Divine Consolation*, §2, DW V, 25.10–13.
[6] Eckhart, Sermon 86, DW III, 491.19–20.
[7] Eckhart, Sermon 86, DW III, 489.20.
[8] Eckhart, *Counsels on Discernment*, §7, DW V, 211.6–10.
[9] Eckhart, *Commentary on John*, n.551, trans. McGinn in *Teacher and Preacher*, 183.

and corporeality are the greatest hindrances to spiritual progress.[10] Still, as God is wholly present in the least thing in its being, even matter cannot be purely nothing. The world is no illusion for Eckhart. Its reality is meaningful and suffused with God. Therefore, Eckhart cannot advocate the contemplative ideal that puts down all that is worldly as if it had no value. However, Eckhart does not leave contemplation behind either.[11] Instead, he takes the provocative stance that contemplation and action are *one*:

> Master Thomas says: the active life is better than the contemplative life, as the active man pours out from love what he received in contemplation. They are the same thing, for man does not apprehend things from anywhere other than the ground of contemplation itself and then make them fruitful in action. This brings contemplation to perfection. Though action happens, it is nothing other than one. It comes out of one end, which is God, and comes back into the same. Just as when I go from one end to the other in a house: that would certainly be motion, but it would be nothing other than one in the same. So in this activity, man has nothing other than one contemplation in God. The one rests in the other and perfects the other.[12]

First, of course, in light of the traditional tension between contemplation and action, it is unusual for Eckhart to claim that they are one.[13] In doing so, he does more than adopt a middle ground. Eckhart's account of divine activity and the soul's participation in it naturally implies the statement that contemplation and action are one. Everything that is God is wholly God, by his thoroughgoing oneness. As the soul itself is divine in its innermost reaches, when man clears away what is created and acts out of this innermost ground, his actions are necessarily divine. Since the innermost ground is one of contemplation and ultimately one of rest and repose, as we will see later, man is at once active and contemplative, just as God is at once at rest and at work. In this way, action and contemplation are one. This is the well-known dynamic of "boiling" or "melting" which occurs interiorly with God while not "adding" anything of multiplicity to God.

10 Eckhart, Sermon 68, DW III, 148.2–3; cf. Sermon 12, DW I, 193.1–2.
11 Cf. Fox, *Breakthrough*, 486.
12 Eckhart, Sermon 104a, DW IV.1, 579.155–581.171.
13 Once again, this is a theme that will sound familiar to Mahayana Buddhists. The understanding, for example, of the *bodhisattva* is of someone who ascends to the divine and then returns to the world to be fruitful and compassionate in action to others. Compare this to Eckhart's interpretation of Scripture where it describes how "a nobleman went to a faraway land to receive a kingdom and then returned." Eckhart, *On the Nobleman*, DW V, 109.1–2; cf. Fox, *Breakthrough*, 518.

When one begins, however, Eckhart does not advocate just any action. Instead, he advises "a beginner who wants to have a good life should consider this analogy: whoever wants to make a circle first sets his foot down and keeps it still until he makes the ring."[14] This means "that their hearts must be constant." This is a version of the hinge metaphor from *On Detachment*. The foot on the outside that describes a circular orbit is in motion while the center, which is the heart, remains constant. With respect to contemplation and action, the metaphor that follows extends the foot and hinge metaphors in an important fashion. He describes the motion of an anchored boat in the following terms: "If [sea travellers] want to sleep, they throw an anchor into the water so the ship will stop. They still rock up and down in the water, but they do not wander about."[15] As a circle is two-dimensional and part of a plane (recalling the importance of the second and third dimensions of the sphere and cone that are projected to circles and thus lose the third dimension), motion in the third dimension does not affect the constancy and motionlessness of the center in two dimensions.

ACTIVITY AND PASSIVITY

The rhetoric of activity and passivity figures centrally in Eckhart's rhetoric of the individual. For something to be active and perform an action, it must be a substantial subject that is capable of having actions attributed to it. Eckhart understands active and passive principles to be fundamental: "The entire universe created by God is distinguished into two principles, the active and the passive. These two can be found in every nature."[16] For something to be active means that it either creates or at least issues forth action that is not caused externally. Specifically, the acted is not acted upon when it acts.[17] Importantly, the action is one-way where the active principle "takes nothing at all from its passive principle" and instead pours action into the passive principle.[18] Further, the relation of actor to acted upon is one of superior to inferior. To have the capacity to be acted upon implies *likeness* between actor and acted upon. Consequently, there is reciprocal love, especially when

---

14 Eckhart, Sermon 81, DW III, 397.4–6.
15 Eckhart, Sermon 81, DW III, 398.1–3.
16 Eckhart, *Book of the Parables of Genesis*, n.21, trans. McGinn in *Essential Eckhart*, 101.
17 Eckhart, *Book of the Parables of Genesis*, n.22, trans. McGinn in *Essential Eckhart*, 101.
18 Eckhart, *Book of the Parables of Genesis*, n.26, trans. McGinn in *Essential Eckhart*, 103.

the action is generation.[19] Since love and desire are at play due to likeness, this straightforwardly implies that "what is passive always thirsts for what is active even when drinking it."[20]

When the boundary between superior and inferior is crossed in action and the superior acts on the inferior, Eckhart identifies two possibilities. The first is that the active principle touches upon the passive principle so long as it is present, but the effect departs as soon as the active principle leaves. Such is the case with sunlight in a medium. The sun spreads light throughout, but that light does not inhere and "take root" in what is lighted. This means that the thing lighted ceases to be lit as soon as the light is taken away. Eckhart explains, "Fire sends its root into water with heat, for when the fire is removed, the warmth remains for a while." This is different in the case of sunlight, which "lights the air and shines through it, but does not send its root into it, for whenever the sun is no longer present, we have no more light."[21] As he explains in another metaphor, sending a "root" means to give possession to the thing, while not sending a root means to loan it instead.[22] This is the relationship between God and creatures. God does not send the "root" (*wurzel*) of being into creatures. If God were to withdraw, creatures would cease to be. As we see here in various forms, the idea of action describes relations from highest to lowest in Eckhart's celestial hierarchy. This is why action itself cannot be a created thing.

Eckhart understands unity of being and unity of activity in different ways, "My body and my soul are united in one being, not as one activity. As my soul is one with my eye in one activity, which is seeing. So, the food I eat has one being with my nature, not united in one activity."[23] Action or movement can be described of both physical and spiritual things, but they are not the same. The action of physical things unites disparate things in order to act. The act of seeing is not just the eye or the soul, but the work of both as a kind of unity, rather like we speak of a single subject who sees. Once again, this is the familiar case. We know what it is like to see and to lift a stone. We know that when we do these things, many powers and things act in concert, which makes them unified in performing the action. As before, we cross from

---

19 Eckhart, *Commentary on Wisdom*, n.28.
20 Eckhart, *Book on the Parables of Genesis*, n.2, trans. McGinn in *Essential Eckhart*, 102.
21 Eckhart, Sermon 41, DW II, 294.7–12.
22 Eckhart, *Book of Divine Consolation*, §2.
23 Eckhart, Sermon 7, DW I, 119.2–5.

familiar to unfamiliar with spiritual things. Spiritual things are not separate like physical things in action. When God works in me, his work is done by him in his entirety and the work is God in his unity.

METAPHORS FOR PASSIVITY

Action transforms what is passive, potentially changing a lower substance into a higher one. For instance, Eckhart understands the process of something catching first and burning up completely in terms of the fire transforming the burning thing entirely into itself. In the same way, he tells us, "We must put on Christ as iron puts on fire, as air does sunlight, and as wool does color. Iron puts on fire such that it becomes entirely fire."[24] The active and passive dynamic at work here speaks to the way Eckhart sees man's transformation. Just as fire is active and iron is passive, so God actively works and the soul passively receives. This is why Eckhart describes the soul as "suffering" or "undergoing" (*lîden*) God: "Only God must be active. You only have to undergo it."[25] Likewise, "the best and most perfectly noble place you can come to in this life is when you are silent and allow God to work and speak."[26] Pure passivity is key. Just as the humble man empties himself (*kenosis*) and compels God to flow into him as if to fill the void, so the purely passive person creates a kind of vacuum of agency whereby God must flow into him and work. Eckhart describes this in the following terms: "It is a divine work when man only follows and does not resist, where he undergoes and lets God work."[27]

"Undergoing" and "passivity" refer to a specific *experience*. In meditation, for example, part of "letting go" through detachment is allowing the calming process to continue. This means not becoming an obstacle or hindrance to it by allowing other thoughts to crowd it out. As Eckhart says of God giving us everything, "the less we strive, the more God will give."[28] The way Eckhart describes a single image displacing God accurately captures how a single thought crowds out the blissful calm of concentrated meditation. The

---

24 Eckhart, Sermon LII, LW IV, 436.5–7.
25 Eckhart, Sermon 103, DW IV.1, 476.23. This is an extension of his statement that the creature desires while God works.
26 Eckhart, Sermon 101, DW IV.1, 355.116–117.
27 Eckhart, Sermon 73, DW III, 270.2–3; cf. Sermon XI.2.
28 Eckhart, Sermon 41, DW II, 297.2.

dynamics he mentions throughout his works about the effort and training required to do this match well with building meditative skill. Further, Eckhart links blessedness with undergoing God: "I am passive in hearing. I am active in seeing. Still, our bliss does not lie in our activity, but rather in that we undergo God."[29]

Another metaphor that Eckhart often employs for passivity is that of the wax seal or stamp. As he says in Sermon 72, "The soul must be re-formed and pressed into the image, which is God's Son."[30] On its own, this depiction is too intelligible and familiar to usefully spur thinking in the right direction. Eckhart continues by saying that the Son is the image of divinity itself, the Godhead, implying that we are molded into a form that is beyond form. He draws us in with an intelligible metaphor, pushes the concept to its breaking point, and then challenges us to think through the metaphor and the inherent shortcomings of our mode of thinking and being. Furthermore, the wax metaphor gives us an example of connoisseurship. Because "God's likeness is stamped into the soul," Eckhart says, it leaves an impression that allows us to tell if a soul has grace.[31] Since God's likeness is something that requires knowledge of God for us to be able to recognize it, this means that only one who has this knowledge (and thus would manifest such grace in turn) can recognize it in others.

The idea of wax being stamped also carries the connotation of force and compulsion. Eckhart explores this in a provocative fashion. He tells us that the just man sees and hears from justice itself. Through this experience, justice "seals and impresses the truth of what it says."[32] This is as close as Eckhart gets to the "force of truth" metaphor that Blumenberg discusses.[33] Ironically, we see and hear only if God and the person who sees and hears are one. This strains the idea of being compelled by the force of truth since it amounts to being compelled by yourself to see the truth that you already are.

To a lesser extent, Eckhart also uses the wax and imprinting metaphor to discuss images and the reception of sensory stimuli and knowledge. He

---

29 Eckhart, Sermon 102, DW IV.1, 421.143–422.145. One could also say, as Fox does, "I undergo hearing." This passive undergoing, as Eckhart describes in quoting Dionysius in the same sermon, implies "unknowing" as well, which amounts to a transformation in the conception of knowledge for the passive and detached individual (Sermon 102, DW IV.1, 424.158–425.162).

30 Eckhart, Sermon 72, DW III, 244.1–2.

31 Eckhart, Sermon 96, DW IV.1, 215.34.

32 Eckhart, *Commentary on John*, n.85, trans. McGinn in *Essential Eckhart*, 154.

33 Blumenberg, *Paradigms for a Metaphorology*, 11.

speaks of seeing something as requiring both the functioning of the eye, due to the proximity of the thing seen, as well as conscious involvement in the act, which enables knowledge to be "imprinted on and transferred to or 'dwell in' the one who sees."[34] This use of 'dwell in' is important since it provides a clue as to the intimacy of what the imprinting metaphor implies: that knowledge is taken into and becomes part of the soul.

Juxtaposing two different passages that use the wax metaphor in the two ways described will elucidate the difference. First, with the imprinting of worldly images, Eckhart tells us, "The soul of Christ naturally has the image of all things which he gave to them. Yet he is not the same image, just as a stamp gives its form to wax while it is not one with it."[35] The second passage bears striking resemblance, but uses the metaphor in the opposite fashion: "If you press a seal into green wax, red wax or cloth, that is completely an image. If the seal is stamped totally into the wax, so that none of the wax is left over but pressed entirely into the seal, then it is one with the seal without any difference. So the soul is wholly united with God like this in image and likeness."[36] In the first case, the wax is not the same as the seal, while in the second case it is. The difference is that the first case refers to the image of worldly things, while in the second case it refers to God.[37]

Eckhart sees the connection between the imprinting of worldly images and the imprinting of the soul with the image of God. He explains, "Being all mixed up with color and sound and corporeal things is indeed a good preparation and, in that way, is certainly useful for progressing. It is just an exercising of the senses whereby the soul becomes awakened and the image of knowledge is naturally imprinted on her."[38] Knowledge of corporeal things lets us know what knowledge is, which is a useful preparation for knowledge of higher things.

The image of wax is particularly useful because wax may be molded with ease into different forms. It does not *resist* being molded. Thus, Eckhart

---

34 Eckhart, *Commentary on John*, n.121, trans. McGinn in *Essential Eckhart*, 169.
35 Eckhart, Sermon 90a, DW IV.1, 63.110–64.115.
36 Eckhart, Sermon 32, DW II, 136.2–137.1.
37 Other examples of this image can be multiplied. For angels imprinting God's will on the soul, see Eckhart, Sermon 35, DW II, 178.3–4, and Sermon 96, DW IV.1, 210.8–211.10. For angels having the "impress of all creatures," see Sermon 72, DW III, 247.7–9.
38 Eckhart, Sermon 36a, DW II, 192.2–5. Though "all mixed up" is colloquial, it carries the desired negative connotation of being confused and intertwined. This is closer to Quint's *verquickt* than Walshe's "involved."

observes, "Saint Jerome says that a piece of pure wax, malleable and good for making this or that out of it, whatever one wants, contains in itself all that one can make with it even if no one outwardly makes anything with it."[39] That it contains within it all possible forms makes wax an artistic medium, something that can accept the intention of the person molding it just as a sculptor manifests his or her intention by sculpting wood or stone. We do not have to remove material from wax to mold it, however. As we will see shortly, this fact prompts Eckhart to use the wax metaphor when speaking of passivity and the sculptor example when speaking of alteration and production.

Eckhart says, "If I want to write on a wax tablet, no matter how noble the things written on it are, they prevent me from writing on it."[40] He says this is an analogy for the heart attaining the highest place through detachment, which "must be in nothingness, for the greatest receptivity is in there."[41] In other words, detachment brings us to a place of complete passivity. Importantly, he identifies complete passivity with "the greatest receptivity," which is the soul's capacity for God. As we will see, Eckhart uses the container metaphor of receptivity and capacity to describe the expansion of the soul by shedding self, as well as for the attuning of the lower powers to become more receptive of God.

ENLARGING, EXPANDING THE SOUL

Being purely passive to receive God implies expanding the soul's capacity. As Eckhart describes this, "God cannot be diminished or increased, for he is measureless and unchanging. So, the soul then must be elevated and enlarged, for she is small and changeable. Therefore she should be elevated above herself and enlarged for God's measurelessness."[42] Eckhart describes receptivity as a kind of passivity and potential. When something dies (Eckhart gives the example of wheat) it yields to potential, which means that only its receptivity remains. In just the same way, he says, the soul "dies" when it becomes entirely passive so that it can become receptive of another nature.[43] This comparison reveals much about what the soul is and is not. When wheat

---

39 Eckhart, *Book of Divine Consolation*, §2, DW V, 55.2–5.
40 Eckhart, *On Detachment*, DW V, 425.6–8.
41 Eckhart, *On Detachment*, DW V, 425.5.
42 Eckhart, Sermon 95a, DW IV.1, 199.303–200.309.
43 Eckhart, Sermon 98, DW IV.1, 235.4–5.

dies, Eckhart seems to say that the matter itself remains and can be formed again into something else. With the soul, Eckhart's comparison implies, the "death" of losing its self and all createdness does not *destroy* the soul, just as the matter that composes the wheat is not destroyed when the wheat dies. Consequently, as the wheat's life is not necessary for the existence of the matter which composes it, neither the self nor any aspect of the soul's createdness are necessary for its being what it is.[44]

The greatest capacity for the soul comes with the greatest stripping away, the losing of all createdness and indeed anything other than God himself. This is what Eckhart had in mind in describing the soul's capacity: "God dwells in the substance of the soul. This, therefore, is higher than the intellect. The highest is to have the capacity for God and to take on God."[45] A few lines earlier, he remarks, "note the way in which Plato argues for the immortality of the soul since it has the capacity for wisdom. How much greater the soul is than even that, for it can take on God."[46] Plato is no clearer on how a soul "participates" in the Forms than the Ancient Greeks were in saying that an individual could be possessed by the gods.[47] Eckhart makes this more explicit. In addition to intentionally extending Plato's argument for immortality in a provocative way, Eckhart pushes the expanding capacity metaphor to its extreme. For Eckhart, even the smallest speck of heaven is wider than all the earth. God himself then is infinite many times over—or, perhaps more simply, he is beyond size. The soul's expansion yields another explosive metaphor. We should hear echoes of the passage in the *Book of the Twenty-Four Philosophers* that describes God as an infinite sphere whose center is everywhere and circumference nowhere. As the soul expands (which, if it has a shape, surely must be spherical since a sphere is the simplest and most perfect shape), we have no trouble conceptualizing an expanding container. However, when it crosses over into infinity, the ideas of "expanding" and "capacity" strain and burst.

---

[44] A different passage may serve to clarify this point: "As grace carries the soul into God, it carries the soul over herself, divests her of self and of all that makes her a creature, and unites her with God. The soul must make room as grace works with her, for she is a creature, until nothing remains other than God and the soul without intermediary" (Eckhart, Sermon 96, DW IV.1, 218.51–54).

[45] Eckhart, Sermon XXIV.2, LW IV, 227.7–9.

[46] Eckhart, Sermon XXIV.2, LW IV, 229.5–6.

[47] If Plato's Forms reoccupy the place of the gods, then this is one solution to the problem of participation in the Forms: there was no need for Plato to explain an experience that was already common for his audience.

Throughout this process, we should not fail to notice that the individual soul persists. At first glance, this is not fundamentally different than Platonism. Created things, including individuals, do participate in the forms and owe their existence to what is higher, since all ultimately are children of the Good. The difference lies in how Eckhart speaks of the individual's relation to that existence. For Plato, while something may participate in the higher forms, it does not become them without leaving its individuality behind, since individuals exist at the temporal level of manifestations, a lower rung than the eternal Forms. For Eckhart, when we are empty of all createdness and even die a bodily death, the soul remains as an individual but not a self. The self is not what makes us individual. The individual soul can be empty of self and still be an individual with the capacity for God. As Eckhart says, "The more barren you are of your self and unknowing of all things, the nearer you come to Him."[48]

Compare this infinite capacity for man to receive with the following passage. In speaking of God's power, Eckhart says that God "is rich. To be rich is to have all things without ever lacking. If I am a man and am rich, I am still not another man.... Therefore, no one is rich other than God alone, for he simply has all things enclosed within himself."[49] Notice also that to lack is to be at a lower level than God since all things, up to and including God himself, desire that which has more being. The particularity of the individual here points to the lack of our capacity to contain all things. Of course, this refers to man insofar as he is created and not insofar as he is divine, as Eckhart explains: "I say that God offers himself to me just as he does to the highest angel. If I were ready to receive as he is, I would receive as he does."[50]

Eckhart tells us, "Just as God is almighty in his deeds, so the soul is bottomless in her ability to undergo."[51] This is the opposite of a metaphor of annihilation or detaching from self. In mysticism, the body and worldly things are sometimes denigrated so that they are as nothing, implying that one is better off escaping from them. Eckhart describes this same dynamic of escaping and leaving behind. However, escape for Eckhart is from what is nothing and lacks being. The individual soul and even the material world

---

48 Eckhart, Sermon 103, DW IV.1, 481.66–482.67. As this sermon makes clear, we must "go out" (*ûzgân*, DW IV.1, 476.24) of all activity, will, and knowing that is ours and thereby constitutes our "self" for us to passively undergo God's coming in and acting.

49 Eckhart, Sermon 47, DW II, 398.3–399.1.

50 Eckhart, Sermon 47, DW II, 399.3–5.

51 Eckhart, Sermon 102, DW IV.1, 424.152–53.

(which is a "footprint" of God) does not fall into this category. In this way, Eckhart's mysticism is thoroughly embodied and "individual" in an ironic and subtle fashion. That is, to use his language, it is individual insofar as the individual is divine. The individual soul is not identified with the self. Instead, by losing the worldly attuned self, the soul actually expands in its capacity. The metaphor of expansion is not merely compatible with an inflated notion of the individual but actively encourages and expresses it.

Finally, to have a capacity for something is akin to potency. Potency is unfulfilled and thirsts for its realization in existence.[52] If man has a capacity for God, insofar as he expands his capacity, so too does he expand his thirst. Eckhart explains this in a fashion that is reminiscent of his mathematical metaphors: "the thing that grows in filling will never be full. If an excellent vessel, a cartload, swells as it is loaded and grows thereby, then it will never be full. So it is with the soul: the more she seeks, the more she will be given. The more she receives, the wider she becomes."[53] Once again, Eckhart clearly does not conceive of the soul's ascent to God as diminishing the individual soul at all, even though it loses its self and all createdness in preparation for its union with God.

CLOTHING, STRIPPING AWAY, AND DETACHMENT

As with Eckhart's other metaphors, his clothing-based metaphors have two forms: familiar and unfamiliar. The familiar, worldly form is where we strip off clothing like any unessential thing that may be taken off, put on, or exchanged without changing who we are.[54] The unfamiliar, spiritual form, found in Eckhart's discussion of Romans 13:14, is where we "put on" Christ.[55] Both forms are unified in the "universal rule that any receptive potency, such as the soul's powers, must always be naked. For example, the power that receives color must be without any color."[56] To be naked is to be receptive without any hindrance.

---

[52] Eckhart, *Sermons and Lectures on Ecclesiasticus*, n.45, trans. McGinn in *Teacher and Preacher*, 175.
[53] Eckhart, Sermon 100, DW IV.1, 26–30.
[54] Cf. Eckhart, Sermon 54b DW II, 565.11–13.
[55] Eckhart, Sermon 24.
[56] Eckhart, *Book of the Parables of Genesis*, n.31, trans. McGinn in *Teacher and Preacher*, 104.

For familiar, worldly things, the metaphor of clothing refers to what takes us in the direction of multiplicity and thus moves away from God. Eckhart tells us that "the very first power to spring from the pure ground is bare awareness. Emerging bare into the marketplace, it is immediately clothed."[57] What goes for this first expression of the soul's powers goes for the rest of them as well. No sooner do we begin to have a mental life than our powers put on the clothing of material things, obfuscating the bare essence of the power. In speaking of going in the other direction, which means moving away from the knowledge and perception of material things, Eckhart says, "if I know something, that would not be unknowing, nor would it be free and bare."[58] This parallels Eckhart's rhetoric about stripping away images in Sermon 2. If I was completely unattached to images, he says, "I would be a virgin, truly unimpeded by all images, as I was when I was not."[59] In this, the virgin has "receptivity."[60]

Since we are talking about a Platonic hierarchy, stripping away also points to increasing abstraction, whereby differentiating aspects of things drop away and progressively more common and universal forms are abstracted.[61] The terminus of this increasing abstraction is the removal of all such qualities, which, of course, crosses over into unfamiliar territory since it is difficult

57 Eckhart, Sermon 94, DW IV.1, 148.66–67.
58 Eckhart, Sermon 103, DW IV.1, 478.41–42.
59 Eckhart, Sermon 2, DW I, 26.2–3.
60 Eckhart, *Enpfenclicheit* (Sermon 2, DW I, 27.5). We hear the same of the higher intellect: "This power is a virgin.... This power takes God entirely bare in his essential being." Sermon 13, DW I, 220.9–222.1.
61 Cf. Eckhart, Sermon 71, Sermon XII. One might even argue, as Davies does, that the details of the language itself pull the listener in the right direction. "Just as Eckhart seeks in his theology to stress that we must always transcend the particular, it is a striking feature of his vocabulary that he moves strongly in the direction of the abstract." He uses "abstract nouns (often of his own composition) which generally end in –heit and which derive from more specific nouns." ... Adjectives that "often end in –keit" "another group of words end in –ung and, according to Quint, generally 'designate the mystical act of cognitive union.'... As Quint points out, these words are more often than not German translations of Latin words ending in -tas or –tis" (*Mystical Theologian*, 189). As an example of Eckhart making abstract words from Sermon 83, he cites "You should wholly sink from your youness (*dîner dînesheit*) and dissolve into his hisness (*sîne sînesheit*)" (*Mystical Theologian*, 190). Eckhart's wordplay works similarly elsewhere. Notice that *einunge* (oneness) and *einöde* (desert) both contain *ein* (one). Likewise, in Latin, *solitudinibus* is the word "desert," making the reference to the solitary or unitary psychological state that much clearer. The most explicit form of this is in *On the Nobleman*, where Eckhart says, *ein mit einem, ein von einem, ein in einem und einem ein êwiclîche* ("one with one, one of one, one in one, and in one one forever," DW V, 119). See Frank Tobin, "Mechthild of Magdeburg and Meister Eckhart: Points of Coincidence," in *Meister Eckhart and the Beguine Mystics: Explorations in Vernacular Theology*, ed. Bernard McGinn (New York: Continuum, 1994), 50.

to imagine any "thing" that is so common as to be everything and is in fact utterly one. Eckhart explains the process this way: "The immaterial powers ascend by abstracting. However, abstraction stops in being, beyond which is God as the cause of being."[62] As he says, "understanding and reason peel away everything and take hold of what is neither 'here' nor 'now.' In this extent, it touches angelic nature."[63]

Eckhart describes the progressive stripping away like this: "Everything attached to the soul should be completely peeled off. The nobler the powers are, the more they peel off. Some powers are so high above the body and so separate from it that they peel away and separate completely."[64] The higher the powers of the soul, the more they strip away. This is straightforward. Lower faculties like sense perception take the world as it is. Higher faculties abstract and strip away what is coarse and individual to arrive at what is universal. This process does not stop even with being, since the intellect is higher: "As the intellect dissolves things into being, it must surpass being too."[65] However, we enter unfamiliar territory when he refers to powers that are "so high above the body and so separate from it that they peel away and separate completely." He surely has the spark in mind, the part of the soul that is divine. It separates "completely" insofar as it is divine and is above all such distinction, division, and separation. Further, separating completely implies a flight into the One. As he explains elsewhere, Christ "must transcend the powers of the soul, which are so many and spread so widely, even those that are in thought, although thought works wonders as it is in itself. One should transcend this thought for God to speak in the powers that are undivided."[66] Notice the paradox at the end: powers that are presumably distinct are also indistinct since they are undivided. Clearly, this passage dwells almost entirely at the unfamiliar extreme of the metaphor. Finally, we have an example of where Eckhart joins the idea of abstraction with the metaphor of expanding capacity in speaking of the light of intellect: "This light separates things from corporeality and temporality. This light is also so wide that it escapes width—it is wider than wide."[67] Here, Eckhart makes it

---

62 Eckhart, Sermon XXII, LW IV, 197.3–4.
63 Eckhart, Sermon 21, DW I, 365.1–3.
64 Eckhart, Sermon 7, DW I, 120.1–4.
65 Eckhart, Sermon XXIV.2, LW IV, 226.3–4.
66 Eckhart, Sermon 72, DW III, 240.5–9.
67 Eckhart, Sermon 73, DW III, 261.1–2.

unusally clear that to take an extreme beyond the most extreme conceivable, "wider than wide," is to transcend that concept.

The different forms of stripping away are inflections of one of Eckhart's most well known and powerful metaphors, detachment. To "cut away" and "separate," what the elements of the word *abegescheidenheit* mean, refers to the shedding of all that is worldly. By detaching from one or two worldly things, we have merely made a mundane change, exchanging one thing for another without having to alter our way of thinking or being at all. However, as we should expect now, the nature of detachment changes when it includes *all* that is worldly. At this point, we give up all images, including our attachment to time and space. After all, our knowledge would not be bare if we still "knew" of such images.[68] As it is for the intellect, so it is for the will: "For a person to possess true poverty, he must be as free of his created will as he was when he did not exist."[69] Likewise, "When everything is detached, abstracted away, and peeled off, nothing at all remains but a solitary 'is.'"[70] This removal of all worldly things means "I must be completely alienated from all that is mine."[71] This makes what is mine foreign to me, just as multiplicity is foreign to God.

Ultimately, to detach from everything is to "go out of yourself and all things and all that you are in yourself."[72] This strips the soul of worldly things and all images that it has in itself, which ultimately means denuding the soul of self.[73] Beyond stripping the powers of the soul, as discussed above, stripping away self is more comprehensive and clearly crosses over into the unfamiliar. In terms of detachment, Eckhart tells us that "detachment does

---

68 Eckhart, Sermon 103, 476.24–26.

69 Eckhart, Sermon 52, DW II, 491.7–9. Another instance of this idea of poverty is in Sermon 74, DW III, 274.7–275.5. Though Sermon 52, *Beati pauperes spiritu*, is well known, Eckhart does not use the poverty metaphor as often as some of the others discussed here. It is also one that he shared with many other writers who spiritualized poverty (not to mention the debate about Franciscan poverty that raged during his lifetime). Eckhart links poverty directly with nakedness: "Being naked, poor, having nothing and being empty transforms nature. Emptyness makes water flow uphill and many other wonders of which we should not speak now" (*Book of Divine Consolation* §2, DW V, 29.11–13). It is extraordinary that he mentions the miraculous in this passage, since he rarely does so.

70 Eckhart, Sermon 45, DW II, 372.5–6. Eckhart also describes this stripping away in one place as "sacrifice" (*opfern*, Sermon 31, DW II, 114.7). We might question why he did not think this particular idea was more useful.

71 Eckhart, Sermon 42, DW II, 304.4–5.

72 Eckhart, Sermon 24, DW I, 419.6–8.

73 Cf. Eckhart, Sermon 76, DW III, 322.4–6.

not want to be anything at all"[74] and that "detachment is so close to nothingness that there is no thing so slight that it can be contained by detachment except God alone."[75]

Once we reach an extreme of stripping away, the metaphor reverses direction and we are told about "putting on" Christ and making God our own. We might say that the apophatic practice of stripping away all names of God yields to God being "omninameable" instead.[76] In this way, the continuum of apophatic and cataphatic forms a kind of circle, where the ends meet at the extremes and one can cross over from one to the other. As we have already seen many times, Eckhart's metaphors share this dynamic. Once we reach the extreme of the worldly and familiar, we cross over into the eternal and unfamiliar. When the clothing metaphor reaches its extreme in the nudity of the soul, the soul then "puts on" Christ.[77]

Equally unfamiliar is the image of God's "clothing" and the idea of God "in his dressing-room."[78] What makes this idea difficult is that the "clothing" that we must strip God of includes things like goodness and truth, ideas that are normally associated with God. Eckhart tells us, however, "Goodness is a garment under which God is hidden."[79] Further, we do this through the intellect: "Intellect pulls off the cloak [of goodness] from God and takes him bare, as he is stripped of goodness and being and all names."[80] Just as the soul is laid bare, so too must God be taken unclothed: "Goodness and justice are God's clothing, for they clothe him. So detach God from of all his clothing and take him naked in his dressing-room where he is uncovered and bare in himself. Then you will abide in him."[81]

Since Eckhart calls out goodness and Plato's highest form is the Good, a few words are needed to stave off the impulse to make too facile a connection and say that Eckhart is distinctly different than Plato here. While it is to some extent true that Eckhart departs from Plato here, we should recall

---

74 Eckhart, *On Detachment*, DW V, 406.8–9.
75 Eckhart, *On Detachment*, DW V, 404.3–5.
76 Eckhart, *Commentary on Exodus*, n.35, trans. McGinn in *Teacher and Preacher*, 54.
77 Eckhart, Sermon 24, DW I, 414.1–2.
78 Eckhart, Sermon 40, DW II, 274.5; cf. Sermon 11, DW I, 183.4.
79 Eckhart, Sermon 9, DW I, 153.5–6.
80 Eckhart, Sermon 9, DW I, 152.6–8; cf. Sermon 7, DW I, 122.5-8.
81 Eckhart, Sermon 40, DW II, 274.3–6. See the notes on my translation for more information on this passage.

that Plato's Good is also a maximal abstraction from which all things flow. In that way, even for Plato the Good is prior to the being of things. Eckhart has clear Neoplatonic roots here, so his talk of detaching even from good may be best understood as referring to the dualistic concept of goodness as distinct from not-goodness, instead of the form of the Good. As I said in the beginning, if we can talk of one notion of divine oneness as different from another, then we have not stripped away enough to arrive at oneness at all.

Stripping the soul and stripping God are ostensibly different, but they are in fact one. Eckhart hypothesizes, "If the soul were bared and stripped of all intermediaries, then God would be bared and stripped and would give himself entirely to her."[82] God must come in to the humble soul, one which is bare of images and self. Here, as well, we reach "the essence of the soul, in which God may only descend in his nakedness."[83] Ultimately, this happens because the clothing that God wears is clothing that we give him. His clothing comprises part of our images. Thus, once we give up those images and lay the soul bare, so too is God laid bare.[84]

REST

If we consider the soul as a door attached to a hinge, the outer man (the door) continues to trace out a circle at each point of its length while the inner man (the hinge) remains motionlessness. The door is the radius of the circle. Since the door moves uniformly, all points on the door trace out circles at different speeds. As we move from the outer edge of the door inward toward the frame, the speed at which each point traces a circle becomes slower and slower until finally, at the hinge, motion stops altogether. Eckhart gives us this metaphor for the inner and outer man in *On Detachment*. It shows that as we approach the innermost reaches of the soul, motion slows to a halt. In fact, the motion of the outer man is possible because of the hinge. The hinge anchors the door just as the eternal anchors the material (as we saw in another metaphor). We might even say that the hinge traces a circle with zero radius so that it is a "circle" of a single, dimensionless point with no motion even though it is in motion.

---

82 Eckhart, Sermon 69, DW III, 165.5–7.
83 Eckhart, Sermon XXIV.2, LW IV, 227.11–12.
84 Cf. Eckhart, Sermon 45 DW II, 367.2–3.

Here again, two forms of this same metaphor are in apparent tension with one another. I believe these two-sided metaphors account for some of the claims of inconsistency levied against Eckhart by some scholars. On the one hand, we have the hinge metaphor, which describes the interior life of the soul. In the interior life, peace and wisdom come with reaching the restful and motionless center. By contrast, the physical world is ordered in the opposite fashion. There, the earth is at the center and tends downward, away from the higher things. Fire is higher and tends upward. At the highest level are the heavens themselves, which are the source of all things below. As with a rotating sphere, the outer shell moves more quickly than the points closer to the center.[85] There is a twofold movement in this metaphor just as in the others. We begin with the lowest of things in the external world, the earth. We move upward in ascending toward the heavens, which have the greatest motion. In opposite fashion, the lowest of things in the interior world involve attachment to temporal things. As we move toward the center of the interior world, we reach a divine point of rest and repose in the soul insofar as it is divine.

Beginning with worldly cares and the motion that inheres in attachment to temporal things, Eckhart tells us that all things seek rest.[86] In its most prosaic form, we can think of this in terms of reaching a state of equilibrium. A stone falls and comes to rest on the ground, where it may lie at rest for a thousand years. Eckhart applies this principle to all levels of the cosmos. Even at the highest level, "the heavens are continually running around and in this running they seek rest."[87] Indeed there is something divine about rest, recalling the dynamics of the hinge metaphor. Further, unrest relates to the self: "All turmoil and unrest come entirely from self-will, whether we recognize it or not."[88] Eckhart identifies self-will with attachment to external things.[89]

---

85 Eckhart, *Commentary on John*, n.247, LW III, 247.7–8.

86 In this and similar metaphors, we should detect an echo of Origen's notion of *apokatastasis*, the return of all things to God.

87 Sermon 7, DW I, 118.8–9.

88 Eckhart, *Counsels on Discernment* §21, DW V, 282.11–283.2. I am particularly indebted to Davies' translation of this passage. Translating *unvride* as "unrest" is very Eckhartian. The term *gesturme* here simply refers to motion with a negative connotation. Our internal "storminess" and "unrest" robs us of our freedom and makes us not-peaceful (*un-vride*). The motion is critical for Eckhart since it separates us from the divine repose that comes with dwelling in God.

89 This is one of the points in the discussion where we arrive at a conclusion that smacks of Buddhism. That this should happen repeatedly does much to explain the fondness that many Buddhists have had for Eckhart in the past century.

While stones do not know of anything higher and cannot "desire" to reach above their station, mankind has the potential for coming to know God and thereby seeking divine repose. As Eckhart says, "the soul will never rest until it becomes wholly one in God."[90] This reveals much about the nature of the soul. After all, on Eckhart's account, simple people do not know to desire God and may achieve a kind of low-level, fleeting rest in the material world. In response to this, Eckhart tells us that the soul naturally seeks God and that the irascible part of the soul in particular has *synderesis*, which is the perpetual drive for God. Synderesis is our natural instinct to "stand against what is impure" and "be evermore lured to the good."[91] Synderesis, for Eckhart, is the human form of perpetual striving for God that all things exhibit. This allows him to say that even in hell, the impulse to strive for God is never completely destroyed: "Evil never totally destroys good, or extinguishes it, or renders it dumb."[92] The impulse never decays because the nature of the subject is not destroyed and synderesis lives in the eternal nature of its form. This is in accord with the Platonic hierarchy, in which there is no form of evil since evil is simply nonexistence. Insofar as things exist, even in hell, they still possess some measure of the Good and the concomitant desire for what is higher. The powers of the soul manifest the practical activity of this striving in their desire for peace. For the soul to achieve this motionlessness, Eckhart tells us that it "must rise above herself to the divine order."[93]

Once the soul arrives at its center, the metaphor of birth becomes important. That metaphor extends the idea that all things are created from their forms. Eckhart tells us that the production of a manifestation of a form occurs "in silence of the efficient cause and the final cause which both properly look to the external creature and both signify 'boiling over.'"[94] Creation is *ebullitio*, 'boiling over,' which to Eckhart is the manifestation of God's principle as creation.[95] Where boiling is the form, boiling over is the manifestation of that form.[96] In the vernacular sermons, Eckhart uses the

---

90 Eckhart, Sermon 21, DW I, 369.10–11.

91 Eckhart, Sermon 20a, DW I, 334.1–3; cf. Sermon 20b, DW I, 348.10–349.2.

92 Eckhart, *Book of the Parables of* Genesis, n.163, trans. McGinn in *Essential Eckhart*, 120.

93 Eckhart, Sermon 31, DW II, 123.2–3.

94 Eckhart, *Commentary on Wisdom*, n.283, trans. McGinn in *Teacher and Preacher*, 172–3; cf. Sermon XLIX.3 n.511.

95 The word "principle" here is used instead of "form" because this is how Eckhart speaks of it. Admittedly, it is not clear how he conceives of God's principle manifesting in the world.

96 Eckhart, Sermon XXV.1, n.258, trans. McGinn in *Teacher and Preacher*, 218; cf. *In Ex.* n.16.

metaphor of melting for this same idea, where "melting inward" (*smilzet in*) corresponds with boiling, and "melting outward" (*ûzsmilzet*) corresponds with boiling over.[97] In language that recalls the image of boiling, he tells us that intellect "goes in and breaks through into the root, where the Son wells up and the Holy Spirit blossoms out."[98] What is important for us here is that the formal emanation occurs "in silence," which is an inflection of the metaphor of motionlessness and repose. In general, begetting is motionless.[99] Thus, for the soul to reach God by way of the higher reason (*ratio superior*), higher reason must be "quiet and silent, where the Father speaks the Word 'without noise.'"[100] Thus, begetting by way of the Father speaking the Word must also be silent. Noise and motion belong to temporal things and consequently are the province of inferior reason.[101] Putting it all together, Eckhart tells us, "The Word lies hidden in the soul. You don't know about it or hear it. Unless room is made for it in the ground of hearing, it will not be heard. All voices and all noises must cease for a pure stillness to be there, a still silence."[102] Eckhart describes the lesser form of this in the human intellect's own process of coming to understand something. We should notice that he uses very similar language for describing this: "When the intellect truly recognizes being, it descends on it straightaway and comes to rest on it, speaking its rational word about the thing it has there."[103] These are specific examples of Eckhart's general principle, "what is produced from something is universally its word."[104]

Eckhart also describes progress toward rest using the metaphor of how light changes over the course of a day, an image he attributes to Augustine.[105] In the morning, the light of creation shines on things. As the soul begins its

---

97 Eckhart, Sermon 18, DW I, 301.6–302.1; cf. Sermon 19, DW I, 314.4–5.

98 Eckhart, Sermon 69, DW III, 180.1–2. He also tells us that God "would have burst if he had not poured himself out completely," a phrase that points to the idea of boiling over, adding color to the idea by also including necessity in the metaphor (Sermon 99, DW IV.1, 260.44).

99 Eckhart, *Commentary on Exodus*, n.159, trans. McGinn in *Teacher and Preacher*, 94.

100 Eckhart, Sermon XXIV.2, LW IV, 228.5–6.

101 Eckhart, Sermon XXIV.2, LW IV, 228.6–7.

102 Eckhart, Sermon 19, DW I, 312.5–9.

103 Eckhart, Sermon 104a, DW IV.1, 592.298–593.302.

104 Eckhart, *Commentary on John*, n.4, trans. McGinn in *Essential Eckhart*, 123.

105 Eckhart, Sermon 19, DW I, 319.12–320.7; Augustine, *On the Literal Interpretation of Genesis* IV, c.23 n.40.

ascent to God, the light gets brighter. As evening draws in, the soul comes to rest in God. Eckhart describes the process as follows:

> The natural light of the soul is the morning. When the soul breaks through itself into the highest and purest part in the light and thus strides into the angel's light, it is midmorning in that light. When the soul then strides up with the angel's light into the divine light, it is midday. When the soul remains in God's light in the stillness of pure repose, that is the evening: it is then hottest in the divine love.[106]

Notice that Eckhart involves the idea of heat in the increasing light to parallel the increase of desire the soul feels as it is inflamed with divine love.

As the soul comes to rest in God, Eckhart also describes this using the metaphor of "dwelling" or "abiding," which Eckharts knows has roots in Scripture as well as in Augustine.[107] The implication is that whatever dwells is at home, at peace and rest, where it dwells. God can find the soul at peace "if He finds us at home and the soul is not betrothed to the five senses."[108] If the soul is at "home" in its ground, then God may come to rest in the soul.[109] As Eckhart dsecribes it, "God is nowhere so properly God as in the soul. Something of God is in all creatures, but in the soul God is godly, for she is his resting place."[110]

What happens when the soul reaches this point of rest? As I argued in the section on joy, delight floods the soul. Eckhart builds a theological mechanism around this observation, telling us that joy increases as one desires worldly things less and that this process reaches its end in unlimited desire (thirst) for God, who pours forth joy without hindrance. We should notice two things about this. First, we can see that people who are content with less and desire less are generally happier for it. Second, we hear from meditative traditions that such desire manifests internally in the anxious motion of the mind. As Eckhart says, "thinking has motion and runs about."[111] When that

---

[106] Eckhart, Sermon 36b, DW II, 199.1–200.2; cf. *On the Nobleman*, Sermon 19, DW I, 319.12–320.7; Sermon 37, DW II, 221.4–222.3.

[107] Eckhart, *Commentary on Exodus*, n.158, trans. McGinn in *Teacher and Preacher*, 94.

[108] Eckhart, Sermon 34, DW II, 164.1–2. My translation departs from Walshe and Quint, who rendered *sponzieren* as though it were modern German's *späzieren* ("to walk" or "to stroll"), instead of Middle High German's *sponsieren* ("betrothal" or "engagement").

[109] Cf. Eckhart, Sermon 101, DW IV.1, 357.134–35.

[110] Eckhart, Sermon 73, DW II, 267.7–8. Regarding the pronouns, the word for "soul" is feminine, while the word for "God" is masculine.

[111] Eckhart, Sermon XXIV.2, LW IV, 227.5–6.

motion stops, "wisdom comes into the mind when the soul rests from the turmoils of the passions and concern for worldly things, when all things are silent to it and it is silent to all."¹¹² Thus, "in this [lack of passion], note the soul's rest."¹¹³ So God and the soul are at home in the divine ground of the soul. The soul comes to rest here and abides in God just as God abides in the soul.¹¹⁴ This is where God speaks his Word in the soul. That speaking is the divine activity. Thus, it is at this point that the metaphor crosses over and we begin to hear of activity instead.

METAPHORS OF ACTIVITY

Eckhart's philosophy of action, leading the active life, is possible insofar as we participate in the Word's creative action. Our action is justified because it is not creaturely action. Fittingly, Eckhart's metaphors of divine and human speech reflect this point. We have two different forms of the metaphor of speaking. The first is the prosaic form of human speech, "Whatever is in me goes out from me. If I only think it, my word reveals it and yet remains within."¹¹⁵ Eckhart juxtaposes this with the other side of the metaphor, that of divine speech. He writes, "To the extent that I am near God, God speaks himself in me."¹¹⁶ Just as all things seek rest, we see an analogous situation with speech: "All creatures want to speak God in all their activity."¹¹⁷

Eckhart often uses art and the artisans as an example of production as contrasted with creation. While production is a kind of bricolage, an assemblage of existing pieces, creation is a special kind of production, a production from nothing.¹¹⁸ An architect who builds a house, Eckhart's favorite example of production, uses existing materials that are separate from himself.¹¹⁹ God does not do this in creation as would Plato's demiurge.

---

112 Eckhart, *Commentary on Wisdom*, n.280, trans. McGinn in *Teacher and Preacher*, 171.

113 Eckhart, Sermon XXIV.2, LW IV, 224.6.

114 In one particularly unusual metaphor, Eckhart says that the soul is "thrust into peace" (Sermon 7, DW I, 118.1).

115 Eckhart, Sermon 53, DW II, 530.1–2; cf. Sermon 38, DW II, 229.1–230.3.

116 Eckhart, Sermon 53, DW II, 530.4–5.

117 Eckhart, Sermon 53, DW II, 531.1.

118 Eckhart, *Book of the Parables of Genesis*, n.9; cf. *In Sap.* n.25.

119 Eckhart, *General Prologue*; cf. *Commentary on Wisdom*, n.27, 36; *Commentary on Exodus*, ns.28, 157; *Commentary on John*, n.30.

The artist, instead, seeks to make what is like himself. Eckhart describes this process in the following terms: "What I make, I make myself and with myself to myself and in myself and press my image entirely into it."[120] Again, this is a notion with Platonic roots. Each copy on a lower rung in the hierarchy of being is an imperfect manifestation of what is higher. Eckhart describes this process of artistic production using language that points to God's act of creation. His language also describes detachment and the ascent of the soul, as if to imply that artistic creation, in its striving to make what is like itself, is like God's creation. For example, in describing a sculptor's chiseling away material to reveal what was already contained within, Eckhart calls this "clearing away [*expurgando*], cutting off [*excidendo*] and drawing forth [*educendo*]."[121] Recall that "cutting off" is the literal image in *abegescheidenheit*, detachment. Regarding this "cutting off," Eckhart remarks, "If a master makes an image from a piece of wood or a stone, he does not place that image in the wood. Rather, he cuts away the shavings that have hidden and covered it up. He does not give anything to the wood. Instead, he takes away from it and removes the covering."[122] This is the same language that Eckhart uses for the uncovering and progressive removing of images that characterizes the return to God. This makes art analogous to our return to God. Our part in that process is "creative," therefore, in the sense of *production*, where we use our own skill to tame passion and remove images. Once that is done, the divine can flow into us by grace.

Eckhart describes the process of art striving for what is above itself: "The work that is 'with,' 'outside' and 'above' the artist must become his work 'within,' by informing him so that he can make a work of art, as it says in Luke chapter one: 'The Holy Spirit will come upon you' (Lk 1:35), that is, so that the 'upon' may become 'within.'"[123] This striving for what is above is sensibly applied to art because Eckhart understands art as more than mere copying. It seeks to render what is universal and therefore above particular things: "A master who makes an image of man does not make it like Conrad or Henry, for he would not portray man, he would portray Conrad or Henry."[124] Thus,

---

120 Eckhart, Sermon 109, DW IV.2, 763.13–14.

121 Eckhart, *Commentary on John*, n.575.

122 Eckhart, *On the Nobleman*, DW V, 113.18–21.

123 Eckhart, *Commentary on John*, n.41, trans. McGinn in *Essential Eckhart*, 136. This also hints at a connection between possession by the Holy Spirit and the creation of art.

124 Eckhart, Sermon 77, DW III, 342.5–6. Similarly, the form in the artist's mind, Eckhart tells us, is "nobler in him than the material" because it is a form and not a manifestation (DW I, 290.4–5).

what art actually does as production ranks below creation. However, what art *strives* to do is to reach higher than itself, just as nature does: "Existence, both in nature and in art, is what everything thirsts and hungers for, seeks and desires. Art and nature labor to and for the end that an effect exist and possess existence."[125] We might hear echoes of Plotinus in Eckhart's own account of art, since both describe art as creation which reaches for divine unity.

We may readily comprehend the idea that things strive to make what is like themselves. They try to reproduce what is in their nature and essence. With mankind, however, the situation has different potential. Since the soul has the capacity even for God, what likeness can such a man hope to produce artistically? Eckhart says, "a picture praises its master, who has imprinted upon it all the art he has in his heart and made it completely like himself."[126] Less like Plato's notion of imitative art as producing pale copies and more like his notion of a "likely story" or image which has the scent of truth (and presumably applies to his own writing), Eckhart's conception of art also has an explosive element when applied to human nature insofar as it has the capacity for God. Speaking more generally, "As far as it can, every agent makes something like itself, and it makes the other itself, that is, makes the other from other into itself. It begins from the other, withdraws from it, and draws it to itself."[127] This same language is used when describing the way that fire burns and the way that God transforms the soul into God: "In the same way, when fire wants to bring wood to itself . . . the hotter the wood becomes, the stiller and more restful it becomes. The more it is like fire, the more peaceful it is until it becomes entirely fire."[128] Eckhart provides a hint of what man would create by comparing what man creates to what God creates. He tells us that, although man has limited power to reproduce something just like himself, God, since his power is unlimited, produces an exact image of himself.[129] If even God strives to create what is like himself, then surely the perfected man who dwells in God would seek to do no less. The artist creates art as a manifestation of the exemplar in his mind, which is a kind of "son."[130] This exemplar is "his living conception."[131] It stands to reason that the soul's

---

125 Eckhart, *Sermons and Lectures on Ecclesiasticus*, n.44, trans. McGinn in *Teacher and Preacher*, 175.
126 Eckhart, Sermon 19, DW I, 318.6–8.
127 Eckhart, *Commentary on John*, n.67, trans. McGinn in *Essential Eckhart*, 146.
128 Eckhart, Sermon 11, DW I, 180.8–9, 11–12.
129 Eckhart, Sermon 38, DW II 238.7-9.
130 Eckhart, *Commentary on John*, n.57, trans. McGinn in *Essential Eckhart*, 142.

ascent implies a similar ascent in the striving of his art. At the extreme, the artist would seek to beget God himself, as we will see shortly.

We might say in general that activity is the result of striving to create: "As far as possible, everything active produces what is like itself."[132] Everything tries to express, manifest, and recreate itself in action. So long as creatures stay within themselves and preserve self-will, rather than allowing God's will to express itself, frustration naturally follows since things do not have the capacity for creation. The important distinction here is between creation and alteration or production. Creation is the giving of being. For Eckhart, this power belongs solely to God. Lesser forms of being, however, can be achieved in alteration or production by artists, artisans, and even animals, as when beavers build dams. Eckhart explains, "No creature can give life. If it was possible for a creature to give life, God could not bear it because he loves the soul so dearly. He wants to give it himself. If a creature gave it, it would be unworthy of the soul. It would consider it as small a thing as a bug."[133] No creature qua creature can create. This tension helps to explain why the soul's *synderesis* manifests as an endless striving toward God. Only in God can this striving reach fulfillment. As Eckhart says, the highest power of the soul "always wants to beget like the father. If it were not hindered," it would give birth just as the Father does.[134] The principal, and most powerful metaphor Eckhart uses for this process is birth—culminating in the birth of the Word in the soul, an idea that speaks directly to the status of the individual soul as divine.

THE SPARK OF THE SOUL

Eckhart's notion of the "spark" primarily builds upon three metaphors: light, fire, and seed. As only a part of the soul that begins for each of us as something covered up by worldly concerns, the spark as light metaphor captures this quality of it being a mere "flash" or light that is glimpsed through a "chink." In linking it with light Eckhart says, "The spark of the intellect, which is the

---

131 Eckhart, *Commentary on John*, n.6, trans. McGinn in *Essential Eckhart*, 124.

132 Eckhart, Sermon XL.3, DW IV, 344.4.

133 Eckhart, Sermon 59, DW II, 630.9–631.3; cf. Eckhart, *Commentary on Wisdom*, n.31, trans. McGinn in *Teacher and Preacher*, 151.

134 Eckhart, Sermon 106a, DW IV.2, 694.87–88. Eckhart describes this in terms of the drive everything has to give birth to what is most like itself. To say that the soul is driven to give birth like the Father does is to say that the soul is one with the Father.

head of the soul, is called the 'man' of the soul, and is as much as a spark of the divine nature, a divine light, a sprout and an imprinted image of the divine nature."¹³⁵ Conveniently, Eckhart gives us a list of metaphors for the spark. As "head" it is spatially the highest and thus the highest in being (*houbet* means both "head" and "apex"). As "man" it goes with its head uncovered and is thus receptive to what is higher. As "imprint" it takes the form of God who is the "seal." The light metaphor works particularly well for Eckhart because he sees light as immediately flooding whenever it is let in, but also, because it does not take "root", leaving just as quickly when it is impeded. Further, light can be blocked by the most mundane of things, which enables him to say that even the smallest worldly thing is big enough to hinder God from coming into the soul. His listeners would have also been keenly aware of the importance of sparks in starting fires for warmth and cooking, two essentials for daily life. This phenomenon is largely hidden from and overlooked by us today due to our use of electricity and the strategies used for creating our artificial living spaces, such that the effects of fire and electricity are hidden. Thus, our homes often function without the irregularities and unevenness that are characteristic of natural things. In other words, fire mattered more in the daily life of Eckhart's audience than it does in ours.

Eckhart describes the ways different people are "alive" to the divine light in order of increasing awareness. He places "the flash of a sword" beneath "a great flash," which is yet beneath those who "receive a great light as if it is day, but still as if through a chink."¹³⁶ A spark, for Eckhart, is the smallest flash of something higher in something lower, since "all that is on earth lives from a spark of an angel."¹³⁷ Likewise, "from [an angel's] work there falls a shaving (just as a shaving falls from a piece of wood that one hews), a flash, where the angel touches heaven with its lowest part."¹³⁸ We see a similar image in Sermon 65: "I take the lowest angel in its pure nature: the smallest splinter or spark that ever fell from him would light the all the world with delight

---

135 Eckhart, Sermon 37, DW II, 211.1–3. Though I render *zein* as "sprout" since it is an important metaphor for Eckhart, the word could also be rendered "ray" for consistency with the metaphorics of light.

136 Eckhart, Sermon 57, DW II, 603.6–604.1, 604.1, 604.6–7.

137 Eckhart, Sermon 42, DW II, 303.6–7; in Sermon 38, DW II, 240.4 we also hear that all things are "green, leafy and bright" (*grüenet, loubet und liuhtet*) from the spark of an angel.

138 Eckhart, Sermon 38, DW II, 243.2–3; cf. Sermon 63, DW III, 79.5–7 for nearly the same image. The image here is clearly one of a spark falling from the sky, but Eckhart does not call it a spark as we might expect. This is probably because this kind of spark is quite different from the spark of the soul, which is more like the smallest spark from which a fire grows.

and joy."[139] This speaks to the incommensurability of different levels since he speaks of the smallest part of the least angel filling all the world below. The spark represents something of a jump discontinuity, a sudden inflow from higher to lower. This dynamic makes the soul's spark capable of something greater that is beyond any scale, analogy, or proportion because its spark is from the Godhead itself and enables the soul to achieve union with God.[140] As Eckhart says, this power "takes God in his oneness and in his desert. It takes God in his wilderness and in his own ground."[141] It is "a spark of intellect that never dies. In this spark, we place the image of the soul."[142]

The way a spark grows and raises the soul is described through the metaphor of fire. In these examples, Eckhart is not referring to the spark of the soul, though the dynamics are similar and should be associated since we are changed into God in the same way. Eckhart says as much in this passage: "Fire changes into itself whatever is joined to it and this takes on fire's nature. Wood does not change fire into itself, but rather fire changes wood into itself. So we will be changed into God."[143] We should remember here that in the Aristotelian cosmos fire naturally moves upward toward the heavens. One of the key details that we get from the fire metaphor is the manner in which sparks are "sons" of fire. Here again, just as "likeness . . . lures the soul into God,"[144] when a fire starts in wood, the spark "forgets and forsakes its father and mother, brother and sister on earth, and hurries to the heavenly father."[145] The fire "forgets and denies" its family (recalling Lk 14:26 among other passages) which are at the same level as it. Ultimately, this forsaking includes forsaking itself,[146] which is necessary for it to rise above itself. We see the same dynamics in the soul. The soul must deny its earthly family and its worldly self to rise above itself and achieve union with God. The spark that starts a fire is the first flash of something greater that has the capacity to elevate.

139 Eckhart, Sermon 65, DW III, 100.1–3.
140 Eckhart, Sermon 20a, DW I, 332.2–333.3.
141 Eckhart, Sermon 10, DW I, 171.14–15.
142 Eckhart, Sermon 76, DW III, 315.6–7.
143 Eckhart, Sermon 6, DW I, 114.5–115.2.
144 Eckhart, *Book of Divine Consolation* §2, DW V, 31.5–6.
145 Eckhart, *Book of Divine Consolation* §2, DW V, 31.9–11.
146 Another example of fire "forgetting" is the following: "When part of a log is thrown into fire, changing into a spark or kind of fire, soon deserts the wood itself from which, through which, and in which it has its whole being as a part of itself, deserts the log by which, through which, and in which it once had its whole being as an intimate part of itself. It flees backward and tends upward, having forgotten itself as it were, as much as it is extinguished while doing so" (Eckhart, Sermon XXX.1, LW IV, 276.9–12).

So too is the spark in the soul something greater (though in a paradoxical fashion since it is one with God) and it enables the soul to rise above itself by forgetting itself. Further, fire "wants" to change other things into fire: "If it could turn everything that is around it into fire, it would do it."[147]

Perhaps the origin of the idea of the spark in Eckhart's writing is found in the seed metaphor in Scripture. Eckhart thinks of the seed as a seed of a tree, which enables other metaphoric possibilities in speaking of trees, branches, and verdant blossoming. He connects the idea of the seed to the spark when he speaks of "the soul, which has a droplet of understanding, a little spark, a twig."[148] Eckhart further explains, "The seed of God is in us. If it has a good, wise, and industrious farmer, it will thrive much more.... The seed of a pear tree grows into a pear tree, a nut seed into a nut tree, the seed of God into God."[149] The Holy Spirit raises this sprout up and causes it to blossom.[150] By analogy, we know this seed will grow into God and not something merely similar because he elsewhere tells us, "Whenever a branch grows from a tree, it carries both the name and the essence of the tree. What goes out is the same as what remains within, and what remains within is the same as what goes out. Therefore the branch is an expression of itself."[151] Further, the spark as the seed of a tree wants to grow just as fire wants to produce fire. Referring the idea to Origen, Eckhart says that since God himself "imprinted and bore it into us, it may indeed become covered and hidden, but it is never extinguished, nor will it go out. It blooms and sparkles, blazes and ceaselessly leans toward God."[152] Finally, the metaphors discussed for the spark all culminate in blossoming and fruition.[153] Eckhart consistently describes this in terms of "greenness."[154] What blossoms becomes green, of course. Greenness has another useful connotation, however: what is green is vibrant and *new*. Eckhart tells us, "All creatures 'green' in God."[155]

---

147 Eckhart, Sermon 84, DW III, 460.7.
148 Eckhart, Sermon 9, DW I, 151.1–2.
149 Eckhart, *On the Nobleman*, DW V, 111.11–13.
150 Eckhart, Sermon 20b, DW I, 344.9–345.1.
151 Eckhart, Sermon 16a, DW I, 259.14–21.
152 Eckhart, *On the Nobleman*, DW V, 111.19–21.
153 For examples, see Eckhart, Sermon 97.
154 Cf. Eckhart, Sermon 106, DW IV.2, 684.13, *grüenende*. For the connection between greenness and Hildegard of Bingen, see chap. 1.
155 Eckhart, Sermon 72, DW III, 247.5.

THE BIRTH OF THE WORD IN THE SOUL

The rhetoric surrounding the birth of the Word in the soul may be the clearest point at which we can say that Eckhart's rhetoric evidences a new conception of the individual. Like his other ideas, the birth of the Word in the soul is not new with Eckhart. The tradition extends back at least to Origen and Hippolytus. Hippolytus says, "The mouth of the Father has begotten a pure Word; this Word appears a second time, born of the saints. Constantly producing saints, it is also itself reproduced by its saints."[156] Similarly, Origen says, "from this seed of the word of God which is sown Christ is born in the heart of the hearers ... the soul conceives from this seed of the word and the Word forms a fetus in it until it brings forth a spirit of the fear of God."[157] Reiner Schürmann cites similar evidence with Origen and Maximus Confessor.[158] He concludes that Eckhart takes the birth of the Word idea further and gives it an "Aristotelian flavor" by having the detached person give birth to the Son of God in activity.[159] Schürmann is right on target in linking Eckhart's alteration with his notion of the active life for the detached person, though this does not result solely from his Aristotelianism. Finally, we also find the idea of God constantly begetting the Son in Eriugena's *Periphyseon*.[160] As it is in Eckhart's extant series of Christmas sermons,[161] the birth of the Word is routinely discussed around Christmas in the form of 1) the eternal birth of Christ, 2) the Incarnation, and 3) the birth of the Word in the soul. Characteristically, Eckhart goes straight to the heart of the matter and focuses on the birth of the Word in the soul.

The two sides of the birth metaphor stand in strong contrast to one another. We have little difficulty understanding worldly birth. The offspring is clearly a product of what gives birth, with animals and even forms and manifestations. With imperfect worldly things that are in the process of becoming, "alteration is concerned with becoming and is a handmaid or servant; along with motion it serves the generation that looks to existence."[162] Since it still

---

156 Henri de Lubac, *The Motherhood of the Church*, trans. Sergia Englund (San Francisco, Calif.: Ignatius Press, 1982), 80.

157 Origen, *Homilies on Leviticus 1–16*, trans. Gary Wayne Barkley, Fathers of the Church 83 (Washington, D.C.: The Catholic University of America Press, 1990), 230.

158 Reiner Schürmann, *Wandering Joy: Meister Eckhart's Mystical Philosophy* (Hudson, N.Y.: Lindisfarne, 2001), 25.

159 Schürmann, *Wandering Joy*, 26.

160 558B; Duclow, *Masters of Learned Ignorance*, 54.

161 Eckhart, Sermon 101, Sermon 102, Sermon 103.

162 Eckhart, *Commentary on Exodus*, n.139, trans. McGinn in *Teacher and Preacher*, 88.

does not achieve being in God, striving for existence continues in worldly things that become other worldly things. Nevertheless, we notice in worldly things a dynamic that continues to be true for anything less than God: "Giving birth always involves plurality and disturbance."[163] Things that are changed in time experience pain and distress in the process. Thus, Eckhart can sensibly use the metaphor of lightning to describe it: "We find an analogy with lightning. Whatever it strikes, it turns toward itself."[164] The image here is rather specific. Eckhart says shortly thereafter that the leaves on trees even turn toward a lightning strike, which is an unusual way of describing how it grabs the attention of things that are ostensibly unable to understand and are unaware of what is going on. The image is apt since he is describing the way that the lower powers pay attention when there is a flash of light from above. They cannot understand it, but they turn and attune themselves toward it. Since alteration and birth are painful, we may then understand why Eckhart describes God as holding back from revealing himself to those who are not ready: "If God gave himself to the soul temporally, it would vex her. Now he gives himself to her in eternity, in a new now, greening without ceasing."[165]

Again in tracing through this metaphor, we find ourselves ascending to God, considering things that are increasingly universal, before crossing over and reaching the crucial second side of the metaphor. Although many things can ascend, for example by being transformed into fire by burning, only the innermost part of the individual soul is capable of the highest form of birth: being transformed into God.[166] This capacity results in some of Eckhart's most shocking rhetoric. This birth of the Word in the soul results in our being born as only-begotten Son—that is, as Christ.[167] Lest there be any confusion about this identification, Eckhart makes it quite clear: "It would be of little value for me that 'the Word was made flesh' for man in Christ as a person distinct from me unless he was also made flesh in me personally so that I too might be God's son."[168] Further, in speaking of Christ's birth as part of a

---

[163] Eckhart, *Commentary on John*, n.130, trans. McGinn in *Essential Eckhart*, 173.

[164] Eckhart, Sermon 103, DW IV.1, 488.127–28.

[165] Eckhart, Sermon 106, DW IV.2, 698.107–9.

[166] Eckhart, Sermon 43, DW II, 325.12–13.

[167] Eckhart, Sermon 30, DW II, 96.7–8; Sermon 18, DW I, 305.3–5; Sermon 99, DW IV.1, 256.14–16; Sermon 22, DW I, 382.8–383.1.

[168] Eckhart, *Commentary on John*, n.117, LW III, 101.14–102.2. Eckhart does qualify this to avoid some of the undesirable conclusions that the so-called Free Spirit heretics might draw: "For what I say here should be understood about a good, perfect person who 'walked and still walks God's way,' not about a carnal, inexperienced person who is entirely far from and knows nothing of

Christmas sermon, Eckhart wonders, "What does it help me if this birth is always happening and yet it does not happen in me? All that matters is that it happens in me."[169] Likewise, "He gives birth to me, his Son, the same Son. I say more: he gives birth to me not only as his Son, but rather, he gives birth to me and me to him, and to me as his being and his nature."[170] And so, as we are all the Son of God as Christ was, though Eckhart tells us that we should understand "'Only-Begotten' in the sense of first of many."[171] Later, we will explore the significance of this idea in the way it alters the idea of Christ and the Incarnation. For now, we should notice that the capacity of the soul to undergo this is straightforwardly implied by the bare fact that the soul in its ground is divine. That simple point enables Eckhart to craft some of his wildest rhetoric. Since God is one and entirely indistinct and beyond all things, anything that God does is one and the same in God: creating the world, coming into the world as Christ, being eternal, and so on. Just as there cannot be many mysticisms because oneness would not be oneness if there were different kinds, so it is with God: God's oneness implies unity in the divine being, the divine action, and the divine Son.[172] Therefore, if we understand that the ground of the soul itself has the capacity for God, it "touches" and is thereby divine, inheriting all of the things and powers that apply to God.

As if this were not enough, Eckhart takes his rhetoric farther by describing this birth as reciprocal. He writes in another sermon, "I have eternally given birth to you and you to me."[173] Similarly, "God gives birth to himself out

---

this birth" (Sermon 101, DW IV.1, 336.8–337.10). Similarly, but without it seeming as much like a caveat, he states, "Where God finds likeness to this [divine] order in the soul, he the Father bears his Son there" (Sermon 31, DW II, 120.4–5). If there is any touch of what is worldly, the birth cannot happen: "As long as you have sorrow in your heart over any thing, even over sin, your child is not born." (Sermon 76, DW III, 325.5–6). These passages should be sufficiently clear as to avoid any possibility of misinterpretation as allowing free license for sin.

169 Eckhart, Sermon 101, DW IV.1, 336.4–5. We might also recall, as Cyprian Smith does, the relevance of Luke 17:21, which reads "the Kingdom of God is within you" (*Way of Paradox*, 102; cf. C. Smith, *Path of Life*, 24). Interestingly, many new translations attempt to mollify this language by using "among" or "in your midst" instead of "within" or simply "in." Ilaria Ramelli concluded after studying the language in detail that the correct translation is "in," the most powerful option, the one which establishes the most intimate relation ("Luke 17:21: 'The Kingdom of God is Inside You' the Ancient Syriac Versions in Support of the Correct Translation," *Hugoye: Journal of Syriac Studies* 12, no. 2 [2009]: 259–86).

170 Eckhart, Sermon 6, DW I, 109.8–10.

171 Eckhart, *Commentary on John*, n.123, trans. McGinn in *Essential Eckhart*, 170.

172 Interestingly, this would be extended in the century that followed by Nicholas of Cusa, who took significant influence from Eckhart. To this list, he might also add "divine potential."

of himself into himself and gives birth again to himself into himself."[174] We should be reminded here of the dialectic of particles whereby each reformulation succeeds principally in reinforcing the intimacy of the relation and the utter oneness of God. The birth can be described as reciprocal because the soul insofar as it is divine is amenable to being described as doing anything that God does. As Eckhart says, "As I speak the word of God, I am a co-worker [*mitewürker*] with God and grace is mixed with the creature [namely, the soul]."[175] As he explains elsewhere in greater detail, when the soul "comes home, she is united with him, and she is a co-worker. No creature works anything other than the Father, who works alone. The soul should never stop until she works as powerfully as God. Then she works with the Father in all His works."[176] As Eckhart is fond of doing, he juxtaposes a statement that seems to exclude a possibility right beside another that claims that very possibility. Proximity helps to emphasize the tension. God works alone. And then we are told that the soul "works all His works with the Father." Finally, the next clause releases the tension by explaining that the soul works as one with God, just as we read elsewhere: "Whenever he is one with God, so he brings forth all creatures with God. He brings blessedness to all creatures insofar as he is one with God."[177] Compare this to another sermon where Eckhart says, "[If I am to know God without means,] God must truly become me and I must truly become God, so completely one that I work together with him, not in the sense that I work and he does something afterwards. Further, I work with what is mine. I work with him as truly as my soul works with my body."[178] He is at pains to insist not only upon unity with God, but also upon the appropriateness of still saying "I" and "mine," and upon the fact that what is God's is equally my own. Put simply, not only am I one

---

173 Eckhart, Sermon 14, DW I, 239.3.

174 Eckhart, Sermon 43, DW II, 320.4; cf. Sermon 22 DW I 383.7-8, Sermon 106a DW IV.2 686.32, Sermon 106c DW IV.2 687.32.

175 Eckhart, Sermon 81, DW III, 398.13–4.

176 Eckhart, Sermon 31, DW II, 125.1–4; cf. Sermon 22, DW I, 387.9–12; Sermon 6, DW I, 106.5 (here, we read that we do all of God's works "with God," *bî gote*, in the same way the Word is "with" God—that is, in the most intimate and unifying way). Less frequently, Eckhart describes this working with God as truly living life: "For your works to live, God must touch you in the innermost part of the soul if they are to live. For there is your life and there alone you live" (Sermon 39, DW II, 259.6–260.1). Finally, our works "live" if "we act within God's kingdom" (Oliver Davies, *Meister Eckhart: Selected Writings* [London: Penguin, 1994], 250–51; see also Jostes manuscript 82, forthcoming in DW IV.2 as Sermon 117).

177 Eckhart, Sermon 40, DW II, 278.8–9.

178 Eckhart, Sermon 70, DW III, 194.14–195.4.

with God, but my identity does not yield to God's. The individual soul does not dissolve into God like a drop of wine in the ocean (a popular metaphor whose shortcomings Eckhart often points out). Instead, Eckhart uses the language of ownership and property, saying that what is his is mine and that this ownership is not partial or incomplete. Perhaps the most extreme example of this rhetoric is found in Sermon 52, *Beati pauperes spiritu*:

> In God's being itself where God is above being and beyond distinction, there I myself was, there I willed myself and came to know myself in creating this man. Therefore, I am the cause of myself on account of my being, which is eternal, and not after my being born, which is temporal. And therefore I am unborn, and after the way of my being unborn so I may never be destroyed. According to the way of my being unborn, I am eternally existing, I am now and eternally will be. . . . In my birth, all things came to be born and I was the cause of myself and of all things; and had I wished, I would not be, nor would all things be.[179]

Here, Eckhart gives us the most paradoxical conclusion of his creating with God: I create myself. This clearly strains our notion of self. We imagine only with great difficulty what it might mean for us to have God in the innermost ground of the soul. Seeing all the various implications is most helpful since it helps us in the process of thinking through a particular idea. This is part of his rhetoric's ability to guide thought. Just as we do not desire what we do not know is desirable, we may not be savvy enough with a new idea to think it all the way through without someone helping us to see what all the implications are.

THE PARADOX OF HUMANITY: THE INTERSECTION OF TIME AND ETERNITY

Man lives at the intersection of time and eternity, Eckhart claims: "The soul was created at the border between time and eternity, and she is touching both. With the highest power she touches eternity. With the lowest power she touches time."[180] Though "all creatures are either body or spirit," Eckhart tells us, "man has two natures: body and spirit."[181] The soul participates in

---

[179] Eckhart, Sermon 52, DW II, 502.7–503.4, 503.6–504.1.

[180] Eckhart, Sermon 47, DW II, 404.3–405.2. In one of the most unusual passages, Eckhart refers obliquely to Prometheus: "Now one may ask: What does our Lord mean when he says, 'Where I am, my servant will be with me'? Perhaps he means that God wants to steal something from God that he wants to impart to the soul" (Sermon 98, DW IV.1, 242.33–243.1).

both but with different faculties. As spiritual, the soul "must pour out into the body."[182] Thus Eckhart uses both sides of his metaphors to speak about man. He makes this explicit: "although the inner man is seen with the outer man in the same place, they are yet more distant from each other than the highest heaven is from the center of the earth, just as heat and form are distant from the substance of fire."[183] They are opposed like form and manifestation, universal and temporal. Still, they comprise the same individual soul.

God and the soul are ostensibly incompatible as creator and created: "Light and darkness cannot coexist, nor can God and creature. If God goes in, the creature must go out at the same time."[184] And so, he asks, "How can the soul undergo God being stamped onto her without dying? I say: everything that he gives her, he gives to her within himself."[185] The soul is not "crushed" and can endure it because God gives himself as himself and the soul endures it in God and not in herself.

For Eckhart, the soul as divine is above both knowledge and love. The rhetoric of love and knowledge applies to the soul insofar as it is created. Eckhart uses the word "compassion" to describe the activity of detached love that is ordered by reason. He tells us that "beyond these two, knowledge and love, is compassion. God works compassion in the highest and purest acts that God can work."[186] This happens in a mind that is well-ordered, meaning one that is governed by reason: "We therefore are compassionate like the Father, not from passion, not from impulse, but when we are compassionate from deliberate choice and the command of reason."[187] Compassion therefore is a deliberate, willed choice that is the province of the intellect.

We should notice that the confluence of the extremes where the ends meet has the effect of not allowing us to identify man only with one side. Since mankind inhabits all points of the continuum, Eckhart does not simply cast aside certain parts of human existence as evil. Importantly, Eckhart thinks that even the lower faculties can be attuned so that they become more receptive to God. This attunement amounts to their being ordered according to reason. Eckhart describes the well-ordered soul as being like an army, with

---

181 Eckhart, *On the Nobleman*, DW V, 109.9–10; 109.7–8.
182 Eckhart, Sermon 107, DW IV.2, 722.15–723.1.
183 Eckhart, Sermon XXII, LW IV, 193.3–5.
184 Eckhart, Sermon 102, DW IV.1, 413.44.
185 Eckhart, Sermon 47, DW II, 408.3–5.
186 Eckhart, Sermon 7, DW I, 123.3–5.
187 Eckhart, Sermon XII, LW IV, 128.10–11.

higher reason in command.[188] Also like an army that has a common goal, the powers "all desire peace, and therefore they all help one other."[189] In ordering the soul according to reason, "the soul's six powers, both the higher and lower powers, must each have a golden ring, gilded with the gold of divine love."[190] This way of thinking enables Eckhart to identify problems like concupiscence as failures of attunement, not ones inherent in the power of desire.[191] This way of thinking allows Eckhart to elevate the value of embodied human existence in general. It cannot rise to the level of the divine since the lower powers cannot be made receptive like the highest power can. Nevertheless, they can be well-ordered and facilitate a life that is governed by the highest power. By consequence, God's will flows through the highest power and the lower powers are still moved (recall that even Christ and the saints are moved), but this does not result in suffering and distress.

The crucial consequence of this for the development of the modern individual is that the valuation of the embodied individual as a whole is elevated. This allows human life, even in its most prosaic forms, to be considered valuable. Once we look more closely at Eckhart's revaluation of natural knowledge, we will see that his rhetoric of the individual very much speaks to what was to come in the development of modern thought. Eckhart's account of detachment is perhaps the clearest sign of this. All that we do in external actions and have within us in our powers can be attuned to God and become well-ordered and receptive of the divine so long as we are detached. This single insight clears the way for the ennobling of all human interior and exterior life, since detachment can coexist with any aspect of them. If individual life generally is worthwhile by dint of God's love and blessedness, does this not imply that even sin rises in value too? Not for Eckhart. Though he does

---

188 Eckhart, Sermon 31, DW II, 122.3–4. This is a twist on Plato's metaphor of the charioteer with two horses, a good one and a bad one that may be set to order with reason.

189 Eckhart, Sermon 31, DW II, 122.6. This is a peculiar comparison since he pairs peace with an army. There is a certain concord follows from a fixed hierarchy, however, since each part serves a definite function and does not create strife by competing with the other parts. This seems to be the kind of *vride* (peace, tranquility, serenity) that Eckhart has in mind.

190 Eckhart, Sermon 83, DW III, 444.2–4. The six powers of the soul include the three lower powers of 1) making distinctions, 2) anger, and 3) desire, as well as the three higher powers of 1) memory (Father), 2) intellect (Son), and 3) will (Holy Spirit).

191 See Eckhart, *Commentary on Exodus*, ns.210, 214. Here, we should perhaps think of the Ancient Greek notion of *harmonia* and Aristotle's notion of *sophrosyne* in particular. We might also think of Origen's comments on *eros* and how we might just as well say that God is *eros*, as discussed on p. 39.

say that *knowledge* of sin is valuable, sin is opposed to detachment. Sin is a mistake in desire, a result of lower powers that are not properly attuned and desire worldly things instead of higher goods.[192] Sin puts us at a distance from God through attachment to worldly things. Although this is obvious for those intimately familiar with his thought, much to Eckhart's frustration, the risk of superficial misinterpretation certainly existed.

RHETORIC OF THE INDIVIDUAL

The paradox of being God and man is strengthened and even made more intense in Eckhart because he does not allow humanity to fall away into divinity. Being human remains all the way to God and the soul remains all the way to the Godhead. We have human nature in common with Christ, who divinized it by being both man and God. Thus, what is human remains all the way to God. What we can say about God when we say "God" can be applied to what is human in us as well. Eckhart describes the individual in the same way that he describes Christ.[193] Insofar as I participate in humanity, which is the same as Christ's humanity and was divinized by him, I am, like him, the image of God. This is the Platonic relation of a temporal individual manifesting an eternal Form and owing its being to that Form and remaining identical with it insofar as it manifests it. For Plato, the soul has the capacity for wisdom in that it can ascend to the realm of the gods by understanding the Forms. Eckhart tells us that in contrast to "the way in which Plato argues for the immortality of the soul since it has the capacity for wisdom," we should see "how much greater the soul is than even that, for it has the capacity for God."[194] Thus, Eckhart takes this further by also talking about the individual breaking through to the Godhead, so as to erase all distinctions and even the possibility of distinctions. Contrary to the typical philosophical rhetoric on the topic, this does not represent a significant break from Plato, the Neoplatonists, and Pseudo-Dionysius. Each expressed mysticism in terms of the notion of the individual that was current when they were writing. Despite the Godhead being the ground (*grunt*) of God and being beyond all distinction

---

[192] Eckhart, Sermon 63, DW III, 79.2–3.

[193] Matthew Fox says that "he deliberately and consciously copies the style of Jesus' sayings" (*Breakthrough*, 219). In other words, not only does Eckhart elevate the individual (which manifests in his rhetoric); he also intentionally mimics Christ's own rhetoric to make the elevation of the individual even clearer. See the discussion of particles (in, through, from, with) starting on p. 147.

[194] Eckhart, Sermon XXIV.2, LW IV, 229.5–7.

and non-distinction (or the more Eckhartian "indistinction"), Eckhart still speaks of the soul as "breaking through" (*durchbrechen*) to the divine ground using the personal language of the soul's activity. To be human is to be distinct from what is not human and cannot reach divine oneness. The soul, however, continues all the way to the Godhead. This is why Eckhart's move is so beautifully modern: we do not have to think of completely emptying ourselves to reach the divine ground because his notion of the individual paradoxically includes oneness.

At the same time, being individual specifically involves denying what we normally consider to be individual: "Be careful not to take yourself in the slightest as you are this person or the next. Rather, take yourself according to free, undivided human nature."[195] As we have seen, this principle results in rhetorical novelty and some of Eckhart's most shocking rhetoric. Others who wrote around Eckhart's time, like Thomas Aquinas, leave us with the distinct impression that the individual has certain set limits and that mystery is largely the province of the divine. Eckhart, by contrast, uses very personal rhetoric even when describing the soul insofar as it is divine: "Intellect looks in and breaks through every nook of the Godhead and takes the Son in the heart of the Father and in the ground and places him in its ground."[196] The description of looking around, taking something, and placing it somewhere strongly implies personal agency and responsibility on the part of the one performing the actions. None of this description implies passivity.

The rhetoric turns on Eckhart's contention that the soul is not limited to what is created: "I say that there is something above the soul's created nature. Some priests do not understand that there is something that is so akin to God and so one with God."[197] The difficulty that many probably had with this rhetoric is that it implies that the individual remains individual in becoming God, which seems to imply that the individual is God. It is understandable that someone could get this impression: "If I am to know God without an intermediary, then 'I' must become 'he' and 'he' must become 'I.' I say more: God must become 'I' and 'I' must become God, as completely one that this 'he' and this 'I' become and are one 'is' in the eternal is-ness act in one activity."[198] He qualifies this, however, by saying that as soon as anything temporal enters,

---

195 Eckhart, Sermon 46, DW II, 382.3–4.
196 Eckhart, Sermon 69, DW III, 178.3–179.2.
197 Eckhart, Sermon 29, DW II, 88.5–7.
198 Eckhart, Sermon 83, DW III, 447.3–6.

there can be no oneness. The difficulty that remains is trying to conceive of a soul that is at once temporal and created while also being divine and eternal. In other words, the difficulty in understanding Eckhart's notion of the individual is the *same* difficulty that people who heard about Christ in the first centuries had in trying to understand how he could be man and God.

This results in some of Eckhart's surprising exegeses. In Sermon 16b, Eckhart reverses the usual sense of Matthew 11:27. Instead of the usual reading of knowledge of God being reserved for the Son alone and not for individuals, Eckhart points to it as a passage that shows us the way to divine knowledge.[199] Since the self can become the Son, Eckhart can elegantly endorse the same passage with a very different meaning.

In each case, Eckhart's individual does not yield as it ascends. He tells us that "we will become knowledgeable with divine knowledge and will be ennobled and adorn our unknowing with supernatural knowledge."[200] That "we" come to divine knowledge tells us that even though God is beyond knowledge, He is not beyond the soul. We hear as well that our "putting on" Christ is done with the passive form of the verb, indicating that it happens passively within.[201] This happens within because God is not something external. In a passage that helps to explain his justification for elevating individuals qua human, Eckhart explains, "since I am the same kind [as Christ] according to humanity, I am so united to his individual being that by grace I am one in his individual being and I am that individual being."[202]

The soul's ascent involves detaching from all that is dualistic in the soul: "If there were neither time nor place nor anything else, all would be one being."[203] Eckhart explains this more fully:

---

199 Milem, *Unspoken Word*, 102n15. Milem may overstate the original passage's exclusion of humanity from knowledge of God. It does allow for the Son to reveal the Father and his knowledge to those whom he chooses. Nevertheless, the point about how Eckhart reverses the usual interpretation, just as he does in other places, is well taken.

200 Eckhart, Sermon 102, DW IV.1, 420.132–33.

201 Eckhart, Sermon LII, LW IV, 437.12.

202 Eckhart, Sermon 67, DW III, 135.9–11.

203 Eckhart, Sermon 44, DW II, 3–4. Compare these statements to the following: "He who is nowhere, who, I say, is not tied down by love of any place, homeland or household, is really everywhere. He who is not affected by any particular created being is thus in all things" (Eckhart, *Commentary on John*, n.112, trans. McGinn in *Essential Eckhart*, 165). This touches on the more practical aspect of how love figures into being everywhere and being in all things.

> If you take away the now of time, you are everywhere and you have all time. This or that being is not all things, for so long as I am this and that or have this and that, I am not all things and I do not have all things. Detach yourself from being this and that and having this and that, and you are all things and have all things. Further, you are neither here nor there, so you are everywhere. Further still, you are neither this nor that, so you are all things.[204]

Notice again that the subject is still "you," despite being this or that. This points to a nondualistic and thus paradoxical notion of the individual and the highest reaches of reason. We simply cannot think through this using our habitual mode of thought. As we ascend through the lower faculties to the higher ones, this kind of rhetoric is appropriate to reaching the extreme, since the self itself is problematized, along with time and space and all possible modes of thought. The soul should be ordered, Eckhart tells us, so that what is superior is above and governs what is inferior, with each superior touching its inferior. The continuum of superior and inferior in the soul is the same as it is for being in general, where the more universal is likewise the superior. With this in mind, consider the statement, "What is outside time is always universal; what is without body and matter is everywhere."[205] The higher reason works with what is more universal. It is thus outside time by way of its abstractions, which push toward what is most universal.[206] Thus, Eckhart naturally concludes that those who leave themselves and all worldly things "truly possess all things."[207] That is, if the soul abides in higher reason, in her ground with the spark, then she abides in God himself. Eckhart even bends scriptural passages in this fashion: "Saint Philip said when our Lord spoke of his Father, 'Lord, show us your Father, and that will satisfy us,'[208] as if he said that seeing him would have been enough for him. We would have far greater satisfaction in nearness to him."[209] In other words, the scriptural metaphor of "seeing" for "knowing" is not strong enough for Eckhart because

---

204 Eckhart, Sermon 77, DW III, 336.1–6.

205 Eckhart, *Book on the Parables of Genesis*, n.162, trans. McGinn in *Essential Eckhart*, 120.

206 Note the similarity in this description to what we see in Plato himself. The ultimate goal with Plato was the contemplation of the Good, the most universal form that enabled all of the other forms to be what they were. Also like Plato, Eckhart moves up a sliding scale of being, where the most universal also has the most being.

207 Eckhart, Sermon 42, DW II, 306.4–5.

208 Jn 14:8.

209 Eckhart, Sermon 58, DW II, 614.6–615.2.

it indicates something temporary and possibly external. He prefers the more permanent "dwelling" or "abiding," which make the soul at home in God.

Eckhart describes the dynamic at work here as follows: "Fellowship with the body prevents the soul from understanding as clearly as the angels can. However, to the extent that we understand without material things, we are angelic."[210] In addition, Eckhart tells us that "a limit has been set [for the highest angels] beyond which they cannot go. The soul can indeed go beyond it."[211] The angels are wholly spiritual and immaterial, as is reason which trades only in universals.[212] The soul can go beyond this, reaching beyond the grasp of the angels by moving into her ground. Eckhart speaks of that ground in the same way he speaks the Godhead: "Know now that all our perfection and all our bliss lie in man going through and going beyond all createdness and all temporality and all being and going into the groundless ground."[213] Here again, Eckhart tells us that the "individual" goes beyond everything and goes into the ground. This implies that the individual soul somehow remains individual throughout, even after shedding the worldly self. Thus, Eckhart writes, "if I were empty and had a fiery inner love and likeness, I would draw God entirely into me."[214] Though paradoxical, the idea is coherent since the soul is both temporal and divine, both God and man. We might therefore expect rhetoric that parallels the soul with Christ, since they have similar status. This is precisely what we find: Eckhart quotes John 14:11, "I am in the Father and the Father is in me," and comments "So then, God is in the soul and the soul is in God."[215] The scriptural passage is spoken by Christ. Eckhart applies it to the soul, with the subtle implication that the soul is like Christ. Thus, we may not be surprised to see statements like this: "If you want to know God, then you should not only be like the Son—you should be the Son himself."[216]

Eckhart, however, does not completely identify the soul with Christ. Although one could be forgiven having that impression (since most of his rhetoric appears to emphasize just this idea), at one point he does address

---

210 Eckhart, Sermon 23, DW I, 408.1–409.1.

211 Eckhart, Sermon 1, DW I, 13.5–6.

212 Eckhart has this in mind when describing the four levels of being (*Commentary on John*, n.83). He places angelic intellect above human intellect because human intellect is still attached to materiality.

213 Eckhart, Sermon 42, DW II, 309.3–5.

214 Eckhart, Sermon 31, DW II, 124.4.

215 Eckhart, Sermon 59, DW II, 635.2–3.

216 Eckhart, Sermon 16b, DW I, 273.5–6.

the difference: "There is no difference between the soul and our Lord Jesus Christ, except that the soul has a coarser being. For his being is by the eternal person. To the extent that the soul renounces coarseness—let her renounce it completely!—so then is she completely the same. Then all that one can say about our Lord Jesus Christ, one can say about the soul."[217] The soul's temporal aspect prevents her from being Christ without qualification (i.e., without an "insofar as"). Eckhart essentially says here that if the soul could divest herself of herself insofar as she is worldly, then she would be Christ. Eckhart explains this dynamic elsewhere: "As the inner man loses the distinctive existence that he has according to the kind of living thing he is, he becomes one ground in the [divine] ground. So too must the outer man be robbed of his own support and entirely take hold of the support of the eternal personal being."[218] So while we are told to be dead to the body and to deny all worldly things, the soul remains embodied in part and thus the "insofar as she is worldly" portion endures. Of course, it is not hard to imagine Eckhart responding that God would have had no reason to create the soul if it were simply God.

Thus, we hear of Paul's being taken up to the third heaven, "He was enraptured insofar as he was a spirit. He remained insofar as he was a soul."[219] For Eckhart, the soul remains a part of the world even when it is enraptured. With respect to this vision of God,[220] Eckhart says, "Does the spirit have no vision of God in the eternal life? Yes and no. Insofar as it is born, it does not look up and see God. But insofar as it is being born, it has a vision of God."[221] He responds with an "insofar as" qualification which refers to the soul's life here and now.

217 Eckhart, Sermon 59, DW II, 632.3–7.
218 Eckhart, Sermon 67, DW III, 134.17–135.3.
219 Eckhart, Sermon 23, DW I, 405.9–10. The phrase does not translate easily, even into modern German. One is tempted to say, "He was enrapt according to his spirit-ness, he remained according to his soul-ness," or "according to his being a soul," which is similar to Quint's rendering, "Er ward verzückt nach seinem Geist-Sein, er blieb nach seinem Seele-Sein." Nevertheless, Paul "remained insofar as he was a soul," which makes the desired point. Further, the Eckhartian "insofar as" may be most appropriate here if *nâch* is indeed his vernacular version of the Latin *in quantum*.
220 The beatific vision, about which there was so much controversy during Eckhart's lifetime and shortly afterward for Pope John XXII.
221 Eckhart, Sermon 39, DW II, 265.3–6. Here, ûfsehen could mean either to "look up" or experience a "furor," a strong emotional surge. As Eckhart is talking about bliss and also about vision, it is not clear which connotation is most desirable, though "looking up" is perhaps better since it implies a directing of attention toward higher things, which makes it a metaphor for spiritual ascent.

Eckhart focuses upon and presses upon the rhetorical detail of the individual remaining individual. As he says in one passage, "When the will is united that it becomes one single one, the Father bears from heaven his only-begotten Son in himself in me. Why in himself in me? Since I am one with him, he cannot leave me out. In that act, the Holy Spirit receives his being and his becoming from me the same as he does from God."[222] Eckhart leaves little space for confusion about whether or not the individual persists in this dynamic. There are several potentially radical aspects of this: the individual soul can reach God Himself; this can be done in this life (with the insofar as qualification); and the individual remains individual throughout. As we saw before with Sermon 52, Eckhart brings together all of these implications there where he says that "I am the cause of myself." Bruce Milem talks about the important shifts in meaning of "I" in this passage.[223] However, this would allow Eckhart to wiggle out of the implication that the same individual soul is intended throughout, which as we have seen is not what he wants to do. Eckhart often insists (via chiasmus and various reformulations the same phrase) that the appearance of such personal pronouns is no accident. On one occasion, for instance, we find "He gives birth to me not only as his Son, but rather, he gives birth to me and me to him, and to me as his being and his nature. In the innermost wellspring, I gush forth in the Holy Spirit."[224] If Eckhart intended the meaning of the pronouns to be different, then his rhetorical strategy seems to push in the opposite direction by emphasizing their uniformity and stamping out any possibility of accident through repetition. Indeed, we might come to a very different conclusion: Eckhart uses "soul" and "I" interchangeably in his rhetoric to refer to the individual soul, even when the soul is considered insofar as it is divine. As McGinn rightly recognizes, we never know if Eckhart is referring to God, the soul, or both, which "is exactly what Eckhart had in mind."[225]

---

[222] Eckhart, Sermon 25, DW II, 11.1–4.
[223] Milem, *Unspoken Word*, 43.
[224] Eckhart, Sermon 6, DW I, 109.9–11.
[225] McGinn, *Mystical Thought of Meister Eckhart*, 49.

7

Metaphors and the Development of Modern Thought

Two main aspects of Eckhart's thought helped lay the groundwork for the development of the modern worldview. First, as we see especially with the nominalists, the compression of the hierarchy of beings enables a reconceptualization of what man is and how people can work creatively. Though Eckhart's thought is tightly intertwined with the medieval view of the cosmos, he plants the seeds for the compression of the hierarchy with respect to the individual, even if the hierarchy itself ostensibly remains intact. Second, the practical focus of Eckhart's theology on individual attainment fits well with the more pragmatic and individualistic modern approach to religion. These considerations will conclude our study of Eckhart's rhetoric and prepare us for reflection on the relevance of Eckhart's thought to the contemporary world.

COMPRESSION OF THE HIERARCHY

In a move that points directly to the collapsing of hierarchical levels, Eckhart says, "The thought came to me last night that God's highness depends on my lowliness; by my lowering myself, God will be raised.... What's more, I thought last night that God should be brought down, not in all but in me. I liked this 'God brought down' so much that I wrote it in my book."[1] We

---

[1] Eckhart, Sermon 14, DW I, 237.3–5, 6–8.

might rightly think of Cicero's comment that Socrates was the first to bring philosophy down from the heavens, signaling the beginning of the thought that what was once inaccessible and divine was now attainable.[2] Readers of Blumenberg might also think of Galileo's similar attempt to raise the Earth to be a star among stars, even if it effectively brought the stars down to Earth.[3] This "bringing down" of God corresponds to the leveling of the celestial hierarchy *within the individual*.[4] Eckhart's metaphor of the sphere collapsing into a circle and bringing the pole and center together applies here, with the qualification that the pole falls instead of the center rising.[5] Eckhart explains further, "What was above is now within. You should go inside yourself, from yourself and within yourself so that he comes to be in you. Not that we take from what is above us, but that we should take into us, and from us into us."[6] Though we see Eckhart use a full-fledged medieval cosmos with regard to the rest of the created world, the soul contains in itself all levels of being since she is herself *capax dei*, capable of God.[7] The hierarchy thereby becomes a continuum of progress for the individual soul within the individual soul.

Another metaphor for collapsing the hierarchy is that of breaking the shell. We encounter this metaphor in Sermon 13: "The foot of the highest sits on the head of the lowest. All creatures do not touch God according to their createdness. Their createdness is what must be broken for the good to come out. The shell must be split in two for the kernel to come out. This

---

[2] Eckhart, *Tusculanae Disputationes*, V.4.

[3] Blumenberg, *Paradigms for a Metaphorology* 107.

[4] This is how Eckhart understands the old theological claim that "it is as true that man became God as it is true that God became man" (Sermon 46, DW II, 380.5–381.1). This claim always had overtones of man's divinization and his being raised up to God or God being brought down to man. Eckhart simply presses this point and brings all its implications into the light of day with his more developed notion of the individual soul and its "spark."

[5] The consequent feeling of loss for us may be because we intuitively sense that the individual is less than God. As Eckhart might say, if we are still attached to what is created within us instead of living as detached individuals who are one with the divinity that has always been there, the idea of having the individual as the center can be disconcerting. In speaking of Galileo's attempt to elevate the earth, Blumenberg describes it as "sobering" rather than joyous. For Eckhart, the collapsing of the hierarchy and loss of all possible purpose is cause for celebration since it elevates the individual to divine joy. Blumenberg, along with most modern thinkers, conceived of the loss of divine providence as a disorienting unmooring from all possibilities for meaning in life. He does not consider the "solution" offered by mystics like Eckhart. Eckhart solves the problem of purpose by an evanescence of the problem. God needs no "why" in his absolute oneness and neither do we once we strip away createdness and return to unity with the divine.

[6] Eckhart, Sermon 14, DW I, 237.9–12.

[7] Eckhart, Sermon XXIV.2, LW IV, 229.6.

all means a growing out."⁸ In this case, the hierarchy is present, but must be broken through like the shell of a nut so that we may get to the kernel. Most creatures cannot rise above their station because they lack the higher intellect that would allow them to see and desire what is higher, thereby lifting them up above themselves to what is more universal. Thus, as we saw before, "If a piece of wood knew God and apprehended how near to it he is, as the highest angel knows it, then the piece of wood would be as blessed as the highest angel."⁹ This is why "even the lowliest creature in God possesses his great sovereignty."¹⁰ Since Eckhart departs from Aquinas and others in his theory of analogy and insists that the transcendentals belong to God alone, he can assert that created things are divine insofar as they manifest the transcendental qualities of being, truth, justice, and the like. Thus, his theory of analogy contains an implicit compression of the hierarchy—with the crucial qualification "insofar as."

We see this as well in his insistence that these things happen "without intermediaries." Eckhart tells us that all beings have their transcendental qualities (being, truth, unity, and goodness) directly from God without an intermediary, but they do not know it.¹¹ God is "brought down" to the entire material world, nut only man has the capacity to become aware of this and see God in all things. This ultimately paves the way for valorizing natural knowledge and man's role in creating it with God.

ECKHART'S COSMOS

Eckhart lived in a distinctly medieval cosmos. This increases the contrast between the medieval and modern elements in his thought. If his both cosmology and conception of approximate knowledge were broadly modern, we might simply conclude that he is more modern than medieval. Instead, however, what we see is a traditional cosmology with rational individuals who straddle the line between ephemeral and eternal in a decidedly different way

---

8 Eckhart, Sermon 13, DW I, 212.2–6.

9 Eckhart, Sermon 68, DW III, 142.4–5.

10 Eckhart, Sermon 52, DW II, 493.4. As Walshe notes, *rîcheit* has many meanings, including wealth, sovereignty, power, and so on (*Complete Mystical Works of Meister Eckhart*, 425n8). This is perhaps why we see quite different translations of this passage in Davies and Colledge. All of these meanings amount to the same thing, though. Even the lowest creature has God's greatness within it. I opted for a rendering that including the connotation of rank and highness, while making clear that it is from God and within God that the creature has it.

11 Eckhart, *Prologue to the Book of Propositions*, LW I.1, 44.6-9.

than they did in the ancient world. We might even be forgiven for wondering if the changing notion of the individual spurred more wholesale changes in worldview that were recognizably modern.

Eckhart saw a clear hierarchy of elements which descended down from the heavens to fire, air, water, and earth. The earth is at the center and the cosmos consists of concentric spheres, with each of the outer spheres moving progressively faster and corresponding to the higher elements. Causality moves from superior to inferior, with superior things being unaffected by the exchange.[12] Effects are present virtually but not formally in their causes. This implies, for example, that the sun is not hot, because heat is in it virtually but not formally.[13] Consequently, lower things receive from their superiors the things that they.[14] By extension, God possesses all things virtually but not formally. Thus, God is not good because he is above goodness.[15] To call God "good" would demean him.[16] God precontains all things virtually and in unity, a dynamic that applies to all levels. Higher things contain many lower things virtually without disrupting their unity. The universe with all its parts proceeds from God as a unity without disturbing his unity.[17] This is why all of the transcendentals, including being, are prior to things rather than in addition to them.[18]

All things desire to return to God. Therefore, their natural motion, metaphorically described as "desire," tends upward. Higher elements lift lower things up; for instance, because the moon is higher than water, it can cause the tides by causing water to flow uphill, contrary to its nature.[19] Eckhart explores the extreme of this: "If a man could and knew how to make a cup completely empty and keep it empty of all things that can fill it, even of air, then without doubt the cup would give up and forget all its nature, and its barren emptiness would lift it up to heaven."[20] The metaphors here, "forgoing"

---

12 Eckhart, *Commentary on John*, n.91.

13 Eckhart, *Commentary on Exodus*, n.123. For example, the ideas of things are virtually present in the mind of God. God is not a manifestation of those things, so the ideas are not formally present in him. Heat is ontologically below the station of the sun. The sun is not hot because the idea of heat is in it *virtually*. Hot things are informed by the idea of heat and thus have heat *formally*.

14 Eckhart, *In Ex.* n.262.

15 Eckhart, Sermon 83, DW III, 441.4.

16 Eckhart, Sermon 9, DW I, 148.6–7. We have no words for what God is, so we speak of God through the "veil of goodness" (*velamen veri*), the "veil of truth" (*velamen boni*), and the "veil of being itself" (*velamen ipsius esse*) (Eckhart, Sermon XI.2, LW IV, 114.4–6).

17 Eckhart, *Commentary on Genesis*, n.3.

18 Eckhart, *General Prologue*.

19 Eckhart, *Book of Divine Consolation*, §2, DW V, 45.6–10.

20 Eckhart, *Book of Divine Consolation*, §2, DW V, 30.5–8.

and "forgetting," are used in service of his general point that being empty of created things lifts the soul to God.[21] Thus the dynamics of the physical world are the same as the dynamics of the soul. That is, the soul lives in a consistent world, where the physics of material things are not divorced from the dynamics of spiritual things. This straightforwardly follows from the fact that Eckhart's cosmos represents a sliding scale of being, like Plato's divided line in the *Republic*. Natural and supernatural are utterly different for Eckhart, but they are not utterly *separate*. Nowhere is this more clearly the case than in the soul, which is both spiritual and corporeal in all ways.

NATURAL KNOWLEDGE AND CURIOSITY

Since Eckhart advocates the life of action and insists that we never cease to be moved by earthly things, does this also make curiosity about the natural world and the pursuit of natural knowledge a viable option? It does, but only in a qualified sense. Since being is the perfection of things, metaphysics investigates created things as well, insofar as they have being.[22] Since God is present in all things in whole, the metaphysician still justifiably investigates even material things without losing sight of the highest.

Since natural knowledge was not something Eckhart focused much on, we must infer from various fragments what he might have thought. His take on it appears to be largely traditional. For instance, "the known object begets itself or its species and gives birth in the knowing power. The begotten species is one common offspring in the object known and in the knowing power, as Augustine says."[23] This is at least similar to Aquinas's *adaequatio intellectus ad rem*, the match of the intellect to the thing. For example, Eckhart refers to "a kind of equivalence of thing and intellect" (*quaedam adaequatio rei et intellectus*) with regard to "the true" (*Verum*).[24] Indeed, for Eckhart, to know a common object is to have an *image* of it. As we will see, although Eckhart insists upon the need for the soul to be purified of images (e.g., Sermon 2), to live at all is to necessarily be involved with images of this sort, which provide a certain motion in the mind. This motion does not need to be a hindrance to the soul, however, so long as it is marked by detachment. Eckhart advocates philosophical speculation that is useful for advancing one spiritually. It is

21 Eckhart, *Book of Divine Consolation*, §2, DW V, 30.8–9.
22 Eckhart, *General Prologue*, LW I.1, 37.8–12.
23 Eckhart, *Commentary on John*, n.109, trans. McGinn in *Essential Eckhart*, 163.
24 Eckhart, *Commentary on John*, n.562, LW III, 490.1.

important for us to notice that the Eckhart does not exclude the pursuit of worldly learning and scientific curiosity, so long as these are pursued with detachment. In fact, such learning may even be in the service of spiritual advancement so long as it is *useful*. It is telling that Eckhart did not follow in the footsteps of Albertus Magnus in this regard and do his own investigation of the natural world. Nevertheless, Eckhart leaves the door for such things wide open. As he put it:

> Can there not be creaturely knowledge in me that does not hinder me in any way, just as God knows all things without hindrance, just as the saints do as well? This is a useful question. Now pay attention to this explanation! The saints see a single image in God and know all things in this image.... [God] has no need to turn from one thing to another as we need to do. In this life, if we could see and know all things in a single image in one glance in a mirror before us, then neither actions nor knowledge would hinder us. However, since we must turn from one to another, we cannot think of one without hindrance to the other.[25]

There can be natural knowledge without hindrance, but only insofar as we see all things in a single image which is the divine oneness in all things.[26] Ultimately, this is not entirely clear. It seems that we can pursue knowledge of individual things so long as we see them in a single image—that is, as God sees them. However, it seems that we cannot pursue such knowledge without turning from one thing to another and thus descending into multiplicity. As Eckhart explains in the sermon, this is because the soul must flow with the powers for them to work at all, but this can bring the soul down. The soul must remove this encumbrance by divine unknowing, which Eckhart describes ironically as knowing. Of course, this problematizes the idea of "knowing." As usual, Eckhart tells us that something is impossible (a soul that knows without being hindered) only to immediately contrast it with the opposite claim (that the soul can have unhindered knowing if it is transformed by divine unknowing). As always, Eckhart's ultimate concern

---

25 Eckhart, Sermon 102, DW IV.1, 417.99–418.105.

26 My reading of this is informed by Eckhart's explanation of Matthew 25:21 in Sermon 64. Eckhart interprets this passage as moving from multiplicity to a unity that transcends all the multiplicitous things, but still contains them: "Now I take a passage, spoken by our Lord: 'Go in, faithful servant, I will put you above all my *good*.' This is understood in three ways. The first way: 'I will put you up above all my *good*,' as 'all my *good*' is spread out in creatures: over the fragmentation, I will put you in oneness. The second way: as it is all united into one, I will put you over the union in oneness, as all good is in oneness. The third way: I will put you in the nature of oneness, where all 'uniting' is taken away" (Sermon 64, DW III, 87.7–89.1).

remains with the individual soul's ascent to God. The question of natural knowledge is a peripheral concern, addressed in this sermon only with regard to whether or not it is a hindrance, not with regard to whether it is valuable in itself. Taking this passage alongside what he says in *On Detachment*, it seems fair to conclude that the pursuit of natural knowledge is not a hindrance for a person, provided that he or she remains detached.

Eckhart's practical concern provides another clue as to his take on the pursuit of natural knowledge. We should notice that he does not oppose any kind of intellectualism. He simply recognizes that some activities facilitate our return to God more productively than others.[27] As *On Detachment* makes abundantly clear, any external work is not valuable in itself, but only insofar as we have the proper interior disposition of detachment. We observe this when Eckhart compares hindrances to words written on a wax tablet: "If I want to write on a wax tablet, no matter how noble the things written on it are, they prevent me from writing on it."[28] Only our attachment to things is a hindrance, not our interaction with them or knowledge of them.

When Eckhart interprets the scriptural passage "I will set you over all my goods," he interprets this as God putting us in the source of blessedness in God himself, as well as "over everything that can be put into words and over everything that can be understood."[29] If we are higher than all things, then we rightly govern all things—that is, we provide order to them just as superior things provide order (*kosmos*) to their inferiors in the Platonic hierarchy. Not only does this sanction natural knowledge (since we are above all that anyone can understand); it also implies that all such knowledge is within us, if we consider man insofar as he is divine.

We have another hint from Eckhart that natural knowledge is valuable, though not for its own sake. He suggests that belief prepares us for knowledge by rushing ahead. As for Plato, this primes us for knowledge and motivates us to get the requisite experience. Knowledge similarly sets the stage for the creation of habit. Eckhart tells us that one master expresses disgust at the idea that anything that we hear or see should take up the space that God can fill. In response to this, he says that being involved with the senses is "a good preparation, and it will certainly help ... to awaken [*erwecket*]" the soul so that the "image of knowledge is naturally imprinted on her."[30] Here,

27 Cf. Fox, *Breakthrough*, 284.
28 Eckhart, *On Detachment*, DW V, 425.6–8.
29 Eckhart, Sermon 65, DW III, 101.5–7.
30 Eckhart, Sermon 36a, DW III, 192.5.

Eckhart explicitly speaks against the idea that we should only be concerned with divine things and give no attention to natural knowledge. In contrast, he says, natural knowledge acquaints us with the form of knowledge and thus prepares us for divine knowledge. At all points, even though Eckhart maintains a tight orbit around God and is perpetually focused on the divine, he does not disavow natural knowledge or in any way forbid pursuing it, especially if it is pursued with detachment.

ECKHART'S PRACTICAL THEOLOGY

Eckhart's theology is rooted in embodied life. This is why he is called a *Lebemeister* as well as a *Lesemeister*. By juxtaposing the most practical aspects and consequences of his thought, we see that Christianity itself—including its dogma, practices, and theology—was eminently practical for Eckhart. As an entrypoint, we will look at Eckhart's notion of living without a why and how it implies a practically focused theology. Next, we will see how other elements of his rhetoric contribute to this. The end result will be a vision of Christianity that has a decidedly different flavor from what we often encounter today, and indeed, what people in Eckhart's day were likely accustomed to as well.

In Eckhart's cosmos, all things have a 'why,' a reason for their existence and direction of their existence, as in Aristotelian teleology. As Eckhart expresses the idea,

> All things in time have a why. If you ask someone: "Why do you eat?"—"So that I have strength." "Why do you sleep?"—"For the same reason." And so it is with all things in time. But if you ask a good man, "Why do you love God?"—"I don't know. For God." "Why do you love truth?"—"For truth"; "Why do you love justice?"—"For justice." "Why do you love goodness?"—"For goodness." "Why do you live?"—"Truly, I don't know! I like living!"[31]

When we speak of life, we refer to being itself, which ultimately belongs only to God. For those things that belong to God alone, we should not be surprised that they do not have a why because "A master says: 'All things have a why, but God does not have a why.'"[32] If everything lives with a why except God and Eckhart recommends that we live without a why, he is recommending

---

[31] Eckhart, Sermon 26, DW II, 27.3–10; cf. Sermon 5b, DW I, 90.11–92.6; Sermon 27, DW II, 45.9–10; Sermon 29, DW II, 180.1–3; Sermon 39, DW II, 253.4–254.3, *Commentary on Exodus*, n.247.

[32] Eckhart, Sermon 59, DW II, 625.7–626.1. Frank Tobin tells us that this may be one of the cases where Eckhart refers to "a master" when he really means himself (McGinn, Tobin, and Borgstädt, *Teacher and Preacher*, 310n3). However, as John Connolly describes the history of the idea of

that we live as God does: "God and hence the divine man does not act for the sake of a why or wherefore."[33] Thus, while Eckhart has a largely Aristotelian teleological conception of the natural world, if man has an "end," then his end is God, for "Our Lord created man for this unity with himself."[34] Thus, at best, Eckhart is only ironically teleological with man, since his end is not an end. It is the erasure of all ends.

Among potential ends are ethical perfection in the virtues, love, and knowledge. Eckhart asks why love is not mentioned among the commandments. He answers that love is the goal of the commandments and not something to be commanded.[35] He further explains that arts always instruct us about means, not about ends.[36] They are *useful* as means, but ultimately the intended end lies outside of them. This must be the case, for Eckhart, because love is involuntary: "We love something so far as we find God in it. Even if I had sworn to do it, I could love nothing other than goodness."[37]

As with the ethical precepts, so too with love and knowledge. Eckhart says that we must surpass our senses: "Move forward, noble soul, put on your walking shoes, which are knowledge and love. Advance thereby above your powers and above your own knowledge ... and spring into the heart of God."[38] This metaphor complements the guiding metaphor of the sermon of "sitting" that is associated with divine repose. As for Aristotle, movement gets us there but is distinct from the end, which is repose. Of course, if love and knowledge are means, then so too are external works and devotional

---

living without a why, he mentions Beatrijs of Nazareth, who used the term and whose work was used by Hadewijch of Brabant and Marguerite Porete, both whom also used the idea (*Living without Why*, 207). Though it would be extraordinary if Eckhart were referring to any of these figures by saying "a master says," he probably was referring only to himself with this phrase, as he did on occasion. Given his connection with the Beguines in his area as part of the *cura monialem*, he would have probably been at least aware of others who used the same idea. The best reason we have for thinking Eckhart knew Porete in particular was that he stayed in the house of the chief inquisitor for Porete's trial in 1311, only one year after she was burned at the stake. Porete, of course, was probably not his source for the idea (if it is not his own) since Eckhart had been using the idea since his earliest work, the *Counsels on Discernment*, in 1294. The most we can conclude is that Eckhart's rhetoric would have left open the possibility that he was not just referring to himself by saying, "a master says."

33 Eckhart, Sermon IV.1, trans. McGinn in *Teacher and Preacher*, 207; cf. Sermon 41, Sermon 102.

34 Eckhart, Sermon 58, DW II, 616.3–4. Here we should see the contrast between this end and the end of man identified as the result of Aristotle's "function" (*ergon*) argument in the *Nicomachean Ethics* 1.7, 1097b24.

35 Eckhart, *Commentary on Exodus*, ns.94, 96.

36 Eckhart, *Commentary on Exodus*, n.95.

37 Eckhart, Sermon 41, DW II, 286.7–8.

38 Eckhart, Sermon 90a, DW IV.1, 68.156–163.

practices, for we have them "so as to catch a man and hold him back from foreign and ungodly things."[39] Shortly thereafter, he even calls such practices "most useful" as correctives.[40] This is because, on its own, "no work is good or holy or blessed."[41] Eckhart understands his approach as practical and focused on the utility of anything that can further our progress toward God: "We must indeed love the things that further our motion toward God. ... If I had the desire to cross the sea and if I wanted a ship, it would be solely because I wanted to cross the sea. As soon as I had crossed the sea, I would no longer need the ship."[42] Buddhists are likely to see a strong parallel between Eckhart's ship and the Parable of the Raft, which carries the same message. Is anything excluded from being a mere expedient?

Eckhart even advises us to give up practices that are not productive since they are not good in themselves. He gives the example of a simple layperson who knows only corporeal discipline and takes up a vow of prayer or something similar. If such a person moves closer to God without the vow, "let him be boldly free of it."[43] The message is clear: if something else works better, do that instead. If only the end matters, then the prescription will be for what is most useful. In a more extreme form, we read, "Whenever a man finds himself well-ordered to true inwardness, he may boldly let go of all externality and such disciplines, even of those where he is bound by vow, from which neither pope nor bishop can release him."[44] In light of this, consider the following statement, "All the gifts that he ever gave in heaven and on earth, he gave all so that he could give one gift: himself."[45] This may not seem shocking until we realize that the "gifts" include Scripture, the Mosaic Law, the Church, and so on. This accords with Eckhart's general principle: everything that God does is meant to bring us back to God. As he says, "He needs our blessedness so much that he lures us to him by any means, whether pleasant or unpleasant. God forbid that he ever permit anything that does not lure us to him."[46] All that happens is ultimately for our own good. This principle's foundation is likewise in utility.

---

39 Eckhart, Sermon 104a, DW IV.1, 603.460–2.

40 Eckhart, *Nützest* (Sermon 104a DW IV.1, 604.469); Sermon 104b has *nützlîchest*.

41 Eckhart, Sermon 105a, DW IV.1, 640.53–54.

42 Eckhart, Sermon 57, DW II, 602.3–6.

43 Eckhart, Sermon 104, DW IV.1, 607.532. This phrase does not appear in 104B, but a similar idea does.

44 Eckhart, Sermon 104, DW IV.1, 604.477–605.485.

45 Eckhart, *Counsels on Discernment*, §21, DW V, 278.16–279.1.

At all times, Eckhart is concerned with divine oneness. All rhetoric, ideas, dogma, Scripture, virtues, physics, and cosmology have this and only this one end: to push us usefully toward divine unity. With virtue, for example, Eckhart calls our perfections "the remedies and aids of the imperfection" and says that they would be "altogether useless if they were in and posited in God."[47] Our virtues and perfections are therefore merely *useful* for remedying imperfections, which amounts to removing hindrances to our ascent to God. In fact, Eckhart's account of virtue is close to Plotinus's notion of virtue as a likeness to the divine which enables one to avoid being hindered by the material world. Eckhart continues, "how can perfections be where they do not perfect and are of no advantage, but rather corrupt and make multiple?"[48] A few sections later, he tells us, "Only those things that are defective and are not able to be self-sustaining are multiplied and numbered."[49] Here, it seems that dogma generally may be included. If dogma is something "true," then we must consider it in light of statements like the following: "The term 'one' adds nothing beyond existence, not even conceptually, but only according to negation. This is not so in the case of 'true' and 'good.'"[50] What is true, therefore, is beneath God in multiplicity: "The True is begotten and not begetting, having its principle from another."[51] Eckhart has a high regard for truth, to be sure, but truth is beneath divine oneness: "Truth is also something added."[52] Eckhart values things that exist beneath divine oneness in terms of their practical utility in effecting our return to God, since they are all secondary to God's oneness.

Though this might sound outrageous so far (we are talking about Eckhart after all), let us now consider what he says about Christ. Surely, if anything in Christian dogma is too sacred to be spoken of in practical terms, it would be the Incarnation. Speaking of Christ's birth in a Christmas sermon, Eckhart says, "What does it help me if this birth is always happening and yet it does not happen in me? All that matters is that it happens in me."[53] Eckhart's statement that Christ's historical birth does not "help" (*hilfet*) me

---

[46] Eckhart, Sermon 73, DW III, 269.2–4.
[47] Eckhart, *Commentary on Exodus*, n.44, trans. McGinn in *Teacher and Preacher*, 57.
[48] Eckhart, *Commentary on Exodus*, n.44, trans. McGinn in *Teacher and Preacher*, 57.
[49] Eckhart, *Commentary on Exodus*, n.51, trans. McGinn in *Teacher and Preacher*, 59.
[50] Eckhart, *Commentary on Wisdom*,. n.148, trans. McGinn in *Teacher and Preacher*, 167.
[51] Eckhart, *Commentary on Exodus*, n.564, trans. McGinn in *Teacher and Preacher*, 188.
[52] Eckhart, Sermon 23, DW I, 401.5; cf. *Commentary on Exodus*, n.58.
[53] Eckhart, Sermon 101, DW IV.1, 336.4–5.

unless it takes place in me derives from a concern for practical utility.[54] If all of creation centers around man and God does everything to effect our return to him, then even Christ's birth, which might otherwise seem to be so lofty and above us, ultimately must be seen in terms of practical utility. Of course, this utility is not for us insofar as we are created, so much as it is a statement of the elevation of humanity generally and recognition of the individual soul insofar as she is divine.

Of course, this passage about the Incarnation is not an outlier. In the Latin works, Eckhart says, "It would be of little value for me that 'the Word was made flesh' for man in Christ as a person distinct from me unless he was also made flesh in me personally so that I too might be God's son."[55] Similarly, when speaking of Mary's grace, which is associated with the Immaculate Conception, Eckhart says, "What does it help me if Mary is 'full of grace' if I am not also 'full of grace'? What does it help me if the Father gives birth to his Son if I do not also give birth to him?"[56] At this point, it seems fair to conclude that nothing is off limits for Eckhart.

We also see this in Eckhart's discussion of Augustine's comments on finding much of Christianity in the books of the Platonists (those whom we generally call Neoplatonists). We may infer that Eckhart has a similarly high regard for the Neoplatonists and Plato in particular since Eckhart calls him "the great priest."[57] As Eckhart describes, Augustine tells us that he read much of the first chapter of the gospel of John in Plato.[58] This may be surprising to those not familiar with Augustine, since it impinges upon the question of the uniqueness of Christianity's message. Augustine mentioned a number of passages from John that he did not find in the Platonists' writings. Of course, Eckhart takes this further:

> But there is still good reason to say (always presupposing the historical truth of the text) that everything that is said here [in the prologue of the gospel of John], the whole verse, is contained in and taught by the properties of the things of nature, morality, and art. The word universally and

---

54 Eckhart, Sermon 101, DW IV.1, 336.5.
55 Eckhart, *Commentary on John*, n.117, LW III, 101.14–102.2.
56 Eckhart, Sermon 75, DW III, 300.7–301.2.
57 *der grôze pfaffe*, Eckhart, Sermon 28, DW I, 67.1.
58 Eckhart, *Commetnary on John*, n.2. Eckhart mentions Plato by name in this context, although Augustine refers to the books of the Platonists. Of course, the "Neoplatonists" thought of themselves as Platonists, so the ambiguity is not entirely misleading.

naturally becomes flesh in every work of nature and art, and it dwells in things that are made or in which word becomes flesh.[59]

Eckhart tells us that he is aware of going beyond Augustine, which is unusual. Although Eckhart cites Augustine more than any other author, he mostly leans upon Augustine and cites him approvingly. Here, however, he extends Augustine significantly on the question of the "Word made flesh." If the prologue to the gospel of John (1:1–14) "is contained in and taught by the properties of the things of nature, morality, and art," then the historicity of Christ's Incarnation is secondary to the incarnation of the Word everywhere and always. This subtle change undermines the claim to unique historical significance that is often thought of as centrally important to Christianity. Eckhart must have recognized this since he saw fit to include the cautionary statement "always presupposing the historical truth of the text." For Eckhart, if God and his teaching are eternal and if God himself is infused in whole in the smallest part of all things, then we have access to God and his teaching everywhere in all things, not just in one set of historical circumstances or one set of books.

Eckhart knew he was doing something different and potentially radical. Thus, as Augustine appealed to Scripture to support his statement that we become what we love, Eckhart refers us to the gospel of Luke's story of a woman who went to Christ and said, "Blessed is the body that bore you and blessed are the breasts that you nursed." Christ responded that this was right, "but rather, blessed is the man who hears my word and keeps it."[60] Eckhart says, "If *I* had said to you, and if they were my own words, that a person who hears the word of God and keeps it is more blessed than Mary.... I will say it again: if *I* had said it—people might be surprised. But Christ himself said it."[61]

In his vernacular sermons, Eckhart's dismissive tone reveals much about his attitude toward particular historical truths which might seem to be so sacred as to be untouchable and thus *above* us. Eckhart quotes "a master" who says, "God became man and thereby We can rejoice that Christ, our brother, has gone of his own power over all the choirs of angels and sits at the right hand of the Father."[62] To this, Eckhart responds, "This master speaks well. But truly, I would not make too much of it. What would it help me if I had

---

59 Eckhart, *Commentary on John*, n.124, trans. McGinn in *Essential Eckhart*, 171.
60 Lk 11:27–28; Eckhart, Sermon 49, DW II, 427.3–6.
61 Eckhart, Sermon 49, DW II, 428.3–6.
62 Eckhart, Sermon 5b, DW I, 86.1–3.

a brother who was a rich man while I was a poor man? What would it help me if I had a brother who was a wise man while I was a fool?"[63] Eckhart says, "I would not make too much of it," but it is difficult to imagine more subtle, subversive rhetoric against historical significance. He seems instead to be saying, "It isn't important at all that Christ ascended unless it also happens in us." In the same sermon, Eckhart says of the passage, "'God sent his only-begotten Son into the world.' You should not understand this with respect to the exterior world, that he ate and drank with us. You should understand it with respect to the interior world."[64] Eckhart does not *deny* the historicity, of course, but his rhetoric consistently downplays historical significance and thus brings such sacrality "down" to the individual soul. Though any one of these statements can shock and usefully provoke thought and movement toward God, taken all together, something more general emerges. This dynamic is characteristic of explosive metaphor, which makes this theme itself explosive. To deny that any one external thing or group of things has significance is a commonplace claim. To downplay *everything* external, that is, *every thing* that can be isolated as a thing, including the historical Incarnation, in favor of inner growth toward God, is something wholly different. Once the metaphor crosses over to something different, the same rhetoric will not do. Even if we follow him this far, exploding in one conceptual dimension is not enough. Eckhart extends this to time as well: "That this birth happens spiritually in Our Lady was more delightful to God than him being born to her bodily. That this birth happens still today, this day in the God-loving soul is more delightful to God than his creation of heaven and earth."[65] Since this birth is eternal, the birth in the individual soul cannot be different than the Incarnation itself which happened in time: "Now notice here where this birth happens. 'Where is he born?' Again I say as I have often said, this eternal birth happens in the soul in every sense that it happens in eternity, no more or less, for it is one birth. This birth happens in the essence and in the ground of the soul."[66] The "where" of Christ's birth is everywhere. The when is every possible when. It is the difference between being large and

---

[63] Eckhart, Sermon 5b, DW I, 86.3–7. I followed Fox's already fluid and effective rendering of the phrase "I would not make too much of it." Colledge and Walshe do not quite capture the blithe tone of it.

[64] Eckhart, Sermon 5b, DW I, 90.3–5.

[65] Eckhart, Sermon 106a, DW IV.2, 686.34–40; 106b has "more worthy of praise," while 106d has "more pleasing," instead of "more delightful," which appears in 106a and 106c.

[66] Eckhart, Sermon 102, DW IV.1, 407.2–6.

transcending spatial dimension, being long-lasting and transcending time by eternity. He goes farther: "Each blessed soul is nobler than the mortal life of our Lord Jesus Christ."[67] Thus, the value of such a birth in the individual soul is *greater* than Christ's historical life. Of course, if we step back and realize that this birth is nothing less than God himself, then the statement seems more sensible. The value of the birth of the Word in the individual soul can only be greater than Christ's mortal life if God himself is born in the soul and the soul herself continues to be an individual soul throughout, though not in the way that we normally think of someone as an individual. If the birth is merely analogous to the Incarnation, then surely its significance is less than Christ's mortal life since that life enabled the Word to be brought to earth for the salvation of all. If the individual soul ceases to be individual in this birth, then the birth does not happen in the individual and such a statement reduces to an assimilation of the soul into eternity, like a drop of water in a cask of wine. In other words, Eckhart's notion of what an individual is enables and shapes his most shocking pronouncements.

Eckhart's comments about Christ stand out, clearly advertising their significance to his audience. Less obvious is the *lack* of personality in his conception of God. The more we read from Eckhart on what God is and does, the more he looks like a necessary force rather than a divine personality. For example, "all the prayers and good works that man can work in time move God's detachment as little as if no prayer or good work had ever happened anywhere in time."[68] This statement does much to remove the possibility of emotion and vicissitude from God, often thought to be essential elements of human personality. Of course, we might notice at this point that personality conceived of in this way necessarily implies imperfection. Without such emotional whimsy and the possibility of being blown here and there by the emotion that builds as a product of a chain of events, such an indiviudal would appear coldly measured and governed entirely by reason. This, of course, fits well with Eckhart's conception of the well-ordered soul. He would object to such an individual being called "cold" since excitation and movement necessarily remain possibilities as a consequence of our being human. Nevertheless, those are human qualities that result from the soul's interaction with a body, not qualities that can be rightly superimposed upon God.

---

67 Eckhart, Sermon 87, DW IV.1, 27.64–65.
68 Eckhart, *On Detachment*, DW V, 414.2–4.

Eckhart consistently depicts God as moving necessarily, not by what we might want to call "free will." We must note however that Eckhart and many medieval authors think about free will very differently than we typically do. For Eckhart, one's will is free if it is one with God—that is, if one's personal will has been entirely annihilated along with all worldly concern as part of the annihilation of self. As he says, "As long as the will remains untouched by all creatures and all creation, then it is free."[69] Eckhart more fully describes what this means in the following words:

> God does not *force* the will. He rather places it in freedom so that it wills nothing other than God himself in such a way that it wishes nothing other than what God himself is and what freedom itself is. The spirit can will nothing other than what God wills. This is not its bondage but its proper freedom. Now some people say, "If I have God and God's love, I can indeed do anything I want." They understand these words incorrectly. So long as you will anything against God and his commandment, you do not have God's love.[70]

Therefore, a will that is corrupted by attachment to worldly things is not free and is subject to their vicissitudes. Only by removing our self and our created will and self can we return to a state of freedom whereupon our will becomes God's will. This enables Eckhart to conclude that "any activity and work that are free are properly divine."[71] Thus, with this understanding of free will, God by definition has free will. We might therefore rightly conclude that free will is present in Eckhart's God, along with his conception of the beatific vision, the one who experiences the birth of the Word, and life in heaven. It simply looks very different than our usual conception of it.

Eckhart makes the necessity with which God acts very clear: "God must perform all of his works from necessity."[72] Already we see that the way God proceeds will be unfamiliar to us. Further, God knows and loves only himself

---

69 Eckhart, Sermon 5b, DW I, 94.2–3.

70 Eckhart, Sermon 29, DW II, 78.2–79.3. This statement also constitutes Eckhart's response to the Free Spirit heresy of his time. Though not a well-formed sect, the Free Spirit heretics characteristically held views that were similar to Eckhart's and, as a result, were often mistakenly associated with him. They claimed that union with God was possible through perfection in this life through austerities and that, upon reaching this lasting state by grace, sin was no longer possible. Eckhart separates himself from any hint of the self-indulgent behavior that could result from this by insisting in this passage that they have misunderstood the will's union with God.

71 Eckhart, Eckhart, *Commentary on Exodus*, n.75, trans. McGinn in *Teacher and Preacher*, 69.

72 Eckhart, Sermon 43, DW II, 319.5–6.

and he knows and loves nothing outside of himself. If God only works in himself and knows in himself, then God does not know or love imperfections, including all kinds of sin. Indeed, this is the case, "God knows nothing but himself.... Therefore God does not see us when we sin. And so God knows us only insofar as we exist in him: that is, insofar as we are without sin."[73] Eckhart also tells us, "he loves nothing in us except insofar as he finds us in him."[74] Again, this points to an unusual notion of personality. We typically think of the possession of our virtues and faults, including the propensity to sin, as being a sine qua non of what makes us who we are. Though Eckhart recognizes that these faults belong to the soul (naturally, since they cannot be God's), they are part of what must be shed in returning to God. In other words, our sins and faults are personal since they are ours but they are not essential to what makes us individual. For Eckhart, we may drop such flaws and other hallmarks of what we think of as personality without ceasing to be individual.

Just as God's personality may seem foreign to us, so too does Christ's. Eckhart tells us that God assumed humanity in Christ, "but not the defects that are personal sins and belong to the soul."[75] Thus, as God "assumed bare human nature and not any particular man. Therefore, if you would be the same Christ and God, then go out from all that the eternal Word did not assume."[76] In other words, even though this notion of personality is unfamiliar, we attain it by emptying ourselves of self. Once this happens, Eckhart observes, "When I let go of self, he must from necessity will for me everything that he wills for himself."[77]

Eckhart tells us that this process is compulsory for God. He must be speaking metaphorically, since the ideas of compulsion and oneness are not otherwise compatible. To have compulsion, we must have two things, one of which compels the other. If an individual is entirely detached, God must flow in: "Detachment compels God to love me."[78] This straightforwardly follows from Eckhart's dynamic of desire where I must desire what I recognize as good. When I make myself like God, God recognizes himself in me and loves

---

73 Eckhart, Sermon 5a, DW I, 78.6–9.
74 Eckhart, Sermon 41, DW II, 286.6; cf. *Book of Divine Consolation* §3.
75 Eckhart, *Commentary on John*, n.102, trans. McGinn in *Essential Eckhart*, 161.
76 Eckhart, Sermon 24, DW I, 420.4–7.
77 Eckhart, *Counsels on Discernment*, §1, DW V, 187.7–9.
78 Eckhart, *On Detachment*, DW V, 402.5.

me as himself. This is not exactly "necessity" in the sense of "compulsion," but it lends itself to some interesting and perhaps useful possibilities for rhetoric. For example, Eckhart says that "God can no more withdraw himself from the soul than he can escape himself."[79] This is why "if God's love for us were taken away, this would take away his being and his divinity, for his being depends on his loving us."[80] Of course, his divinity depends on loving us, because his love for us *is* his being. Likewise, God "cannot refuse the man of humility and great desire. Wherever I cannot force God to do all things that I will, it is from a lack of humility or desire in me."[81] We first encounter such rhetoric with our conventional ideas about what it means to impose our will on something. The metaphor draws us in with its ostensible radicality, only to lead us down a useful pathway of thought.

---

[79] Eckhart, DW IV.1, 132.69; cf. *Counsels on Discernment*, §1.

[80] Eckhart, Sermon 41, DW II, 287.3–4.

[81] Eckhart, Sermon 100, DW IV.1, 273.22–23; cf. Sermon 15, DW I, 246.9–18; Sermon 48, DW II, 415.1–9.

8

The Relevance of Eckhart Today

Why does Eckhart appeal to us? In other words, why would someone think to read something like Meister Eckhart's works today? We like to say that a religious writer is worth reading because he or she expresses a good argument or has pleasantly insightful things to say. This cannot be right, though. Those factors only touch on our conscious awareness of why we *think* we want to read someone. They are at least partly confabulations that support our culturally popular conception of a will that is entirely self-driven, as if everything we did with religion was a conscious choice that we were wholly responsible for choosing.

We know this isn't true. I may choose to go to one shop over another when I buy fresh bread, but I do not choose to like pumpernickel over rye. This is why I would like to begin the discussion of why we read Eckhart by at first avoiding terms like belief, faith, truth, and even desire. Those terms are loaded with other implicitly accepted ways of speaking that freight in assumptions about the will, what religion is, and how the mind works. Instead, let us begin at the lowest possible level: we will simply observe that encountering certain things—whether they be works of art, experiences of one kind or another, or Meister Eckhart's sermons—catalyzes recognizable *movement* in the mind. I say "recognizable" because the question of whether this is *my* mind or a notion of mind that spills over into other people and the surrounding world can be safely left aside for now. This is not because it is an irrelevant question. It can be left aside because that is not the way we are likely to begin thinking about it. If I were to suggest a different notion of mind, we would have to consciously entertain whether it was viable. Instead, I want to appeal to where we *actually* begin, the notion that we have before we have an opportunity to think about it. Whether it is "right" or "true" in some objective sense is irrelevant for the entirely pragmatic purpose here.

I must pause for a moment to note how ironic it is that Eckhart and theologians in general are often more sensitive to this than philosophers are. Since the goal for Eckhart is to help carry his listeners from where they are back to divine oneness, he must be sensitive to where they begin. If the goal instead were to prove something or argue forcefully for the truth of one position or another, as is often the case in philosophy, then the particular disposition of the listener does not matter so long and he or she is sufficiently rational to enable the force of truth to work its magic.[1] What's more, it may even be well known that the starting point is in no way "true" or even relevant to what will come later. As Eckhart said (citing Augustine) Scripture has something to offer everyone, from the smallest child to the most sophisticated theologian. That is a testament to how *useful* the words are, independent of how *true* they are.

To find a theological idea beautiful is like hearing a new piece of music that resonates with us. We may not understand it at first. Perhaps we need to hear the piece a few times before the roots of attraction take hold. William James tells us that we rush to abstract when presented with only a few recognizably similar examples. Eckhart accomplishes this through metaphorical repetition. When attraction takes root, attention is catalyzed and we are compelled to return to the idea so as to partake in its beauty and, perhaps, to search out what we know that we do not yet understand. Eckhart's paradoxes work in this way. They confound the mind and leave no space for familiar thought to domesticate them. Conscious attention and rethinking are required, which provide an opening for the possibility of new experience. This is the key to the Socratic method as well. If we remain comfortable in our present knowledge and way of seeing the world, we have no reason to apply energy to question our assumptions.

To begin thinking about something, we must overcome the inertia of remaining comfortably and unthinkingly where we are. Once we set an idea or activity down—even for a moment—we must overcome inertia to pick it back up again. In other words, we first try the low-energy approach of using existing habits of thought. We only reevaluate what we think when we see the need to do so. Once we do reevaluate it and question our assumptions, we have momentum that keeps us moving. Eckhart's insistence upon paradoxes antagonizes the facile use of our existing habits. It provides a persistent

---

[1] "Force of truth" is Hans Blumenberg's phrase. For example, see his discussion of the history of the idea in chap. 1 of *Paradigms for a Metaphorology*, 6–12.

irritation (as in the Socratic "gadfly" metaphor) that does not allow us to rest content with our current understanding, precisely because it defies a restful state of understanding. Paradoxes are not compatible with a state of quiet conceptual equilibrium. They poke at us, nagging us to continue thinking through them. This catalyzes persistent motivation. It is also an indication that a nerve has been struck, attention has been provoked, and the groundwork for belief can then be laid.

This is why "movement" is a useful way to begin thinking about Eckhart's appeal. Eckhart's modern readers are not homogeneous in their beliefs or affiliations. This is to say that Eckhart elicits movement in people independent of their social and theological ties. When I feel movement (enjoyment, interest, and motivation) in reading Eckhart, I might subsequently think that he has catalyzed *desire* to read more, do more, understand more, or even to do something more specific, like to return to God. Recognizing a desire is not necessary for movement. We lean toward pleasant sounds, look toward what stimulates interest, and even move toward things without necessarily thinking that we have an identifiable "desire for" something. To make claims outside of merely observing movement risks invoking some notion of truth or particular model of mind which can be accepted or rejected. This is all in concert with Eckhart's talk of God as beyond goodness and truth. Just as the oneness of God is prior to any notion of truth, perhaps we should not be surprised that a productive way of approaching Eckhart is with a similarly phenomenological approach that assumes as little as possible about objective reality and truth. Since we are talking about personal spiritual progress and not about theological truth, movement in the right direction is ultimately the only thing that matters. The concepts that we use along the way are like the raft in the Buddhist Parable of the Raft. So is the notion of the individual who moves: the individual appears in the Parable of the Raft as a rhetorical expedient even though self is precisely the illusion that is broken through.

This may all seem like unnecessary phenomenology, but herein lies the rub: this is pure Plato. While philosophy nowadays often acts as though the onus is upon the reader to have an inexhaustible fount of motivation, impelling us to do whatever is necessary to get to truth, Plato did no such thing. Socratic dialectic achieves its goal of philosophical midwifery precisely by being attuned to the motivation of the interlocutor and audience, capitalizing on the place from which they begin. This is all fairly well known and obvious to anyone who has studied Plato, though it does provide an amusingly ironic contrast with modern treatise-writing.

What is not so obvious is the dynamic of *beauty* in Plato. I did not begin with beauty because that term is just as loaded as belief, truth and faith. Yet if we allow ourselves to expand what the notion of beauty includes to be more sympathetic with Plato's use of it, we can understand Eckhart's appeal in a way that he, with his strong Neoplatonic influences, would have very much appreciated. How did Plato think about beauty? Beauty is the vehicle that carries us to the divine. He described an ontological hierarchy, a sliding scale of being, whereby the things on top have more being—more existence—than the things below. People have more being than their shadows. A real horse has more being than a painting (an imitation) of a horse. The real thing is necessary in both cases for the shadow and the painting to exist at all. Similarly, the Forms are necessary for the things to exist. The idea of Horse is necessary for individual manifestations of it (the horses) to exist, which enables paintings of them and their shadows to exist. Prior to all that and at the top of the hierarchy is the Good, the unity from which all things flow and upon which they depend for their existence.

Given this setup, it is not obvious that beauty would be the vehicle that carries us up the hierarchy. We might think that knowledge or truth should have that distinction. Knowledge cannot do it for Plato, though. The world of temporal things is the realm of *doxa*, opinion. Knowledge is only possible with the eternal Forms themselves. That truth cannot be the way, either, is less obvious. To see this, we must pay attention to Plato's comment that all things are children of the Good. If everything that exists ultimately came from The Good (remembering that there is no form of Evil since evil is merely a lack of being), then we have a hierarchy that all overflows from the utter oneness of the Good. If the Good is wholly one and all things are but imperfect manifestations of it, then the possibility of anything being "true" must point to one of the lower Forms and not to the Good itself, since any formulation of "truth" and "knowledge" as distinct from "falsehood" can only arise with multiplicity. This is the Platonic version of Eckhart's argument that the oneness of God is above truth. This is why Eckhart speaks of the "veil of truth" (*velamen veri*) alongside the "veil of goodness" (*velamen boni*) and "veil of being itself" (*velamen ipsius esse*).[2] It is as if the mind will take any opportunity to stop along the way and rest content with knowledge. Eckhart, like any good mystic, insists upon the mystery and resists any attempt to stop before reaching utter oneness and breaking through to the divine ground.

---

2 Eckhart, Sermon XI.2, LW IV, 114.4–6. See also the discussion on p. 127.

It must, then, be *beauty* that is the way higher things *appeal* to us and thereby incite *movement*. Understood like this, beauty is a precondition for any movement back to oneness. Now it is an open (and fascinating) question why we are naturally attracted to things that are ontologically higher in the Platonic sense. In other words, we are undeniably attracted to mathematics, ideas, archetypes, and divine oneness, though we all differ in the intensity of our attraction toward each of these, and this intensity waxes with familiarity. As Eckhart would say, we are born with a drive to return to God. As Schopenhauer observed, we enjoy art for the temporary reprieve from willing that it provides us. What this really means is that we are drawn to experiences where our normally overpowering notion of self is temporarily set aside. This happens when we experience music and art, when we get caught up in a group activity, when we get in the "zone" in sports, and when we have a religious experience. In other words, we are naturally drawn toward *immediate* experiences since the nature of an immediate experience is that we are consumed with the present moment to the exclusion of any notion of self. Kenosis is the sine qua non of immediate experience.[3]

Are all experiences of beauty moments of self-emptying immediate experience? They are immediate in the same way that smelling chocolate chip cookies is immediate. However, this is not necessarily self-emptying. To invoke Schopenhauer's notion, it does not provide a reprieve from willing. The opposite happens. Experiences like that water the desires. Since desire is anything that keeps us focused on the selfish aims of the will, such experiences do not draw us upward in the Platonic hierarchy. They keep us down at the level of individual manifestations. There is subtlety here, though. We should not think that upward movement is only created by the contemplation of God and other obviously upward-directed experiences. While smelling a cookie might water desire, savoring it *is* an immediate experience that provides a reprieve from willing. Though I chose the example of cookies since I think they best fit the rhetorical exigence of this particular situation, Plato leapt to the more contentious example of beautiful bodies. He tells us that observing one beautiful body leads us to appreciate the beauty of bodies in general (first abstraction) and then to beauty in general (second abstraction). The mixture of beauty and sexuality, while provocative and worth considering in this context, is not necessary to make the point; it

---

3 I especially like this idea when we consider the idea of kenosis to imply a metaphorical "pouring out" of self, recalling Eckhart's metaphysics of flow.

may, in fact, distract from the point. Cookies do not have this problem. Put very plainly, the contemplation of beauty of any kind can be immediate and self-emptying so long as one remains in the experience of beauty and does not proceed to indulge in the associated desire for individual instances of it. This is simply a reformulation of Eckhartian detachment, the same point that was made when considering the legitimacy of pursuing natural sciences.

Insofar as the experience of beauty precedes our conscious deliberation and is not subsequently sullied by willed pursuit of some object of desire, it is immediate and self-emptying. At the very least, this is a useful way of thinking about it. This comment about what is useful should be understood as a response to rhetorical exigency in the same way that Plato's "truthlikeness" does. Plato tells us in the *Timaeus* that his description may not be the truth, but it at least looks like it.[4] My comments that follow can be understood not only as an explanation of Eckhart, but also as an extension of Plato's own claims about truthlikeness insofar as beauty may be Plato's solution to Meno's paradox. Something having the semblance of truth is another way of saying that it has beauty, owing to its carrying a scent of the truth. Insofar as we recognize this by dint of our natural attraction to divine oneness, we are inspired to move in a spiritually productive direction.

Beauty accomplishes something specific for us with spiritual progress: it enables us to rush ahead and gives us motion in the right direction before we have personal experience and knowledge. If beauty is an experience that motivates us to move usefully before we know, then *faith is a kind of beauty*. Eckhart's rhetoric does not elicit movement by invoking faith, but the outcome is the same. He compels us by way of beautiful speech and paradoxes that push us in the direction of returning to unity with God by dislodging habits which constitute obstacles to spiritual progress.

Nothing being off-limits for Eckhart is endearing to people today. The push for greater individual autonomy in thinking and importance that rose in the late medieval world and culminated in the Enlightenment motto *sapere aude* manifests today in a sense that people are entitled to think for themselves, disbelieving by default claims to religious truth. This sense forms a backdrop against which new possibilities for belief and thought, ultimately culminating in action, are considered. The result is often that new religious ideas are not taken seriously enough to even listen to or read, much less think through.

---

4 Plato, *Timaeus* 29d.

Eckhart appeals to many today because he downplays what such people have difficulty believing and focuses instead on what they can see for themselves by turning inward. Let us begin with half a quote from Huston Smith: "How many men and women today feel themselves driven to atheism because the only version of theism they have encountered is too anthropomorphic, too person- (and therefore in the end too self-) centered, too moralistic-because-dualistic to fit the shape the God-vacuum assumes in their mystically inclined souls?"[5]

Those who struggle with modern ideas of faith will find Eckhart's depiction of Christianity to be a breath of fresh air, useful to them because it draws out what is beautiful in Christianity while downplaying what they often find most difficult to accept. His Christianity is not anthropomorphic, dualistic, or moralistic. He does not emphasize the blind faith popularly spoken of today or the historical significance of Christ. In fact, he does not emphasize any exclusive access to truth in Christianity at all. Eckhart's God is not jealous, whimsical, or angry—without a recognizable personality in the way we are accustomed to expect when someone speaks of a god. These details constitute barriers for many people who stand on the outside looking in, unable to believe in them. Eckhart has a lot to offer such people. As Cyprian Smith says, what Eckhart says to us "is very different from what we are used to. If we are attracted by it and gravitate towards it, that is surely because it is something we need, something we are short of, like a missing vitamin in our diet."[6] Though a study in Eckhart's metaphors can only hint at it, Eckhart's rhetoric simply "works" for many people, just as some music resonates with us.

Instead of taking an authority's word about God, Eckhart simply tells us to look inside and detach from all the dross of the material world (which we often suspect is corrupting and problematic anyway). Then, God *must* come in and we will see for ourselves.[7] We will then be among those who are familiar with inner things and have tasted the wine in the cellar to say firsthand that it is good.[8] In other words, Eckhart does not prescribe blind

---

5 H. Smith, "Preface" in *Essential Eckhart*, xv–xvi.

6 C. Smith, *Way of Paradox*, 14.

7 Those who are familiar with the dynamics of meditation may recognize something insightful here. When one finally achieves one-pointed concentration and is wholly focused, a rush of quiet bliss often follows. Eckhart would likely call this a first taste of the divine.

8 "Those who have never been familiar with inward things do not know what God is. Like a man who has wine in his cellar but has never tasted it, he does not know that it is good" (Eckhart, Sermon 10, DW I, 164.5–8).

faith or unquestioning acceptance. Instead, he tells us that faith is *useful* in the same way that having confidence in a teacher is, with the understanding that we will later come to experience it and know.[9] Rushing ahead of certainty and reason, faith motivates us to move in the right direction even when we do not know for certain that it is the right direction. This makes faith a willed antagonism of disbelief while at the same time having confidence in what one will see firsthand in the future. This is not an abandonment of reason, which might either feel like giving up or simply appear impossible to a modern individual.

In addition to providing a pragmatic account of faith, faith also answers the sophistic paradox: how can we know how to look for truth if we do not already have it? Also called Meno's Paradox, it was originally expressed in Plato's *Meno* in the following terms: How can I go looking for what virtue is if I do not already know what it is? Though this is often discussed in philosophical circles as an epistemological problem, the motivational and intentional (in the sense of giving direction to thought) are at least as important as the implications for epistemology, if not more so. It is more important when knowledge is not the final end. For Eckhart and many other mystics, knowledge is not the end because even truth itself is not the end of the road. It is not the divine ground. In such a circumstance, even the appearance of such a paradox being epistemological is itself a mere pragmatic expedient. We expect it to be about knowledge since that is our habitual mode of thinking. Thinking that it is epistemological is enough to motivate us to try to logically untangle the paradox. In doing so, it pushes us like an explosive metaphor to the point where the notion of knowledge itself strains and may break. Since Socrates ultimately claimed that he did not know (and so the Oracle who told Chaerephon that Socrates was the wisest man in Athens must be mistaken), his injunction to consider this paradox from an epistemological standpoint must ultimately be a pragmatic expedient, part of his overarching service as a "philosophical midwife" who helps others to give birth to philosophical experiences. The dynamic here is worth exploring at length because Eckhart and Plato share it.

Given the foregoing discussion on faith, I believe we can imagine how Eckhart might respond to E. M. Cioran's quip, "What advantage would having faith be to me, since I understand Meister Eckhart just as well without

---

9 This is the closest idea to faith that we see in Buddhism as well.

it?"[10] Faith enables us to rush ahead. Eckhart's message extends far beyond Christianity. This does not mean, however, that the recognizably Christian elements are (as Schopenhauer implied) merely burdensome excrescences.[11] In a word, they help to catalyze useful motion since they fundamentally appeal to people in a particular historical circumstance.

Cyprian Smith has the right response to Schopenhauer. He says that Eckhart wanted to remind us that the Church and its sacraments are instruments, means to an end: "Theology, liturgy, church hierarchy and pastoral works—these are ultimately only means and instruments; they are not God himself."[12] Eckhart would have appreciated this. If they are seen as anything more than instruments, then we mistake the way for the end and deify the instruments. Of those who take God in only one way Eckhart says, "They take the way instead of God."[13] Smith summarizes the point: "[Eckhart] is no iconoclast or revolutionary in the sense of wanting to overthrow the existing church order; but he wants us to regard that order for what it truly is: a framework within which to seek union with the transcendent God."[14] This is a critical point to bear in mind when considering my ideas on the future of religion and why Eckhart appeals to us today.

Some people love Christian images while others are repelled by them. Regardless of what we would consciously assert, almost all of us in the modern West are *moved* to some sort of reaction by them. This tells us that the images *work* for us at a fundamental level. They create movement in people before the conscious mind has the opportunity to pass judgment on them. We can decide to reject the scent of fragrant flowers because of some negative association or conscious decision to try and push the experience away, but we cannot control the visceral emotional and physical reaction we have before those thoughts arise. We see this in the way that even those who reject Christianity are still attracted to films that borrow from a recognizably Christian mythos.

Eckhart so clearly fits with modern needs because he gives people a metaphorically legitimate place to begin with mysticism. He speaks to incredulous people about mysticism through images and ideas that are already

---

10 E. M. Cioran, *Drawn and Quartered*, trans. Richard Howard (New York: Seaver Books, 1983), 65. As cited by Milem, *Unspoken Word*, 177.

11 Davies, *Mystical Theologian*, 19.

12 C. Smith, *Way of Paradox*, 128.

13 Eckhart, Sermon 5a, DW I, 82.6.

14 C. Smith, *Way of Paradox*, 128.

familiar and appealing. Mysticism is notoriously difficult and approached only by the few. Its esotericism constitutes a barrier to entry. Christianity, especially in Eckhart's narrative of it, appeals to people on all stages of the path. We should recall that both Eckhart and Augustine, who said that the Bible offers something for everyone, recognize that we have to start somewhere and that we must be moving in order to progress.[15] The key here is that Eckhart does not provide an *argument* that appeals to people at all stages of spiritual development.

We are accustomed to thinking that a good teacher must address a student's particular needs in order to be effective. We are not as comfortable—again due to our inheritance of rugged individualism—with knowing that we are not being given the "truth" up front, or even worse, that we are being lied to for educative purposes. We know that training is required to build skills, and we valorize individual effort in doing so because it is "honest" in the sense that the individual knows the target and undergoes the training (with its concomitant delayed gratification) to achieve the desired outcome. We do not, by contrast, know what to think of a situation where we cannot know what the outcome is (the Sophistic paradox) and so we do not even know how to aim. If God is not *like* anything that we have experience with and we must undergo a cataclysmic change in worldview to start to understand him, then how can we be given the "truth" and aim for a target when the notions of "truth" and "God" must be understood in terms of what we already know? This is where some version of *faith* is necessary. Faith gives us a push so that we can overcome spiritual stasis and get moving toward God. Cyprian Smith observes that "there have to be projections in the beginning; without them the spiritual life cannot get started. At first one's notion of God is distorted by our personal needs and emotions; it takes time for all that to be refined and purified."[16] He continues, "Atheism and rationalism strip away the projection and leave us with nothing. That leads to nihilism and despair. [Eckhart] strips away the projections in such a manner as to unveil the truth behind them that is life-giving."[17] Nihilism causes despair because we do not know where to go or how to begin. Even to those who cannot begin with projections—or perhaps even *especially* to those who have no other starting place—Eckhart shows a path forward, which is enough to spur movement and allow them

---

15 Eckhart, Sermon 51, DW II, 467.3–7; Sermon 101, DW IV.1, 358.139–42.
16 C. Smith, *Way of Paradox*, 32.
17 C. Smith, *Way of Paradox*, 35.

to begin. In this way, the modern age is unusually open and well suited to mysticism, which may explain its growing popularity despite its difficulty.

The historical figure of Christ causes difficulty for many today for the same reasons that other aspects of faith do. As we saw, Eckhart does not believe that Christ, the Virgin Birth, and the Incarnation have significance simply because they are historical facts. Though he does not doubt that they happened, as historical facts alone they are of little consequence for his theology. While much of Eckhart's theology and rhetoric builds upon the Incarnation as divinizing humanity, his account is too Platonic to treat the Incarnation only as a contingent fact of history. To emphasize the way that Eckhart's theology is based on the historical fact of the Incarnation is to take an overly philosophical stance on his theology, as if he were merely constructing arguments that were susceptible to judgment by common philosophical standards of reason and truth. By contrast, Eckhart's notion of the continuous and endless birth of the Word (i.e., the Incarnation) in the soul points to a leveling of history, taking the individual from the linear time of history to the atemporality of eternity which is forever everywhere and everywhen. With a nod to Johannes Tauler's (and later, C. F. Kelley's) suggestion that Eckhart speaks *in divinis*, from the standpoint of eternity, I suggest that Eckhart's theology is rooted in the divine ground and makes practical expedients of anything short of that ground insofar as it can be used as a vehicle to help move the soul toward the divine.

Against this backdrop of eternity, we might read implicitly here that the historicity of Christ should be understood alongside other practical expedients for those who are at a certain place on the path and to those who are susceptible to finding beauty in the idea. The theological significance of Christ for Eckhart lies in the divinization of humanity. If humanity is divine, then my humanity is Christ's humanity, which is God in his entirety. The inflation of the individual in this way may represent something of an ironic return to the archetypal. As the individual rises to divinity, its accidents are shed and it becomes *archetypal*. The difficulty we have with that now is the same difficulty people have with the beatific vision: it seems to exclude the elements of our personality that we take to be essential features of our humanity. For Aristotle, the defining feature of what makes us human is not our imperfections and personal eccentricities. It is our reason. Eckhart extends this aspect of Aristotle (already compatible with the Dominican emphasis on the primacy of knowledge) and points to the divinity that is prior to knowledge, prior to truth, and prior to love. For Eckhart, therefore, the essence of humanity is to have one foot in time and the other in eternity, just as Christ does. In other words, paradox is in the ground of what it is to be human. Such paradoxes subtly affirm what we already feel: contemporary physicalism, the idea that we are just deterministic machines, living and dying with the brain, is just not all there is to life. We are revulsed by the idea of an inert, meaningless world where we are just cogs in a machine. We want to reject it, but we don't know how. So we remain in a nihilistic void of meaning, mired in stasis. Eckhart gives us the push we need with images we understand, subtly affirming what we already feel about the more-than-individual nature of our mental life, enabling us to move away from meaninglessness and toward divine oneness. Buddhism offers much of the same psychology and mysticism, but clothed in unfamiliar images. Eckhart provides a unique combination of what is appealing about Buddhist mysticism with the images that are naturally appealing to us in the West. That's why Eckhart appeals to us and is important for us today.

God is necessarily one and unique for Eckhart, which is not an exclusive doctrine that prefers one particular conception of God over all others. Instead, Eckhart argues that one conception of God *is all there can be* according to reason: "It is impossible to have two indistinct things, for the indistinct and the One are the same.... God is indistinct and indistinction itself. Therefore, it is impossible for many gods to exist ... if two gods are put forth, there will not be two gods: either none of them or one of them will be God."[18] We might think at first that this is not straightforwardly Platonic. If we recall though, that the roots of Platonism extend into the Pythagorean, Parmenidean, and other Presocratic philosophical circles that often spoke of oneness and the divine, we might recognize the Neoplatonic as a reformulation that was both a product of its time and also a return to its roots. Eckhart's God is not one that requires belief. A God with specific characteristics requires belief because belief is a choice of one thing among many possibilities. Such belief amounts to belief in the rightness of those qualities that make a particular conception distinct. Divine oneness is, as Eckhart so memorably put it, distinct in its indistinction. Consequently, undifferentiated oneness is not something that we can be wrong about since being right or wrong appeals to truth as a higher arbiter. Any possible notion of truth will only be coherent in multiplicity. If we strip away enough layers, we strip away the possibility of truth itself. What is left is not a "what" at all—though Eckhart might call

---

18 Eckhart, *Commentary on Wisdom*, n.146, LW II, 484.6–8, 10–11.

it a "something" or declare that God is "omninameable," while at the same time embracing apophatic negation. The negation of negation is not a *claim*. It is not the sort of thing that one can be wrong about. Consequently, belief does not apply.

The idea of the Incarnation was made possible by a reconceptualization of the individual. Ancient polytheism emphasized the yielding of the temporal individual to the archetypal and eternal. What was individual was precisely what was not eternal. Even in the years following the time of Christ, the idea of a God-man was opposed because it seemed self-contradictory for an individual to be eternal. If we take the notion of the Incarnation as a single event, an unusual intermixing of temporal and eternal, and extend what is paradoxical to its maximum, then we have Eckhart's formulation: the divine, eternal oneness of God which is maximally significant is present in his entirety in the smallest and ostensibly least meaningful part of the temporal world. Everything has its being from God without intermediary, and being belongs solely to God. Therefore, anything that exists is intertwined with God in the closest and most complete way possible. Further, for man in particular, since we all share our humanity with Christ, we also have the eternal birth of Christ within us, happening at each moment. In all cases, Eckhart takes the paradox to the extreme, where it can break through all of the boundaries of our thinking and all that which keeps us tied to our world of images and apart from God.

Eckhart is most useful today in his emphasis on living "without a why." People today have difficulty deriving meaning and significance from a world of lifeless efficient causes. Meaning comes from aesthetics and purpose.[19] This is a blend of Plato and Aristotle. For Plato, beauty was special because it was the vehicle to the divine. Beauty is a nonconceptual feeling, an attraction to something that we somehow sense can be a vehicle back to the oneness of the Good. Similarly, Aristotle's world was suffused with meaning because each thing had its own *telos*, or end, as part of its *ergon*, or function. To know a thing's function was to have knowledge of its final cause, the "why" of its existence. Blumenberg observed that a world where meaning is presupposed in all things makes each thing open to an investigation of its "why."[20] Further,

---

[19] With aesthetic meaning, we should think of Plato's account of Beauty in the *Phaedrus* and *Symposium*. With meaning that derives from purpose, we should think of Aristotle's teleology insofar as the telos of something is less a goal than it is the proper activity of that thing.

[20] Blumenberg, *Paradigms for a Metaphorology*, 54. Blumenberg comes close to equating meaning with teleology here since he says that a world full of meaning would imply that everything had

if we lose certainty at the most basic level of what an individual thing even is, any meaning or significance based on those things becomes suspect as well. In other words, our current understanding of the physical world demands skepticism all the way down. Eckhart's insistence on living without a why short-circuits this problem. The problem of meaning evanesces with the self.[21] To live without a why is also to not *need* a why.[22] Ironically, this restores meaning by eliminating the need for it. If nothing is sacred, then that opens up the possibility for *everything* to become sacred. This is a felt and lived experience, not an argument: When natural philosophy's investigations of physical reality increasingly showed it to be lifeless causal interactions, theology of the Late Medieval world often emphasized God's transcendence rather than his immanence and indwelling, creating the problem of the *deus absconditus*, the hidden God. This left every aspect of physical reality and the total of our experience in it entirely separated from God. This was *felt* as a loss of God and a loss of the very possibility of lived meaning, opening us to existential dread and despair. When the soul returns to divine oneness, we *break through* the dam that holds back the very possibility for meaning with the *deus absconditus*, suddenly overflowing and flooding the world and everything in it with meaning.

A similar situation arises with the natural and supernatural. We too often associate the supernatural with the miraculous. This puts it in direct opposition to the modern worldview. As Kohàk observes, "Nature appears dead to us in great part because we have grown accustomed to thinking of God as 'super-natural,' absent from nature and not to be found therein."[23] Eckhart's

---

a purpose. That is, nothing would be meaningless. We should distinguish, however, between the *understanding* that things have meaning and the *feeling* that things have meaning. To say that things are rationally meaningful is to imply that things have reasons for being, which is teleological. By contrast, to say that things *feel* meaningful refers, it seems to me, to the *motion* with which one lives in the service of a particular intention. Though intentions may have proper Aristotelian ends—such as when I intend to build something—the most pleasant kind of intentionality comes from engaging in an activity for its own sake—in other words, living without a why.

21 We see the same dynamic with the Parable of the Poison Arrow in Buddhism. Ultimately, eschewing unnecessary questions results in one's seeing firsthand that they are unnecessary. The solution of the problems is found in the dissolution of the problems.

22 Bruce Milem noticed a similar possibility as well, though he did not mention living without a why in this context: "Detachment serves as an image of God by challenging the worth and necessity of creation considered simply by itself. This challenge, paradoxically, may for some restore to the world the value that it initially took away, since it sees the world as an expression of mysterious creativity" (*Unspoken Word*, 111).

23 Kohàk, *Embers and the Stars*, 182.

intensification of meaning by insisting on God being present in all things breaks this boundary. This is perhaps another useful shade of meaning in his metaphor of "boiling over." Smith tells us, "Ideally there should be no distinction in our lives between the sacred and the profane at all.... We want the holy to overflow all boundaries and engulf everything."[24] The opposites meet and enable the possibility of everything taking on meaning as we shed what we mistakenly believe to be good in worldly things. Nihilism, a vacuum of meaning, is the other possibility that is regrettably common today. It is often accepted with resignation, for lack of anything else we feel to be believable. It is here that Eckhart's thought is most useful. He shows us how to revive meaning without necessarily throwing out our way of understanding the physical world.

More should be said about the viability of living "without a why." Purpose is an aesthetic experience. Purpose does not need to be an individualistic experience. When we think of someone living with an overarching sense of purpose and meaning, we typically understand this in terms of goals and ends. This is because we confabulate our own lived meaning and others' meanings in just this kind of a conceptual way. That is, we tell the story in accordance with how we customarily think of the mind and the self. The real results, however, are lived in each moment and have little resemblance to this story. At any given moment, what is the experience of living with meaning? We rush ahead, moving confidently, unhesitatingly in some direction without anxiety. It is an experience of wholeness, uncorrupted by doubt and worry, lacking nothing, fulfilling and complete. While we normally associate fulfillment with a self that is filled with meaning, there is nothing about this experience that requires a self. In fact, ironically, reflective self-consciousness may be precisely what is *not* present in the whole and fulfilling experience of living with meaning. Meaningful living is possible without a self. In fact, the experience of aesthetic immersion, flow, and acting with purpose is precisely *not* an individual experience. Living without a why feels suffuse with meaning. It only seems paradoxical that utter meaninglessness should feel meaningful. When mysticism strips away all possibility of meaning, if the self is not simultaneously stripped away, then the cup of meaning becomes painfully empty. Effacing the self shrinks the cup. We cannot feel emptiness if the self is gone: the vessel itself has departed. Nihilism's emptiness is a feeling of lack that cannot happen if the possibility of lack has been removed.

24 C. Smith, *Path of Life*, 107.

I would like to extend Lévi-Stauss's idea of the "total understanding" that is central to traditional societies' religions. As he says, "If you don't understand everything, you don't explain anything."[25] This description and the idea of a total "understanding" limits the scope to knowledge, truth, and explanation unnecessarily. Instead, I would like to offer the idea of a *complete experience*, bringing together insights from Lévi-Strauss, Schopenhauer, and Nietzsche in the service of something new. A complete experience is one that engenders a feeling of wholeness and not just total understanding. This reframes Levi-Strauss's notion as an experience instead of a concept. Coeval with this feeling arising is the silencing of will and desire, enabling us to be in the flow and in the moment with an immediate experience that lacks nothing. The need for and identity of the self drop away with the will and desires. This creates the feeling of wholeness.

Consider the case of sound: what we hear can readily be ambient and all-encompassing. If it is poignantly beautiful too, then a feeling of wholeness can arise for some listeners as beauty enters and the self leaves. Schopenhauer reserved a special place for music since it carried the potential for providing a temporary reprieve from willing. A complete experience and one of flow characterizes those moments. They produce, in other words, a higher, more sublime feeling of wholeness where the will and the self leave and only immediate aesthetic experience remains.

When Nietzsche spoke of the death of God, the idea might be usefully interpreted to mean that a complete worldview revolving around a distinct God was no longer possible. Religion viably functions when it grounds every aspect of one's worldview. This does not mean that it provides all the answers or even makes any dualistic claims. It simply means that religion cannot fully function when it is compartmentalized and not comprehensive. If science or some other aspect of culture takes the place of religion in determining part of a worldview, unless religion can ground that too, then the viability of what was previously a living option (William James) or living myth (Joseph Campbell) falters.

Implicit in this description is a solution, one which gives additional force and scope to Huston Smith's words that bookend this chapter. Eckhart's God is not nameable, nor does it compete with investigations of the natural world. If divine oneness is prior to truth and therefore prior to the possibility of thinking any claim, then the possibility of contradiction and tension with

---

25 Lévi-Strauss, *Myth and Meaning*, 17.

science can only manifest at a level posterior to the divine. Though it is certainly esoteric in the form that points to mystical experience and unity with the divine, as an expression of Christianity, it may still be *complete*. If so, then it points the way to identifying viable, living forms of religious expression for today.

Eckhart is a bridge between East and West, a bridge between the exclusivism and dogmatism of folk Christianity before the "death of God" and the direction that Western religion may go in the future. Figures like Eckhart will be increasingly important as we collectively think through and adopt the features and practices of religions that will be living, breathing options for people today. The Western intellectual trajectory since Kierkegaard and Nietzsche has been to valorize and exalt individual religious experience and to separate it from and show it as more fundamental than any given philosophical conception of truth. Mysticism is a part of that, but the applicability is far wider than the coterie of mystics. Eckhart places truth beneath divine unity. The implication of this, which is not obvious, is that it pushes us to begin again understanding Christianity from the starting point of religious experience instead of truth. Ironically, this does not change what the core of esoteric Christianity has always been with divine oneness, but it points to a seismic shift in popular Christianity for those whose experience has not reached beyond the predominant cultural standard of truth. If we see the history of popular Christianity as a series of such changes, then we might see the next movement more clearly insofar as the possibilities are latent and discoverable in the intellectual currents of today that comprise the substrate in which thoughts and feelings arise.[26] Now let us allow Huston Smith to have the last word by completing the other half of his thought:

---

26 This points to the possibility of a larger metaphorological project that looks to metaphor to understand the cultural movements antecedent to more superficial changes and chronicles how these changes coincide with the changing of important philosophical currents. For the Late Medieval world, for example, we could look to Heinz Heimsoeth's book (*Six Great Themes*) that charts the changes in metaphysics during that time and then extend this into theological and popular religious circles. Regarding the "substrate in which thoughts and feelings arise," this wording points to and reflects Blumenberg's own in describing how metaphorological investigation can uncover material such as this: "Everywhere in the language of philosophy, indications can be found that answers to these questions have always already been given in a subterranean stratum of thought, answers that, although they may not be contained in the systems in propositional form, have never ceased to pervade, tincture, and structure them" (*Paradigms for a Metaphorology*, 7). The addition of "feelings" stretches his idea to encompass all immediate experience. Note that we need not subscribe to his model of "questions" being posed by our circumstances to make good use of this style of thinking as an indication of a new, productive mode of thinking.

As the theism they see seems childish and sentimental, some in this camp accept materialism as the only way to live without lying, while others gravitate to Zen or Vedanta or Sufism where their drive for total self-transcendence ... is recognized and welcomed at the door. No task is more important for the Church than to let such persons know that behind its outer doors that are always open stands another that is closed—closed though accessible to those who knock.... Meister Eckhart will be among those waiting to welcome those who enter.[27]

---

[27] H. Smith, "Preface" in *Essential Eckhart*, xvi.

Abbreviations of Frequently Cited Works

CRITICAL EDITIONS OF THE MEISTER ECKHART'S WORKS

DW I   Quint, Josef. *Meister Eckharts Predigten 1–24*. Stuttgart: Kohlhammer, 1958.

DW II   Quint, Josef. Meister *Eckharts Predigten 25–59*. Stuttgart: Kohlhammer, 1971.

DW III   Quint, Josef. *Meister Eckharts Predigten 60–86*. Stuttgart: Kohlhammer, 1976.

DW IV.1   Steer, Georg, Wolfgang Klimanek and Freimut Löser. *Meister Eckharts Predigten 87–105*. Stuttgart: Kohlhammer, 2003.

DW IV.2   Steer, Georg, Wolfgang Klimanek and Freimut Löser. *Meister Eckharts Predigten 106–110*. Stuttgart: Kohlhammer, 2003.

DW V   Quint, Josef. *Meister Eckharts Traktate*. Stuttgart: Kohlhammer, 1963.

LW I.1   Weiss, Konrad. *Magistri Echardi Prologi. Expositio libri Genesis. Liber parabolarum Genesis*. Stuttgart: Kohlhammer, 1964.

LW I.2	Sturlese, Loris. Magistri *Echardi Prologi in opus tripartitum et expositio libri Genesis secundum recensionem Cod. Oxoniensis Bodleiani Laud misc. 222 (L). Adiecta sunt recensiones cod. Amploniani fol. 181 (E) ac codd. Cusani 21 et Reverensis 72/1056 (CT) denuo reconitae. Liber parabolarum Genesis editio altera*. Stuttgart: Kohlhammer, 1992.
LW II	Fischer, Heribert, Josef Koch and Konrad Weiss. *Magistri Echardi expositio libri Exodi. Sermones et lectiones super Ecclesiastici cap. 24, 23–31. Expositio libri Sapientiae. Expositio Cantici Canticorum cap. 1,6*. Stuttgart: Kohlhammer, 1992.
LW III	Christ, Karl, Bruno Decker, Josef Koch, Heribert Fischer, Loris Sturlese and Albert Zimmerman. *Magistri Echardi expositio sancti Evangelii secundum Iohannem*. Stuttgart: Kohlhammer, 1994.
LW IV	Benz, Ernst, Bruno Decker and Josef Koch. *Magistri Echardi sermones*. Stuttgart; Kohlhammer, 1956.
LW V	Geyer, Bernard, Josef Koch, Erich Seeberg and Loris Sturlese. *Magistri Echardi opera Parisiensia. Tractatus super oratione dominica; Responsio ad articulos sibi impositos de scriptis et dictis suis. Acta Echardiana*. Stuttgart: Kohlhammer, 2006.

Bibliography

Adams, David. "Metaphors for Mankind: The Development of Hans Blumenberg's Anthropological Metapohorology." *Journal of the History of Ideas* 52, no. 1 (1991): 152–66.

Aertsen, Jan A. "Ontology and Henology in Medieval Philosophy (Thomas Aquinas, Meister Eckhart, and Berthold of Moosburg)." In *On Proclus and His Influence in Medieval Philosophy*, edited by E. P. Bos and P. A. Meijer, 120–40. Leiden: Brill, 1992.

Ancelet-Hustache, Jeanne. *Master Eckhart and the Rhineland Mystics.* Translated by Hilda Graef. New York: Harper Torchbooks, 1957.

Ancelet-Hustache, Jeanne, and Mangin Éric. *Maître Eckhart: Sermons, Traités, Poème: Les Écrits Allemands.* Paris: Seuil, 2015.

Aristotle. *Aristotle's Metaphysics: A Revised Text with Introduction and Commentary.* Edited by W. David Ross. 2 vols. Oxford: Clarendon Press, 1924.

Asad, Talal. "Medieval Heresy: An Anthropological View." *Social History* 11, no. 3 (1986): 345–62.

Ashley, Benedict M. "Three Strands in the Thought of Eckhart, the Scholastic Theologian." *The Thomist* 42, no. 2 (1978): 226–39.

Augustine. *Augustine Confessions*, Volume 2: *Commentary, Books 1–7*. Translated by James O'Donnell. Oxford: Oxford University Press, 2012.

———. *Sancti Augustini opera: Enarrationes in Psalmos 101–150*. Translated by Franco Gori. Austria: Verlag der Österreichischen Akademie der Wissenschaften, 2001.

———. *Homilies on the First Epistle of John.* Translated by Boniface Ramsey. Hyde Park, N.Y.: New City Press, 1990.

Augustine, *On the Trinity.* Translated by Edmund Hill. Hyde Park, N.Y.: New City Press, 2012.

Bassler, O. Bradley. "Theology and the Modern Age: Blumenberg's Reaction to a Baconian Frontispiece." *New German Critique* 84 (2001): 163–92.

———. *The Pace of Modernity: Reading with Blumenberg.* Melbourne: re-press, 2012.

Beccarisi, Alessandra. "Philosophische Neologismen zwischen Latein und Volksprache: 'istic' und 'isticheit' bei Meister Eckhart." *Reserches de théologie et philosophie médiévale* 70 (2003): 329–58.

Beierwaltes, Werner. "Primum est dives per se: Meister Eckhart und die 'Liber de causis.'" In *On Proclus and His Influence in Medieval Philosophy*, edited by E. P. Bos and P. A. Meijer, 141–69. Leiden: Brill, 1992.

Blamires, David. "Eckhart and Tauler: A Comparison of Their Sermons on 'Homo quidam fecit cenam magnam' (Luke XIV.16)." *The Modern Language Review* 66, no. 3 (1971): 608–27.

Blumenberg, Hans. "Die Ontologische Distanz. Eine Untersuchung *über* die Krisis der Phänomenologie Husserls." Unpublished habilitation diss., University of Kiel, 1950.

———. "Wirklichkeitsbegriff und Wirkungspotential des Mythos." In *Terror und Spiel: Probleme der Mythenrezeption*, edited by Manfred Fuhrmann, 11–66. Munich: Fink, 1971.

———. "The Life-World and the Concept of Reality." In *Life-World and Consciousness. Essays for Aron Gurwitsch*, 425–44. Evanston, Ill.: Northwestern University Press, 1972.

———. *The Legitimacy of the Modern Age*. Translated by Robert M. Wallace. Cambridge, Mass.: MIT Press, 1985 [*Die Legitimität der Neuzeit*, Erneuerte Ausgabe, 1966. Frankfurt am Main: Suhrkamp, 1996.].

———. *Work on Myth*. Edited and translated by Robert M. Wallace. Cambridge, Mass.: MIT Press, 1985 [*Arbeit am Mythos*. Frankfurt am Main: Suhrkamp, 1979].

———. "An Anthropological Approach to the Contemporary Significance of Rhetoric." In *After Philosophy: End or Transformation*, edited by Kenneth Baynes, James Bohman and Thomas McCarthy, translated by Robert M. Wallace, 429–58. Cambridge, Mass.: MIT Press, 1987.

———. *Genesis of the Copernican World*. Translated by Robert M. Wallace. Cambridge, Mass.: MIT Press, 1989 [*Die Genesis der kopernikanischen Welt*. Frankfurt am Main: Suhrkamp, 1975].

———. *Shipwreck with Spectator: Paradigm of a Metaphor for Existence*. Translated by Robert M. Wallace. Cambridge, Mass.: MIT Press, 1997 [*Schiffbruch mit Zuschauer: Paradigma einer Daseinsmetapher*. Frankfurt am Main: Suhrkamp, 1979].

———. *Care Crosses the River*. Translated by Paul Fleming. Stanford, Calif.: Stanford University Press, 2010 [*Die Sorge geht über den Fluss*. Frankfurt am Main: Suhrkamp, 1987].

———. *Paradigms for a Metaphorology*. Edited by Robert Savage. Ithaca, N.Y.: Cornell University Press, 2010 [*Paradigmen zu einer Metaphorologie*, 1960. Frankfurt am Main: Suhrkamp: 1998].

———. *Laughter of the Thracian Woman: A Protohistory of Theory*. Translated by Spencer Hawkins. New York: Bloomsbury, 2015 [*Das Lachen der Thrakerin. Eine Urgeschichte der Theorie*. Frankfurt am Main: Suhrkamp, 1987].

Boer, Theodore de. *The Development of Husserl's Thought*. Dordrecht: Springer, 1978.

Bond, Lawrence. *Nicholas of Cusa: Selected Spiritual Writings*. New York: Paulist Press, 1997.

The Book of Causes. Translated by Dennis J. Brand. Milwaukee, Wis.: Marquette University Press, 2012.

The Book of the Perfect Life: Theologia Deutch—Theologia Germanica. Translated by David Blamires. Walnut Creek, Calif.: AltaMira Press, 2003.

Brient, Elizabeth. "Transitions to a Modern Cosmology: Meister Eckhart and Nicholas of Cusa on the Intensive Infinite." *Journal of the History of Philosophy* 37, no. 4 (1999): 575–600.

———. "Hans Blumenberg and Hannah Arendt on the 'Unworldly Worldliness' of the Modern Age." *Journal of the History of Ideas* 61, no. 3 (2000): 513–30.

———. *The Immanence of the Infinite: Hans Blumenberg and the Threshold to Modernity*. Washington, D.C.: The Catholic University of America Press, 2002.

———. "Meister Eckhart and Nicholas of Cusa on the Where of God." In *Nicholas of Cusa and His Age: Intellect and Spirituality: Essays Dedicated to the Memory of F. Edward Cranz*, edited by Thomas P. McTighe and Charles Trinkhaus, 127–50. Boston: Brill, 2002.

———. "How Can the Infinite Be the Measure of the Finite? Three Mathematical Metaphors from *De docta ignorantia*." In *Cusanus: The Legacy of Learned Ignorance*, edited by Peter Casarella, 210–25. Washington, D.C.: The Catholic University of America Press, 2006.

———. "From Vita Contemplativa to Vita Activa : Modern Instrumentalization of Theory and the Problem of Measure." *International Journal of Philosophical Studies* 9, no. 1 (2010): 19–40.

———. "Blumenberg Reading Cusanus: Metaphor and Modernity." In *Erinnerung an das Humane: Beiträge zur phänomenologischen Anthropologie Hans Blumenbergs*, edited by Michael Moxter, 122–44. Tübingen: Mohr Siebeck, 2011.

Browning, Don. "William James' Philosophy of Mysticism." *Journal of Religion* 59, no. 1 (1979): 56–70.

Brunner, Fernand. "L'analogie chez Maître Eckhart." *Freiburger Zeitschrift für Philosophie und Theologie* 16 (1969): 333–49.

Byers, Sarah. "The Meaning of Voluntas in Augustine." *Augustinian Studies* 37, no. 2 (2006): 171–89.

Campbell, Joseph. *Masks of God: Primitive Mythology*. New York: Penguin, 1991.

Caputo, John D. "The Nothingness of the Intellect in Meister Eckhart's 'Parisian Questions.'" *The Thomist* 39, no. 1 (1975): 85–115.

———. "Fundamental Themes in Meister Eckhart's Mysticism." *The Thomist* 42, no. 2 (1978): 197–225.

Cassirer, Ernst. *The Individual and the Cosmos in Renaissance Philosophy*. Translated by Mario Domandi. New York: Harper, 1963.

Certeau, Michel de. "Mystic Speech." In *Heterologies: Discourse on the Other*, translated by Brian Massumi, 80–100. Minneapolis: University of Minnesota Press, 1986.

———. "The Gaze of Nicholas of Cusa." *Diacritics* 17, no. 3 (1987): 2–38.

Cioran, E. M. *Drawn and Quartered*. Translated by Richard Howard. New York: Seaver Books, 1983.

Claus, David. *Toward the Soul: An Inquiry into the Meaning of 'Psyche' before Plato*. New Haven: Yale University Press, 1981.

Cohn, Norman. *The Pursuit of the Millenium: Revolutionary Millenarians and Mystical Anarchists of the Middle Ages*. 3rd ed. New York: Oxford University Press, 1970.

Colledge, Edmund. "Meister Eckhart: His Times and His Writings." *The Thomist* 42, no. 2 (1978): 240–58.

Colette, Jacques. "Mystique et Philosophie." *Revue des sciences philosophiques et théologiques* 70, no. 3 (1986): 329–48.

Connolly, John. *Living without Why: Meister Eckhart's Critique of the Medieval Concept of Will*. New York: Oxford University Press, 2014.

Counet, Jean-Michel. "Ontologie et itinéraire spirituel chez maître Eckhart." *Revue Philosophique de Louvain* 90, no. 2 (1998): 254–80.

Davies, Oliver. "Why Were Meister Eckhart's Propositions Condemned?" *New Blackfriars* 71 (October 1990): 433–45.

———. "Hildegard of Bingen, Mechthild of Magdeburg and the Young Meister Eckhart." *Mediävistik* 4 (1991): 37–51.

———. *Meister Eckhart: Mystical Theologian*. London: SPCK, 1991.

Demkovich, Michael. "Meister Eckhart and the Controversial Corrections of Aquinas." *New Blackfriars* (May 2010): 335–44.

Dietrich, Paul. "The Wilderness of God in Hadewijch II and Meister Eckhart and His Circle." In *Meister Eckhart and the Beguine Mystics*, edited by Bernard McGinn, 31–43. New York: Continuum, 1994.

Dobie, Robert. "Ontological Philosophy of Religion." *The Journal of Religion* 82, no. 4 (2002): 563–85.

———. "Science and Mysticism in the Middle Ages: Meister Eckhart's Synthesis." *Medieval Mystical Theology* 19, no. 1 (2010): 15–34.

Dreyfus, Hubert. "Merleau-Ponty and Recent Cognitive Science." In *The Cambridge Companion to Merleau-Ponty*, edited by Taylor Carmen and Mark B. N. Hansen, 129–50. Cambridge: Cambridge University Press, 2004.

Duclow, Donald. "'My Suffering is God': Meister Eckhart's Book of Divine Consolation." *Theological Studies* 44, no. 4 (1983): 570–86.

———. "Hermeneutics and Meister Eckhart." *Philosophy Today* 28, no. 1 (1984): 36–43.

———. "Nicholas of Cusa in the Margins of Meister Eckhart: Codex Cusanus 21." In *Nicholas of Cusa in Search of God and Wisdom*, edited by Gerald Christianson and Thomas M. Izbicki, 57–69. Leiden: Brill, 1991.

———. *Masters of Learned Ignorance: Eriugena, Eckhart, Cusanus*. Burlington, Vt.: Ashgate, 2006.

Dupré, Louis. *Passage to Modernity: An Essay in the Hermeneutics of Nature and Culture*. New Haven: Yale University Press, 1993.

———. "Unio Mystica: The State and the Experience." In *Mystical Union in Judaism, Christianity, and Islam*, edited by Moshe Idel and Bernard McGinn, 3–23. New York: Continuum, 1996.

"Eckhart: The Man," The Eckhart Society, December 14, 2015, http://eckhartsociety.org/eckhart/eckhart-man.

Eckhart. *Meister Eckhart: A Modern Translation*. Translated by Raymond Blakney. New York: HarperOne, 1942.

———. *Meister Eckhart: Selected Treatises and Sermons*. Translated by James M. Clark, and John Skinner. London: HarperCollins, 1958.

———. *Parisian Questions and Prologues*. Translated by Armand A. Maurer. Toronto: Pontifical Institute of Mediaeval Studies, 1974.

———. *Meister Eckhart: The Essential Sermons, Commentaries, Treatises and Defense*. Translated by Edmund Colledge and Bernard McGinn. Mahwah, N.J.: Paulist Press, 1981.

———. *Meister Eckhart: Teacher and Preacher*. Translated by Bernard McGinn, Frank Tobin, and Elvira Borgstädt. Preface by Kenneth Northcott. New York: Paulist Press, 1986.

———. *Breakthrough: Meister Eckhart's Creation Spirituality in New Translation*. Translated by Matthew Fox. New York: Doubleday, 1991.

———. *Meister Eckhart: Selected Writings*. Translated by Oliver Davies. London: Penguin, 1994.

———. *The Complete Mystical Works of Meister Eckhart*. Translated by Maurice O'Connell Walshe. New York: Crossroad, 2010.

Eliade, Mircea. *The Sacred and the Profane: The Nature of Religion*. New York: Harcourt Brace Jovanovich, 1987.

———. *The Myth of the Eternal Return*. Princeton, N.J.: Princeton University Press, 2012.

Evans, C. de B. *Meister Eckhart by Franz Pfeiffer*. 2 vols. London: Watkins, 1924–31.

Flasch, Kurt. "Predigt Nr. 52: 'Beati Pauperes Spiritu.'" In *Lectura Eckhardi: Predigten Meister Eckharts von Fachgelehrten gelesen und gedeutet*, edited by Georg Steer and Loris Sturlese, 163–99. Stuttgart: W. Kohlhammer, 1998.

———. *Meister Eckhart: Philosopher of Christianity*. Translated by Anne Schindel and Aaron Vanides. New Haven: Yale University Press, 2015.

Forman, Robert K. C. *Meister Eckhart: The Mystic as Theologian: an Experiment in Methodology*. Rockport, Mass.: Element, 1991.

———. *Mysticism, Mind and Consciousness*. New York: SUNY Press, 1999.

Franke, William. "Varieties and Valences of Unsayability." *Philosophy and Literature* 29, no. 2 (2005): 489–97.

Freddoso, Alfred J. "Medieval Aristotelianism and the Case against Secondary Causation in Nature." In *Divine and Human Action: Essays in the Metaphysics of Theism*, edited by Thomas V. Morris, 74–118. Ithaca, N.Y.: Cornell University Press, 1988.

Gandillac, Maurice de. "La 'dialectique' de Maître Eckhart." In *La mystique rhénane, Colloque de Strassbourg, 16-19 mai 1961*, edited by Johannes Tauler, 59–94. Paris: Presses universitaires de France, 1963

Garside, Bruce. "Language and the Interpretation of Mystical Experience." *International Journal of the Philosophy of Religion* 3, no. 2 (1972): 93–102.

Gascoigne, Neil, and Tim Thornton. *Tacit Knowledge*. Durham, UK: Acumen, 2013.

Geyer, Bernard. "Albertus Magnus und Meister Eckhart." In *Festschrift Josef Quint anlässlich seines 65. Geburtstages überreicht*, edited by Hugo Moser et al., 121–26. Bonn: Semmel, 1964.

Gill, Christopher. "The Ancient Self: Issues and Approaches." In *Ancient Philosophy of the Self*, edited by Paulina Remes and Juha Sihvola, 35–56. New York: Springer, 2008.

Gilson, Étienne. *Reason and Revelation in the Middle Ages*. New York: Charles Scribner's Sons, 1950.

——. *History of Christian Philosophy in the Middle Ages*. New York: Random House, 1955.

——. *The Spirit of Medieval Philosophy*. Translated by A. H. C. Downes. Notre Dame: University of Notre Dame Press, 1991.

Haas, Alois. "Die Problematik von Sprache und Erfahrung in der deutschen Mystik." In *Grundfragen der Mystik*, edited by H. Balthasar, W. Beierwaltes and Haas, A, 73–104. Einseideln: Johannes Verlag, 1974.

——. "Mystische Erfahrung und Sprache." In *Sermo Mysticus: Studien zu Theologie und Sprache der deutschen Mystik*, 18–36. Freiburg, Schweiz: Universitätsverlag , 1979.

——. "Das Paradox: Herausforderung des abendländlische Denkens." In *Das Mystische Paradox*, edited by Paul Geyer and Roland Hagenbüchle, 273–89. Tübingen: Stauffenburg-Verlag, 1992.

——. "Dichtung in christlicher Mystik und Zen-Buddhismus." *Zen Buddhism Today* 9 (1992): 86–116.

——. "Correspondances entre la pensée eckhartienne et les religions orientales." In *Voici Maître Eckhart*, 373–83. Grenoble: Jérôme Millon, 1994.

——. "The Nothing of God and its Explosive Metaphors." *The Eckhart Review* 8, no. 1 (1999): 6–17.

Harries, Karsten. "The Infinite Sphere: Comments on the History of a Metaphor." *Journal of the History of Philosophy* 13, no. 1 (1975): 5–15.

——. *Infinity and Perspective*. Cambridge, Mass.: MIT Press, 2001.

Heimsoeth, Heinz. *The Six Great Themes of Western Metaphysics and the End of the Middle Ages*. Translated by Ramon Betanzos. Detroit: Wayne State University Press, 1994.

Hopkins, Jasper. *On Learned Ignorance* (De Docta Ignorantia) *by Nicholas of Cusa*. Minneapolis: Arthur J. Banning Press, 1981.

Hunt, Anne. *The Trinity: Insights from the Mystics*. Collegeville, Minn.: Liturgical Press, 2010.

James, William. *Psychology: Briefer Course*. London: Macmillan, 1892.

———. *Talks to Teachers on Psychology: And to Students on Some of Life's Ideals*. New York: Henry Holt, 1899.

———. *The Varieties of Religious Experience: A Study in Human Nature*. New York: Longmans, Green, 1902. Reprint New York: Collier-Macmillan, 1961.

———. *A Pluralistic Universe*. New York: Longmans, Green, 1909. Reprint Arc Manor LLC, 2008.

———. "A Pluralistic Mystic." *Hibbert Journal* 8 (1910): 739–59.

———. *Radical Empiricism*. New York: Longmans, Green, 1912.

———. *On Some of Life's Ideals*. New York: Henry Holt, 1929.

———. "A Suggestion about Mysticism." In *Understanding Mysticism*, edited by Richard T. Woods, 215–22. Garden City, N.Y.: Doubleday, 1980.

Johnson, D. Clint. "How Mysticism Can Point the Way to Tolerance: Recognizing a Common Ground of Nonconceptual Experience in Meister Eckhart and Zen." In *Atone: Religion, Conflict, and Reconciliation*, edited by B. Adebayo A., Hayes, and S. Lundy, 135–51. Lanham, Md.: Lexington Books, 2018.

———. and Lisa Barbanell Johnson. "Reinventing the Stress Concept." *Ethical Human Psychiatry and Psychology* 12, no. 3 (2010): 218–31.

Jones, Claire Taylor. "The Trouble with Verbs: Meister Eckhart and the Tropology of Modistic Grammar." *Mystics Quarterly* 35, no. 3–4 (2009): 99–126.

Jostes, Franz. *Meister Eckhart und seine Jünger: ungedruckte zur Geschichte der deutschen Mystik*. Berlin: De Gruyter, 1972.

Kahn, Charles H. "Discovering Will from Aristotle to Augustine." In *The Question of 'Eclecticism': Studies in Later Greek Philosophy*, edited by John M. Dillon and A. A. Long, 234–59. Berkeley: University of California Press, 1988.

Katz, Steven. "Language, Epistemology, and Mysticism." In *Mysticism and Philosophical Analysis*, edited by Steven Katz, 22–74. London: Sheldon Press, 1978.

Keele, Rondo. *Ockham Explained: From Razor to Rebellion*. Chicago: Open Court, 2010.

Kellenberger, James. "The Ineffabilities of Mysticism." *American Philosophical Quarterly* 16, no. 4 (1979): 307–15.

Kelley, Carl Franklin. *Meister Eckhart on Divine Knowledge*. New Haven, Conn.: Yale University Press, 1977.

Kertz, Karl G. "Meister Eckhart's Teaching on the Birth of the Divine Word in the Soul." *Traditio* 15 (1959): 327–63.

Kieckhefer, Richard. "Meister Eckhart's Conception of Union with God." *The Harvard Theological Review* 71, no. 3–4 (1978): 203–25.

Köbele, Susanne. *Bilder der unbegriffenin Warheit: Zur Struktur mystiche Rede im Spannungsfeld Von Latein und Volkssprache*. Tübingen: Franke, 1993.

———. "Predigt 16b: 'Quasi vas auri solidem.'" In *Lectura Eckhadi: Predigten Meister Eckharts von Fachgelehrten gelesen und gedeutet*, edited by Georg Steer and Loris Sturlese, 43–74. Stuttgart: W. Kohlhammer, 1998.

Kohàk, Erazim. *Embers and the Stars: A Philosophical Inquiry into the Moral Sense of Nature*. Chicago: University of Chicago Press, 1984.

Kristo, Jure. "The Interpretation of Religious Experience: What Do Mystics Intend When They Talk about Their Experiences?" *Journal of Religion* 62, no. 1 (1982): 21–38.

Ladner, Gerhart B. "Medieval and Modern Understanding of Symbolism: A Comparison." *Speculum* 54, no. 2 (1979): 223–56.

Lakoff, George, and Mark Turner. *Women, Fire and Dangerous Things: What Categories Reveal about the Mind*. Chicago: University of Chicago Press, 1987.

———. *More than Cool Reason: A Field Guide to Poetic Metaphor*. Chicago: University of Chicago Press, 1989.

———. "Contemporary Theory of Metaphor." In *Metaphor and Thought*, edited by Andrew Ortony, 202–51. Cambridge: Cambridge University Press, 1993.

———. *Philosophy in the Flesh*. New York: Basic Books, 1999.

Lakoff, George, and Mark Johnson. *Metaphors We Live By*. Chicago: University of Chicago Press, 1980.

Lanzetta, Beverly. "Three Categories of Nothingness in Eckhart." *Journal of Religion* 72, no. 2 (1992): 248–68.

Laurent, M.-H. "Autour du procès de Maître Eckhart. Les documents des Archives Vaticanes." *Divus Thomas* 39 (1936): 331–48, 430–47.

Leff, Gordon. *Medieval Thought: St. Augustine to Ockham*. Atlantic Highlands, N.J.: Humanities Press, 1958.

Lentzen-Deis, Wolfgang. "Les prédicateurs sont comme des boulangers." In *La Prédication et l'Eglise chez Maître Eckhart et Nicolas de Cues*, edited by Marie-Anne Vannier, 107–18. Paris: Cerf, 2008.

Lerner, Robert E. "The Image of Mixed Liquids in Late Medieval Mystical Thought." *Church History* 40, no. 4 (1971): 397–411.

———. "New Evidence for the Condemnation of Meister Eckhart." *Speculum* 72, no. 2 (1997): 347–66.

Lévi-Strauss, Claude. *Myth and Meaning: Cracking the Code of Culture*. New York: Schocken, 1995.

Lévy-Bruhl, Lucien. *La Mythologie Primitive*. New York: AMS Press, 1978.

Libera, Alain de. *Le problème de l'être chez Maître Eckhart: Logique et métaphysique de l'analogie*. Geneva: Cahiers de la revue de théologie et de philosophie, 1980.

Lichtman, Maria. "Marguerite Porete and Meister Eckhart: The Mirror of Simple Souls Mirrored." In *Meister Eckhart and the Beguine Mystics*, edited by Bernard McGinn, 65–86. New York: Continuum, 1994.

Lossky, Vladimir. *Théologie negative et connaissance de Dieu chez Maître Eckhart*. Paris: Vrin, 1960.

Lubac, Henri de. *The Motherhood of the Church*. Translated by Sergia Englund. San Francisco, Calif.: Ignatius Press, 1982.

Mangin, Eric. *Maître Eckhart ou la profondeur de l'intime*. Paris: Seuil, 2012.

Matsen, P. P., P. B. Rollinson, and M. Sousa. *Readings from Classical Rhetoric*. Carbondale, Ill.: SIU Press, 1990.

McGinn, Bernard. "Eckhart's Condemnation Reconsidered." *The Thomist* 44, no. 3 (1980): 390–414.

———. "St. Bernard and Meister Eckhart." *Cîteaux* 31 (1980): 373–86.

———. "The God Beyond God: Theology and Mysticism in the Thought of Meister Eckhart." *The Journal of Religion* 61, no. 1 (1981): 1–19.

———. "Meister Eckhart on God as Absolute Unity." In *Neoplatonism and Christian Thought*, edited by Dominic O'Meara, 128–39. Albany, N.Y.: State University of New York Press, 1982.

———. "Love, Knowledge, and Unio Mystica in the Western Christian Tradition." In *Mystical Union and Monotheistic Faith: An Ecumenical Dialogue*, edited by Moshe Idel and Bernard McGinn, 59–86. New York: Macmillan, 1989.

———. *The Foundations of Mysticism: Origins to the Fifth Century*. New York: Crossroad, 1992.

———. *The Growth of Mysticism: Gregory the Great through the 12th Century*. New York: Crossroad, 1994.

———. "The Changing Shape of Late Medieval Mysticism." *Church History* 65, no. 2 (1996): 197–219.

———, ed. *Meister Eckhart and the Beguine Mystics: Hadewijch of Brabant, Mechthild of Magdeburg, and Marguerite Porete*. New York: Bloomsbury, 1997.

———. "A Prolegomenon to the Role of the Trinity in Meister Eckhart's Mysticism." *The Eckhart Review* 6, no. 1 (1997): 51–61.

———. *The Mystical Thought of Meister Eckhart: The Man from Whom God Hid Nothing*. New York: Crossroad, 2001.

———. "'Evil-Sounding, Rash, and Suspect of Heresy': Tensions between Mysticism and Magisterium in the History of the Church." *The Catholic Historical Review* 90, no. 2 (2004): 193–212.

———. *The Harvest of Mysticism in Medieval Germany (1300–1500)*. New York: Crossroad, 2005.

———. "Mystical Language in Meister Eckhart and His Disciples," *Medieval Mystical Theology* 21, no. 2 (2012): 214–32.

Meconi, David Vincent. "Becoming Gods by Becoming God's: Augustine's Mystagogy of Identification." *Augustinian Studies* 39, no. 1 (2008): 61–74.

Milem, Bruce. *The Unspoken Word: Negative Theology in Meister Eckhart's German Sermons*. Washington, D.C.: The Catholic University of America Press, 2002.

———. "Meister Eckhart's Vernacular Preaching." In *A Companion to Meister Eckhart*, edited by Jeremiah Hackett, 337–57. Boston: Brill, 2013.

Milne, Joseph. "The Desire for God, the Ordering Principle of Nature." *Medieval Mystical Theology* 22, no. 1 (2013): 45–58.

Mojsisch, Burkhard. *Meister Eckhart: Analogy, Univocity and Unity*. Translated by Orrin F. Summerell. Amsterdam: Grüner, 2001.

Mojsisch, Burkhard, and Virginie Riant. "«Ce moi»: la conception du moi de maître Eckhart. Une contribution aux «Lumières» du Moyen-Age." *Revue des Sciences Religieuses* 70, no. 1 (1996): 18–30.

Moran, Dermot. "Edmund Husserl's Phenomenology of Habituality and Habitus." *Journal of the British Society for Phenomenology* 42, no. 1 (2011): 53–77.

Moreschini, Claudio. *A Christian in a Toga, Boethius: Interpreter of Antiquity and Christian Theologian*. Göttingen: Vandenhoeck and Ruprecht, 2014.

Morgan, Ben. "Developing the Modern Concept of the Self: The Trial of Meister Eckhart." *Telos* 116 (1999): 56–80.

Morris, Charles. "Mysticism and its Language." *Writings on the General Theory of Signs*, 456–63. Boston: De Gruyter Mouton, 2013.

Murk-Jansen, Saskia. "Hadewijch and Eckhart, Amor intellegere est." In *Meister Eckhart and the Beguine Mystics*, edited by Bernard McGinn, 17–30. New York: Continuum, 1994.

Newman, Sara. "Aristotle's Notion of 'Bringing-Before-the-Eyes': Its Contributions to Aristotelian and Contemporary Conceptualizations of Metaphor, Style, and Audience." *Rhetorica: A Journal of the History of Rhetoric* 20, no. 1 (2002): 1–23.

Nicholls, Angus. *Myth and the Human Sciences: Hans Blumenberg's Theory of Myth*. New York: Routledge, 2014.

Origen. *Origen: An Exhortation to Martyrdom, Prayer, and Selected Works*. Translated by Rowan Allen Greer. Classics of Western Spirituality. New York: Paulist Press, 1979.

———. *Homilies on Leviticus 1–16*. Translated by Gary Wayne Barkley. Fathers of the Church 83. Washington, D.C.: The Catholic University of America Press, 1990.

Otto, Rudolf. *Mysticism East and West. A Comparative Analysis of the Nature of Mysticism*. New York: Macmillan, 1932.

———. *The Idea of the Holy*. London: Penguin, 1959.

Pasqua, Hervé. "Le statut méontologique de la créature selon Maître Eckhart." *Annuario Filosófico* 44, no. 1 (2011): 129–57.

Pépin, Jean. "'Stilla aqvae modica mvlto infvsa vino, ferrvm ignitvm, lvce perfvsvs aer'. L'origine de trous comparisons familières a la théologie mystique médiévale." In *Miscellanea André Combes I*, 331–75. Paris: Vrin, 1967.

Pfeiffer, Franz. *Meister Eckhart (Deutsche Mystiker des Mittelalters Bd.2)*. Aalen: Scientia Verlag, 1962.

Proclus. *The Elements of Theology: A Revised Text with Translation, Introduction, and Commentary.* Edited by E. R. Dodds. Oxford: Oxford University Press, 1992.

Plato. *Euthyphro, Apology, Crito, Phaedo, Phaedrus.* Translated by Harold North Fowler. Loeb Classical Library 36. Cambridge, Mass.: Harvard University Press, 1914.

———. *The Dialogues of Plato, Volume Two.* Edited and translated by Benjamin Jowett. New York, N.Y.: Random House, 1937.

Poulakos, John. "Kairos in Gorgias' Rhetorical Compositions." In *Rhetoric and Kairos: Essays in History, Theory, and Praxis*, edited by Phillip Sipiora and James S. Baumlin, 89–96. Albany, N.Y.: State University of New York Press, 2002.

Quint, Josef. "Mystik und Sprache: Ihr Verhältnis zueinander in der spekulativen Mystik Meister Eckharts." *Deutsche Vierteljahrsschrift für Literaturwissenschaft* 27 (1953): 48–76.

Radler, Charlotte. "In Love I Am More God: The Centrality of Love in Meister Eckhart's Mysticism." *Journal of Religion* 90, no. 2 (2010): 171–98.

Ramelli, Ilaria. "Luke 17:21: 'The Kingdom of God is Inside You' The Ancient Syriac Versions in Support of the Correct Translation." *Hugoye: Journal of Syriac Studies* 12, no. 2 (2009): 259–86.

Riel, Gerd Van. "Augustine's Will, an Aristotelian Notion?" *Augustinian Studies* 38, no. 1 (2007): 255–79.

Rubenstein, Richard. 2003. *When Jesus Became God: The Epic Struggle over Christ's Divinity in the Last Days of Rome.* New York: Harcourt Brace, 1999.

———. *Aristotle's Children: How Christians, Muslims, and Jews Rediscovered Ancient Wisdom and Illuminated the Dark Ages.* Orlando, Fla.: Harcourt, 2003.

Ruh, Kurt. *Meister Eckhart: Theologe, Prediger, Mystiker.* Munich: C.H. Beck, 1985.

Savage, Robert. "Laughter from the Lifeworld: Hans Blumenberg's Theory of Nonconceptuality." *Thesis Eleven* 94 (2008): 119–31.

Schmoldt, Benno. *Die deutsche Begriffssprache Meister Eckharts.* Heidelberg: Quelle and Meyer, 1954.

Schürmann, Reiner. "The Loss of Origin in Soto Zen and Meister Eckhart." *The Thomist* 42, no. 2 (1978): 281–312.

———. *Wandering Joy: Meister Eckhart's Mystical Philosophy.* Hudson, N.Y.: Lindisfarne, 2001.

Sells, Michael. *Mystical Languages of Unsaying.* Chicago: University of Chicago Press, 1994.

Senner, Walter. "Meister Eckhart in Köln." In *Meister Eckhart: Lebensstationen-Redesituationen*, edited by Klaus Jacobi, 207–37. Berlin: Akademie, 1997.

———. "Meister Eckhart's Life, Training, Career, and Trial." In *A Companion to Meister Eckhart*, edited by Jeremiah M. Hackett, 7–84. Boston: Brill, 2013.

Slingerland, Edward. "Conceptual Metaphor Theory as Methodology for Comparative Religion." *Journal of the American Academy of Religion* 72, no. 1 (2004): 1–31.

Smith, Cyprian. *The Way of Paradox: Spiritual Life as Taught by Meister Eckhart.* London: Dartman, Longman and Todd, 1987.

———. *The Path of Life*. York: Ampleforth Abbey Press, 1995.

Smith, Huston. "Preface." In *Meister Eckhart: The Essential Sermons, Commentaries, Treatises and Defense*, edited by Colledge and McGinn, xi–xvi. Mahwah, N.J.: Paulist Press, 1981.

Stace, W. T. *Mysticism and Philosophy*. New York: Macmillan, 1960.

Steer, Georg, and Loris Sturlese. *Lectura Eckhardi: Predigten Eckharts von Fachgelehrten gelesen und gedeutet*. Stuttgart: W. Kohlhammer, 1998.

Sturlese, Loris. "Mysticism and Theology in Meister Eckhart's Theory of the Image." *The Eckhart Review* 2, no. 1 (1993): 18–31.

Suzuki, Daisetz T. *Mysticism: Christian and Buddhist*. New York: Harper, 1957.

Théry, Gabril, OP. "Edition critique des pièces relatives au procès d'Eckhart continues dans le manuscrit 33b de la bibliothèque de Soest." *Archives d'histoire doctrinale et littéraire du moyen âge* 1 (1926): 129–268.

Tobin, Frank. "Eckhart's Mystical Use of Language: The Contexts of *eigenschaft*." *Seminar* 8 (1972): 160–68.

———. "Creativity in Interpreting Scripture: Meister Eckhart in Practice." *Monatshefte* 74 (1982): 410–18.

———. *Meister Eckhart: Thought and Language*. Philadelphia: University of Pennsylvania Press, 1986.

———. *Henry Suso: The Exemplar, with Two German Sermons*. New York: Paulist Press, 1989.

———. "Mechthild of Magdeburg and Meister Eckhart: Points of Coincidence." In *Meister Eckhart and the Beguine Mystics: Explorations in Vernacular Theology*, edited by Bernard McGinn, 44–61. New York: Continuum, 1994.

———. *Mechthild of Magdeburg: The Flowing Light of the Godhead*. New York: Paulist Press, 1997.

Tuchman, Barbara W. *A Distant Mirror: The Calamitous 14th Century*. New York: Ballantine Books, 1987.

Turner, Denys. *The Darkness of God: Negativity in Christian Mysticism*. Cambridge: Cambridge University Press, 1995.

Ueda, Shizuteru. *Die Gottesgeburt in der Seele und der Durchbruch zur Gottheit. Die mystische Anthropologie Meister Eckharts und ihre Konfrontation mit der Mystik des Zen-Buddhismus*. Gütersloh: Mohn, 1965.

Underhill, Evelyn. *Mysticism: A Study in the Nature and Development of Man's Spiritual Consciousness*. 12th. ed. New York: World, 1965.

Undusk, Rein. "Infinity on the Threshold of Christianity: The Emergence of a Positive Concept Out of Negativity." *Trames* 13, no. 4 (2009): 307–40.

Vannier, Marie-Anne. "Déconstruction de l'individualité ou assomptionde la personne chez Eckhart?" In *Individuum und Individualität im Mittelalter*, edited by Jan A. Aertsen and Andreas Speer, 622–41. Berlin: Walter de Gruyter, 1996.

Wackernagel, Wolfgang. "Establishing the Being of Images: Master Eckhart and the Concept of Disimagination." *Diogenes* 41, no. 162 (1993): 77–98.

Wallace, Robert. "Introduction to Blumenberg." *New German Critique* 32 (Spring–Summer 1984): 93–108.

Walshe, Maurice O'Connell. *A Middle High German Reader*. Oxford: Clarendon Press, 1974.

Wetz, Franz Josef. "The Phenomenological Anthropology of Hans Blumenberg." *Iris: European Journal of Philosophy & Public Debate* 1, no. 2 (2009): 389–414.

White, Lynn. "Medieval Engineering and the Society of Knowledge." *Pacific Historical Review* 44, no.1 (1975): 1–21.

Yount, David J. *Plotinus the Platonist: A Comparative Account of Plato and Plotinus' Metaphysics*. London: Bloomsbury, 2014.

Zum Brunn, Emile, and Alain de Libera. *Métaphysique du verbe et théologie négative*. Paris: Beauchesne, 1984.

PART II

Eckhart's Sermons
Translator's Note

The following translations were made using the critical editions of Eckhart's works. I translated all of the sermons that had not been previously translated into English that were currently available in the critical editions, including sermons 54a, 106, 107, 108, and Kurt Flasch's 1998 revision of the manuscript for sermon 52. I translated the sermons that had not been translated since C. de B. Evans translated them in 1924 and 1931, before the critical editions were available, including sermons 87, 88, 89, 90a, 90b, 91, 92, 93, 94, 95a, 95b, 96, 97, 98, 100, 106a, 106b, 106c, and 106d. I also translated others that were important for my study of Eckart's rhetoric, including sermons 2, 24, 40, 64 and XXIV,2. In each case, I benefitted from the notes in the critical edition and the translations available in English, French, and German. In all cases, I kept the numbering convention of the critical edition for the sermons, using numbers for the vernacular sermons and Roman numerals for the Latin sermons. I opted for translations that show a distinct preference for the formatting and phrasing found in the original. Even when paragraphs breaks and sentence structure are not as natural to us in writing, we receive the rhetoric naturally when read aloud.

The single most important and unique aspect of these translations is that I tried in all cases to preserve the metaphorical character of the words in the original. Eckhart chose his words carefully and used metaphors consistently. Similarly, where the repetition of a particular metaphor was more important than choosing the most natural word in English, especially for consistency throughout a sermon, I opted to preserve the metaphor. In existing translations in English and other languages, metaphors are sometimes obscured by subtle changes in word choice. I hope that the present translations are as true to Eckhart's spirit as they can be while also being living, vibrant expressions of his ideas.

Sermon 52
Beati pauperes spiritu,
quoniam ipsorum est regnum caelorum[1]

Blessedness opened its mouth of wisdom and said: "Blessed are the poor in spirit, for theirs is the kingdom of heaven."

All the angels and all the saints and everything that has ever been born must be silent when the wisdom of the Father speaks. For all the wisdom of the angels and of all creatures is pure foolishness before the groundless wisdom of God—and this wisdom has said that the poor are blessed.

Now there are two kinds of poverty. There is an external poverty, which is good and very praiseworthy in men who willingly do it for the love of our Lord Jesus Christ, since he had it himself when he was on earth. I do not want to say any more now of this poverty. But there is another poverty, an inner poverty, about which our Lord's word is to be understood when he says, "Blessed are the poor in spirit."

I urge you to be like this so that you understand this teaching. For I tell you by eternal truth that if you are unlike the truth I now want to speak of, you will not understand me.

You have asked me what poverty is in itself and what a poor man is. This is how I will answer.

Bishop Albert says that a poor man is one who has no satisfaction in anything God ever created—and this is well said. Further, we may say still more and take poverty in a higher sense: a poor man wills nothing and

---

[1] Mt 5:3. This translation is from Kurt Flasch's 1998 revision of Josef Quint's critical edition. This sermon appears first here because it is arguably Eckhart's most famous sermon. Despite its popularity, Flasch's revision has not been completely translated into English until now. Bruce Milem translated large sections of it in 2002.

knows nothing and has nothing. I will now speak of these three points. I urge you, for the love of God, to understand this truth if you can. If you cannot understand it, do not worry yourselves over it, for the truth I want to speak of is such that few good people can understand it.

First, we say that a man is poor who wills nothing. There are some people who do not understand this very well. They cling to their egos[2] with attachment in penitential and external practices, which they regard as very important. God have mercy on those who know so little of divine truth! These people are called holy because of their external actions.[3] Yet inside they are donkeys, for they do not understand the difference [between outward appearances and] divine truth. These people say that a poor man is one who wills nothing. They go on to explain that a man should live so that he never fulfills his will in anything and further that he should incessantly strive so that he fulfills the most beloved will of God. These people are all right[4] because their intentions are good. For that we should commend them. May God in his mercy give them the kingdom of heaven. But for all that, I say in divine truth that these are neither poor men nor do they resemble poor men. They are regarded highly in the eyes of those who know no better. Yet still I say: they are donkeys who are ignorant of the truth. They should have the kingdom of heaven by their good intentions. Yet still, they know nothing of this poverty of which we wish to speak.

If someone were to ask me what a poor man is who wills nothing, I would say that as long as a man has his own will that he wills to fulfill the most beloved will of God, that man does not have that poverty of which we want to speak. For this man still has a will with which he wills to satisfy God's will, and this is not true poverty. For, if a man has poverty, then he should be as free of his created will as he was when he was not. For I say to you by eternal truth: so long as you have a will to fulfill the will of God and you have

---

[2] The language is ambiguous here. The words *sich behalten* are perhaps closest to our colloquial expression "to bogart" something, or to jealously keep it for yourself. Since the expression is reflexive, it could also mean "to keep or cling to one's self," which is the sense that both Schürmann ("hold fast to their selfish I") and Davies ("cling to their own egos") use. Colledge simply translates it as "attached," absorbing the word *eigenschaft* as well, just like Walshe does in translating it as "cling with attachment."

[3] The word translated as "actions" here is *bilden*, which is also Eckhart's word for "images." The word means "image," "appearance," and "work (activity)." Conveniently for Eckhart, the word for "images" also implies activity. Thus, to be free of one's images, as he suggests in Sermon 2, is to likewise be free of activity.

[4] More literally, "It is well with these people," as with the archaic expression "All is well with these people."

the desire for eternity and for God, you are not poor. For a poor man is one who wills nothing and desires nothing.[5]

When I stood in my first cause, I had no God and I was my own cause. I willed nothing and I desired nothing, for I was a free being, knowing myself by savoring truth. I willed myself and willed no other thing. What I willed, I was, and what I was, I willed, and so I stood free of God and all things. What's more: when I went out from my free will and I received my created being, then I had a God. For before there were creatures, God was not God. Further still: he was what he was.[6] When creatures came to be and received their created being, then God was not God in himself, but rather, he was God in creatures.

Now we say that God, insofar as[7] he is God according to them, is not the supreme end of creatures. Great riches such as that are possessed by even the lowliest creature in God. If it were the case that a fly possessed reason and through reason could seek the eternal abyss of divine being out of which it comes, then we say that God with all that he is as God would not be enough to fulfil or satisfy the fly.[8] Therefore, we pray to God that we may become free of God and that we take on the truth and enjoy eternity where the highest angel and the fly and the soul are one[9]—there I stood and willed what I was,

---

[5] This pairing of desire (*gebert*) and will (*wil*) in two different terms shows why previous instances of *wil* in this section should be translated as "will" instead of "want." The Dominicans are famously opposed to the Franciscans over the issue of the primacy of love or will versus knowledge. This sermon directly addresses the issue. Thus, the three-part structure that Eckhart uses for this sermon should be translated as *will* (not want), knowledge, and possession. In ascending order, we have the solutions given by the Franciscans, the Dominicans and, finally, the way of detachment from possession advocated by Eckhart himself. If the terms are not translated consistently in light of this theme, it can be easily masked by translation.

[6] In both meaning and phrasing, this seems clearly to refer to Exodus 3:14, "I am he who is 'I am,'" *sum qui sum*.

[7] Eckhart's "insofar as" (*in quantum*) principle is often discussed in the context of his Latin works. In German, he often uses *nâch* to convey the same idea, as he does here. I find it useful to translate such instances as "insofar as" to make the allusion to this principle clearer. Of the existing translations in English, only Davies makes the same choice.

[8] In three places in this section, Eckhart uses a similar word to track a progression. First he tells us that Albert says that a poor man has no "contentedness" or "satisfaction" (*genüegede*) in created things. Then he says that so long as one still has an individual will to will the satisfaction (*genuoc*) of God's will, one is not poor. Finally, he says that God is not enough (*genuoc*) to satisfy or fulfill the fly with reason that seeks the divine abyss. The metaphor here is one of *rest*. The soul is a home for God when he can rest, dwell, or abide there, as we read in Sermon 40. The soul passively "suffers" or "undergoes" (*lîden*) God and allows God to act in her. The persistence of a similar term in this sermon shows how pervasive Eckhart's metaphorical themes are even when they are not discussed directly.

[9] Though *glîch* means "equal," as Walshe, Schürmann, Fox, and Colledge rendered it, Eckhart here refers to the undifferentiated likeness of all things in the godhead, which is oneness. This

and was what I willed. We also say that if a man is poor in will, then he must will and desire as little as he willed and desired when he was not. It is in this way that a man is poor who wills nothing.

Second, a man is poor who knows nothing. We have sometimes said that a man should live as if he did not live, either for himself, for truth, or for God. Yet we now say otherwise and want to go further: a man who would have this poverty should live so that he does not even know that he is not living in any way for himself, for truth, or for God. Further still, he should be so free of all knowing that he neither knows, nor recognizes, nor is he aware that God lives in him. Further still, he should be free of all knowing that lives in him. For when man stood in the eternal nature of God, nothing else lived in him. Further still, he was himself what lived there. So we say that a man should stand as free of his own knowing as he was when he was not. He should let God act as he will and let man stand free.[10]

Everything that ever came from God is directed to some genuine[11] activity. And so, it is the proper activity of man to know and love. Now the question is, in which one does blessedness lie most of all? Some masters say that it lies in loving. Others say it lies in knowing and in loving, and what they say is better. Yet we say that it lies neither in knowing nor in loving. Further still, there is a something[12] in the soul from which knowing and loving flow. It itself neither knows nor loves like the powers of the soul do. Whoever knows this knows where blessedness lies.[13] This something has neither before nor after. It is not waiting for anything to arrive, for it can neither gain nor lose. Therefore, it is so deprived that it does not know that God acts in it. Further, it just is itself, delighting in itself as God does. And so we say that a man

---

was Davies's choice as well, perhaps thinking as I do that it reads more powerfully this way. This accords with the oneness implied by each thing standing or remaining in their first cause. The list includes something material (the fly), immaterial (the angel), and the soul which crosses all boundaries as created and uncreated. The only "place" where these are all "alike" is the godhead.

10 Though I believe it is important to translate *ledic* consistently and render it as "free" so that one can see the continuity in Eckhart's language, one could easily say "unengaged," "void" (Schürmann), or even "idle" (Walshe), since Eckhart here pairs the work of God's activity with the freedom of man's passivity.

11 Walshe alone has captured the Aristotelian sense of this sentence. For Aristotle, each thing has an activity that is proper to it. This is its *ergon*, its "function." In this and the sentence that follows, Eckhart clearly has this principle in mind when describing the "proper" (*eigen*) work of man.

12 Eckhart often refers to the spark of the soul as a "something" (*etwaʒ* or *eineʒ*).

13 This is an ironic use of "knows" here, of course, to be juxtaposed paradoxically with the "something" that is described as beyond knowing and loving in the previous sentence.

should stand so free and empty that he neither knows nor is he aware[14] that God acts in him: only then can he possess poverty.

The masters say of God that he is a being and a rational being and that he knows all things. Yet I say that God is neither being nor a rational being nor does he know this or that.[15] Therefore, God is free of all things and so he is all things. For a man to be poor in spirit, he must be poor of all his own knowing so that he knows no thing, neither God nor creature nor himself. Therefore it is necessary that a man should prepare himself[16] so that he does not know and is not aware of God's activity. In this way, a man can be poor of his own knowing.

Third, a man is poor who has nothing. Many people have said that not having the material things of the earth is a perfection, and this is indeed true in a sense: when it is done willingly. But this is not the sense in which I mean it.

I have said before that a poor man does not even will to fulfill God's will and, still further, that he lives so that he is free of his own will and of God's will just as he was when he was not. We say of this poverty that it is the highest poverty. Secondly, we say that he is a poor man who knows nothing of God's activity within him. He stands as free of knowing and awareness as God is free of all things, which is the purest poverty. But the third is the greatest[17] poverty, of which we will now speak: when a man has nothing.

Now pay serious attention here! I have sometimes said, as a great master[18] says, that man should be as free of all things and all activity, both inner and outer, so that he may be a proper place for God in which God can act.[19] Now we say otherwise. If it is the case that a man stands free of all creatures and

---

14 The word translated as "aware" here is *bekenne*. It means "to acknowledge" or "to recognize." Here, it means to have any conscious awareness of a thing such that it is present to mind. Eckhart is emphasizing the utter emptiness and poverty of this. In English we can say that a complete lack of recognition is something that a person is "unaware of." In this sentence, the verbs are *enbekenne* (un-aware) and *enwizze* (un-knowing).

15 As we see elsewhere, *noch diz noch daz*, which means "neither this nor that" is Eckhart's German version of his Latin phrase *hoc et hoc*, which refers to any given "this or that" of the world.

16 The reflexive use of the word *bereite* is different in the new critical edition than *begernde*, which has often been translated as "desire." The connotation of *bereite* is similar, insofar as "readying oneself" is an act of will (although it more generally implies cultivation of oneself), while "desiring" is a more specific activity.

17 Notice how he tells us of the "highest" poverty and "purest" poverty, only then to immediately contrast these with the "greatest" poverty. Eckhart's sermons abound in this sort of paradoxical juxtaposition.

18 A single letter in Flasch's 1998 revision of the critical edition makes a difference here. Instead of referring to "great masters," Eckhart instead refers to "a great master," which could be himself.

19 Though it is natural to say "external works" when referring to activities like prayer and penance, the phrase "inner works" is not as clear. Further, by using "activity" and "act" here, I have attempted to preserve Eckhart's passive and active metaphorics that are at play in this sermon.

God and his own self, and if God finds a place in him to act, then we say: as long as that is in a man, then he is not poor with the greatest poverty. God does not intend in his activity for a man to have a place in him wherein God may act. For poverty of the spirit is when a man remains so free of God and all his activity that if God is to act in the soul, he must himself be the place in which he will act—and this he does gladly. For if he finds a man this poor, God undergoes his own activity[20] and God is his own proper place for activity, so that God is an actor in himself. Here, in this poverty, a man brings about[21] the eternal being that he was and that he is now and in which he should eternally stay.

Yet there is a problem. Saint Paul says, "all that I am, I am from the grace of God."[22] Now my words seem to be above grace and above being and above understanding and above willing and above all desire—so how can Saint Paul's words be true? To this, we answer that Saint Paul's words are true: it was necessary that the grace of God was in him, for the grace of God acted in him so that the accidental entered into the essential. When grace completed and perfected its action, Paul remained what he was.

So I say that man should remain so poor that he should not be or have any place in which God can act. When man clings to place, he clings to distinction. Therefore I pray to God that he make me free of God, for my essential being is above God if we take God to be the beginning of created things. For in the same being of God where God is above being and above distinction, there I was myself, I willed myself, and I knew myself to create this man. Therefore I am the cause of myself according to my being, which is eternal, and not according to my becoming, which is temporal. Therefore I am born, and insofar as I am born I am mortal. Insofar as I am unborn, I have eternally been, I am now, and I shall eternally remain. What I am insofar as I am born will die and become nothing, for it is temporal. Therefore, it must decay in time.

---

20 Flasch's revision is substantially different here. Quint's version of the text said that God acted while man remained passive. Flasch's version has God "undergoing" his own action, which implies that God is both completely active and passive, a richer paradox in the new version.

21 Here, *ervolget* is difficult to translate into a natural-sounding phrase in English because the idea Eckhart is expressing is not one we are accustomed to hearing. Previous translations used more muted terms like "attains," "enters" or "recovers." The word is related to the modern German *erfolgen*, which means 'to effect" or "to bring about," implying that the subject plays an active role in causing the object. What we have then is a peculiar phrase where someone "brings about" or "effects" eternal being. It sounds wrong, but only because we are not accustomed to giving birth to God. Compare with the later passage: "I was the cause of myself and of all things."

22 1 Corinthians 15:10.

In my birth all things were born, and I was the cause of myself and of all things. If I had willed it, I would not be, nor would all things be. If I was not, then God would not be. That God is God, of that I am a cause. If I was not, then God would not be God. But you do not need to know this.

A great master says that his breaking-through is nobler than his flowing out. That is true. As I flowed from God, all things spoke: God is. But this cannot make me blessed, for I spoke[23] myself to be a creature. Further, in this breaking-through where I stand free from my own will in God's will and stand free from God's will and all his actions and from God himself, then I am above all creatures, and I am neither God nor creature. Still further: I am what I was and what I should remain now and forevermore. There I receive an imprint[24] which raises me above all the angels. In this imprint I receive such riches that God cannot satisfy me insofar as he is God or by way of all his divine actions. For what I receive in this breaking-through is that God and I are one. There I am what I was, and there I neither increase nor decrease, for there I am an immovable cause which moves all things. Here, God finds no place in man, for what man attains with this poverty is what he has been and eternally should remain. This is where God is one with the spirit. This is the greatest poverty that one can find.

Whoever does not understand this, let him not trouble his heart with it. For so long as a man is not like this truth, he will not understand these words. For this is an unconcealed[25] truth which comes from the heart of God without a medium.[26]

That we may live so as to find it eternally, so help us God. Amen.

---

23 Flasch's text differs importantly here. Quint's *bekenne* means "know" while Flasch's *bejehe* means "bespeak" or simply "spoke." This complements the instance of "spoke" (*sprâchen*) in the previous sentence, alluding to the speaking of God's creative word.

24 Translating *îndruk* as "imprint," as Walshe does, is important since stamping or imprinting is an important metaphor for Eckhart. As with Sermon 2, *enpfâhe* could mean both to receive (passive) or conceive (active).

25 The word *unbedaht* (unconcealed) would have sounded very close to *unbedâht*, which means "unknowing," which would be consistent with Eckhart's stripping away of "knowing" along with "loving" or "willing" to arrive at "having" in this sermon.

26 This is the much-discussed *âne mittel* passage in Quint, now emended to *sunder mittel* by Flasch. The "medium" or "middle" refers to intercession, which precludes direct contact. This effectively tells us that his rhetoric sounds peculiar because it directly touches God. This stands out as a commentary on how Eckhart viewed what ministerial rhetoric was capable of doing. This is different than saying "Eckhart's view on language," since his words do not merely *refer* so much as they induce or catalyze ontological change in his audience's souls.

Sermon 2
*Intravit Iesus in quoddam castellum
et mulier quaedam, Martha nomine,
excepit illum in domum suam*[1]

I have spoken a few words first in Latin that are written in the Gospel and mean this in German: "Our lord Jesus Christ went up into a little castle and was received[2] by a virgin, who was a wife."

Ah yes, now listen carefully to these words: it must be from necessity that the person who received Jesus was a virgin. A person is rightly spoken of as a virgin if he is free of all foreign images, as free as he was when he was not. See, now one may ask, how a person who is born and proceeds in a rational life can also be free of all his images, as when he was not. He knows many things, after all, which are all images. How then can he be free? Now take note of this explanation which will make you understand: were I so rational that all rational images were in me that all people had ever received and all those that were in God himself, and if I were without attachment, having not grasped[3] with attachment in doing or leaving anything undone, without looking to past or future, then I would stand free and unhindered in this present moment in God's dearest will in uninterrupted doing. In truth, I would be a virgin, truly unimpeded by all images, as I was when I was not.

---

1 Lk 10:38.

2 *Enpfangen*—to receive or conceive. This dual meaning is important for Eckhart in this sermon. The Latin *excepit* has the same connotations, meaning both "receive" and also "draw out."

3 In Middle High German, *begriffen* as a verb means "to grasp," while as a noun it means "concepts" (i.e., things that are grasped). Thus, Eckhart's audience would have heard both the pair "attachment/grasped" and also "attachment/concepts," which works nicely for his purposes.

Yet I say: that a man is a virgin takes nothing from him. It takes nothing from all his works and all he ever did. He remains virginal and free without any hindrance to the highest truth, as the unhindered and free Jesus is maidenly in himself. As the masters say, oneness is through likeness and likeness alone.[4] In this way so must a man be a maid, a virgin, who shall receive the maidenly Jesus.

Now mark well what I say and look carefully![5] For now if a man always remained a virgin, then no fruit would come from him. For him to become fruitful, from necessity he must be a wife. "Wife" is the noblest word that one can say of a soul, much nobler than "virgin." For a man to receive[6] God in himself, that is good, and in the receptivity he is a virgin. That again God becomes fruitful in him, that is better. The only gratitude for a gift is to be fruitful with it. And there is the spirit of the wife in giving birth again in gratitude. There she gives birth to Jesus back into God, into his fatherly heart.

Many great gifts are received in virginity and are not again born back into God in return in wifely fruitfulness with grateful praise. The gifts all spoil and come to nothing, so that man becomes neither blessed nor better through them.[7] His virginity is useless to him, for he is not a wife as well in his virginity with all fruitfulness. Therein lies the loss. I have said on that account: "Jesus went up into a little castle and was received by a virgin, who was a wife." That must be from necessity, as I have made known to you.

Married people bring forth little more than one fruit in a year. But now I mean other married people: all of those who are bound with attachment to prayer, fasting, vigils and all kinds of exterior exercises and mortification. Any attachment to any works takes away the freedom to attend to God in this present now and follow Him alone in the light in which he shows you what to do and what to leave undone, renewed and free in every present moment, as if you did not possess, nor desire, nor even could do anything else. Every

---

4 Cf. *In Ioh.* ns.556, 558.

5 As *vlîze* can mean "zeal" or "assiduous," there is a connotation of energy that isn't quite captured by saying 'look carefully!' We don't normally say 'look with energy!'

6 Edmund Colledge has "conceives" and "conceiving" here for *enpfæhet* and *enpfenclicheit* (*Essential Eckhart*, 178). Since *enpfæhet* can mean "receive" or "conceive," this isn't necessarily wrong, but here Eckhart is still talking about the limitation of the virgin in her receiving. The conceiving is giving birth to the Son back to God, which is the province of the wife. This conception is what Eckhart refers to in the next sentence. Saying that a man "conceives God," and then saying that God becoming fruitful in him is better (which means that he conceives God), would be strange. This would be like saying that "man conceives God, but it is better if man conceives God." Note that Bruce Milem and Reiner Schürmann both chose "receive" here.

7 Cf. Sermon XLIII, n.432.

attachment or premeditated work that deprives you of this freedom in each new moment, I now call a "year." For your soul brings forth no fruit if it has not done that work that possessed you with attachment, having neither trust in God nor in yourself unless you accomplished the work that you have grasped with attachment. Otherwise, you have no peace. Therefore you do not bring forth any fruit until you have done your work. I reckon that as a year, and your fruit is small indeed, for it comes from attachment to the work and not from freedom. I call these married people, for they remain bound to attachment. They bring forth little fruit, and what they do bring forth is indeed small, as I have said.

    A virgin who is a wife is free and unbound, without attachment. She is equally near God and herself at all times. She brings forth many fruits, and these are great, neither less nor more than God himself is. This virgin who is a wife makes this fruit and this birth, giving birth and bringing forth every day one hundred or one thousand fruits, even without number, by giving birth and bearing fruit out of the noblest ground. Or to say it even better: yes, out of that same ground the Father is giving birth to His eternal Word, and from there she fruitfully gives birth with him. For Jesus, the light and likeness of the fatherly heart—as Saint Paul said, he is the glory and likeness of the fatherly heart and he powerfully shines through the fatherly heart—this Jesus is united with her and she with him. She radiates and shines with him as one single one [*ein einic ein*[8]] and as a pure and clear light in the fatherly heart.

    I have also said more: there is a power in the soul which touches neither time nor flesh. It flows out of the spirit and remains in the spirit and is wholly spiritual. In this power God is all at once verdant and blossoming in all the joy and in all the glory that He is in Himself. That is a joy so heartfelt, a joy so incomprehensible, an abundance of which no one can speak. For the eternal Father gives birth to his Son in this power ceaselessly. Also, this power is giving birth to the Son along with the Father and to itself in this one power of the Father. If a man had an entire kingdom or all the goods of the earth and let it go purely through God and became one of the poorest men who ever lived on earth, and God gave him as much to suffer as he ever gave a man, and he endured all this unto his death and God gave him a single glance for him to see of how He is in this power: his joy would be so great that all this

---

8 *Ein einic ein*—difficult to render in English since "a," "single," and "one" neither sound alike nor look alike. Eckhart's expression probably stood out to his listeners, so my rendering, "one single one," sounds a little odd so as to stand out in the same way—at least, it stands out in a way "a single one" does not.

suffering and poverty would then be too little. Yes, if God then never more gave him the kingdom of heaven, he would have already received so great a reward for all that he ever suffered, for God is in this power as He is in the eternal now. If the spirit were united with God for all time in this power, the man could not grow old. God made the first man in this now, and in this now the last man will pass away. I say, in this now, they are alike in God and there is not more than one now.[9] Now see, the man lived in one light with God. On that account there is not in him either suffering or the succession of time, but an eternal likeness. From this man all wonder has truly been taken away. All things stand in him in their essences. Therefore, he receives nothing new from things to come nor from anything that happens, for he lives anew for all time in the single now without ceasing. Such is the divine sovereignty in this power.

There is another power that is also incorporeal. It flows out of the spirit and remains in the spirit and is entirely spiritual. In this power God is ceaselessly gleaming and burning with all his riches, with all his sweetness and with all his delight. Truly, in this power is so great a joy and such an immeasurably great delight that no one can fully reveal it or speak of it. Yet I say: if there were a single man to rationally look herein and glimpse in truth for a single moment the delight and joy that is in there, all that he may suffer and all that God would have had him to suffer would be too little for him and indeed nothing. I say yet more: it would be at once a joy and a resting place for him.

If you would rightly know whether your suffering is yours or God's, then you should listen closely to this: if you would suffer for yourself, in whatever way it is, that suffering causes you pain and is a burden for you to carry. But if you suffer for God and God alone, that suffering does not do you harm and is not a burden for you to carry, for God carries the burden. In good truth! If there were a man who wanted to suffer through God and purely through God alone,[10] and more if all at once the suffering that all men had ever suffered and that all the world bears, that does not do him harm and is not a burden for him to carry, for God carries the burden. If someone placed a hundredweight on my neck and another carried it, then it would be as

---

9 Cf. Sermon XVII, n.168.

10 Colledge has, "If there were a man who wanted to suffer for the love of God and purely for God alone." The addition of "for the love of" instead of "through" (for *durch*) does not seem to be implied by the manuscripts. Here, it seems, Milem's translation is clearer than Colledge's and Schürmann's.

pleasant to carry a hundred of them as one. For it would not be a burden to me nor would it do me harm. Said briefly: whatever a man suffers through God and God alone, God makes it light and sweet for him, as I said in the beginning when our sermon began: "Jesus went up into a little castle and was received by a virgin, who was a wife." Why? It must necessarily be that she was a virgin and also a wife. Now I have told you that Jesus was received, but I have not told you what this little castle is. I want to talk about this now.

I have sometimes said that there is a power in the spirit that alone is free. I have sometimes said that it is a guardian of the spirit. I have sometimes said that it is a light of the spirit. I have sometimes said that it is a spark.[11] Yet I say now: it is neither this nor that.[12] And still, it is a "something"[13] that it is higher above this and that than heaven is above earth. Therefore, I name it now in a nobler mode than I have ever named it, since it denies nobility and denies all modes and is above them. It is free of all names and naked of all forms, at once unhindered and free, as God is unhindered and free in himself. It is so completely one and simple, as God is one and simple, that one with modes cannot peer into it. In this same power that I have spoken of, God is blossoming and verdant with all his godhead and spirit in God. In this same power the Father is giving birth to his only-begotten Son as truly as in himself, for he truly lives in this power. And the spirit gives birth with the Father to the same only-begotten Son and to himself, the same Son, and is the same Son in the light and is the truth. If you could look upon this with my heart, you would understand well what I say, for it is true and the truth itself speaks it.

Now see and listen well! So one and simple is this little castle above all modes,[14] I say to you and I mean, in the soul, that this noble power that I have

---

11 Cf. Sermon LV, n.547.

12 *weder diʒ noch daʒ—weder... noch* = "neither... nor." *Diʒ und daʒ* (as we see repeated again in this form a few lines later) is clearly the German version of Eckhart's *hoc et hoc* in Latin, meaning "this and that." He uses that particular locution when referring to all the things of this world, all the things we call "this" and "that."

13 *ein waʒ*—Milem, Colledge and Schürmann all have this as "a something." It is a peculiar construction that recalls the modern German *etwas* or *was*, which can both mean "something" (and indeed, some manuscripts have *etwa* or *etwaʒ*). Elsewhere, Eckhart makes much of a long tradition of giving weight to the *erat* in John 1:1: *In principium erat verbum*. We are told (as is traditional) that *erat* is the most perfect and substantial form of *esse* and, as such, it is appropriate for God. Perhaps here as well we are to hear that the spark is "a was" (i.e., past of "to be") since *was* sounded the same as *waʒ* when spoken.

14 *wise*, "way," "mode." Though "mode" is a bit awkward in his first use of it at DW II 39.6, its use as a technical term makes the rest of that otherwise strange sentence in DW II 40.1 much more sensible. The idea is that the godhead cannot be seen in any mode. Previous translations

spoken of is not even worthy to peer for one single moment for one glance within the little castle and the other power that I have spoken of. There, God is gleaming and burning with all his richness and with all his delight. It never dares to peer within, so truly one and simple is this little castle. And so far above all modes and all powers is this single one that God himself can in no mode and in no power peer into it. In good truth and so truly as God lives! God himself never peers into it for a single moment and has never peered in, insofar as he possesses himself according to a mode and out of the attachment to his persons. This is good to notice, for this single one is without modes and without attachment. And therefore: should God ever peer into it, it must cost all of his divine names and attachment to his persons.[15] He must leave them all at once, if he should ever peer inside. Insofar as[16] he is a simple one, without all modes and attachment: there he is neither Father nor Son nor Holy Ghost in this sense and is nevertheless a something that is neither this nor that.

You see, as he is one and simple, so he comes into that one that I call a little castle in the soul. Otherwise, he does not come into it in any way. Only in this way does he come in and is he inwardly there. With this part, the soul is like God and otherwise not. What I have said to you is true. I lay the truth before you as a testimony with my soul as a pledge.

That we may be in a little castle, which Jesus may go up into and be received and eternally abide in the way as I have spoken, may God help us in this. Amen.

---

have tried different approaches: Colledge ("way," "fashion"), Milem ("way"), and Schümann ("fashion," "mode").

15 *persônlîche eigenschaft*—I think Eckhart meant for this to sound odd. It has the ring of "personal" as in "my own, what I am attached to" and also as "personly," as in "relating to the persons of the Trinity." I am tempted to render it "personly attachment" to emphasize the unusual form.

16 Note that *sunder als* ("only" or "separately as") and *als verre* ("as far") can be rendered "insofar as," perhaps being German forms of Eckhart's *inquantum* principle that was so important to his defense. Cf. Sermon XXIV, n.247.

Sermon 24
Induimini dominum Iesum Christum[1]

Saint Paul said: "Put on," internalize "Christ."

When one takes off himself, he puts on Christ, God, blessedness, and holiness. When a boy tells of strange[2] things, one believes him, yet when Paul promises great things, you do not hardly believe it. He promises you—if you take off yourself—God, blessedness, and holiness. It is wondrous:[3] if a man should take off himself, then in his taking off himself, he puts on Christ, holiness, and blessedness and he becomes very great. The prophet wondered about two things. The first: what God did with the stars, the moon, and the sun. The other wonder is about the soul, that God has done and does such great things with it and for its sake and because he does whatever he can for it. He does many great things for its sake and is entirely occupied[4] with it, and that is from its greatness, in which it is made. How great it is made—notice that! I make a letter of the alphabet according to the likeness that the letter has in me, in my soul. It is likewise with God. God has made all things generally according to the image that he has in Himself of all things and not according to Himself. He has made some things differently

---

1 Rom 13:14.

2 The connotation of "unfamiliar" in the word *vremdiu* may be important since unfamiliar things inspire wonder, as with Eckhart's "novel and unusual" rhetoric.

3 The repetition of words relating to "wonder" is important for the philosophical overtones of *thaumazein*: all philosophy begins in wonder. Eckhart would have read this in Aristotle's *Metaphysics* (982b12), though the idea was originally expressed in Plato's *Theaetetus* (155d).

4 The word *unledic* means "occupied" (Colledge) or 'busied' (Walshe), though it may be significant that *ledic* means "free" and is a significant word for Eckhart. Thus, *unledic* is "not free" or "un-free."

according to something[5] which emanates out of Himself, such as goodness, wisdom, and what one says of God. Yet he has neither made the soul according to an image that is in Him alone, nor according to that which emanates out of Him, as one says of Him. What's more: He has made it according to Himself—yes—according to all that He is, according to nature, according to being, and according to his activity which flows out and yet remains within, and according to the ground where he remains within Himself, where he is giving birth to his only-begotten Son, where the Holy Spirit blossoms forth: God created the soul by this activity of flowing forth yet remaining within.

It is then natural for all things that the higher always flows into the lower, just as long as the lower are accommodating toward[6] the higher. For the higher receive nothing from the lower. Further, the lower receive from the higher. For, God is above the soul now, so God is always flowing into the soul and can never fall away from the soul. The soul indeed falls away from Him, and as long as man holds himself fast under God, so is he receiving the unmediated, bare divine inflowing from God and he is not under other things: under neither the fearful, nor the lovable, nor the hateful, nor any thing which is not God. Now cast yourself completely under God, so you receive the divine inflowing, whole and bare. How does the soul receive from God? The soul receives from God not as a stranger, as the air receives light from the sun. Air receives according to the foreignness[7] of the light. But the soul receives God not according to the foreignness of God, nor as under God. For what is under is something other, foreign, and distant. The masters say that the soul receives as light from light, for in that there is no foreignness or distance.

There is something in the soul, in which God is bare, and the masters say it is nameless and it has no name of its own. It is and has no being of its own, for it is neither this nor that, neither here nor there. Yet it is what it is in an other and the other in it. For that which it is, it is that in an other and

---

5 That it is a "something" (*etwaz*) that emanates is significant for Eckhart. He puts weight into calling God a "something" as opposed to a "nothing."

6 The word *gevüege* means "accomodating," "courteous" or "well-bred," which adds color to the idea Eckhart expresses. We might therefore read *zuogevüeget* as "courteous toward."

7 "Foreign" (*vremdicheit*) here refers to what is dualistic and thereby distant from God, perhaps meant to complement the "strange" (*vremdiu*) stories the boy tells in the beginning of the sermon. Eckhart repeats versions of the word *vremd-* which means "strange," "foreign," or "unfamiliar."

the other in that.[8] For another flows into this and this into the other. This is what Paul means by, unite yourselves in God, in blessedness! For in here the soul takes its entire life and being, and from here she draws her life and being. For this is entirely in God and all else is outside. Therefore, the soul is always in God according to this. It remains, then, unless the soul is carried away to the outside and silences[9] it within you.

A master says: God is so present in this, that it may never turn away from God and God is always present to it and within it. I say that God has always been in this, eternally and without ceasing. And in this, man is one with God in this sense. Grace does not belong here, for grace is a creature and that place has nothing to do with creatures. For in the ground of divine being, the three persons are one being. There the soul is one according to the ground. Therefore, if you like, all things are yours, and God too. That is: go out of your self, all things and everything that you are presently yourself. Take yourself in according to what are you in God.

A master says: human nature has nothing to do with time, it is completely untouched, and it is more within and closer to a man than he is to himself. And therefore God assumed human nature and united it with his Person. Then, human nature became God, for he assumed bare human nature and not any particular man. Therefore, if you would be the same Christ and God, then go out from all that the eternal Word did not assume. This eternal Word assumed no particular person. Therefore, go out of whatever makes you a particular person and whatever you are. Take yourself according to bare human nature so that you are the same to the eternal Word as human nature is to him. For your human nature and his have no separation: his is one, for whatever it is in Christ, it is in you. Therefore, as I said in Paris, all that the Holy Scripture and the prophets ever said of Christ[10] is fulfilled in

---

8 This probably sounded just as confusing to his audience. Eckhart's antecedent for "that" (*jenem*, a "that" as differentiated from another alternative, just as in modern German) is unclear. Walshe explains that this "that" refers to the part of the soul that is not the nameless something. The fact that Eckhart repeats almost the same phrasing in two consecutive sentences may indicate that he had difficulty in expressing the idea (DW I, 418.2–3, 3–4).

9 The word *verlesche* is difficult to translate here. It means "extinguish" or "efface," though Eckhart clearly does not mean that this part of the soul can "die." Since being "carried off" and "distracted" by (*ûztrage*) things other than God implies the 'fading" into the background and "silencing" (also appropriate for *verlesche*), "silences" carries the right connotation for this context.

10 Quint adds "of Christ" here, which he says was likely omitted because it was evidently the basis for article twelve of *In agro dominico*.

the just man. For if you are just right, everything that was foretold in the Old and the New Testament will be fulfilled in you.

How should you come to be just right?[11] There are two ways to understand this according to the words of the prophet, who said: "The Son was sent in the fullness of time."[12] "Fullness of time" is of two kinds. A thing is full at the time when it is at its end. So the day is full in its evening. And so, as all time falls away from you, so is time full. The other is: time comes to its end in eternity, for there all time has an end. In eternity there is neither before nor after. There, all that is, is present and new. There you see immediately all that has ever happened and ever will happen. There is neither before nor after, it is all present. In this present seeing, I possess all things. That is the "fullness of time" and in this way I am just right. And in this way, I am truly the only Son and Christ.

God help us so that we come to our "fullness of time." Amen.

---

11 I tried to preserve Eckhart's wordplay here between *gerehten* ('just' as in justice) and *reht* ("right"), even though the latter occurs in the idiom *ist dir reht* ("if you are as you should be," "if everything is right with you").

12 Gal 4:4.

Sermon 40
Manete in me
Beatus vir qui in sapientia morabitur[1]

Our Lord Jesus Christ says in the Gospel, "Abide in me!" He also says in the Epistle, "Blessed is the man who dwells in wisdom." The two passages carry the same meaning: Christ's words, "Abide in me!" and the passage from the Epistle, "Blessed is the man who dwells in wisdom."

Now observe what a man should have for him to dwell in God. He should have three things. First, he must renounce himself and all things, being attached neither to any thing the mind has internally grasped[2], nor abiding in creatures that are in time or eternity. Second, he must not love this good or that good. He should only love that good from which all good flows.[3] For no thing is delightful or desirable except to the extent that God is in it. Therefore, one should not love a good thing except to the extent that one loves God in it. One should not love God because of Heaven or because of any thing. One should love Him only for the goodness that He is in Himself. For whoever loves Him for some other thing does not abide in Him, but instead abides in the other thing that he loves. Therefore, if you want to abide in Him, you should love Him for nothing other than Himself. Third, you should not take God as being good or just. You should only take him

---

[1] Jn 15:4, Sir 14:22.

[2] The manuscript varies here. Walshe has "not remain attached to anything that is grasped by the senses within" which is perhaps not optimal. The variations include "anything under the Sun." The word *sinne* can be either "senses" or "mind," while the variation in spelling between manuscripts makes it *svn*, or Sun. Nevertheless, the point is clear: get rid of attachment to all ideas about worldly things.

[3] Cf. Sermon XXXIII, n.333.

in His pure, naked substance as He takes Himself. Goodness and justice are God's clothing, for they clothe him. So detach[4] God from of all his clothing and take Him naked in His dressing-room where he is uncovered and bare in Himself.[5] Then you will abide in Him.

He who abides in Him has five things. First, there is no difference between him and God. They are but one. The angels are innumerable. They do not make up any particular number, for they are without number because of their great simplicity. The three persons in God are three without number, but they have multiplicity. Yet between man and God there is no distinction and no multiplicity. There is nothing other than one.[6] Second, he takes his blessedness from the same purity where God takes His purity and resides. Third, he has one knowing with God's knowing, one work with God's work, and one understanding with God's understanding. Fourth, God is being born all the time in that man. How is God born all the time in that man? Take note of this! Whenever that man bares and uncovers the divine image that God created in him by nature, God's image will be revealed in him. We should notice God's revelation in the birth. To say that the Son is born from the Father is to say that the Father reveals His mysteries to him in a fatherly way[7]. Therefore, as that man more and more clearly uncovers God's image in himself, so God will be that much more clearly born in him. And so, God's continuous birth should be understood by way of understanding how that man[8] uncovers the bare image and the Father shines in him. Fifth, that man is continuously being born in God. How is that man continuously being born in God? Notice this! As the image is bared in that man, so then is he like God. For that man is like God's image by that image, as God is bare according to

---

4 The word for "detach" here is *abegescheiden*, which is the same root as *abegescheidenheit*, "detachment," the chief virtue for Eckhart. Eckhart enjoins us to detach or cut away God's clothing, stripping him bare of this and that concept, including goodness and justice.

5 Cf. Sermon XXIV.2, n.247.

6 Cf. Sermon XI.2, n.118.

7 The phrase *der vater veterlîche offenbârende ist sîne tougene* literally means "the father is fatherly revealing his mysteries," which probably sounded odd to Eckhart's audience as well.

8 The manuscripts vary with this sentence. Walshe and Quint translate this as saying that the Father does the uncovering, which is not consistent with what Eckhart says a few lines earlier. One manuscript is missing the ostensible subject *der vater* (DW II, 276), which gives us reason to suspect that other alterations may need to be made. Fortunately, as is his habit elsewhere, Eckhart restates the same idea here that he just explained in the preceding sentences. If this is the case, my alteration is justified since "that man" should be the one who does the uncovering of the divine image while the Father is the one who then shines. That is, I suspect *der mensch* is either implied or missing in this sentence.

his essence. The more that man bares, the more he is like God. The more he is like God, the more he is united with Him. We should understand the continuous birth of that man in God as that man shining with his image in God's image, as God is bare according to his essence, and with which that man is one. And so the oneness of that man and God should be understood by the likeness of the images. For man is like God according to the image. Therefore, as we say that man is one with God and is God by oneness, we are considering him insofar as he is part of the divine image, and not insofar as he is created. In doing so, we consider man as he is in God, not according to his creatureliness. As we consider man insofar as he is in God, we do not deny his creatureliness, which would mean the denial of him insofar as he is creaturely, as if he did not have creatureliness and we were considering him only according to the claim that God is in him, which means one considers him as God.[9] For Christ, who is God and man, as one takes him according to his humanity, one then denies him according to his divinity—not that one denies his divinity, but only that one denies him according to it. So then should we understand Augustine[10] when he says: "Man is whatever he loves. If he loves a stone, he is that stone. If he loves a man, he is that man. If he loves God—now I will not dare to say anything further, for if I then say that he is God, you might stone me. I will point you to Scripture instead." Therefore, as man nakedly yields to God with love, so will he un-form, inform, and transform[11] in the divine uniformity where he is one with God. He has all this in his abiding within. Now notice the fruit that this man brings forth. Whenever he is one with God, so he brings forth all creatures with God. He brings blessedness to all creatures insofar as he is one with God.

The other passage from the Epistle says: "Blessed is the man who dwells in wisdom." It says "in wisdom": wisdom is a motherly name. A motherly name has the property of passivity. Activity and passivity are both in God. For the Father is active and the Son is passive by having the property of being born. The Son is the eternally born wisdom in which all things remain with distinction. Therefore, he says: "Blessed in the man who dwells in wisdom."[12]

---

9 As Walshe and Tobin both recognize, this is a very difficult sentence since it is ambiguous and complex. As Tobin says, it is an exposition of Eckhart's "insofar as" principle. Fortunately, the surrounding comments that Eckhart makes help to resolve the ambiguities.

10 Augustine, *In ep. Ioh. ad Parthos* tr. 2 n.14.

11 Unform, inform, and transform all have *bild* as their root, an important term that Eckhart uses elsewhere to mean "image."

12 Cf. Sermon XXXIV.1, n.340; Sermon LV.1, n.535.

Now he says, "blessed is the man." I have said before[13] that two powers are in the soul: one is the man and one is the woman. Now he says, "blessed is the man." The power which is in the soul that is called "man" is the highest power of the soul in which God shines bare. For in the power is nothing other than God and the power is always in God. Further, should man take all things in the power, he would not take them insofar as they are things, but only insofar as they are in God. Therefore, a man should always abide in this power, for all things are equal in it. If a man abided in all things equally and taking all things insofar as they are equal in God, then he would possess all things. If he strips away what is coarse and takes things insofar as they are equal, then they would be delightful and desirable. Insofar as he does this, he possesses them. God cannot help but to give by the oneness of his nature. He must give you everything, all that He has created and Himself. Therefore, a man is blessed if he continually dwells in the power and if he continuously dwells in God.

Our dear Lord Jesus Christ, help us so that we should continuously dwell in God. Amen.

---

13 Cf. Sermon VIII, n.93; Sermon XXI, n.205; *In Sap.* n.99.

Sermon 54a
Unser herre underhuop und huop
von unden ûf sîniu ougen und sach in den himel[1]

Our Lord raised his eyes and carried his gaze on high to heaven and said: "Father, the time has come. Glorify your Son that your Son may glorify you. To all those you have given to me, I give them eternal life. Eternal life is that they know you as the one true God."[2]

A pope wrote these words: as our Lord raised his eyes, he thought of something great. The sage said in the Book of Wisdom that the soul is carried to God by divine wisdom.[3] Saint Augustine[4] also said that all of God's works and teaching of humanity are an image and figure of our holy life and our great dignity before God. The soul must be purified and made subtle in light and in grace, totally detached and stripped of all that is foreign to the soul and also of the part that is itself. I have often said: the soul must be totally denuded of all that is "accident" and carried on high in purity and flow back into the Son as it flowed from him. For the Father created the soul in the Son. That's why it must flow back into him as bare as it flowed from him.

Now he said: "He raised his eyes and carried his gaze on high."[5] These words have two meanings. The first is evidence of pure humility. If we are to ever reach into God's ground and into his innermost, we must first come

---

1 For reasons that are unclear, this sermon was not included in the otherwise-complete collection of translations of the sermons made by Maurice O'Connell Walshe for DW I–III, sermons numbering 1–86. To my knowledge, this is the first translation of this sermon in English.

2 Jn 17:1–3,11.

3 Wis 7:28.

4 Augustine, *De cons. Evang. I*, c. 35 no. 53.

5 Jn 17:1.

into our own ground and into our innermost in pure humility. The masters say that the stars pour all of their powers into the ground of the earth, into nature, and into the element of earth, and therein produce the purest gold.[6] To the extent that the soul reaches into the ground and its innermost being, so then does the divine power pour out completely in it. It works there very secretly and reveals itself much in three great works. The soul also becomes very great, elevated into the love of God which is like pure gold. Such is the first meaning of "he raised his eyes."

The second is that the soul must carry itself on high in humility, with all its faults and sins. It must position itself and bow under the door of the mercy of God, as God melts outward in compassion. It must also carry on high its virtue and its good works. It must place itself with those under the doorway where God melts outward by way of goodness. So must the soul follow and order itself according to the image: "He raised his eyes."[7]

Next he said, "He carried his gaze on high." A master said that he who would be clever would know to put water over wine so that the power of wine could act therein: the power of wine would make the water into wine. If it was well placed above the wine, it would be better than the wine. At the very least, it would become as good as the wine. The same goes for the soul that is well ordered in the ground of humility. It climbs up and is drawn on high into the divine power. It never rests before having gone straight to God and having touched him in his nakedness. It rests entirely on the inside. It seeks nothing outside. It does not stand next to God or near God. Rather, it flows straight into God, into the purity of being. There also is the being of the soul, for God is pure being. A master says: in God, who is pure being, nothing at all comes that is not also pure being. It is thus the soul's "being" that reaches up to God and into God.

That's why he says: "He carried his gaze on high, toward heaven." A Greek master says that "heaven" signifies the "house of the sun." Heaven pours its power into the sun and into the stars. The stars pour their power into the earth and produce gold and precious stones of such a kind that the precious stones have the power to do wondrous works.[8] They have the power to attract flesh and bone. If a man approaches them, he would be hindered and could not free himself unless he had the necessary tricks to escape. Other

---

6 Cf. Sermon XIII, n.150; *In Gen. II* n.210.

7 Cf. Sermon IX, n.100.

8 Cf. Sermon XXXVI.1, n.369.

precious stones attract bone and iron. Each precious stone and each plant is a little house of the stars which conceals in itself a celestial power. Further, just as heaven pours its power into the stars, so then do the stars pour theirs in turn into precious stones, plants, and animals. The plant is nobler than the precious stone because it has a life that grows. It would disdain to grow under the material sky if there was not in it a spiritual power from which it received life. Also, just as the lowest angel pours his power into the heavens, moves it, and directs its revolution, so does heaven pour its power very secretly into each plant and animal. From this, each plant has the property that it takes from heaven and what surrounds it in every direction like the heavens. The animals raise themselves higher. They have an animal and sensory life and yet remain in time and space. But the soul in its natural light, in that which it has from the highest, raises itself above time and space, to equal the angelic light and work with it intellectually in heaven. Thus, the soul must ceaselessly elevate itself in intellectual work. There where it finds something of the divine light or divine likeness, it must make its home, without coming back until it climbs still higher. And so, it must constantly elevate itself in the divine light and also reach above to all the houses, up to the contemplation of God, pure and naked, with the angels in heaven. That's why [John] said: "He looked to the sky and said: 'Father, the time has come. Glorify your Son so that he may glorify you.'" As the Father glorified the Son and as the Son glorified the Father, it is better to be silent than to speak. Only the angels may speak of it.

Now I will say a little about the words he said: "All those you gave to me." For the one who grasps the true sense, "all that you gave me" means: I gave them "eternal life," the same as the Son in the first emanation and in the same ground and in the same purity and in the savor where he had his own beatitude and where he possessed his own being: "This eternal life, I gave it to them"[9] and no other. I sometimes offer this common meaning. But tonight I depart from it, although it is found truly in the Latin words that I often said. You should pray it and speak it boldly!

He says further: "Eternal life is knowing him as the one [true God]." If two men recognize God as one, and the first understands him as a thousand and the other recognizes God as "more than one" but less than [a thousand], then he would recognize more of the "one" God than the one who recognized him as a thousand. The more God is recognized as one, the more he is recognized as all. If my soul were sensible, noble, and pure, then whatever it knows

9 Jn 10:28.

would be one. If an angel knew one thing and it was ten, and if another nobler angel knew the same thing, it would not be for him more than one. That's why Saint Augustine says: if I knew all things but I did not know God, I would know nothing. And if I knew God and I did not know anything else, I would know all. The more someone knows God strictly and deeply as one, the more he or she knows the root from which all things sprout. The more someone knows as one the root and the kernel and the ground of the Godhead, the more he or she knows all things.[10] That's why he says: may they know you as the one true God. He does not say "wise" God, nor "just" God, nor "powerful" God, but only the "one true God." He means that the soul must detach and strip away all that is added to God by thought and knowledge, and grasp him in his nakedness as pure being: insofar as he is the "true God." That's why our Lord says: "Eternal life is that they know you as the one true God."

May God help us so that we may reach the truth which is pure being and so that we may abide in it eternally. Amen.

---

10 Cf. *In Ioh.* n.107.

Sermon 64
Die sele die wirt ain mit gotte vnd nit veraint

The soul is one with God and not united. Think of this by way of a parable: as one fills a vessel with water, so the water in the vessel is united to the vessel but not one with it. For where the water is, the wood is not. And where the wood is, the water is not. Now take the wood and throw it in the middle of the water. Still, the wood is only united with it and not one with it. It is not like this with the soul. The soul becomes one with God and not united. For where God is, there the soul is. And where the soul is, there God is.

Scripture says: "Moses saw God face to face."[1] The masters speak against this and say: where two faces appear, one does not see God. For God is one and not two. For whoever sees God, sees nothing apart from one.

Now I will take the passage I spoke of in the first sermon:[2] "God is love, and he who is in love is in God, and He is in him."[3] To him who is in love, I would mention a little passage that Saint Matthew said: "Go in, faithful servant, into the joy of your Lord."[4] Now I take a passage, spoken by our Lord: "Go in, faithful servant, I will put you above all my 'good.'"[5] This is understood

---

1 Ex 33:11.
2 Sermon 63.
3 1 Jn 4:16.
4 Mt 25:21.
5 In characteristic fashion, Eckhart cobbles together pieces of the original and makes important changes. Matthew 25:21 in the Vulgate reads, *Ait illi dominus eius: Euge serve bone, et fidelis: quia super pauca fuisti fidelis, super multa te constituam; intra in gaudium domini tui* This means, "And his Lord said to him: Well done, good and faithful servant. Because you have been faithful over a few things, I will make you ruler over many things. Enter into the joy of your Lord." Eckhart changes "many things" to "all my good," which could be singular (referring to what is good) or plural (referring to many goods—that is, many things) and may refer to God's goodness, contra

in three ways. The first way: "I will put you up above all my 'good,'" as "all my 'good'" is spread out in creatures: over the fragmentation, I will put you in oneness[6]. The second way: as it is all united into one, I will put you over the union in oneness, as all good is in oneness. The third way: I will put you in the nature of oneness, where all "uniting" is taken away. There, God is the soul's, as if he is God so that he may be the soul's. So completely does the soul become one with God that if God were to hold back from the soul as much as a single hair of his being or his is-ness where He is in Himself, he would not be God. Consider a passage from Scripture, where our Lord says: "I ask you, Father, just as you and I are one, that they might also become one with us."[7] Take another passage from Scripture, where our Lord says: "Where I am, my servant should be there too."[8] The soul becomes so completely one is-ness, which is God and nothing less. This is entirely true, as God is God.

Dear children, I implore you to understand this one meaning! I ask this through God and I ask you to become fit for this and closely preserve this meaning for my sake. As I said before, though all who are in oneness are without images, they must not imagine that they would be better off in images than in not going out from oneness. For whoever would do this would be wrong. One may even say it was heresy. You should know that in oneness is neither Conrad nor Henry. I will tell you how I think of people: I flow myself out to them so that I forget myself and all men, and for them I give myself over into oneness.

God help us to stay in oneness. Amen.

Walshe's translation as 'good.' This is in line with DW III. 88n1 which includes commentary on this and many manuscript versions that have the singular in quotes.

6 Here, *ain* is rendered as "oneness" for clarity since Eckhart's *ain* (one) is set in contrast to *zertailung* (fragmentation or division).

7 Jn 17:21.

8 Jn 12:26.

Sermon 87
Ecce, dies veniunt, dicit dominus,
et suscitabo David germen iustum

Jeremiah said these words: "Behold, the days are coming, said the Lord, and I will raise up a righteous seed for David."[1] Solomon said: "Good news from a faraway land is like cold water for a thirsty soul."[2]

According to the way of sin, man is far from God.[3] That's why heaven is like a faraway foreign land to him, and the good news was from heaven. Saint Augustine said of himself when he was not yet converted that he stood at a distance from God in a strange land of unlikeness.[4]

It's a sorrowful thing for man to be separate from that without which he cannot be joyful. If one took the most beautiful creatures that God created out of the divine light under which they stand—for to the extent that all things stand beneath the divine light, they are delightful and at ease[5]—and if

---

[1] Jer 23:5.

[2] Prv 25:25.

[3] Cf. Sermon 57, DW II, 597.6; Sermon XVII.4, n.172.

[4] Augustine, *Conf.*, VII.10.16: *et inveni longe me esse a te in regione dissimilitudinis*. In Sap. n.166; *Sermo die b. Augustini Parisius habitus* n.5; Sermon IX, n. 102; Sermon 44; Sermon 93.

[5] This pair of descriptors, *lustlich und behegelich*, is challenging to translate because the connotations play upon two of Eckhart's important metaphors, divine repose and delight. They refer to something that is quietly and comfortably lovely. Divine passivity for Eckhart is entirely quiet, at peace and pure delight. In this way, God is the resting place of the soul. The other important metaphor in this passage is divine light and the fact that this light does not "take root" in the things it lights. Eckhart explains, "Fire sends its root into water with heat, for when the fire is removed, the warmth remains for a while." This is different in the case of sunlight, which "lights the air and shines through it, but does not send its root into it, for whenever the sun is no longer present, we have no more light" (Sermon 41, DW II, 294.7–12). The goodness in things, in Platonic fashion, is directly from the Good, which is God. We are sinful insofar as the light of the Good

it was the will of God and if he allowed them to be taken outside of the divine light and they became manifest in a soul, she would have neither pleasure nor contentment in it,[6] but rather they would be dreadful.

Still more sorrowful is that man is separated from that without which he cannot be.[7]

What is utterly sorrowful is that he is separated from that which is his eternal joy.

That's why it was good news, as the prophet says: "Behold, the days are coming, said the Lord, and I will raise up a rightful seed for David."[8] When the old fathers knew sorrow inside themselves,[9] they cried out with their appeals to heaven. They were then drawn into God with his spirit and let into the divine wisdom to which God must give birth.

That's why the good news was like "cool water for a thirsty soul."[10] For it is true that God gives his kingdom like a drink of cool water to a good heart.[11] And so it is satisfying.[12] And I consider this with regard to my soul: whoever offers a good thought in the eternal love through which God became man will be saved.[13] That's why man must fear neither the devil, nor the world, nor his own flesh, nor our Lord God. For Saint Paul said: the Son is given to us as a promise, he who is the wisdom of the Father, he who must give a wise teaching for all our foolishness and wrongdoing. Saint Paul said further:[14] he is given to us as a champion who will win all of our needs for us. We must pray whether the Heavenly Father has to receive our prayers or not. If the Father wanted to fight against us, he could not do it, for the same power and wisdom that the Father has, the Son has alike with him. The Son was given entirely to us as a champion, and he paid so dearly for us that he will not

---

is absent from us. Eckhart follows Augustine (and ultimately Plotinus and Plato) in describing evil as a privation of the good that lacks its own existence (evil was not a Form for Plato, but was instead the absence of Good and thereby lacked existence according to his sliding scale of being as described by the "divided line" in the *Republic*). Cf. Sermon 112.

6 Cf. Sermon 60.

7 Cf. Sermon XVI, Sermon 93.

8 Jer 23:5.

9 Ps 50:7.

10 Prv 25:25.

11 Mt 10:42.

12 Eckhart uses *genuoc* and similar words to refer to being satisfied, as one is after eating. This is part of the need and satisfaction metaphor.

13 Cf. Sermon 93; *In Gen. I* n.157; Sermon 91; Sermon 41.

14 Cf. Rom 8:33–34; Heb 7:25; 1 Jn 2:1–2; 1 Cor 15:57; Sermon XLV, n.461.

abandon us. And the Father cannot deny him for he is his wisdom. He cannot fight against him for he is his power. That is why man must not fear God. He may boldly[15] go toward God with all that he is.

When man was cast out of paradise, God placed three guards there.[16] The first was the angelic nature, the second a fiery sword, and the third was that it was double-edged.

Angelic nature means as much as purity.[17] When the Son of God came to earth, he who is "a pure mirror without stain," he broke apart the first guard and brought innocence and purity to human nature on Earth. Solomon said of Christ: "He is a pure mirror without stain."[18]

The fiery sword means the divine fiery love without which man cannot enter into the kingdom of heaven. Christ brought it with him and broke apart the second guard. For He had that same love for man before He created him. *Et in caritate perpetua dilexi.* Jeremiah said: "God has loved you with eternal love."[19]

The third guard is the sharp-edged sword, which was human sorrow. Our Lord took it upon Himself to the greatest extent, as Isaiah said: *Vere languores nostros ipse tulit.* "He truly took our sorrows unto himself."[20] That's why he came to earth, took the sins of man upon himself, wiped them out and saved man. Now the kingdom of heaven is open once more without any guards. That's why man can boldly go toward God.

We should notice something else that he says: "I will raise up the righteous seed for David *or* the fruit."[21] One can see this in that the angel touched the water at a certain time.[22] As a result, it attained so great a power that it healed people of all kinds of ills. Much greater is that the Son of God touched human nature in the body of Our Lady. For from that, all human nature became blessed.[23]

---

15 That he should "boldly" (*küenlîche*) go is an unusual idea for Eckhart, though we see this same word used in Sermon 54a and Sermon 104.

16 Gn 3:24.

17 Cf. Sermon 77; Sermon 78; Sermon XXVII.3, n.275; Dionysius, *De Div. Nom.*, C.4 §22.

18 Wis 7:25–26.

19 Jer 31:3.

20 Is 53:4. Cf. Jn 1:29, 1 Pt 2:24, 1 Jn 3:5.

21 Jer 23:5.

22 Jn 5:4.

23 Cf. *In Ioh.* ns.286, 288; Augustine, *De Trin.*, 1 XIII, c.14.

It is a still greater blessing that God through his own nature touched the water of the Jordan in which he had been baptized.[24] Through that He gave his power to all waters: so that when man is baptized, he is purified of all sins and becomes a child of God.[25]

The greatest blessedness[26] is that God comes to be born and manifest himself in the soul by spiritual union. From that, the soul is more blessed than from the body of our Lord Jesus Christ without his soul and without his divinity, for each blessed soul[27] is nobler than the mortal body of our Lord Jesus Christ.

The interior birth of God in the soul is a consummation of all her blessedness, and that blessedness accomplishes more for her[28] than Our Lord becoming man in the body of Our Lady, Saint Mary, or even that he touched the water. God never carried out or did anything for man that would help him more than a bean if he was not united with God in a spiritual union, one where God will be born in the soul and the soul will be born in God, and so God carries out all his work.[29]

May God help us so that this should happen for us. Amen.

---

24 Mt 3:13–17, Mk 1:9–11, Lk 3:21–22, Jn 1:29–34.

25 Cf. Sermon 60.

26 We find a repetition of various forms of *sælic*, which means "blessed," "joyous" or "blissful." For more information on Eckhart's metaphorics of joy, see the section on joy in chap. 5.

27 Cf. Sermon 32.

28 Cf. Sermon 101.

29 Cf. *In Ioh.* n.117; Sermon 5b; Sermon 22; Sermon 38; *Counsels on Discernment*, §21.

Sermon 88
Post dies octo vocatum est nomen eius Iesus[1]

Post dies octo vocatum est nomen eius Iesus. On the eighth day, his was the name "Jesus."[2] "No one says the name 'Jesus' except through the activity[3] of the Holy Spirit."[4]

A master says: in any soul where the name of Jesus comes to be spoken, it must happen in eight days.[5]

The first day is when he gives his will to the will of God and he lives in Him.[6]

---

1 Lk 2:21.

2 It is unsurprising that Eckhart likes Luke 2:21, since it contains a seemingly paradoxical juxtaposition. Luke 2:21 first tells us first that the child was given the name "Jesus" after the customary eight days. In the next clause (that Eckhart does not include), we hear that "his name was called Jesus, which was so named of the angel before he was conceived in the womb." Thus, we have the paradox of waiting eight days to name him Jesus and his already being named Jesus even before he was conceived. This fits well with Eckhart's enjoining the reader to paradoxically make himself or herself so that "[I am] as I was when I was not" (Sermon 2, DW I, 26.2).

3 It is important here that Eckhart tells us that the Holy Spirit "works" or causes and inspires action, since action for Eckhart is properly divine (in contrast with the long-standing tradition of exalting contemplation over action, see Sermon 2), especially here since the act is one of *speaking* the name of the Son, just as God spoke the Word which is the Son. Thus, to speak the name of the Son is to create alongside the Father, which can only be done in and through God. See Sermon 81: "As I speak the word of God, I am a co-worker with God and grace is mixed with the creature" (DW III, 398.13–14).

4 1 Cor 12:3. Cf. Sermon XXIII, n. 217–25.

5 Though *ahten* is clearly "eighth" here, it is worth noting that the word also means "outstanding" as an adjective, and "contemplation, reflection" as a noun) It is also worth noticing that the first day matches Augustine's conversion experience in the *Confessions*. That experience, Eckhart seems to say, is only the beginning of the speaking (birth) of the Word in the soul.

6 Cf. Sermon 25.

The second day is a luminous illumination[7] of divine fire.

The third day is when the soul swells for and runs around[8] God.

The fourth day is when all of man's powers are attuned to God.[9] A master[10] says: when the soul is touched by eternal things, it is set in motion. By being set in motion, it is heated. By this heating, it is expanded so that it can receive so much goodness.[11]

The fifth day, it is a dwelling-place[12] in God.

---

7 There is word play in the original here. Eckhart's words, *beglîmende beglîmunge*, sound even closer to one another than "luminous illumination." The only connotation that is not captured is that *beglîmende* also refers to light that comes from something *smoldering*, which complements the divine fire metaphor in this passage. Metaphorically, then, one both burns with *fire* and gives off *light*. Cf. *Sermo die b. Augustini Parisius habitus* n.11.

8 Eckhart's image is peculiarly specific here, where the soul circumnavigates or runs around (*umbegeloufen*) God. We should perhaps think of the hinge metaphor whereby the closer to the center of the circle one "orbits," the less motion there is, until one finally arrives at rest at the center point. Eckhart often used mathematical metaphors of this kind, and only on occasion (e.g., Sermon XXIV.2) made them more explicit and geometrically detailed. Cf. Song 3:2; Sermon 69, Sermon 97, Sermon 108.

9 Cf. Sermon 19, *Counsels on Discernment*, §20.

10 Cf. Sermon 68.

11 This passage is full of metaphors. To attune the powers to God is to master them (like one tames the bad horse of desire in Plato's account). For Eckhart, the "powers" are the interior (higher) and sensory (lower) powers. To be "touched" by an eternal thing is to have an experience of it that is above the powers, not just an understanding that is contained within the higher powers. To be set in motion is to have activity that is like the divine activity. This corresponds with heat since fire is the highest (physically and ontologically) terrestrial element which, like all other elements tends upward and turns lower things into itself (since all things strive to recreate themselves or what is most like themselves in others). To "expand" is something that Eckhart elaborated upon in Sermon XXIV.2, where he describes the soul as expanding so that it has even a capacity (*capax*) for God (see also Sermon 95a, Sermon 96, Sermon 98, Sermon 103 and especially Sermon 100, DW IV.1, 26–30: "The thing that grows in filling will never be full. If an excellent vessel, a cartload, swells as it is loaded and grows thereby, then it will never be full. So it is with the soul: the more she seeks, the more she will be given. The more she receives, the wider she becomes"). To expand one's capacity is also to expand one's *potential* in the Aristotelian sense, which concomitantly expands one's thirst for God (*In Eccl.* n.45). We should also think of expansion like the infinite sphere metaphor that Eckhart often alluded to from the *Book of the XXIV Philosophers*, where we hear that "God is an infinite sphere whose center is everywhere and circumference nowhere" (*Deus est sphaera infinita cuius centrum est ubique, circumferentia nusquam*). As with his other explosive mathematical metaphors, we are guided to think of a sphere of ever-increasing radius until finally it has the capacity for all things, like God (cf. Sermon 47, DW II, 398.3–399.1).

12 Here, *înstân* could also be "persistence" or "indwelling" since the word literally means "in" + "dwelling," "remaining," or "standing." For Eckhart, to "dwell" or "abide" with God is to reach God and share in his peace. As we hear in Sermon 52, however, if the soul is aware of remaining within God, then there is still a distinction between the soul and God, and one must press on. Cf. Sermon 3, Sermon 13a.

The sixth day is when God melts[13] the soul.
The seventh day is when the soul is united with God.[14]
The eighth day is the savoring[15] of God.
This is when the name of Jesus is given to the child.

---

13 The word *zerlæȝet* is translated here as "melts." Melting is not one of Eckhart's most common themes, but we do see *smilzet în* (melting inward) and *ûȝsmilzet* (melting outward) elsewhere as vernacular equivalents of the Latin terms *bullitio* and *ebullitio*, "boiling" (generating the three persons) and "boiling over" (creating the world) (Sermon 54a, DW II, 552.7–8; Sermon 18, DW I, 301.6–302.1; Sermon 19, DW I, 314.4–5). By this "day," the soul has risen into the "boiling" or "melting" of the godhead and has transcended all but the most primal acts of creation.

14 Cf. Sermon 32, Sermon 58, Sermon 82.

15 Though Eckhart often uses the metaphor of *taste* to allude to the most intimate experience of God, *gebrûchen* may refer to "reveling" or "delighting" in God. Still, unlike the choice of "melting" above, "savoring" is metaphorically consistent with Eckhart's rhetoric elsewhere, since he seems to intend to refer to a completely consuming, blissful experience. Cf. *Counsels on Discernment,* §20; Sermon 52, Sermon 80, Sermon 84.

Sermon 89
Angelus domini apparuit

Angelus domini apparuit ... The angel of the Lord appeared to Joseph while he slept and he said: "Take the child ..."[1]

A master[2] said that Scripture is in its meaning like a flowing stream which overflows on all sides, becoming deep, then driving forth and flowing usefully.[3] Saint Augustine[4] said: Scripture is usefully concealed in its meaning in such a way that one cannot immediately find the primary truth. That's why one finds various useful and delightful teachings which are right around the primary truth. As Moses said, the waters are above and below us.[5] Who can figure this out?[6]

The saints ask why Our Lord God created man last, after he had created all creatures. The most hidden reason and true sense may be that He created the perfection of all creatures entirely in man. Hence, the Holy Trinity conferred[7] when they went to create man and said: *Let us make man in our image.*[8] So we see that this image of the Holy Trinity was created in

---

1 Mt 2:19–20.

2 Cf. *Prol. In Gen. II* n.2, LW I, 449.4–450.10.

3 Augustine, *Conf.*, XII.27.37. "For just as one dammed spring is more fertile than several streams, it provides a flow into greater areas than any one stream which is led from the same source to many places."

4 Cf. Sermon 22, Sermon 51.

5 Gn 1:7.

6 Cf. *In Gen. I*, ns.88, 131, 133.

7 Cf. *In Gen. I* n.120, Sermon 109.

8 Gn 1:26.

the soul.⁹ Secondly, the angelic nature that it possesses in common with the angels[10] and the likeness and complete perfection of all creatures were created in man in such a way that God might behold in man His perfection and that of all creatures as if He were looking into a mirror.[11] So we see that man is the best among all creatures.[12] Moses wrote four books that were useful. After that, he wrote a fifth. It was the smallest and best and is called the truth of all Scripture that God commanded and Moses placed in the ark.[13] Saint Augustine wrote many books as well. He also wrote a small book last in which were written all the things that people could not understand in the others. He had this with him and around him at all times and it was the dearest to him. It is altogether this way with man:[14] God made him as a handbook that He looks at, plays with, and delights in. That is why man commits a great sin whenever he defiles this holy order.[15] For on the last day, all creatures will cry out "woe" unto the one who does that.

Now, we must consider that that after Herod's death, Joseph had to return again to the land which God emptied of those who were hindrances.[16] God must also empty it of sin so that the soul may be set aright,[17] if God should dwell with her. Saint John said: *The true light came into the world and the world received it not.*[18] He means: it found no place where it could stay.[19] That's why it was not received. A master[20] says: if you want to receive and

---

9 Cf. Sermon II.1, n.3, Sermon 14.

10 Cf. Sermon 43.

11 Cf. Sermon 96.

12 Cf. *In Gen. I* ns.132, 182.

13 Dt 31:26.

14 Cf. *In Gen I* n.121.

15 Cf. *Counsels on Discernment*, §22, Sermon 57.

16 Mt 2:19–20.

17 The Middle High German term *reht* (right, well) in all its forms (here, *gereht*) does not have a modern English equivalent that does not sound archaic. We come close to it when we say "you're all right," but closer when we say "all is right with you." It refers to putting something in a condition that best suits it, such as "righting" a ship when we set it upright. Here, Eckhart echoes his previous contention that the soul must be readied by putting it in a condition that is able to receive God.

18 Jn 1:9–11.

19 The word for "stay" here is *behaften*, which carries the connotation of adhering, attaching, and sticking to. In this case, Eckhart chose a colorful word for resting since God was metaphorically spoken of as light.

20 Cf. Sermon 69.

know God with a pure heart, then cast out your joy, fear, and hope. That is the first thing, how one should make room[21] for God.

The second is peace,[22] which was in the land where God was born. We think thereby that the entire earth belonged to and was subject to one king.[23] I show this as well by the three kings who came from a faraway land.[24] So then, all peace should be in the soul. It is the right peace as long as the lowest is subordinated to the highest.[25]

---

21 See the description of the metaphorics of expansion in the section on enlarging and expanding the soul in chap. 6.

22 Note that "peace" (*vride*) carries the connotation of tranquility and rest, recalling Eckhart's metaphorics of rest.

23 Lk 2:1.

24 Mt 2:1–2.

25 Cf. Sermon 31, Sermon 113.

Sermon 90a
Sedebat Iesus docens in templo

Sedebat Iesus docens in templo. The gospel says that "Christ sat in the temple and taught."[1] That he sat signifies rest.

For while seated, one is more capable of bringing forth pure things than when walking or standing. Sitting signifies rest;[2] standing, working; walking, impermanence.[3]

That's why the soul must be seated, so to speak, in a humility bent below all creatures. Then she comes to a quiet peace.[4] She gains peace inside a light. The light will be given to her in silence, there on the inside where she sits and abides.

Albert[5] said it as well: this is the reason that the masters must sit to teach the arts. For the coarse spirits, that is to say the coarse blood, move to the head and dim the understanding. But whenever man sits, the coarse blood sinks and the luminous spirits rush up to the head. Memory will then be illuminated.

That's why Christ was seated in the temple—that is, in the soul.[6]

The other piece is that he was teaching. What did he teach? He taught how our understanding must work. For whoever should teach, teaches according to what he is himself. Therefore, since Christ is an understanding, he teaches our understanding.

---

1 Lk 2:46.
2 Cf. Sermon 31, Sermon 35, Sermon XXXVI.1; *In Sap.* n.280.
3 Cf. Sermon 23, Sermon XXVII.2; *Counsels on Discernment*, §17, 22.
4 Regarding peace and the metaphorics of rest, see the section on rest in chap. 6.
5 Albertus Magnus, *Super Matthaeum*, 5,1.
6 Cf. Sermon 1.

Christ had four kinds of art and wisdom.[7]

The first is divine.[8] From this He understands that which is by eternal providence: not only that which is and must be, but further then, all that God can do if he wills it.

With this art, he saw into the hearts of men, and all works which belong to God, He worked them with His art. Christ was able to do this with this art that is God.

Christ's other art, which is creature,[9] is that art that was poured into his soul when he was created, and it is supernatural.

That's why she savors God and beholds God in his being. In this art, nothing can go to or from Him. By this art, he was able to recognize all that God has ever created or will create. Yet he did not enter into the infinite of which it knows not. This light is creature and nevertheless, by his soul, it is supernatural.

The third knowledge is what He possesses along with the angels, which have in them the image of all things.

Saint Dionysius said about this: when God created the angels, he gave them the image of all things, which they have naturally.[10] Christ's soul also naturally has the image of all things which he gave to them, yet he is not the same image, just as a stamp gives its form to wax while it is not one with it.[11] By this knowledge, he did not take more or less from them. With it, she can come to know all things that have happened, but not those that must happen, as an angel is not aware of things to come, unless they are revealed to him. He does not possess this by nature.

The fourth knowledge that He had was through the senses. For whatever the senses take hold of from the outside, they carry spiritually into the imagination,[12] where the intellect's insight grasps it. Thus, he has a capacity to progressively acquire as we do. Master Thomas said: he had a capacity for progressively acquiring by the power of the senses.

Now we should pay careful attention to what he teaches us with these arts.

---

7 Col 2:3.
8 Cf. Aquinas, *Summa Theologiae*, III.9.1, I.22.1; *Comp. theol.*, I.216.434.
9 Cf. Aquinas, *Comp. theol.*, I.216.435.
10 Dionysius, *Divine Names*, c.7 n.2.
11 For more on Eckhart's metaphorics of stamping and imprinting, see the section on metaphors of passivity in chap. 6.
12 Cf. Sermon 70.

The first art, which is God, from which all things flowed, with it he taught us how we must convert and order all things to their first source: the latter has a place in men, in whom all multiplicity is gathered together and all corporeal things are carried up into God, and in their first source, which is God. And whenever man comes to this and attains oneness with God, then first and foremost, he turns all things to their first cause.[13]

On this, Saint Bernard said: Lord, what is man, that you should have so great a love for him?[14]

He is a good in which all multiplicitous things are gathered together in a oneness. He teaches us this with the art that God is. What does he teach us with the art that is supernatural? With that, he teaches us that we should surpass everything that is natural.

First, we must surpass our own senses and, from there, thoughts and illusions. Now walk forward, noble soul, put on your walking shoes, which are knowledge and love. Walk thereby beyond the acts of your powers and beyond your own intellect and beyond the three hierarchies[15] and beyond the light that strengthens you and leap into the heart of God, in his hiddenness: therein, you must become hidden from all creatures. He teaches us this with this supernatural art.

That's why Saint Paul said: You are dead and your life is hidden with Christ in God.[16]

What did he teach us with the natural art that he shares with the angels, who have the images of all things within them? The soul also has the capacity for grasping all things.

That's why she must remain in herself, for truth comes from within, not from without.

That's why Saint Augustine said: Oh Lord, how many have gone out of themselves to search for the truth and not yet gone into themselves.[17]

So they have not found the truth, for God is the innermost interiority of the soul. He teaches us this with the natural art.

What does he teach us with the progressive art? It is how we must order our outer man.

---

13 Cf. Sermon 5b.

14 Bernard of Clairvaux, *In dedicatione ecclesiae*, Sermo V, n. 3, 7.

15 See Dionysius's description of the hierarchies. The three are likely the earthly, heavenly, and divine.

16 Col 3:3.

17 Augustine, *Expositions on the Psalms*, 4, no. 9. Cf. Sermon XIV.2, Sermon 102.

The order reaches perfection with contemplation: man himself. For man to know himself is better than knowledge of all created things.

Christ taught them. Who are those whom he taught? They are the simple ones. Who is truly simple? They are those who neither injure nor deceive anyone with anything, those who cannot be deceived by anyone.[18] They are the truly simple people.

May God help us to this right[19] simplicity. Amen.

---

18 Prv 12:21.

19 The word for "right" is *reht*, for which there is no direct English translation. See Sermon 89n3.

Sermon 90b
Sedebat Iesus docens in templo

Christ sat and taught.[1] Three things are signified by these words. The first is: he sat. That is a kind of rest.

While seated, one is more capable of bringing forth pure things than when standing or walking. Sitting signifies rest; standing, working; walking, impermanence.

That's why the soul must be seated, so to speak, in a humility bent below all creatures. That's why she comes to a restful peace. She gains peace inside a light. The light will be given to her in silence, there on the inside where she sits and abides.

About this, Bishop Albert[2] said that this is the reason that the masters must sit to teach the arts. For the coarse spirits, that is to say the coarse blood, move to the head and dim the understanding. But whenever man is seated, then the coarse blood sinks to the bottom and the luminous spirits flow up to the head. Memory will then be illuminated.

That's why Christ was seated in the temple—that is, in the soul.[3]

The other thing is that he was teaching. What was he teaching? He taught how our understanding must work. For whoever should teach, teaches according to what he is himself. Therefore, since Christ is an understanding, he teaches our understanding.

Yes, now listen carefully to these words. This is what a very great master[4] says about the arts. Christ has a twofold art in him.

---

1 Lk 2:46.
2 Albertus Magnus, *Super Matthaeum*, 5,1.
3 Cf. Sermon 1.
4 Peter Lombard, *Sent.*, III d.13 n.8.

The first art, which he has by divinity,[5] is that which understands all that the Father understands in being and in the persons and all that he has done and now does and as yet must do and that which he could do if he willed it. This he understands in being and also in the image of all that is in the intermediary person[6] and that the Father beholds in the Son, and the Son in the Father according to the Persons. Although God is one according to being, there is still distinction in the Persons in speech. He has this from divinity, though no creature can have it. That is God and is in no way creature.

Christ's other art, which is creature,[7] is the capacity to receive and to be filled. In this capacity, He has imprinted the images which are in the intermediary Person, to the extent that it was possible, so that the soul may understand all things, those which are created and those which are still to be created. But what God could still do if He willed and what can never come to light, she does not understand. This belongs to God alone. This light is creaturely and yet it is supernatural according to His soul. Nevertheless, where it is his soul, she beholds God there as she still does today.

The third art is what she has in common with the angels. It is that all things are imaged in her. About this, Saint Dionysius says: When God created the angels, he gave them the image of all things. They have this naturally. Likewise, Christ's soul has the image of all things in her naturally. This is apprehended properly as his own image that he gave to her, and yet nevertheless he is not this image: as the seal gives its form to the wax, it does not become mixed with the wax.

The fourth that Christ has is a progressive art. It latches onto bodily sense, as we might describe further here. Now pay attention to the ability he has in each art.[8]

The first art is that of God, as He understands that which is by eternal providence: all that has happened and now is and forever will be and may then happen if he wills it and what will yet never come to light. But for all that, this is being according to His being and not according to itself.

With this art, he saw into the hearts of men. And all works which belong to the godhead, He works them with His power. Christ was able do this by this art which is God.

---

5 Cf. Aquinas, *Summa Theologiae*, III.9.1, I.22.1; *Comp. theol.*, I.216.434.
6 That is, the Son.
7 Cf. Aquinas, *Comp. theol.*, I.216.435.
8 Cf. Sermon 14b.

Christ's second art, which is creature, is spoken of with regard to the soul and was poured into her at her creation and is beyond nature.

That's why she savors and beholds God in his being. Therein, nothing can go to or from Him. With this art, he is able to understand all that has ever happened and now is and ever shall be, except for God's potential for potential,[9] if he wills it, that is his endlessness without break, which is hidden.

The third knowledge is what He possesses along with the angels, which have in them the image of all things. The soul of Christ has this. It is in him in a natural way.

Thereon, nothing is taken from or added to it. With it, she can come to know all present things and those now coming to be, but not those which must come to be, as an angel is not aware of things to come, unless they are revealed to him by God. He does not possess this by nature.

The fourth knowledge that He had was through the senses. For whatever the senses take hold of from the outside, they spiritually carry into the imagination,[10] and the intellect beholds it. Thus, he has a capacity to progressively acquire as we do. So spoke a greater master, Thomas, that he had a capacity to progressively acquire by the power of the senses.

Now pay careful attention to what he taught us with these arts.

The first art, which is God, from which all things flowed—with this art, he taught us how we must convert and order all things to their first source: this takes place entirely in the soul of men in whom all multiplicity is gathered together and all corporeal things in their first source, which is God. And whenever man comes to this and attains oneness with God, then first and foremost, he turns all things to their first cause.[11]

About this, Saint Bernard said: Lord, what is man, that you should have so great a love for him?[12] This he determines himself: he is a good in which all multiplicitous things are gather together in a oneness. He teaches us this with the art that God is.

Now observe what he taught us with the art that is supernatural. With that, he teaches us that we surpass all naturalness.

---

9 Potentiality was an important concept for Aristotle in that it helped to solve the problem of change (i.e., metaphysically, how can we explain one thing changing into another?). What we may have here is a rare foreshadowing of how Nicholas of Cusa would later expand the idea.

10 Cf. Sermon 70.

11 Cf. Sermon 5b.

12 Bernard of Clairvaux, *In dedicatione ecclesiae*, Sermo V n. 3, 7.

In the first place, we must surpass our own senses, and from there, thoughts and illusions. Now walk forward, noble soul, and put on your walking shoes! What are the soul's walking shoes? They are intellect and love. Walk thereby beyond the acts of your powers and walk beyond your own intellect and walk beyond the three hierarchies[13] and walk beyond the light that strengthens you and leap into the heart of God in his hiddenness: therein, you must become hidden from all creatures. He teaches us this with the supernatural art.

That's why Saint Paul said: You are dead and your life is hidden with Christ in God.[14]

Now observe that he teaches us with the natural art, that he shares with the angels, who have the images of all things within them? The soul also has the ability to grasp all things in herself.

That's why she must remain in herself, for the truth comes from within and not from without.

That's why Saint Augustine said: Oh Lord, how many have gone out of themselves to search for the truth and who have not yet gone into themselves.[15]

That's why they have not found the truth, for God is the innermost interiority of the soul. He teaches us this with the natural art.

Now observe what he teaches us with the progressive art. It is how we must order our outer man, to say things very briefly.

The order reaches perfection in contemplation: man himself. If man knows himself, that is better than knowledge of all things.

Christ taught them. Who are those whom he taught? They are the simple ones. Who are the simple ones? They are those who deceive no one with anything, those who cannot be deceived by anyone.[16] They are truly simple people.

Let God help us to this simplicity. Amen.

---

13 See Dionysius's description of the hierarchies. The three he has in mind are probably the earthly, heavenly, and divine.

14 Col 3:3.

15 Augustine, *Expositions on the Psalms*, 4, no. 9. Cf. Sermon XIV.2, Sermon 102.

16 Prv 12:21.

Sermon 91
Voca operarios, et redde illis mercedem suam

"Call the laborers and give them their wages."[1]

These words of the Lord, with which He invites the laborers to his vineyard, mean that our Lord invited all men to return to him in two ways.

Firstly, with the creation of all creatures that he made so beautiful and noble. Secondly, with death and the last days.

A master says that God made the world and all things for man, and man for him.[2] But I want to give a deeper sense to it, that He made Himself for Himself, and man for Himself, and Himself for man. And the love that God has for the soul so exceedingly dazzled and overflowed that He created all creatures in order to reveal his glory to the soul.[3] And he is so very eager draw the soul to him and to lure her to his love that he acts as if he had forgotten all that is in the kingdom of heaven and on the earth, and attends only to the way that he can best draw each soul to him.

That's why he made many creatures, so that his glory would be revealed in many ways. And yet he made no creature so perfect that they do not have pain or likeness placed in them.[4] And so all creatures are messengers, pointing to God, for they proclaim all the glory of God and point man in the direction of God. God placed two things in creatures: those are pleasure

---

[1] Mt 20:8. This sermon is particularly rich in metaphors.

[2] Peter Lombard, *Sentences*, II d.1 c.4 no. 6.

[3] Here we see an unusual reference in the vernacular to the well-known notion of *ebullitio*, "boiling over," from Eckhart's Latin works. For an additional instance of being dazzled (*verblendet*), see Sermon 55. Cf. Sermon II.2, Sermon VI.4, Sermon 12, Sermon 6, and *In Sap.* n.59.

[4] Cf. *In Gen. I* n.72; *In Ioh.* n.538; Sermon 43, Sermon 60, Sermon 81, Sermon 84, Sermon XLIV.3, n.446; and Augustine, *Conf.*, X.6.8, XI.4.6.

and serenity with which he lures men who are noble in that they recognize that pleasure and perfect rest are in God.[5] The good man will be lured with pleasure and serenity. And the base man, he pushes along with pain. That's why pain is placed into a creature, so that if he does not heed the glory and pleasure of God, he is struck by pain and pushed toward God.[6] Just as the mind of people is miraculous, so the way toward God is miraculous. One can be lured with pleasure, another can be struck with sickness and discomfort.[7] Just as Saint Paul was miraculously converted when he was on the way to persecute the Christians, when God struck him down and enveloped him with his light.

And Saint Augustine was converted on the day when he could no longer overcome the pleasure that he had from the miraculous trap God had laid for his soul in order to convert her.[8]

And a teacher[9] says that God behaves as if he had forgotten all creatures and contemplates with all zeal in what way He might draw the soul to Him, and how to reveal himself and be loved by her; He acts as if his life and his nature might come to an end,[10] for his life and his nature consist in his revealing himself and being loved.

That's why God, who is simple, has spread[11] himself out among all creatures so that the soul can in no way turn away from God and toward creatures without finding God's likeness in them. No sinner could ever have pleasure in sin if there was not some likeness of God in it in some way, as is the case in honor, joy, and pleasure. That is why many a man forsakes friends and goods, but he cannot forsake honor: It is alluring to him from the start, and thereby he follows what is most like God.[12] For God said, "I will not give

---

5 The word *gemach* means "ease," "serenity," or "quiet rest." Cf. Sermon 73, *Book of Divine Consolation*, 46.16.

6 For another instance of God pushing someone along (*nâchschürgen*) or simply pushing (*schürgen*, modern German *schieben/stoßen*), see Sermon 70.

7 Cf. Sermon 82.

8 Augustine, *Conf.*, IX.6.14.

9 See Sermon VI.1, n.55; Sermon X, n.104.

10 Cf. Sermon 26, Sermon 41, Sermon 47, Sermon 73, Sermon 103, Sermon 109, Sermon VI.1, ns.55, 56.

11 Cf. Sermon 66.

12 Cf. Sermon XXXVIII, n.387.

my honor to another."[13] A gloss says in speaking of a psalm: "There is no one who will give his honor for the honor of a friend."[14]

There are three reasons for which the soul cannot have satisfaction in creatures.[15] The first is that they have division. The satisfaction of drink is not the satisfaction of food nor that of clothing: each leads in a way from itself up to the other and turns ever further toward God. Therefore, there is no satisfaction there.[16]

The second: creatures are corporeal and fall into corruption and weariness,[17] which is why there is no progress in them. The more I look long at a white cloth or the light of the sun, the more my sight is dulled and darkened. There is no creature so beautiful or so noble that one can look at it for long without it becoming tiresome to do so. But spiritual knowledge has progress without end. The more I know of spiritual things, the more purely and more eagerly my senses want to know more.[18]

The third: God's gift to the soul is not offered starting from the vessel from which she flowed out. Unless all the gifts and pleasure God could give were offered out of the vessel that God is, the soul would have no savor in it, and it would not give the soul any pleasure at all.[19]

God is nothing other than pure being,[20] and creatures are from nothing and nevertheless have a being from the same being.[21] But yet the soul does not have a taste for creatures that is another vessel. No matter how pure and noble a drink is, if it is poured into a dirty glass, it will be disgusting.[22] It's

---

13 Is 42:8.

14 Cf. Sermon XXXVIII, n.379.

15 Cf. Sermon 52, Sermon 41.

16 Cf. Sermon 60, Sermon 93.

17 Here, *verdroʒʒenheit* is rendered as "weariness" while a few lines later, *verdrôʒʒlich* is rendered "becoming tiresome." This is a crucial and vivid description for Eckhart since he, rather insightfully, points out that all created things, no matter how beautiful, fall into corruption and we eventually tire of them. Since beauty in Platonic philosophy is the principal vehicle that carries us to the Form of the Good (identified by Christian theologians as God), Eckhart's insight here compels us to recognize the shortcomings of pursuing the ineluctably limited nature of the worldly things we find attractive.

18 Cf. *In Ioh.* n.372.

19 Cf. Sermon 16b, Sermon 59, Sermon 65.

20 Cf. Sermon 7, Sermon 9, Sermon 23, Sermon 37, Sermon 54a, Sermon 57.

21 Cf. Sermon 4, Sermon 5b, Sermon 20b, Sermon 57, Sermon 59.

22 The final word in this passage is *unedeler*, which means "more ignoble" and is entirely consistent with Eckhart's use of *edel* (noble) in the first portion of the sentence. However, simply saying that something is "ignoble" in English does entirely capture the sentiment. If Eckhart were

the same therefore with all the gifts and the honor that God can give: if they are not offered from himself, they have no value.[23]

A teaching says that the Father has a Son and a Holy Spirit, and through them both he has come down to man.

We can further show that heaven is immeasurably greater than earth, and that the angels in heaven are more numerous than all the people on earth. The masters declare that the angels most nearly reveal God. That's why they must also be very numerous.[24]

Daniel saw that a thousand of God's servants and ten times a hundred thousand were by him.[25] And God truly acted as if he had forgotten all his lordship and turned all at once to a man and put forth his love. That's why God says: "Woe to the man who falters in love for me."[26]

So much for the first point, what God provides with the character of creatures.

That's why Scripture says: "O woeful death, how utterly bitter is your memory to one who has added to his things of this world with all love. But to good people, it is very sweet and joyous."[27] It is nothing more than a crossing over from death to life. And it accomplishes a joyful exchange, for the good man gives pain and misery in death for eternal joy.[28]

Suppose that someone could come by an herb and whoever had it with him would never become old or sick. One would pay dearly for this herb. Such is death. Whoever keeps it in his memory never becomes old in sin.

---

to say that food had gone bad or did not taste right, he could use the word *unedel*, even though we are not likely today to describe bad food as "ignoble" (however true that might be). To both capture the sense of bad taste (which is an important metaphor for Eckhart that he makes much of in this sermon) and imply that something is vulgar (not noble), while at the same time giving a natural description of what it is like to drink from a dirty glass (emphasis on the *experiential* quality of the metaphor), "disgusting" was the best choice.

23 This is an important point that is too easily passed over since it is not a given for us. Here, Eckhart emphasizes that absolutely everything has its being and its value from God and that it has no value and is nothing apart from God. It is a strong injunction for us to turn to God and to God alone and—importantly—not to turn our backs on creatures entirely since God has spread Himself out in them, however partially and imperfectly they manifest God. This tells us to relish (again: *taste*) the beauty of all creation while never losing sight of God, who is the fountainhead of all being and meaning.

24 Cf. Sermon 4, Sermon 74.

25 Dn 7:10.

26 Sir 41:11.

27 Sir 41:1–3.

28 Prv 31:18.

For Scripture says: "In all your actions, be aware of your end and you will never sin."[29]

Thirdly, we must consider the wages of which he speaks: "Call the laborers and give them their wages." No one must trouble himself about what he said—namely, that we must give the laborers their wages. If he is old or sick and if he is not able to perform bodily works, then let him stick to inner spiritual works like good will and love toward God, which are nobler and greater to God than outer works.[30] Therein he claims his reward.

Our Lord God lures us with a reward just like a sheep with a branch: whenever we now want to have it go somewhere else, one points to it with a green branch.[31]

God indicated us that there is a reward. Yet he did not say what the reward is. If God were to say what the reward is, he would have to leave all his power. If anything[32] were in God, it would keep quiet and would not proclaim the reward, and so it would remain unspoken.[33] All that God is and can be, that is the reward.[34] Thus, all his being and his power must speak the reward. And if all the power which is in all souls was placed into one soul, she could not receive the smallest reward which comes from the smallest work that God has ordained in eternal love; she would dissolve and perish.

I swear, let my soul be banished to hell on the day of judgment, that what I will say now is true: If all the power of all the souls and all the angels and all the creatures were completely taken up in one soul, she could not receive the least reward for a good thought which had been thought in eternal love, unless she dissolve, melt, and perish.[35]

---

29 Sir 7:40.

30 Cf. Sermon VII, n.82; Sermon IX, n.96; Sermon XLVII.1, n.488; *Book of Divine Consolation*, 40.15–20.

31 The phrasing and metaphorics here are subtle and crucial. God does not bring or carry us somewhere else. He *points* to where we should go and *lures* us to choose that path, just as one lures a sheep to choose the path one wants it to take by showing it a green branch. Here, as elsewhere, it is salient that the branch is *green*, since this is an important metaphor for Eckhart which indicates (continuous) rebirth. See the discussion of things that are greening, verdant, and blossoming in the section on the spark of the soul in chap. 6.

32 Eckhart uses "something" (*etwaz*) to refer to an indescribable something in God, which plays with the boundary of what is nameable and what is not by calling it by a nonspecific name. Here, the word is *iht*, but the meaning is similar.

33 *Ungesprochen* can mean "unspoken" (with reference to God's speaking the Word) and also ineffable or beyond words.

34 Cf. *In Sap.* n.70; Sermon, XII.2, n.141.

35 Cf. Sermon 47, Sermon 97.

What counsel might she have heard if she must receive all the reward that God is, for the soul must become elevated herself above herself and above all creatures and must come to be carried over[36] into divine being and in the likeness of divine nature? Can she do it?

The reward from another could also become tiresome, since it is eternal.[37] God found a heavenly remedy for this and renewed Himself therewith, and with it brought eternity into time and time into eternity. This happens in the Son, for when the Son pours into eternity, all creatures are poured into him.[38] That's why the Son is eternally born for all time and without ceasing, and all the pleasure and perfection of creatures is gathered together in him and shall be poured[39] without ceasing, ever new. That's why his birth today is always new, as it was with the first beginning,[40] so that the reward can be given as a gift to the soul out of a new vessel, fresh and perfect, and so her reward remains forever joyful without growing weary.

From here I can say no more, God can say no more, except let this perfect reward become ours. God help us to this. Amen.

---

36 Note that being "carried" is passive, playing into Eckhart's metaphorics of activity and passivity. Cf. Sermon 8, Sermon 17, Sermon 39, Sermon 70, Sermon 73, Sermon 76, Sermon 82, Sermon 86.

37 Cf. Sermon 8.

38 Cf. Sermon 19, Sermon 47, Sermon 53, Sermon 60.

39 *Geschenken* as the past of "to pour" or "to bestow upon" may read more naturally as "to bestow upon" in this sentence, but the metaphorics of flow are important and clear, with "to pour," as is the idea that gifts pour from Christ. Cf. Sermon 101, Sermon 106A; Sermon XV.1, n. 153; Sermon XXIII, n. 223; *In Eccl.* n.23; *Book of Divine Consolation*, 43.28–44.5; *In Ioh.* ns.8, 197, 412.

40 Cf. Sermon 31, Sermon 43, Sermon 53, Sermon 57; *In Sap.* n.161; Albertus Magnus, *Sup. Matt.* 6.9.

Sermon 92
Cum sero factum esset[1]

When evening entered and the day had fallen, and his disciples were gathered together, God came in.[2] As the day of bodily pleasure falls and the evening of ephemeral things descends upon the soul and all her powers gather together and are covered over, the light of all truth shines in the soul.[3]

That is why man must die to sin and all causes of sin.

What's more, he must die to nature as if it were nothing in itself, purely seeking the glory of God and nothing for himself.[4]

---

1 The full passage reads: "Then the same day at evening, being the first day of the week, when the doors were shut where the disciples were assembled for fear of the Jews, came Jesus and stood in the midst, and saith unto them, Peace be unto you" (Jn 20:19, KJV). Here, as elsewhere, Eckhart bends the text somewhat and emphasizes ostensibly commonplace elements to tease out the hidden meaning. This kind of interpretation had a longstanding tradition and Eckhart is not too unusual in his practice of it, though it is not as common today.

2 Jn 20:19. Eckhart uses two forms of the same word here, "entered" (*intrat*) and "came in" (*trat în*). This wordplay is not in the Latin.

3 Speaking of a "canopy of night" or of darkness as "blanketing" things is a common metaphor for us and seems to be what Eckhart is appealing to here. This metaphor-rich sentence describes the day (activity) of bodily pleasures (worldly concerns) as falling (out of heaven) and the night (of passivity and rest) blanketing and muffling the bodily pleasures (bringing rest) to enable the light (associated with divinity) to shine freely. This sentence is a good example of how densely packed Eckhart's rhetoric can be with metaphor. Cf. *In Ioh.* n.708.

4 Cf. Sermon 13a.

Further, one must be God's own[5] so that God may joyously work his proper work in the soul.[6] Adam was so completely God's own before he fell that his will was united with God in such a way that divinity shone through the will in the lowest powers so that they could not work unless commanded by the will. There, God speaks his proper work and may move about in the soul.

That's why Christ said: *All power is given to me in heaven and earth and Jerusalem*. It is as if he meant: it is imparted to me to work in the soul that dwells in peace. In her, the power to work my own work is given to me.

Whatever works its own work works joyfully, just as the Holy Spirit does in the soul. What does it work? Twelve fruits, which set man in order man to God and to the good life.[7]

The first three set man in order to God.

The first is love, which raises man above all ephemeral things and puts him in God, whom he loves.[8] For the soul that is enveloped by the fire of true love, all that comes to him accidentally is immediately consumed in the fire of love.[9]

The second fruit is spiritual joy that comes from pure awareness that makes a man light[10] to all good things and raises him above himself. When this happens, he rejoices.

---

5 The word for "own" here is *eigen*. Eckhart has something specific in mind with this term, recalling Aristotle in the sense of a defining quality and something that rightfully belongs to a thing. This little word is easily missed since it occurs in contexts without Eckhart drawing attention to it as significant. I have tried to consistently render it as "proper" so that it may be readily identified.

6 Cf. Sermon 10, Sermon 73, Sermon 82, Sermon 109.

7 Gal 5:22–23.

8 The language may seem strange here to those unfamiliar with the reference. Augustine says we become what we love (*De Trin.*, VIII.iv.9), an idea that Eckhart uses as well (*In Ex.* n.206). For man to be "placed" or "set" man in God has the implication of putting something where it belongs, in the place that it proper to it. Further, placing something is a form of "arranging" or "ordering" it, thus continuing with the metaphor of *ordering* the soul, an originally Platonic idea (cf. the discussion in the *Republic* and the *Phaedrus* of the well-ordered soul and taming the "bad horse" that pulls the chariot of the soul). So, love has the effect of transforming us into what we love and setting us in our proper place, viz., in God.

9 Cf. *Counsels on Discernment*, §12.

10 To become "light" to all good things here is to become light in weight, that is, not being dragged to earth like the lower elements (earth and water), but instead being drawn upward to heaven like the higher elements (air and fire). In Plato's ontology, the metaphor of "up is good, down is bad" applies. The elements are ranked according to their tendency to move down (earth and water), to be suspended in air (as one can see that air does when trapped under a glass that is submerged in water), and to move ever upward apparently without bounds toward the heavens (fire). According to this system, love, especially love of God, is naturally associated with fire.

The third is the peace of the spirit, which makes God a dweller in the soul.

The next three set man in order for his fellow Christian.[11]

The first is kindness, which is the act of wishing goodness with all his heart for everyone.[12]

The second is being true,[13] which is the act of wishing for his fellow Christian as he does to himself.

The third is gentleness, which is when a man behaves with people so that he troubles no one.

The third three fruits set a man in order against future suffering.

The first is patience, where a man is tame[14] under the burden of suffering, so that he does not act like a horse that wears down before the end of a journey under the burden that it must carry.

The second is long-suffering, that man looks for no way out of suffering.

The third is sweetness,[15] which no pain can lessen or make bitter.

The fourth three fruits order man to himself.

The first is self-restraint;[16] the second, continence; the third, self-control, that one does not take too much of things, so that one could take more, so desire ever remains sober.

---

[11] Cf. Sermon XXXIII, n.334.

[12] Though we are more likely to "wish good things" or "have good wishes" for someone, the important connotation here is that we wish for good for everyone, where good is understood Platonically to mean that which is good for you and brings you closer to the Good, to God.

[13] This is being true in the sense of being loyal or faithful.

[14] The use of *getwedic* (tame or submissive) is an unusual image for Eckhart, though it is in concert with his metaphorics of passively undergoing.

[15] Sweetness (*süezgemüete*) is another unusual metaphor for Eckhart, though he again connects sweetness with goodness in Sermon 113.

[16] The word translated as self-restraint is *mâze*, which had special meaning for the medievals. It referred to self-restraint or appropriately measured behavior in accordance with chivalry.

Sermon 93
Quae est ista, quae ascendit quasi aurora[1]

Quae ista quae ascendit quasi aurora consurgens, pulchra ut luna, electa ut sol? This verse is written in the Book of Love: "Who is the one who rises like the dawn, beautiful like the moon, resplendent as the sun?"

We should notice in these words three dignities of Our Lady.

The first is her birth, which is referred to when he says that she "rises like the dawn."

The second dignity of her holy life on earth is referred to when he says: "beautiful like the moon."

The third dignity that she has, as she is the mother of God, is referred to when he says: "resplendent like the sun."

First, likening her to a dawn suggests two things to me: for one, that the dawn has light and darkness in itself at the same time. For another, that it is called the end of night and the beginning of day.

This means that the birth of Our Lady was an end of sorrow and a beginning of joy for our ancient fathers, for before that time, they could do nothing to get themselves to heaven.[2] Yet now our Lord is satisfied with very little: for a glass of fresh water,[3] he gives his Kingdom of Heaven to a pure heart, and that is enough.[4] That's why Christ says, "blessed are those who are

---

1 Song 6:9.

2 Cf. Sermon 86, Sermon 87.

3 Mt 10:42.

4 Cf. *In Gen.* n.157; *In Ex.* n.240; Sermon 86.

pure in heart,"[5] but he does not say that they must do a lot of fasting nor that they must do great works.[6]

Saint Bernard says: "Would to God that it should happen that we should have great desire for the birth of Our Lord, as the old fathers had, for we take greater delight in desiring corporeal things than there is in presently having them."[7] Yet it is not this way with spiritual things: we take greater delight in presently having them than in desiring them.[8] To think of that right longing of the old fathers is enough to make you cry.

The other is higher still. The birth of Our Lady is pointed to by it, and also that this dawn has both light and darkness in itself. Also pointed to is that Our Lady was conceived in sin, and her body and her soul were united in original sin, and thereafter she was unified with the Holy Spirit and was born holy.[9] And that's why we celebrate her birth. The perfection of the love of Our Lord is indicated to us through that, for He never created a purer creature that would be as noble, and further still he does not want to make them so perfect that the soul would be or could be unified with her in love. God indeed wants the soul to see and hear what God is not, but he does not want her to have love for something other than him, for he created her for her oneness.[10]

He alone cast truth upon created things,[11] but they are not the truth themselves as God is the truth himself. Moreover, the truth is in creatures in many ways, as six of them is more than two, and so on. And the soul by nature searches for the truth.[12] If she were to find any creature that was truth itself, she would rest there. That's why Our Lady says:[13] "I sought rest in all things and have rested in the land of my Lord God." Further, Saint Noah sent forth a dove to see if she might find rest anywhere. But she found nowhere to set her feet. This refers to every rational soul[14] that finds no rest in creatures

---

5 Mt 5:8, Cf. Sermon 5b; Sermon 21.
6 Cf. Sermon 32, Sermon 33.
7 Bernard of Clairvaux, *Sermon II super Cant.* c.1 n.1.
8 Cf. Sermon 41, *In Ioh.* n.302.
9 Cf. Sermon 58, Sermon 96, Sermon V.2, n.42.
10 Cf. Sermon XIV.1, n.151. The extra "her" in "He created her for her oneness" is awkward, but it appears in the original: *er hât sie ze sîner einunge geschaffen.*
11 Cf. Sermon 60, Sermon 77.
12 Cf. Sermon 10, Sermon 84; *On the Nobleman*, 116.10; *In Ioh.* n.671.
13 Cf. Eccl 24:11; Sermon 60, Sermon 86, Sermon XLIV.
14 Cf. Sermon 28, Sermon 80, Sermon 93, Sermon XVI; *Book of Divine Consolation*, 11.20–22.

with regard to right truth. That's why she turns again toward her Creator as a dove to the Ark, for the soul is called a dove in the Book of Love.[15]

By nature, the soul loves nothing other than goodness.[16] That's why I say, and it is true:[17] every man who steps with understanding in his heart finds that he has love for nothing other than perfect goodness.[18] And that's why God gave no creature perfect goodness. For if the soul found perfect goodness in creatures, she would unify herself with them. God knows well that love is a unifying power: she unites herself to what she loves completely. And so God does not go to any creature, for love takes man outside of himself and orders him to that which he loves.[19] That's why the soul of Saint Mary Magdalene was more united to the dead body of Our Lord Jesus Christ than to her own. That's why she forgot all that she heard before.[20] Saint Augustine says: "The soul is more properly herself where she loves than where she gives life."[21] And Saint Paul says: "I live and yet do not live, Christ lives in me."[22] All creatures call out to man: you seek truth and goodness,[23] which we are not. Seek God, for he is both truth and goodness. That's why Saint Augustine said: "Seek what you seek, but it is not where you seek."[24] He says in another book that man has joy and delights in sin.[25] If he were to change his ways, he would truly find it in God. In all things, man searches for a blessed[26] life and a joyous light. Satisfaction and perfection are not found in any creature,

---

15 Song 1:15.
16 Cf. Sermon 41, Sermon 84.
17 Cf. Sermon 2, Sermon 4, Sermon 6, Sermon 41, Sermon 47; *Book of Divine Consolation*, 13.13.
18 Cf. Sermon 97.
19 Cf. *In Ex.* n.257; Sermon VI.4 n.73.
20 Cf. Sermon 56; *In Ioh.* n.705.
21 Cf. Sermon 6; Sermon 102; Sermon XVII.3, n.170; *In Ioh.* n.469. Note that the soul (*anima*) is the animating principle of the body.
22 Gal 2:20, cf. Sermon 44.
23 Cf. Sermon 84.
24 Augustine, *Conf.*, IV.12.18.
25 Augustine, *Homilies on First John*, tr.4 n.4.
26 I chose to consistently render *sælic* as "blessed" instead of "joyous," which is also possible. Eckhart has a theology of joy. While he uses many words for it, versions of *sælic* are his favorites, probably since it has overtones of being a specifically divine joy. We see that here, where he says that man has "joy" (*liep*) and "delights" (*sich vröuwen*) in sin, but he recommends a conversion (a turning about, *kêren*, just as in Latin) to God and attaining thereby divine joy, becoming blessed (*sælic*).

always moving from one to another: satisfaction in clothing is not satisfaction in food nor that of drink.[27]

Through all things, we must search for satisfaction in the perfection of Our Lord.[28] That's why Saint Augustine said: "Seek what you seek, but it is not where you seek." For the perfectiaon of all creatures is in God. And if the perfection of all creatures was not in God, then the soul could never have perfect satisfaction nor rest in God. Therefore, the soul wants to have the entirety of the complete perfection in God. If some perfection was outside of God in creatures, she would want then to have it, and would forego the greatest for the least, and would be punished.

Saint Augustine said: It is a great foolishness for the soul to be without that which is everywhere, and for her not to be with that without which she cannot be, and for her not to love that without which she cannot love.[29]

I say, and it is true, that God can no more withdraw from the soul than he can renounce himself. In proportion to her being able to catch sight of Him and her being ready to receive Him by likeness, He must give Himself to her through natural wisdom, and also to each creature insofar as its capacity to receive. This can be explained by a metaphor: I am standing here, and if many mirrors were held around me, my likeness must be reflected by all the mirrors. I cannot prevent this any more than I can withdraw from myself. The clearer the mirror, the more perfect the likeness. Therein can one truly know God's indwelling in creatures.[30] That's why Saint Augustine said: "Old new goodness, how can I have found you so late? Old, for you are eternal, and new, for you are pleasing at all times."[31] Saint Augustine said it again: I looked for you and I found that I was far from you in the land of unlikeness, not too far away, for you are everywhere, and not that I was hidden from you, for you know all things, but only that I hid myself in unlikeness in such a way that I did not know you.[32]

---

27 Cf. Sermon 79, Sermon 91.

28 Cf. Sermon 32, Sermon 41.

29 Cf. Augustine, *De Trin.*, XIV.12.16; Augustine, *Conf.* IV.6.11. Cf. Sermon 87; Sermon 100; Sermon 112; Sermon XVIII, n.180; Sermon XXX.2, n.319.

30 Cf. *In. Gen. I* n.301; Sermon 9; Sermon 57; Sermon 69.

31 Augustine, *Conf.*, X.27.38. Only the first sentence in Eckhart's quote is from the *Confessions*. The original reads, "Late, I loved you, beauty so ancient and so new. Late, I loved you!" (*Sero te amavi, pulchritude tam antiqua et tam nova, sero te amavi!*). Eckhart compresses this to a more curious paradoxical formulation, "alte niuwe güete" (DW IV.1, 132.76).

32 "I looked for you and I found that I was far from you in the land of unlikeness" is from Augustine's *Confessions*, VII.10.16. The remainder of the passage is not. Eckhart does not distinguish the two.

So that is the first point, that "Our Lady rose like the dawn."

The second: "beautiful as the moon." Our Lady is like the moon in two ways: as she is the lowest of the planets and the smallest, except for the one which is the smallest. This refers to Our Lord Jesus Christ, for he was the smallest by humility and just after him came Mary.[33] Saint Bernard said: "The chastity of Our Lady much pleased God, but it was by her humility that she became the mother of God."[34] The second way is the face that the moon shines more than the other stars. It is because she is lower than the other planets. This way indicates the perfect compassion of Our Lady for when the moon waxes, all creatures are stronger and more alive, they become receptive while it wanes. So, it is with the earth. It is the smallest below the elements and the lowest, and each of them is ten thousand times heavier than the other, water, air and fire.[35] That's why the earth floats in the middle of the heavens, for all the power of the stars is funneled together into the other elements and moves through them, while only on the earth is the power of the stars united by way of the fixity of the earth, which does not circle like the other elements. That's why the power of light produces unbelievable things on earth.[36] And so it is the same with Our Lady: she received all perfection that God can place in any creature.[37]

So we must explain by allegory with which people our Lord God is present. We can explain this in two ways, by true humility and kindheartedness. Many people think that they are humble, while they are far from it. For whoever thinks himself to be the lowest and most wretched of all creatures, that man receives whatever goodness and perfection of Our Lord works in all creatures. The other is by kindheartedness, which we should explain by compassion: if another man's eye distresses him, this would not distress me, for it is not mine. Though insofar as I am one with him, it distresses me. If I am more united to Our Lord than to myself, when my eye is distressed, this does not distress me. Why? It is not mine. So it is for everything that

---

33 Cf. *In Gen. I* n.101.

34 Bernard of Clairvaux, Sermon I, n.5; Cf. Sermon XII.1, n.122; *In Ioh.* ns.90, 318.

35 Cf. *In Gen. I*, n.56.

36 Cf. Sermon 36b; Sermon 44; Sermon 54a; Sermon 54b; Sermon XII, n.150; Sermon LV.2, n.542; *In Gen. I* n.109; *In Gen. II* n.208; *In Ioh.* n.268.

37 Cf. Sermon XIV.1, n.151.

disturbs[38] me, it does not disturb me, for I am not my own.[39] That's why Saint Augustine said: "Our Lord acts as if he had greater delight in our joy[40] than we do, and greater pain in our suffering than we do."[41]

The third dignity of Our Lady is pointed to when he says: "brilliant like the sun." The sun is a vessel of light and is not light itself, for it has the light in itself and pours it into all creatures, for none of them can be born or become perfect without the help of light. Indeed, it does not shine at night but flows into the stars. It is called the first vessel of light since it produces great things in the noble stones and in many other things on earth, so that we may find the power of divine works even in the stones.[42] So it is with Our Lady. That's why she is a vessel of light, for she brought us the true light in the world.[43]

Let God, who is the true light, help us so that we may be illuminated and filled with divine light. Amen.

---

38 The metaphors span the continuum of order and disorder. What troubles me (causes me woe) also disturbs me and throws me into disarray, *gewerren*. This is in contrast to his metaphorics of the well-ordered and resting soul that is one with God.

39 Cf. Sermon 2; *Book of Divine Consolation*, 53.20; *Counsels on Discernment*, §1; *In Ioh.* n.683.

40 The word *sælicheit* means both joy and blessedness. Eckhart uses this word to refer to divine joy. It is in this way that we can say that Eckhart has a theology of joy and that a spirit of play informs his preaching.

41 Cf. Sermon XLV, n.456.

42 Cf. Sermon 54a.

43 Konrad von Megenberg, *The Book of Nature*, II.4; Thomas Cantimpratensis, *Liber de natura rerum*, XVII.7.

Sermon 94
Non sunt condignae passiones huius temporis[1]

Non sunt condignae passiones huius temporis ad futuram gloriam, quae revelabitur in nobis. Saint Paul says: "All the sufferings of this time are not worthy of the future glory which will be revealed in us."

Saint Augustine says: They are unworthy.[2] That means that one said to the other, "You do not speak truly." But if he says, "You speak falsely," that would say more.

"They are not worthy." The apostles "went with joy from the council that they were judged worthy of suffering outrages for God."[3] A good man who has virtue would have a great joy if he were worthy to have to suffer anything for God. The man who has the right scent of God and would be kindled from the fire of love would leave all the world as easily as a bean.[4] Saint John says in the Apocalypse: "Sell all that you have, . . . and buy fiery gold"[5]—that is, love—for whoever has that, has all things. A just and good man, who is by rights as he should be, so easily and so joyously suffers pain, purgatory, and all things for God which no one can speak of;[6] for he who

---

1 Rom 8:18.
2 Cf. Sermon XI.1, nos. 112–15; XI.2, nos. 116–21; Augustine, *De diversis quaestionibus LXXXIII*, 67.
3 Acts 5:41. Cf. *Book of Divine Consolation*, 49.3–5.
4 Cf. *Book of Divine Consolation*, 56.7–10; Sermon 3, Sermon 30, Sermon 42, Sermon 59.
5 Rv 3:18, Mk 10:21, Lk 18:22.
6 The phrase here, of course, has the common meaning of "unspeakable things," which serves to emphasize Eckhart's point. The phrase may also have a subtler connotation of "things that cannot be said," though, which would be lost if it were translated less literally.

has it, knows it.⁷ Christ said "I'm thirsty" after all of his sufferings.⁸ He means that he must suffer more for the blessedness⁹ of humanity. This is the "sufferings of the world."

There are sufferings of another world. Our life is divided in two: one consists of suffering and the other consists of action.¹⁰ With work, we merit all of our wages. With suffering, the wages are taken in. All the world cannot know how God strives and lures the soul thereby.¹¹ Our profit lies in acting, but it is small and meagre. And that's why our wages do not lie in action, but rather in suffering.¹² He always aims for the best for us, for we can do little with action and suffer much, give little and take much.¹³ Someone can take a mark while he cannot give a penny. He would sooner take a lot than a little. The greater and better a thing is, the more joyous one is in taking it. For this, He laid down our wages in our suffering, since he can give us much and we can receive much of it.

Suffering is completely naked, action possesses something. I cannot act unless I already possess it and it is in me. But suffering possesses nothing; it is naked. A master says: Wherever one must come to be from two, one must necessarily go out of oneself and die to oneself. He must change himself into another and become one with him.¹⁴ For any sense to perceive something, it must be naked of all knowledge: this eye in its ground must be denuded of all color for it to know color, the ear of sound for it to hear something, and so with each other sense. And insofar as each sense goes out of itself, it

---

7 This is one of the passages where Eckhart clearly refers to the irreplaceability of religious experience.

8 Jn 19:28.

9 It is worth noting here in particular that the word *sælicheit* has a particular meaning for Eckhart in addition to the usual story of Christ suffering for mankind's salvation. He also means that Christ suffered so that mankind could be "joyous" in the sense of reveling in the joy that comes with experiencing union with the divine. Christ thereby underwent (*lîdenne*, "to suffer" or "undergo") suffering to make possible the self-emptying (kenosis) of man that is necessary to achieve union with God.

10 The dichotomy here is between passivity and activity. The word *lîden*, which is translated here as "suffering" to be consistent with the preceding paragraph, also means "undergoing" in the sense of what must be passively taken in from outside. For more detail on the passive and active dichotomy in Eckhart, see the sections in chap. 6 on activity and passivity.

11 Cf. Sermon 68, *Counsels on Discernment*, §12.

12 Cf. Sermon XI.1, n.112; Sermon XI.2, n.117; *In Ioh.* n.677.

13 Cf. *Counsels on Discernment*, §11.

14 Cf. Sermon IX, n.100; Sermon XI.2, n.117; Sermon 27, Sermon 49, Sermon 65.

can then receive more, and becomes one with what it receives.[15] So, the soul should and must go out of herself if she is to receive God;[16] so, she comes to be united with God and works all his divine works with Him.[17] This is the reward that Christ sought, after all his works and sufferings, when he said: "Father, I pray to you in order that they may be one as we are one."[18]

God is not satisfied with suffering as the only reward; God wants much more to do and to give to us once more the ability to reap and attain the reward by willingly and joyously undergoing troubles for God.[19]

"The sufferings of the present time are not worthy; they are unworthy with future clarity which shall be revealed in us."[20]

"Revealed": for something to be revealed in us, it must be in us. All the powers that are covered in the soul must fall away if God is to be uncovered and revealed in us.[21] When God created the soul, he implanted himself in her and covered her. It's the vine of God within, where He is Himself the plant.[22] As soon as He created nature, yes and even before He created it, He was ready to implant Himself there.[23]

No one can know God. Saint Philip said, "Lord, show us and point out the Father and it will be enough for us."[24] We sing to Our Lady: "Show that you are the mother."[25] If you are the mother of God, show him to us, for in doing so, you help us. Show that you are our mother, for if you are our mother, then you help us. Reveal yourself as a mother since you have a child, for these go together: to be a mother, she must have a child. "Show us the Father": to be

---

15 Cf. *Sermon VIII*, n.93; *Sermon XXXVIII*, n.384; *In Ioh.* n.100, 396; *Parisian Questions*, II n.2; I n.12; *In Gen. II* n.31; *Book of Divine Consolation*, 28.9–29.4; Sermon 12, Sermon 71, Aristotle, *De Anima*, II.7.

16 Cf. *Counsels on Discernment*, §4.

17 Cf. *In Ioh.* n.241; Sermon 31.

18 Jn 17:20–21.

19 Cf. Sermon 49.

20 Rom 8:18. The word *entdaht* can mean both "revealed" (as in revealed wisdom or to uncover something), but it is literally the opposite of "decking" (clothing) something. This is an instance of the metaphorics of clothing and nudity.

21 Cf. Sermon 17, Sermon 40; *On the Nobleman*, 114.3–7, 114.12–14.

22 Mt 21:33, Mk 12:1.

23 Cf. *On the Nobleman*, 111.9–21, 113.1–9; *Proc. Col. I* n.22; Origen, *Homilia IV in Psalmum*, XXXVI; *In Gen. II* n.193.

24 Jn 14:8.

25 Cf. Sermon XIV.1, n.151; Sermon 93.

a father, he must have a child.[26] These also go together, we cannot take one without the other: Whoever knows the Father knows also knows the Son.[27] All that the Father gives birth to is born in the Son.[28] If we should know Him, we must be children. "If we are children, surely then we are also heirs."[29]

Blessedness lies therein where we know God, not from the outside as when we gaze at things.[30] All that we know from the outside through distinction is not God.[31] Knowledge of God is a life which flows out of the God's being and the soul, for God and the soul have one being and are one in being;[32] for all activity flows out from God while remaining within.[33] The soul knows God there where she is one in and with the being of God. And that is true blessedness, where the soul has life and being with God. And that is God's knowledge, where all other forms of knowledge and being fall away. The soul does not know herself or of other things, except that she is in God and God in her and all things in Him.[34] All that is in God, she knows it with Him and she works all of his works with Him. There is nothing, she knows nothing except in God and God in her.

The very first power that emanates from the purest ground, is a naked awareness:[35] emerging bare into the marketplace, it is immediately clothed and shrouded. Only when she is within does she cast herself upon pure being, yet she immediately covers herself with a shroud, it is true; she knows true being. Still, the will wants nothing unless it appears good at first glance or shines forth goodness.[36]

He says: "What will be revealed in us."[37] "In us": the word "us" means a naked being. If we would come to the point that this "clarity" is revealed in us, the soul must be stripped of hope, fear, joy, sorrow, and all that may come

---

26 Cf. *In Ioh.* n.115; Sermon 26, Sermon 53.

27 Jn 14:9.

28 Cf. *In Ioh.* n.641; Sermon 27, Sermon 29.

29 Rom 8:17; cf. Sermon XIV.1, n.151.

30 Cf. Sermon XI.2, n.120; *In Gen. I* n.296; *In Gen II* n.83; Sermon 54b, Sermon 61.

31 Dionysius, *Celestial Hierarchy*, c.2 n.5; cf. Sermon 73.

32 Cf. Sermon 49.

33 Cf. Sermon 30.

34 Cf. *On the Nobleman*, 116.28–117.2; Sermon 72.

35 Cf. Sermon XI.1, n.115; XI.2, ns.120, 121; Sermon 3; Sermon 7; Sermon 9; Sermon 23; Sermon 40; *Proc. Col. I*, n.147; *Proc. Col. II*, n.122.

36 Cf. Sermon XXIV.2, n.247; Sermon XI.1, n.115.

37 Rom 8:18.

over her.[38] Then God bares himself to her and gives himself to her with all that he can do.

The second thing: one must look within and not without, for Saint Paul says: "The Kingdom of Heaven is in you."[39]

The third: in the most intimate, it is here that something[40] will be revealed.

Let God help us so that we may nakedly know. Amen.

---

38 Cf. Sermon 22; Sermon 69; *In Ex.* n.12; Sermon XI,2, n.119.

39 Lk 17:21. See also Ramelli's article for more detail on the question of how to translate "in" in this passage. She concludes that the most intimate option is the correct one, despite some translators' attempts to tame the passage and make it less mystical. Ramelli, "Luke 17:21."

40 We should perhaps think of Eckhart's use of *etwaʒ* (something) to indicate something close to God that is unnamable.

Sermon 95a
Os suum aperuit sapientiae

"Beatus homo qui invenit sapientiam."
"Blessed is the man who finds wisdom."[1]
It is a twofold wisdom and also a twofold blessedness which come from wisdom.

One wisdom is transitory, which is understanding and being able to arrange[2] ourselves according to time, as a kind of art where we can guard ourselves against misfortune and can arrange ourselves in accord with chance. Whoever can do so becomes a rich man and is called blessed by earthly wisdom. What is more, earthly wisdom is a scent of eternal wisdom.[3]

That's why Our Lord God gave the soul two kinds of powers, that she might serve Our Lord God temporally with the lowest powers and so that she may serve Our Lord God in eternity with the highest powers.[4]

A master said: The soul is a point[5] or an end, where time and eternity collide, and the soul is not however made of time or of eternity, but she is a nature made of the nothingness between the two. If she were made from

---

1 Prv 3:13.

2 This common metaphorical theme in Eckhart is not easily rendered in English. The idea is captured in the archaic English "right," as when we say, "to set things aright," or "all is in right order," meaning "as it should be." For Eckhart, this refers to the mind being trained or structured according to what is *proper*, which means its right function, recalling Aristotle's notion that things are virtuous when they are in accord with the function that is proper to them. In this way, metaphors like this complement the more easily translated appearances of *eigen* as "proper."

3 Cf. Sermon 54b, Sermon 105, Sermon 112.

4 Cf. *Counsels on Discernment*, §20.

5 The variations here circle interestingly around the same idea: the soul is a *punct* (Sermon 95a: "point," "center point," "point in time") or an *ort* (Sermon 95b: "beginning," "boundary," "birth"), and also an *ecke* (Sermon 95a and Sermon 95b: "end," "edge"). In all cases, the

time, she would be transitory. Else if she were made from eternity, she would be unchangeable.[6]

Saint Augustine said: the soul is made of such a noble, heavenly nothingness, that it is more delightful for us to search our whole lives than for us to one day find it.[7] That's why the soul is noble, for she collides with both time and eternity. If she leans toward temporal things, she will be unsteady. If she sinks down into eternity, she will be steady and strong. And with the strength and constancy, she overcomes over all changeable things.[8]

The other wisdom is eternal, and it is one source of the divine purity and a fountain of divine truth. And from this wisdom, one becomes eternally blessed.

The one who would come to this wisdom must have six things in him.[9]

The first is humility; the second, constant diligence; the third, inwardness; the fourth, a searching silence.

No work is so perfect that it does not hinder inwardness. We can more inwardly hear the Mass than speak it. If a preacher sought much inwardness during the Mass, he might do something that would be harmful.

My advice is to seek inwardness before and after, and whenever one wants to perform an action, to do it properly. If a preacher seeks inwardness in preaching, he may not do well with his teaching. What satisfies me is to have just as much inwardness in preaching as I may have in thinking about it.[10]

The fifth is strangeness. He who can be a stranger in his own home is willingly strange.

The sixth is poverty. He is beneficially poor who can make himself poor of all things which are not God.

This is how we must come to divine wisdom.[11]

After that, we must observe which people come to divine wisdom.

---

metaphors indicate that the soul touches time and eternity at infinitesimal closeness without being of time or eternity.

6 Cf. Sermon 23; Sermon 32; Sermon 47; Pseudo-Augustinus, *De Spiritu et anima*, c.47; Albertus Magnus, *De anima lib.*, 1 tr.2 c.2.

7 Cf. Sermon 7; Sermon 32; Sermon 43; Sermon XLVII, n.482.

8 Cf. *Counsels on Discernment*, §9.

9 Cf. *In Ioh.* n.685; Hugh of St. Victor, *Didascalicon*, III c.12.

10 This paragraph, which does not appear in 95b, may be an addition by the redactor of 95a.

11 The difference between 95a and 95b is particularly interesting here. Where 95a speaks of divine wisdom, 95b says "blessed in this life." These two are not so much in any tension with one another as much as they represent different approaches to expressing the same idea.

On this, Solomon says: *Os suum aperuit sapientiae*, which means, "She opened her mouth of wisdom." This signifies the blessed soul. The mouth is the highest power of the soul; it is there that the soul will delight in God.

This power must always become elevated and open to divine consolation. And what she receives from God, she must pour into the lower powers.

If we want to take God and grasp him with the inferior powers, God would need to abase himself and descend to our knowledge, for we can neither know nor grasp God through any things that are available to us.

A master said: All that one can say of God is God. Another master said: all that one can say of God is not God. And both have truth.

Saint Augustine said: God is power, wisdom and goodness.[12] Saint Dionysius said: God is above wisdom, above goodness, and above all that we can say about him.[13]

Why are many names given to Our Lord in Scripture?

There are two reasons.

The first is that one cannot grasp his nobility with *any* of these words, because he is above and outside of all nature, and has a nobility that is not naturally caused. Sometimes one calls it a power, sometimes a light; he is above all light. That's why we call him by this and that, because he is not properly any of these things. If one could grasp his nobility with any words, he would keep the names secret.

Whoever can most know God, denies the most to Him, as we may show by way of a boat. If I wanted to describe a boat to someone who had never seen it, I would say: It is neither a rock nor a blade of grass. I would have straightaway shown him something about the boat.

Two masters were at their prayers.

One called upon Our Lord for his power and for his wisdom.

The other said: Silence, you blaspheme God! God is so high, beyond all that we can say: if God was not so humble, if the saints had not expressed it, and if God would not have accepted it from them, I would never dare praise Him with words.[14]

By this reverential knowledge, the soul comes to a reverential awe, and through the awe, God will be sown into the soul and the soul dies away into

---

12 Cf. Sermon 9.
13 Cf. Dionysius, *Mystical Theology*, c.5. Cf. Sermon 71.
14 Cf. Sermon 53, *In Ex.* n.174.

God.[15] That's why Our Lord said: "If a grain of wheat does not fall to the earth and die, no fruit can come from it."[16]

The soul must have this death through the knowledge of God, through which she herself decomposes and all things that are not God become foul-smelling to her. Then God pours Himself into her by grace, roots himself by grace, and grows by love.[17]

Saint Elizabeth demonstrated this well: however costly and noble a purchase may be, one gives all things for wisdom.[18] That's why Saint Elizabeth joyously renounced her principality and became a poor person.

On this, Scripture says: "Her light was not extinguished throughout the night," which means: In troubles, she will be found just.[19] That's why her light shall shine in eternal life.

However perfect a man may be, if he loses some worldly good, his heart will move and sadden him. This is a certain thing: when a man loses something against his will and he undergoes it patiently, he attains a greater reward, as if he willingly gave it to Our Lord God, for he would be doing so by his own will. Further, by patience, he gives both his will and his goods to Our Lord God.[20]

If someone is found impatient in adversity, his wickedness is not from the pain, but rather the wickedness comes to be revealed in the pain and appears in the man like a copper coin: while it is not in the fire, it shines pure silver; but when it comes into the fire, it will reveal it is copper. It is the copper, not the fire, that does this for him.[21]

That's why Our Lord God tested the saints with pain, that they would be found right in all virtues and so that they would shine in the night and in the eternal life forever.

The third is: how we should "taste" divine wisdom. Four things help us with this.

---

15 Cf. *On the Nobleman*, 110.7–10, 111.17–20, 113.1–5.
16 Jn 12:24–25. Cf. Sermon 49.
17 Cf. Sermon 73.
18 Cf. Sermon 32, *Counsels on Discernment*, §4, 23.
19 Prv 31:18. Cf. *Book of Divine Consolation*, 8.4–8.
20 Cf. Sermon 49.
21 Cf. *In Ioh.* n.76; *In Sap.* n.119.

The first is likeness, that we should make ourselves like God by purity,[22] like glass or transparent things are to the sun.

The second is the divine light, which shines through in the purity of the soul as the sun shines through glass or water.[23]

The third is oneness, which comes from likeness as light from light.[24]

The fourth is the measure,[25] that God would have measured out the soul. Yet God cannot be diminished or increased,[26] for He is measureless and unchanging. And further, the soul then must be elevated and expanded, for she is small and changeable. So it is for God's measurelessness that she should be elevated above herself and expanded.[27]

A master says that man is a small thing, yet he may become elevated above himself.[28] So the soul first receives perfect joy from God, in accordance with her measure of it. Why does God not taste all souls in the same way? It is from their not being ordered to God.[29]

Let God taste us and set us in order so that we could never be distinct from Him. Amen.

---

22 Cf. Sermon 96.

23 Cf. Sermon 23.

24 Cf. Sermon 2; Sermon 44; Sermon XXIX, n.297; *In Ioh.* n.556, 558.

25 The word *maze* has the meaning of "measure," in the sense of having the proper measure of something that befits the thing or situation. Cf. Sermon 47; *In Eccl.* n.64.

26 Cf. Sermon 62; Sermon 71; Sermon 75; *In Ex.* n.90; Sermon XXXIV.2, n.345.

27 Cf. Sermon XXII, n.213; Sermon XXXII, n.328; Sermon 34; Sermon 60; Sermon 84.

28 Seneca, *Natural Questions*, I Preface no. 5. Cf. *In Ioh.* n.282.

29 Cf. Sermon 47, Sermon 85.

Sermon 95b
Os suum aperuit sapientiae

"Os suum aperuit sapientiae."
A master said: "A good woman opened her mouth of wisdom"[1] and "she tasted and saw how good her profits[2] were" and that purchased eternal joy for her. That's why "her light was not extinguished throughout the night," that is to say, in the night of discontent.[3]

I have said about the two kinds of wisdom: one is divine; the other is not divine, and yet it is from God like a ray from the sun.

It is a gift of God and a scent of divine nature. With this wisdom we acquire in ourselves, we become blessed in this life.[4]

A master said that the soul is a beginning[5] or an end where both time and eternity collide, yet she is not made of either time or eternity, but she is a nature made of the nothingness between the two. If she were made from time, she would be transitory. If she were made from eternity, she would be unchangeable.[6]

---

1 Prv 31:26.

2 Eckhart is translating the Latin *negotiatio*, which refers to business. The Middle High German word *kouf* is more general than its successor in modern German, *kauf*. It refers to trade or negotiation. Here, Eckhart is telling us that she *experienced* what she had gained by *tasting* it, which is the most intimate form of experience (see the section on taste in chap. 5). This parallels the passage in Sermon 10, "Like a man who has wine in his cellar but has never tasted it, he does not know that it is good."

3 Prv 31:18. Cf. Sermon 72, Sermon 86.

4 Cf. *In Gen.*, n. 286, 287. See Sermon 95a n.3.

5 See Sermon 95a n.5.

6 Pseudo-Augustine, *De Spiritu et Anima*, c.47.

So she is that which is not made from time or eternity, for she is changeable and not transitory.[7]

Saint Augustine said that the soul is made from the noblest and most heavenly nothingness, and that it is more delightful for us to search our whole lives than for us to ever be able to find it.[8] That's why the soul is so noble that she collides with both time and eternity. If she inclines toward temporal things, she will darken.[9] And if she sinks down into eternal things, she will be strong and steady. With strength and with constancy, she overcomes all changeable things.[10]

Our Lord God gave the soul two kinds of power to help her, that she may serve God with the lower powers in time and so she may serve God in eternity with the highest powers.

A master was asked how we should come to wisdom. Among other features, he described six things that man should have.[11]

The first is a humble heart, the second is a constant diligence, the third is a restful heart, the fourth a silent searching.

Nevertheless, no work is so perfect that it does not hinder inwardness. One may have more inwardness in hearing the Mass than in speaking it. Were someone to have a very great inwardness in saying the Mass, he might do something that would be harmful.

All of the skill of which a man is capable is shown in his activity. Does a man sing well? We hear it through his singing. Just the same, we know a truly wise man by his silence.

The fifth is voluntary poverty. He is beneficially poor who can make himself poor of all things which are not God.

The sixth is a strange land. He who is a stranger in his own house, that is right poverty.

With these six things, one attains the wisdom with which one becomes blessed in this life.

The other wisdom is an inflowing of divine purity and is a fountain of divine nobility and is God himself.[12]

---

7 See Sermon 95a n.6.

8 See Sermon 95a n.7.

9 That she "darkens" (*vervinstern*) should be understood in contrast to Eckhart's metaphorics of light. Light is divine and affects what it lights without itself changing by the interaction.

10 See Sermon 95a n.8.

11 See Sermon 95a n.9.

12 Cf. Sermon 81.

No one can grasp this wisdom through temporal things. Man would be seriously foolish to want to make God temporal, and he who would like to grasp him with his inferior powers would have serious disdain for God. God remains for him ungrasped through all creatures.[13]

That's why the sage said: "A good woman opened her mouth of wisdom."

This is nothing other than that you should open your desire to what is highest and abide in the highest power of the soul.[14] It is akin to God so that He cannot deny anything to this power, and this power must then receive much sweetness and wisdom from God, and also much consolation and truth, and this she then pours into the rest of the soul.[15]

The saints say that there is a mode that suits temporal life and there is another mode that suits eternal life. Yet we must always first begin with things here and should then become complete in eternal life with eternal wisdom.[16]

A master said to another: Do you know something that God is? No, he replied, I do not know what God is. Of Him, I know well that I know what he is not, for no one can know God except from within God's nature.[17]

Further, no one can come to be in another living nature if he is not first of all dead to his own nature.[18]

Ah, so why is it then that Scripture gives Him so many names?[19] It says that he is all-powerful, wise, and good.

There are three reasons.

The first reason is that God is not enclosed in any nature. I stand here and now, and I am not a lion. Why is this? Because I am a man. I am thus enclosed within the nature that God has ordered within me, so that I cannot move into another nature. So it is with all creatures that God created. God is beyond all nature and is not nature himself.

The second reason is that we cannot give any likeness to God.[20]

---

13 Cf. Sermon 32, Sermon 61.
14 Cf. Sermon 54.
15 Cf. Sermon 27, Sermon 29, Sermon 40.
16 Thomas Aquinas, *Summa Theologiae*, II.182.2. Cf. Sermon 3, Sermon 20a, Sermon 80.
17 Cf. *In Ex.* n.184; Sermon 20a.
18 Cf. Sermon XLVII.1, n.486; Sermon 45.
19 Cf. Sermon 53.
20 Cf. Sermon XXXVII, n.375; Sermon 71.

Saint Augustine gives him many names.[21] He says that He is wisdom, while Saint Dionysius says: No, no, he is above wisdom.[22] He said that He is a light. No, no, he is above light. He said that he is a being. No, no, he is above being. He said that he is an eternity. No, no, he is above eternity. All that one can say is not God.[23]

No one can grasp the nobility or grandeur of God with any words.

I say "man" and with that I grasp human nature. I say "earl" and with that I grasp the lordship of the earl. I say "angel" and with that I grasp angelic nature. I say "God" and with that I cannot grasp the divine splendor or the divine lordship.[24] In one place, Saint Augustine said to a master: Many are the things that God is. A good man. What is a good man? A good rock. What is a good rock? A good angel. What is a good angel? Take away the angel, take away the rock, take away the man, take away all three; there is the pure good which is God.

The third reason that Scripture gives Him so many names is because He is not like any nature and because we cannot come to his knowledge by any likeness. The highest creature that God created has an angelic nature and is as unlike God as is the nature of the smallest blot that you would ever see with your eyes.[25]

A saint said: Lord, is it suitable to you that we praise you? Another said: Is it suitable to you that we are silent about you?

Two masters wanted to pray.

One said: Thanks be to the good and all-powerful God!

The other said: Silence, you blaspheme God! God is too high above us for us to praise him with any words. If God were not so humble, if the saints had not expressed it, and if He did not take them on himself, I would never dare praise Him with words.[26]

The more one denies what is His, the more one praises Him. The more unlikeness we add to him, the closer we get to His knowledge, as I will say with the help of a comparison.[27] If I wanted to tell someone what a boat is

---

21 See Sermon 95a, n.8.

22 See Sermon 95a, n.13.

23 Bonaventure, *De Triplici Via*, III.7.

24 Cf. *General Prologue* n.8; *In Ex.* n.17; *Book of Divine Consolation*, 25.1–7. Notice the progression from worldly lordship to spiritual lordship to divine lordship.

25 Cf. Sermon 61.

26 See Sermon 95a n.14.

27 Note that *glîchnisse* is the word for "metaphor," "comparison," "parable," and "likeness."

who has never seen one, whatever he sees, he sees well what is not a boat. If he sees a stone, he sees well that a stone is not a boat. The more he sees what was not created as a boat, the closer he comes to knowledge of boats. So it is with God. The more one adds unlikeness to him, the closer one comes to His knowledge. For all that Holy Scripture can bring forth altogether denies what is His.[28] We should say the word "humble" to express that he is all-powerful.

As the soul comes to knowledge that God is unlike all natures, she arrives at a miracle, gets driven back, and comes into silence.[29] God calmly lowers himself into the soul,[30] and she will overflow[31] with grace, as Our Lord said through the prophet: "The tree which is planted near flowing water will bring forth much fruit."[32]

The soul must die in suffering as Our Lord said.[33] That is shown by the grain of wheat that falls on the earth: it cannot bear any fruit if it does not die first.[34]

The death of the soul must be through the knowledge of God, where she must flee from herself, and all things that are not God become stinking and tasteless to her. She must be rooted in faith and grow through love.[35]

Saint Elizabeth demonstrated this well: however costly and noble a purchase it may be, one gives all things for eternal wisdom.[36] That's why she joyously renounced her fiefdom and became a poor person.

On this, Scripture says that "Her light was not extinguished throughout the night," which means: In troubles, she will be found just.[37] That's why her light shall shine in eternal life.

However perfect a man may be, if he loses some worldly good, his heart will move and sadden him. This is a certain thing: when a man loses something against his will and he undergoes it patiently, thereby he attains a

---

[28] Cf. Sermon 36b; Sermon 45; *In Ex.*, ns. 172–73.
[29] Cf. Sermon 36a; Sermon 36b; Sermon 101.
[30] Cf. Sermon XXIX, n.296; Sermon CVII; *In Ioh.*, ns.304, 311, 581, 585; *In Sap.* n.60; Sermon 22.
[31] This may be a rare occurrence of "boiling over" (*ebullitio*) in the vernacular sermons. Cf. Sermon XXII, n.206.
[32] Cf. Ps 1:3; Sermon 44; Sermon XXII, n.206.
[33] Cf. Sermon 8; Sermon 49; Sermon 52; Sermon 92.
[34] See Sermon 95a, n.16.
[35] See Sermon 95a, n.17.
[36] See Sermon 95a n.18.
[37] See Sermon 95a n.19.

greater reward than if he would give his will to God. And whoever does this gives his will and his goods through patience to our Lord God.[38]

If someone is found impatient in adversity, his impatient wickedness is not from the pain, but rather the wickedness comes to be revealed in the pain and appears in the man like a copper coin: while it is not in the fire, it shines pure silver, but as soon as it enters the fire, it shows that it is copper. It is the copper, not the fire, that does this for him.[39]

That's why Our Lord tested the saints here with pain, that they would be found right in all virtues and so that they would shine in the night and in the eternal life forever.

The other is: in whomever should "taste" divine wisdom, four things arise.

The first is likeness, that we should make ourselves like God by all purity.[40]

The second is divine light, which shines through the soul like the sun through a glass.[41]

The third is oneness, which comes from likeness, and right oneness comes from like things as light from light.[42]

The fourth is the measure, that God has measured out the soul.[43] Yet God cannot be diminished or increased,[44] for He is measureless and unchanging, rather, the soul must be elevated and expanded, for she is small and changeable.[45] That's why she must be elevated beyond herself and in whatever way she expands, it is very small in comparison with the measurelessness of God.[46]

A master says that man is a small thing, yet he may become elevated above himself.[47] So the soul first receives perfect joy from God, in accordance

---

38 See Sermon 95a n.20.
39 See Sermon 95a n.21.
40 See Sermon 95a n.22.
41 See Sermon 95a n.23.
42 See Sermon 95a n.24.
43 See Sermon 95a n.25.
44 See Sermon 95a n.26.
45 *wandelhaftic* can mean "imperfect," "changeable," and "inconstant." To wander is to lack rest, which would be consistent with Eckhart's metaphorics for a soul that has not expanded infinitely to have the capacity for God. See Sermon 96, Sermon 100, Sermon XXIV.2.
46 See Sermon 95a n.27.
47 See Sermon 95a n.28.

with her measure of it. Why does God not taste all souls in the same way? That is from their not being ordered to God.[48]

Let God help us so that we will be ordered in our souls so as to become truly savory for God. Amen.

---

[48] See Sermon 95a n.29.

Sermon 96
Elisabeth pariet tibi filium

Elisabeth pariet tibi filium et vocabis nomen eius Johannem. Elizabeth shall give birth to a son and he shall be called John.[1] The Angel said these words when *he appeared to Zacharias*.

There are two ways an angel can reveal itself. For example, as a body that he takes from the elements. An angel is capable by nature of making a tree manifest[2] in a moment that takes many years to grow from a seed.[3] Human nature is capable of transforming food into flesh and blood.[4] So it is even more possible that, by divine power, wine and bread be transformed into the body of God.[5] The second way an angel reveals itself is by the likeness to the divine light, pointing to God's will in the soul, and binds God's will to the light and imprints it upon the soul.[6] Just as the words I will say are not the things I want to speak about, but only a manifestation of the thing of which

---

1 Lk 1:13.

2 Here we see one word repeatedly used, *bewîsen*, that has been translated as "manifest," "manifestation," "indicate," and "pointing to." It is an important word since it tells us about the relationship between an active, tangible force in the world and the ultimate goal of that force. Note that this is not merely a question of sign and signified. An angel reveals itself as a likeness to the divine light so that we might be able to take that light in and have the necessary experiences of visceral, full-bodied (not merely conceptual) understanding so as to move us closer to God. This sermon is unusual in that Eckhart makes this relationship explicit, even telling us that his words are mere manifestations of what he wants to speak about. Notice what he says next, though: the meaning is carried into the soul. This is the experience of internalizing the ideas, not merely conceptually understanding them. We should also sense something Platonic going on in his characterization of the ideas and how they may be intuited via imperfect manifestations.

3 Cf. Sermon V.1, n.31; *In Ioh.* n.294.

4 Cf. Sermon 20b, Sermon 65, Sermon 108.

5 Cf. Sermon 6.

6 Cf. Sermon 8, Sermon 12, Sermon 35, Sermon 78.

I want to speak, so I bind my words to the air with a voice, and the air carries them to your ears, and they will be then brought into the soul.[7] In the same way, some spiritual people point with a finger to what they mean,[8] so the angel reveals himself in a likeness, which is spiritual, and points to the will of God in the soul.

Now, we must notice the first word that the angel said: *Elizabeth shall give birth to a child.*[9] With *Elizabeth* is included[10] in what state the soul should be so that the grace of God should come to be born.[11] *John* signifies as much as *in he whom grace is.*[12] The child *shall become great* and *is born holy.*[13] That's why we seek to reach three kinds of birth, that they may become purified in their mother's body. Saint John was so pure that he could not commit a mortal sin. And Our Lady was so full of grace that she never committed a mortal sin or an everyday sin. And Our Lord Jesus Christ was absolutely pure, for he was conceived from a pure conception[14] that he never fell from original sin. Just as the woman was barren,[15] so should the soul be unfruitful, in which the grace of God will be born, thinking neither of the contentment or discontentment of people, but of God alone.[16]

Each action flows from a being. If there were no being, there would be no activity.[17] In the same way, warm things come from fire—if there were no fire, there would be no warmth—and all cold things come from water, and all dry things come from earth, and all very earthly things are thoughtless, cold and able to undergo much, so all perfection of the soul lies in the heat where the living action acts.[18]

---

7 Cf. *In Ex.* n.169; Sermon 101.

8 Cf. Sermon 36a.

9 Lk 1:13. Cf. Sermon 11, Sermon 32, Sermon 95b.

10 That is, saying that *Elizabeth* shall give birth tells us that to know Elizabeth is to know the state the soul needs to be in order to give birth.

11 Isidore of Seville, *Etymology*, VII c.10 n.2.

12 Cf. Sermon XVII.6, n.179; *In Ioh.*, n.167; Isidore of Seville, *Etymology*, VII c.9 n.12.

13 Lk 1:15.

14 As he does elsewhere in his vernacular work, Eckhart often engages in wordplay with the dual meaning of *enpfâhen*, "received" and "conceived." We should interpret such passages in light of his metaphorics of passivity and receptivity. Cf. Sermon 93; Albertus Magnus, *In Luc. 1:15*.

15 Lk 1:7. Cf. Sermon 10; Sermon 43; *In Gen I* n.191.

16 Cf. Sermon 32.

17 Cf. Sermon IX, n. 97; Sermon XIII, n.150; *In Ioh.* n. 634.

18 Cf. Sermon XXXVIII, n.384, Sermon 17, Sermon 20a, Sermon 26, Sermon 33, Sermon 57, Sermon 88, Sermon 97, *Book of Divine Consolation* 32.2–5.

By three things, we can notice whether grace is in the soul. The first, that the soul is god-colored, for she comes from divine being.[19] The second is that she makes the soul like God and imprints God's likeness into the soul and makes her god-colored in the way that she presents herself as a god to the devil, which is from the nobility of grace.[20] Third, by the fact that the soul is not satisfied unless she completely has all perfection. For a pagan master said: all perfection of the soul resides where she has a likeness to God, the angels and all creatures,[21] as I have often said before: the likeness and the perfection of all creatures was created in the angles in a spiritual way, before being created in creatures.[22] Now, the soul should be like the angels in the kingdom of heaven. Whatever the angels possess was promised to the soul. Whatever the angels received, she shall come to be given.[23] That's why the soul is never satisfied unless she reaches the point where the perfection of all creatures is undivided, without any distinction.[24]

We should notice in the second place the way grace works in the soul, as we can demonstrate through the image of the axe.[25] Three things must be in her. The first: an appropriate form and that she is smoothed.[26] So the soul must be purified and cleansed of sin, incapable of sin, as a sinful man is not capable of good without grace and without likeness to God. And however much good he does, it will never profit him. Second: that it is sharpened. So the soul must be sharpened in all divine and virtuous acts. Third: that the ax works the desire of the worker unto the end. So grace carries the soul into God and carries the soul over herself and robs her of self and all that is creaturely and unites the soul with God.[27] Grace works with the soul as

---

19 Cf. *In Ioh.*, no. 521; Sermon 43; Sermon 101.
20 Cf. Sermon 31, Sermon 33, Sermon 54b, Sermon 81, Sermon 82.
21 Avicenna, *Metaphysics*, IX.7. Cf. Sermon IX.1, n.112; Sermon LV.4, n.550; *In Gen*. n.115; Sermon 17; Sermon 37; Sermon 93; Sermon 113.
22 Cf. Sermon IX, n.109; LV.4, n.550; XLVIII.1, n.502; Sermon 37; Sermon 72; Sermon 77; Sermon 81; Sermon 90; Sermon 98.
23 Cf. *Counsels on Discernment*, §23; Sermon 15; *Proc. Col. I* n 57.
24 Cf. Sermon 3, Sermon 66.
25 Aristotle, *De Anima*, II.1.
26 This is an unusual metaphor for Eckhart. The sense of *gesliffen* (modern German *geschliffen*) is the smoothness and polish, such as the blade of an axe obtains when sharpened. To smooth something is to homogenize the surface by removing variations in height. In that sense, it falls under the general heading of Eckhart's metaphorics of oneness.
27 Cf. Sermon 82.

long as it takes for her to empty[28] herself, for she a creature is, so that there is nothing more left but God and the soul without intermediary.[29] Amen.

---

28 Cf. Sermon 89.

29 Cf. Sermon IX, n.99; LII, n.522; Sermon 20a; Sermon 21; Sermon 38; Sermon 48; Sermon 49; Sermon 81.

Sermon 97
Qui manet in me

Qui manet in me et ego in eo, hic fert fructum multum. Christ said: "Whoever remains in me and I in him will bring forth great fruit."[1]

This saying is divided into three parts. The first is: "He who remains or lives in me"; the second is: "and I in him"; the third: "shall bear great fruit."

Regarding the first, Saint Paul said: "Your life is hidden with Christ" in God,[2] and distinctly as well: inasmuch as "you are dead" with him and "resurrected" with him, so your life with Christ is hidden with the heavenly Father.[3]

Now we must consider who the people are who live in God.

It's a sign of these people, that they are warm,[4] that there is not in them any laziness, aversion, or complaint toward divine works. We see that water does not freeze where it originates. This happens because the sun raises water from the bottom of the mountain, raising it to the peak of the mountain and calls it forth from the mountain, whence it flows. It is the heat that works this; that's why it is warm and lively at its spring. And the further it flows, the colder and more impure it becomes. It is the same with men: the further he is from God, the sicker, colder, and more distasteful he is.[5] Ambrose

---

1 Jn 15:5.

2 Col 3:3. Cf. Sermon LV.2, n.543.

3 Cf. Sermon 35, Sermon 90a.

4 It is possible that several rhetorically subtle things may be going on here. First, a *zeichen* is a sign or mark, like a stamp. This recalls Eckhart's metaphor of imprinting. Second, though *warm* means warm as in "welcoming," it is close to *warmâl*, which means a distinctive mark or, in modern German, *wahrzeichen*—an emblem or landmark.

5 The word *unsmachaftiger* means "apathetic" or "listless," but since *smachaftic* means "savory," the image is literally one of taste, which is an important metaphor for Eckhart. Cf. Sermon 96.

teaches in a book, which speaks of the flight from worldly pleasures and their pursuit, "and we should search for God in God."[6] Man is below and God is above. That's why man must raise himself above the world by divine love. Love breaks into God and drives the soul into God and makes manifest all things in God.[7] Insofar as the soul is able to understand or grasp, the power of love draws her up to the highest there is in God, who is goodness, and with goodness she flows out with God in all divine works, and in the goodness God creates heaven and earth.[8] That's why Our Lord also said: whoever finds a faithful[9] and wise servant, who is so faithful that he does not seek his advantage, but the honor of God alone?[10] To the servant who remains in service by humility, to him I will promise: all that God is and can be, that man will truly receive it.[11]

The second is that Our Lord says: "whoever abides in me and me in him."

Saint Bernard would have it that it is more significant that God is in us than that we are in God.[12] That God should put his being in us and move and live in us means that the soul is arranging herself according to God,[13] according to eternity and according to God's immutability,[14] and so she works and lives according to him insofar as God measures it out to her and gives himself to her.

I put forth a third sense about that as well, that God is wholly all of the soul's being and life, and that she only has taste for God alone in all his movements and works.[15] A certain sign that God lives in the soul is that the

---

6 The little word *bî* in "God in God" (*got bî gote*) should remind us of Eckhart's well-known *bîwort* passage in Sermon 9. Cf. Ambrose of Milan, *De Fuga Saeculi*, 1.4.

7 The parallel structure of "into . . . into . . . in" should be a clue that Eckhart is pointing us toward the relationship implied by the use of "in" in the Bible, which is the most intimate possible. Cf. Sermon VI.1, n.52; Sermon 60; Sermon 84.

8 Cf. Sermon 37.

9 *Getriuwe* is a word with a peculiarly medieval meaning. It refers to being true and faithful, with connotations of loyalty and honor, as with the oath between a vassal and lord. For a sense of how lofty the concept was at this time, recall that in *Parzifal*, God is called *ein triuwe*. Walshe, *Complete Mystical Works of Meister Eckhart*, 45.

10 Mt 24:45, Lk 12:42.

11 Cf. Sermon 9; Sermon 75; *Counsels on Discernment*, §21.

12 Bernard of Clairvaux, *Super Cantica Sermo*, 71 n.10.

13 Acts 17:28; Rom 11:36; cf. Sermon IV.1, ns. 20–28; Sermon IV.2, ns.29–30; Sermon XXV.2, n.267; Sermon 8; Sermon 73; Sermon 76; Sermon 81.

14 1 Tm 1:17; cf. Sermon XLV, n.452.

15 Cf. Sermon 4; Sermon 54b; *Counsels on Discernment*, §6.

soul is a resting place.[16] I say that God seeks nothing other than rest in all his works; and thus the soul can do nothing more pleasing to him than to be at rest. The soul can never be so like him than when she is at rest, when she restfully keeps still.[17]

The third is that Our Lord says: "Whoever lives in me and I in him will bring forth great fruit."[18] If I wanted to say now what this fruit is, I would not know how; what I do not know, I know it indeed. A master said: whoever knows God so far as to know that he is unknowable to all creatures, knows God eminently. And whoever knows clearly that we cannot know God, knows God altogether perfectly.[19] So, no one can perfectly know the fruit that God promised us, unless it is by certain signs.

We may observe six signs.

The first is that the soul becomes run down[20] through her vices like an old building that falls down[21] when you shake it; it is a sign that one wants to build it anew, if the one who breaks it apart has the space for it[22] or the price to pay. It is like this when the soul completely gives herself over to God with all her powers to his works.[23]

The second sign is that the true virtues start up in the soul, from which consistency, certainty, and freedom of awareness come next.[24]

---

16 Sir 24:11.

17 Cf. Sir 24:11; Sermon 22; Sermon 60; *In Sap.* n.27.

18 Jn 15:5; cf. Sermon 57.

19 *Book of the XXIV Philosophers*, XXIII. Cf. Sermon 9, Sermon 23, Sermon 25, Sermon 53, Sermon 71.

20 Cf. Sermon 57.

21 The words for "run down" (*nidervellic*) and "falls down" (*nidervellet*) are inflections of the same word.

22 This otherwise peculiar comment makes sense if we translate *stat* as "space" or "room" instead of merely "place." This makes the comment part of Eckhart's metaphorics of capacity or space. He tells us that the soul must expand when filled to continue to make room for what God gives, ultimately claiming that the soul has the capacity for God (*capax dei*). Sermon XXIV.2, LW IV, 250.6.

23 Cf. Sermon 4.

24 Cf. Sermon 92, DW IV.1, 104.21–23: "The second fruit is spiritual joy that comes from pure awareness that makes a man light to all good things and raises him above himself."

The third sign is that the root of divine things thrusts powerfully into the heart, then the man becomes aware[25] that he does not have a taste for or take pleasure in anything other than divine things.[26]

The fourth sign is that all that which has become dry and cracked from sin will moisten, greening and growing from grace.[27]

The fifth sign is that all the powers of the soul are illuminated so that no stain of sin or unknowing remains, the soul becomes entirely one light. Nevertheless, the divine light does not enter[28] into the soul by an open door, but secretly and concealed, so that the soul scarcely knows that it comes, when God comes or goes from her; and God has done this by his goodness, making his presence so secret and concealed. If God were to openly enter into the soul, she could not withstand[29] it; she would altogether dwindle away and vanish from love and joy. If God were to openly withdraw from her, she could not withstand[30] that either; she would necessarily dwindle away from suffering and die. For the divine light and the pleasure are so overpowering that the soul cannot undergo these two without being blown back, as the eye cannot withstand the light of the sun unless it is concealed in the air.[31]

The sixth sign is that everything that would fall to ruin and cool[32] in the soul and in the body is gathered in God and consumed entirely by divine love.

---

25 *Entseben* can also mean "to taste," as in when one becomes aware of something by getting a taste of it.

26 Cf. Sermon 27; *On the Nobleman*, 112.13.

27 Cf. Sermon 57.

28 This is the same word that was translated above as "thrust," giving us reason to compare what Eckhart says here about divine light entering the soul to what he says above about the root of divine things entering the heart.

29 Eckhart uses versions of the word *lîden* to speak of passively "undergoing" something. Though passively undergoing is a good thing in his metaphorics, if the soul is not ready for it and does not yet have the capacity for it, then she cannot receive it.

30 See previous note.

31 Cf. Sermon 31, Sermon 32, Sermon 45, Sermon 47, Sermon 56, Sermon 57, Sermon 95b, Sermon 107.

32 *Verkalten* is the opposite of melting, which is an important metaphor for Eckhart. We are to understand that everything that would cool and solidify in the soul would instead be consumed and melt in divine fire.

Sermon 98
Nisi granum frumenti cadens in terram mortuum fuerit, ipsum solum manet[1]

The masters say that this grain of wheat dies so completely that it loses its form, its color,[2] and its being.[3] Insofar as the wheat's nature is like the stone's, it does not rest anywhere other than in its receptivity. Thus, the soul must die so that she may become receptive to another being. It is necessary to conduct oneself toward things that happen as if one were dead. Otherwise, God will never entirely be your being.[4] He indeed gives various endowments, illumination, and consolation that are thought to be great and are actually great. Yet God never gives himself to you at all if you do not give yourself completely to him.[5] The more fully the soul dies to herself, the more fully God becomes her being, and so there does not remain anything other than one being, for my body and soul are no more than one being.[6]

Now Our Lord says: "Whoever hates his soul, protects it."[7] The word "soul" does not belong to the nature of the soul. We can no more find a name

---

1 Jn 12:24–25.

2 Cf. Sermon 32.

3 Albertus Magnus, *Enarrationes in Iohannem* (ed. Borgnet, XXIV 483). Cf. Sermon 8, Sermon 27, Sermon 65, Sermon 94, Sermon 107.

4 Cf. Sermon XI.1, n.112; *In Ioh.* n.396; Sermon 101; *On Detachment*, 424.9–425.10.

5 Cf. Sermon 27.

6 Cf. Sermon XI.2, n.117; Sermon XLVII.1, n.486; Sermon LV.2, n.543; Sermon LV.4, n.556; Sermon 7; Sermon 8; Sermon 12; Sermon 45; Sermon 65; *Proc. Col. I* ns.65, 70.

7 Jn 12:25.

for the nature of the soul than for God.[8] The soul does not grow old either.[9] Further, we should hate where she has a view out of the body and into it,[10] for it is hateful.[11] That's why the soul says in the Canticle: "Daughters of Jerusalem, do not see me as tan. Two things were done to me. The first: The sun discolored me. The other: The children of my mother fought against me."[12] I had a disorderly[13] love for all that is temporal and all that the sun ever shines upon. They are "my mother's children who fought against me," and not my father's, for the latter are completely orderly. "Therefore, do not say that I am tan.[14] I am beautiful and noble by my nature and I am graceful."[15]

"He who hates his soul" in this world "conserves it."[16] Augustine speaks of a twofold world and calls the soul a world, and in each angel there is a spiritual world;[17] for all that God created is imaged[18] in each angel in a much more noble way than in it is in itself, for it is present in an immaterial way.[19]

---

8 Cf. Sermon LV.4, ns.547–48; *In Ioh.* n.528; Sermon 38.

9 Cf. *In Sap.* n.135; Sermon 2; Sermon 43.

10 Eckhart uses two different words here: "looking out" (*ûzluogen*) and "seeing in" (*însehen*). In addition to the way that they complement one another and refer to all that is corporeal by pointing to what is inside and outside of the body, they have additional connotations. To look out of the body may refer specifically to the act of seeing anything and being aware of the outside world. Just as its equivalent in English, the word *însehen* means insight into and understanding of something. Thus, Eckhart seems to be telling us that we should hate the soul insofar as she looks to the corporeal world or even to the particular experience of the world we have as individuals.

11 Cf. Sermon 16b; Sermon 17; Sermon 20a; Sermon 34; Sermon 38; Sermon L; *Counsels on Discernment*, §3.

12 Song 1:4–5.

13 The word here is *unordenlîche*, "disorderly," in the sense of being improper, unbecoming, and against the established order. The important connotation here is that love of temporal things *disorders* the soul in the sense that it works against the proper ordering of a soul to make it ready to receive God.

14 Song 1:5. Cf. Sermon LV.4, n.552, 554; Sermon 17.

15 Song 1:4.

16 Jn 12:25; cf. Sermon 17.

17 Augustine, *Contra Academicos*, III.17.37; cf. *In Gen. I* n.78; *In Gen. II* n.67; *In Eccl.* n.10; Sermon XIX, n.195, 196; *In Ioh.* n.449.

18 The word for "imaged" is *erbildet*, which might be more naturally translated as "formed" or "revealed." Its root, *bild*, or "image," provides a clue to what Eckhart is doing here since the angels have the *image of* all creation in them immaterially.

19 Cf. Sermon X, n.109; Sermon XI.1, n.112; Sermon XLVIII.1, n.502; Sermon LV.4 n.550; *In Gen. I*, n.115; Sermon 17; Sermon 37; Sermon 72; Sermon 77; Sermon 81; Sermon 90b; Sermon 96.

The truth of it is there,[20] for the truth is in the angels, though that is rather the tip of the needle[21] in relation to the first truth.[22]

Now Our Lord says: "Whoever wants to serve me, let him follow me"[23] ... and nothing more than following him. Yet certain people follow only as long as all is well with them.[24]

We could say now: Our Lord wants too much. He does not want more than to be able to become one with us.[25] For corresponding to the love is the gift: since "God is love," he gives himself completely.[26] The soul possesses in her a natural image of that, she is wholly in all her members and in each.[27] When the soul was created, he gave her in the ground of being[28] the power to work wholly in all of her members and in each one in particular.

Now one may ask: What does our Lord mean when he says, "Where I am, my servant will be with me"?[29] Perhaps he means that God wants to steal something from God, that he wants to impart to the soul.[30] In the first emanation, where the Son shines forth from the Father while staying entirely within,[31] in there—even before the Son is born—he wants to become one with the soul while still staying within, there where there is no view of the outside, there where the soul is becoming with the Son.[32] The birth amounts

---

20 In both this phrase, "The truth of it is there" and the last phrase of the previous sentence, "than it is in itself," the antecedent for "it" seems to be "all that God created." Thus, the truth of all that God created is revealed better in the angels than in the material world because it is immaterial in the angels. Thus, "the truth of [what God created] is there [in the angels]."

21 Cf. Sermon 20a, Sermon 43, Sermon 48, Sermon 59, Sermon 69, Sermon 73.

22 Cf. Sermon XI.1, n.114; Sermon LIV.2, n.533, *In Gen. I* n.204, *In Gen. II* n.154, Sermon 89.

23 Jn 12:26.

24 Cf. Sermon 11; Sermon 13; Sermon 59; *In Ioh.* n.230, 529.

25 Cf. Sermon VI.1, n. 55; Sermon 9; Sermon 18; Sermon 73; Sermon 80.

26 1 Jn 4:16; Sermon LV.2, n.540; Sermon 22; Sermon 59.

27 Cf. Sermon *In Sap.* n.135; Sermon 9; Sermon 35; Sermon 71; Sermon LV.4, n.556.

28 Cf. Sermon 45.

29 Jn 12:26; cf. *In Ioh.* ns.525, 529, Sermon 64.

30 This is an unusual reference to Prometheus, who stole fire from the gods. Eckhart's formulation is appropriately paradoxical. Cf. *In Ioh.* ns.22, 640; Sermon XLV, n.455; *In Gen. II* n.147.

31 This is a densely philosophical and metaphorical statement: Neoplatonic emanation, flowing forth, perhaps translated as "sparking" or "flashing" forth while remaining (resting) within.

32 The difficulty in translation here is not so much with the word as it is with what Eckhart means by it. The word *gewirdet* is a form of *werden*, to become. It could mean that the soul arrives with, becomes with, or happens with the Son. Given the context, where Eckhart repeatedly emphasizes the soul's becoming, it seems reasonable to think that he intends for this passage to point to the soul's act of becoming as happening with and being joined to Christ as one. That is, his words are

to becoming; her becoming is in the eternal birth. There she becomes so purely one that she has no being other than the same being, which is His, which is soul-being.[33] This being is the beginning of all the works that God performs in the kingdom of heaven and on earth. It is the origin and ground of all divine works. The soul gathers together her nature, her being, and life, and she is born in the godhead. Right there is her becoming.[34] She becomes so completely one being that there is no distinction, except that He stays God and she stays soul.[35]

---

meant to indicate an intimacy relation between the soul and the Son (see the dialectic of particles section for more on this practice). cf. Sermon 3; Sermon 7; Sermon 16b; Sermon 17; Sermon 19; Sermon 22; Sermon 24; Sermon 28; Sermon 72; *In Ioh.* n.169; *Book of Divine Consolation*, 46.6–9.

33 *Daʒ sêle-wesen.*

34 Cf. *In Ioh.* n.8; Sermon 6; Sermon 20b; Sermon 41; Sermon 44; Sermon 46; *Book of Divine Consolation*, 44.27–45.3.

35 Cf. Sermon 6; *Proc. Col. I* n.54.

Sermon 100
Et quaerebat videre Iesum, quis esset

Saint Luke writes to us: "When Our Lord walked the earth in human nature, there was a very rich man who wanted to see Jesus. He could not see him because of the crowd, for he was short."[1]

A saint said: he is properly rich who has much of God and virtue.[2] The one who has many goods and little of God is poor and is in no way rich, for all things are like nothing to God.[3] Hence the words of a lord who was praised by his servants for having much power and wealth. The lord said: "Truly, they did not praise me in the slightest, for they forgot the greatest thing of all for which I am to be praised. I am not to be praised because I have much power and wealth. Rather, I am to be praised because I am able to have my flesh wait on my will."[4]

That man, who wanted to see Jesus, surpassed the crowd and climbed up a tree in so that he might see Jesus. Then Our Lord said: "come down quickly, for I must be with you today."[5] Whoever wants to see Jesus must surpass

---

[1] Lk 19:2–3. Cf. Sermon 57.

[2] Augustine, *De civitate Dei*, VII.12.

[3] Cf. *In Ioh.* n.279, 356; Sermon 20b; Sermon 69; Sermon 77.

[4] Though I aim to stay as close to the original as possible, translating this passage more literally would result in awkward or at least archaic-sounding English: "For I am empowered to stay my body, for whatever I will." The idea is that the Lord has the power to make the desires of the flesh pause and wait (*gebeiten*) on the dictates of the will. This is the Platonic idea (found in the *Phaedrus*) of taming the bad horse of bodily desire and having a well-ordered soul (as described in the *Republic*) so that the rational part of the soul (not the will per se for Plato, since he did not have such a conception, but what became the will for the platonically leaning early church fathers) rules over the spirited (honor-seeking or angry) and appetitive (animal desire) parts of the soul.

[5] Lk 19:5. Eckhart modifies this passage in a somewhat surprising way. The passage reads, "for today I must abide at thy house" (KJV). Normally, Eckhart would take the opportunity to use the

all things.⁶ What does it mean for a man not to swiftly surpass all things? It means that he has not tasted God. If he had tasted God, he would swiftly surpass all things,⁷ and not only surpass, rather, he would break through all creatures.⁸ Whatever his love might let go of, he will break through.⁹

That we cannot see God comes from the smallness of desire and the multitude of creatures. Whoever desires a very great thing is great.¹⁰ Whoever would behold God must have very great desire.¹¹ He knows that resolute desire and abject humility work wonders.¹² I say that God is capable of doing all things, but he is not capable of denying anything to the man who is humble and greatly desiring. And if I cannot force God to do everything I want, that is because of my lacking either humility or desire.¹³ I say on my life and I say with certainty: by desire a man could come to pass through a steel wall, as we read of Saint Peter: when he saw Jesus, thanks to his desire, he walked on water. I say truly that his desire could change his nature so that he could walk on water.¹⁴ Now I say: a thing that grows when filling up will never become full. For example, take a vessel, a carrying cart, with a load that causes it to swell. If it grows therewith, it will never become full. This

---

metaphorics of rest in one's house (soul). Here, however, he takes a more direct route and says, "I must be with/in (*bî*) you today." To be *bî* Jesus recalls Eckhart's famous *bîwort* passage of Sermon 9 where he says we must be *adverbs or with-words* (*bîwort*) to God, seeking to be close to him at all times, just as Venus traces a tight orbit around the sun. For more information on Eckhart's use of in, by, and with, see the section on the dialectic of particles in chap. 4.

6 This is one instance of a metaphor Eckhart develops elsewhere in saying that the intellect rashly "runs ahead" of understanding with knowledge, even though it does not understand where it is going, so as to begin the motion that is necessary for progress. In Sermon 3, he explicitly juxtaposes "running ahead" (*loufet vor*) with "surpassing" (*vürloufet*) in saying "knowledge runs ahead, surpassing and breaking through" (DW I 49.1–2). The "breaking through" is Eckhart's well-known *durchbrechen*, whereby the soul breaks through God and God breaks through the soul (e.g., Sermon 29, DW II, 76.3–77.1).

7 Cf. Sermon 59, Sermon 73.

8 Cf. Sermon XXIV.2, n.247; *In Ioh.* n.292; Sermon 3; Sermon 52; *Counsels on Discernment*, §6.

9 Cf. Sermon 69.

10 This may recall the Augustinian idea that we become what we love, as Eckhart cites elsewhere (Sermon 40, DW II, 78.1).

11 Cf. Sermon 5a; Sermon 45; Sermon 54b; *Counsels on Discernment*, §10.

12 Cf. Sermon XXIV.2, n.245; *In Ex.* n.261; *In Ioh.* n.90; Sermon 54b; Sermon 71; Sermon 74; *Sermo Paschalis*, a.1294; *Parisius habitus* n.8.

13 For more on "forcing" and "enforcing," see the list of metaphors in Sermon 106c. Cf. Sermon 13; Sermon 14; Sermon 15; Sermon 20a; Sermon 22; *Proc. Col. I* n.57; *Proc. Col. II* n.29.

14 Mt 14:29. Cf. Sermon 23.

refers to the soul: the more she seeks, the more she will be given; the more she receives, the wider her girth becomes.[15]

Who is Jesus? He has no name.[16] Where do we see God? Wherever there is neither yesterday nor tomorrow: where there is today and now, one sees God.[17] What is God? A master says: if I was compelled to say something about God, then I would say that God is something[18] that no sense can reach or grasp. I know nothing else about him.[19]

Another master says: whoever knows God as he is unknowable, knows God.[20] Now Saint Augustine comes and falls into the conversation and says: God is the highest and most supreme thing that is common to all enjoyment.[21] He means to say that God is something in which all creatures must necessarily be.[22] For if they fall out of the hand of God's mercy, they fall into the hand of divine justice. They must always remain in him. Man must necessarily take his being from God and so have enjoyment, yes, in God Himself, as he will. Whoever does not want to have eternal enjoyment and satisfaction in God Himself must take it from things which are so contemptuous that they are far beneath his footwraps. Since all creatures must necessarily take their being from God,[23] it is necessary that even the damned in hell abide in something of his being.[24] Although they do not remain in God in blessedness, still they must remain in Him against their wills in damnation.[25] What foolishness it is to not want to be with that without which one cannot be![26]

---

15 Cf. Sermon 23, Sermon 70.

16 Lk 2:21; 1 Col 12:3; cf. Sermon XXIII, ns. 217–25; Sermon 88. This is closely related to Eckhart's mathematical metaphors.

17 Cf. Sermon XXIV.1, n. 235; Sermon 6; Sermon 11; Sermon 53.

18 Here again we see Eckhart describing God as an *etwaz*, something unnameable, the same description he gives for the spark in the soul.

19 Cf. *In Ex.* n.184; Sermon 42; Sermon 95b.

20 Cf. Sermon 110.

21 Cf. Sermon XXV.1, n.258; Sermon XLIX.3, n.258, 511; Sermon VI.1, n.53; Sermon 9; *Collatio in Libros Sententiarum*, n.2; *In Ex.* n.262.

22 Cf. Sermon XXIX, n.296; Sermon 8; Sermon 9; Sermon 10; Sermon 71.

23 Cf. Sermon 19, Sermon 45.

24 We see again here the reference to God as a something. We are told that the damned in hell even persist and exist, abiding in God's being. Thus, we see both the metaphorics of rest and of God being a "something" (in all cases, an *etwaz*). Cf. Sermon XVII.4, n.176; *In Gen.* n.243; *In Ioh.* n.226; Augustine, *De Libero Arbitrio*, III.7.20.

25 Cf. Sermon 6; Sermon XVII.4, n.176; *In Ioh.* n.226; *In Gen. II* n.164; *In Gen. I* n.243.

26 Cf. Sermon 87, Sermon 93.

Now Saint Augustine says: what is God? He is something of which one can think of nothing better.²⁷ And I say: God is better than one can think. And I say: God is something, an I-don't-know-what, I truly don't know what. He is all that is being rather than nonbeing, existent rather than nonexistent. All that desire can desire is entirely removed from and small compared to God. He is above all that desire can desire.²⁸ Just as I preached at Paris,²⁹ so I say now—and I truly say it boldly: all those at Paris cannot grasp with all their skills what God is in the smallest creature, even in a fly. Yet I say now: the entire world cannot grasp it. All that one can say and think of God is not quite God.³⁰ What God is in Himself, no one can reach unless he is ravished in a light which is God Himself.³¹ What God is in the angels is wholly remote and no one knows it. What God is in the God-loving soul, no one knows apart from the soul in which he is. What God is in inferior things, I know somewhat, but it's utterly slight.³² Whenever God stoops to knowledge, all natural sensuality falls away.³³

That we may be ravished in a light which is God himself and therein be eternally blessed, let God help us to this. Amen.

---

27 Augustine, *De doctrina christiana* 1, c.11. Cf. Sermon VI.1, n53; Sermon XXIX, n. 295; Sermon XXX.2, n.320.

28 Cf. Sermon 42.

29 Cf. Sermon 14, Sermon 15, Sermon 24.

30 Cf. Sermon 9, Sermon 35, Sermon 36b, Sermon 53, Sermon 71.

31 Cf. Sermon 68, Sermon 70, Sermon 71.

32 We should perhaps think of Sermon 107 where he says that "all creatures become slight [*enge*] or entirely nothing" to the soul in which God shines. Eckhart seems to envision a process by which corporeal things become ever slimmer until they vanish entirely in significance before God. Cf. *Sermo Paschalis*, a.1294; *Parisius habitus* n.13.

33 Eckhart uses the same word (*vellen*) to describe God's "lowering himself" or "stooping" to be knowable and also to the vanishing or falling away of natural sensuality. This is typical of Eckhart's use of this word. In Sermon 92, he uses it to describe how the day of sensuality falls, dropping away and making way for the light of truth to shine in the soul. The image is one of allowing an obstacle to fall away, as though one were holding it up and could simply let it go. Once the hindrances to God fall away, the soul rests peacefully and blissfully in God. It is not difficult to see why Buddhists have taken a liking to Eckhart's ideas and his way of describing them, since this story is similarly told there. Cf. Sermon 71.

Sermon 106a
Aemulor enim vos Dei aemulatione

For I am jealous of you with godly jealousy[1]
In the name of Our Lord. We read on the day of the Virgin, for which they have a wedding, that Saint Paul said: "I have promised and entrusted you to one man, to Christ," who is power,[2] new,[3] and greening.[4]

The masters ask if the Son is born. We say: no.[5]

The masters ask if the Son should be born. We say: no.

We shall answer the masters: The Son is perfectly born and shall be born perfectly:[6] ceaselessly new and greening.[7]

Saint Paul said: Christ is "divine power and divine wisdom."[8] In this power, God created all things, for his wisdom is there and his power.

Christ is *a man* who is new and greening at all times.

Now Saint Paul says: "to this man, I promised and entrusted you."[9]

---

1 2 Cor 11:2.

2 1 Cor 1:24.

3 Rv 21:5. Cf. Sermon 84 DW III 463.2–5; *Prol. Gen.* n.18, LW I, 162.10–163.1. Cf. Sermon XV.2, n.155, LW IV, 147.12–13; *In Eccli.* n.21, LW II, 248.10–12; *General Prologue* n.18; *In Sap.* n.161, LW II, 497.1–9; Sermon 2, DW I, 32.1–4 and 40.4–41.2.

4 The idea of "greening" (*grüenende*) is part of Eckhart's metaphorics of blossoming, though a connection to Hildegard of Bingen has also been suggested. See chap. 1 for more detail on this.

5 Cf. Sermon 25, Sermon 27.

6 Peter Lombard, *Sent.*, I d.9 c.4. Cf. Sermon 1.

7 Cf. *Book of Divine Consolation*, 44.1; Sermon 75; Sermon 91; Sermon 101; *In Ioh.* ns.8, 40; Sermon XXIII, n.223; *In Eccl.* n.21; *In Gen. I* n.171; Sermon XV.1, n. 153.

8 1 Cor 1:24.

9 2 Cor 11:2.

Just as there is an external marriage between woman and man, there should also be a marriage between the soul and God.

Hence, one gives a virgin to a man owing to the expectation of a birth.[10]

Hence God created the soul to give birth to His only-begotten Son.[11]

When this birth happened spiritually in Our Lady, that was more delightful to God than when he was born corporeally to her.

When this birth happens today in the God-loving soul,[12] this is more delightful to God than when He created heaven and earth.[13]

The masters say and the saints as well—and it is entirely true—that the soul is wider than the heavens.[14]

Saint John said in the Apocalypse: "He who sat on the throne said: 'I make all things new.'"[15]

Saint Augustine said: God's speaking is His giving birth and his giving birth is His speaking.[16]

God never speaks any more than one word.[17] And this is so delightful to Him that he never wants to say anything else.[18] And if God were to abandon this Word-speaking[19] even for the blink of an eye, heaven and earth would cease to exist.[20]

Saint Augustine said: just as there is a marriage between woman and man, there is also a marriage in the soul.[21] The soul's highest power, which is always striving for God, is the man.[22] The lowest power, which is susceptible to change in corporeal things, is the woman.

---

10 Peter Lombard, *Sent.*, IV d.30 c.3 n. 2.
11 Cf. Sermon 23, Sermon 38, Sermon 78, Sermon 87, Sermon 110.
12 Cf. Sermon 20a, Sermon 36b, Sermon 100.
13 Cf. Sermon 31, Sermon 43.
14 Cf. Sermon 20b, Sermon 38, Sermon 42, Sermon 107; Sermon XLVIII.1, n.501.
15 Rv 21:5.
16 Augustine, *Conf.*, IX.7.9; Cf. *In Gen. I* n.8; *In Gen. II* ns.47, 110; *In Ioh.* n.641; Sermon 27; Sermon 49; Sermon 102.
17 Jb 33:14, Ps 61:12. Cf. Sermon 30, Sermon 53.
18 Cf. Sermon 19.
19 *wort-sprechen.*
20 Cf. Sermon 4; *Responsio Proc. Col. II* n.106; Augustine, *De Gen. ad litt.*, IV c.12.
21 Cf. Augustine, *De Diversis Quaestionibus*, LXIV.7. Eckhart, *In Gen. II* n.129; Sermon XXI, n. 205; Sermon VIII, n.93; Sermon LV.1, n.535; *On the Nobleman*, 113.25–114.5; Sermon 11; Sermon 108. Peter Lombard *Sent.*, II d.24 c.8 n.1, 3.
22 Cf. Sermon 32, Sermon 33, Sermon 34, Sermon XVIII.

The highest power, the man, must constantly remain naked, but the lowest power, the woman, must constantly remain covered so the lowest power is drawn to the highest.

Nature inherently directs her action at all times toward likeness.[23] At all times, she wants to give birth like the Father does. And if she were not hindered, then at all times a son would be born and never any woman. Now God does this by means of His unhindered goodness,[24] but He hinders nature. As a result, a woman will be born, and this never happens otherwise for the birth of a woman.

If there were not any men, or rather only one, and if there were neither time, nor Place, nor matter, he would renew himself in all ways like the Son to the Father.[25]

God said: I made all things fruitful so why would I not be fruitful myself?[26]

God first gives birth to His likeness in a God-loving soul, then to Himself, and nothing less than Himself.[27] So, the one who is the Son of God in eternity is the son of the soul and her child: God and the soul have a child with each other.[28] If God gave himself to the soul in time, it would vex[29] her. So now he gives himself to her in eternity in a new now, greening without ceasing.[30]

She is so eager that she never wants to rest before she reaches the source.[31]

Philip affirmed this when he said: "Lord, show us your Father and that will satisfy us."[32]

---

23 Cf. *In Gen. I*, n.98; Sermon 22; Sermon 38.
24 Cf. *Counsels on Discernment*, §19.
25 Cf. Sermon 50, Sermon 60, Sermon 91.
26 Eph 3:14. Cf. Sermon XXXV, n.362; Sermon 43; Sermon 59.
27 Cf. Sermon 26; *On the Nobleman*, 110.5–10.
28 Cf. *In Gen. II* n.150.
29 The word is *verdriuʒe*, which could be translated as "vex," "disturb," "bother," or "annoy." The idea here, as elsewhere, is that only God giving Himself in eternity is enough to satisfy the soul.
30 Cf. Sermon 20a, Sermon 25.
31 Augustine, *Conf.*, I.1.1. Cf. Sermon 69.
32 Jn 14:8. Cf. *In Ioh*. n.560.

Just as the eternal Son of God gushes forth[33] from the fatherly heart, so He gushes into a God-loving soul.[34]

Corporeal things are those that act outwardly; spiritual things are those that act inwardly.[35] The fruit of a tree is at first in the tree. Next, it blossoms forth and hangs from the tree. At last, it falls from the tree.

Spiritual things are those that act inwardly. When this birth happens once in a man's soul, he is closely united to God.[36] The more often this birth happens, the more profoundly man will be united with the fatherly heart.

This birth must happen above here and now. "Here" is place. "Now" is time. It must happen in eternity.[37]

May the Father, Son and Holy Spirit help us so that we will be born in Him and so that He may give birth to Himself in us. Amen.

---

33 This is a vigorous metaphor for flow, where the Son gushes forth (*quillet uz*) from the Father and into the soul. We should notice the uncontrollable, even violent activity of boiling over, *ebullitio* in the Latin works. Cf. Sermon 2, Sermon 75.

34 Cf. *In Ex.* n.16; Sermon 28; Sermon 35; Sermon 81; Sermon XLIX.3, n.511; Sermon XXV.2, n.263.

35 Cf. *In Ioh.* n.669; Sermon 9.

36 Cf. Sermon 24; Sermon 34; Sermon 40; *Counsels on Discernment*, §20.

37 Cf. Sermon 10, Sermon 42.

Sermon 106b
Aemulor enim vos Dei aemulatione
For I am jealous of you with godly jealousy[1]

About the virgin, Saint Paul said: "I have promised and entrusted you to one man, to Christ,"[2] who is power[3] and greening.[4]

The masters ask if the Son is born. We shall answer them: no.[5]

They ask if he will be born. We shall answer them: no.

The masters respond: He is perfectly born and will be perfectly born:[6] new and greening without ceasing.[7]

Saint Paul said: "Christ who is divine power and divine wisdom."[8] Through power, God created all things. This power is wisdom. Where His wisdom is, there is his power.

"This man, to Christ," who is power and greening, to "him I promised and entrusted you."[9]

Just as there is a marriage between woman and man, there should also be a marriage between the soul and God.

---

1 2 Cor 11:2.
2 2 Cor 11:2.
3 1 Cor 1:24.
4 See Sermon 106a n.4.
5 See Sermon 106a n.5.
6 See Sermon 106a n.6.
7 See Sermon 106a n.7.
8 1 Cor 1:24.
9 2 Cor 11:2.

Hence, one gives a virgin to a young man for the expectation of a birth.[10]

That's why God created the soul, so that he might give birth to His Son in her.[11]

When this birth happened in Mary in a spiritual way, for God this was more worthy of praise than when [His Son] was physically born to her.

Even today, if he comes to be born in the soul of a man, this is more delightful to God than when He created heaven and earth.[12]

The masters say—and it is also true—that the soul is wider than the heavens.[13] Saint John said: "He who sat on the throne said: 'I make all things new.'"[14]

Saint Augustine said: God's speaking is His giving birth and His giving birth is His speaking.[15]

God never speaks any other than one word.[16] This is so delightful to Him that He never wants to speak any other.[17] If God would leave this word unspoken, even for the blink of an eye, heaven and earth would cease to exist.[18]

Saint Augustine said: just like there is a marriage between woman and man, there is also a marriage in the soul.[19] The highest in the soul is the man.[20] The lowest is the woman. The man must always remain naked. The woman must remain covered. This way, the lowest is drawn to the highest.

Nature inherently directs her action always toward likeness.[21] An apple tree gives birth to another apple tree without the help of another apple tree, a pear tree to another pear tree. Each thing bears in itself its own seed.[22] If there were only a single man on earth, he would renew himself.

10 See Sermon 106a n.10.
11 See Sermon 106a n.11.
12 See Sermon 106a n.13.
13 See Sermon 106a n.14.
14 Rv 21:5.
15 See Sermon 106a n.16.
16 See Sermon 106a n.17.
17 See Sermon 106a n.18.
18 See Sermon 106a n.20.
19 See Sermon 106a n.21.
20 See Sermon 106a n.22.
21 See Sermon 106a n.23.
22 Cf. Sermon XL.3, n.404; Sermon 28; Sermon 47; Sermon 84; Sermon 9; Sermon 110; *In Ioh.* n.4; *In Sap.* n.49, 231; Albertus Magnus, *De animalibus*, XVI tr.1 c.14, n.73.

God said: I make all things fruitful, so why would I not be fruitful myself?[23]

God first gives birth to his likeness in man, then to Himself, and nothing less than Himself. Thereby, The Son of God is the son of the soul in eternity: God and the soul have a child with each other.[24] If God would give Himself to the soul in time, it would vex[25] her.

He gives Himself in eternity, freshly greening.

Philip affirmed this when he said: "Lord, show us your Father and that will satisfy us."[26]

Just as the eternal Son of God gushes forth[27] from the fatherly heart, so He also gushes into the man's soul.[28]

Corporeal things act outwardly, spiritual things are those that act inwardly.[29] The fruit of a tree is at first in the tree. Next, it blossoms forth and hangs from the tree. Then it falls.

Spiritual things act inwardly. When this birth happens in a man's soul, he will be drawn closely into God. When this happens once more, he will be driven even more deeply into God. The more and more often this birth happens, the more and more closely the soul will be united with God.

This birth does not happen once a year, nor once a month, nor once a day; it happens more than a thousand times a day in a soul that is ready.[30]

Where must this happen? Beyond here and now. "Here" is place. "Now" is time. It must happen in eternity.[31]

May God give birth to Himself!

---

23 See Sermon 106a n.26.
24 See Sermon 106a n.28.
25 See Sermon 106a n.29.
26 See Sermon 106a n.32.
27 See Sermon 106a n.33.
28 See Sermon 106a n.34.
29 See Sermon 106a n.35.
30 Cf. Sermon 2; Sermon 37; Sermon 43; Sermon 99; *In Gen. II* n.191–92.
31 See Sermon 106a n.37.

Sermon 106c
Aemulor enim vos Dei aemulatione

For I am jealous of you with godly jealousy[1]

Saint Paul said: *I have promised and entrusted you to one man.*[2] This man is Christ, the Son of God. He is perfectly born and will be perfectly born:[3] ceaselessly new and verdant.[4] He is divine power and divine wisdom.[5] Through them, God created all things.

Just as there is an external marriage between woman and man, there should also be a marriage between God and the soul.

Hence, one gives a woman to a man and then awaits a birth from her.[6]

That's why God created the soul, so that His only-begotten Son would be born in her.[7]

When this birth happened spiritually in Our Lady, that was more delightful to God than that he was physically born to her.

And whenever this birth happens in a man's soul, it is more delightful for God than when he created heaven and earth.[8] The soul is wider and nobler than the heavens.[9]

---

1 2 Cor 11:2.
2 2 Cor 11:2.
3 See Sermon 106a n.6.
4 See Sermon 106a n.7.
5 1 Cor 1:24.
6 See Sermon 106a n.10.
7 See Sermon 106a n.11.
8 See Sermon 106a n.13.
9 See Sermon 106a n.14.

In the Apocalypse, Saint John said: "He who sat on the throne said: "'I make all things new.'"[10]

Saint Augustine said: God's speaking is His giving birth and His giving birth is His speaking.[11]

He never speaks any more than one word.[12] This is so delightful to Him that He never wants to speak any other.[13] And if God would leave this word unspoken, even for the blink of an eye, heaven and earth would cease to exist.[14]

Saint Augustine said: just as there is a marriage between woman and man, there is also a marriage in the soul.[15] The highest in the soul is the power that looks to God, which is the man.[16] The lowest in the soul is the power that looks to external things, which is the woman. The man in the soul must at all times remain naked. The woman must remain covered. The lowest should be drawn toward the highest.

Nature inherently at all times wants to give birth like the Father does. And if she were not hindered, then at all times a son would be born and never any woman.

God said: I made all things fruitful, so why would I not be fruitful myself?[17]

God gives birth first to his likeness in the soul, then to himself as He is in eternity. The Son of God is the son of the soul. So God and the soul have a child, which is God.[18] If God gave himself to the soul in time, it would quickly vex[19] her. She is so eager. So now he gives himself to her in eternity in a new now, freshly greening without ceasing.[20] The soul is eager that she never wants to rest before she reaches the source.[21]

---

10 Rv 21:5.
11 See Sermon 106a n.16.
12 See Sermon 106a n.17.
13 See Sermon 106a n.18.
14 See Sermon 106a n.20.
15 See Sermon 106a n.21.
16 See Sermon 106a n.22.
17 See Sermon 106a n.26.
18 See Sermon 106a n.28. Notice that this version extends and clarifies the versions in Sermon 106a and Sermon 106b.
19 See Sermon 106a n.29.
20 See Sermon 106a n.30.
21 See Sermon 106a n.31.

Saint Philip affirmed this when he said: "Lord, show us your Father and that will satisfy us."[22]

Just as the Son gushes forth[23] out of the fatherly heart, so He gushes into the soul.[24]

Corporeal things act outwardly, spiritual things act inwardly.[25] The fruit of a tree is from the first in the tree. Next, it blossoms forth and hangs from the tree. At last, it falls from the tree.

Spiritual things act inwardly. The soul, in which this birth happens once, will be closely united to God. Beyond this, the one in whom this birth happens once again will be still more closely united to God.[26] The more often this birth happens, the more inwardly the soul will be united with the fatherly heart so that she attains an attachment to God, an embrace, an imprinting, an inflowing, a sealing in, a closing in, a penetrating into, an enveloping, a melting in, an emblazoning, a pressing into, an indwelling.[27]

This birth must happen beyond here and now. "Here" is place. "Now" is time. It must happen in eternity[28] in a new now.

---

22 See Sermon 106a n.32.
23 See Sermon 106a n.33.
24 See Sermon 106a n.34.
25 See Sermon 106a n.35.
26 See Sermon 106a n.36.
27 This list is a kind of metaphorical catalogue. All words in the list have an în- prefix (including some that do not normally take that prefix) which indicates a movement *into* something. As discussed in the section on the dialectic of particles in chap. 4 (e.g., Eph 4:6, "One God and Father of all, who is above all, and through all, and in you all"), this list of metaphors serves to emphasize interiority and sameness while antagonizing the potential for misinterpretation by overly emphasizing any one word's meaning. Here, Eckhart may as well be saying "*inside* in every conceivable way!" As with Eph 4:6, being *above* and *in* at once defies logic and points us beyond the language of any one metaphor. The very first thing mentioned is that the soul attains an "attachment" or "clinging" (*anehaften*) to God. The word "enclosing" has connotations of physically encircling and also comprehending something by surrounding and boxing it in. The word *velzen* means "to ornament," possibly ornamenting in an obvious and showy way ("to emblazon"). Elsewhere, Eckhart asks how we may know if a soul has had contact with God and answers that we know this by several outward *signs*. This "emblazoning" the soul receives may be this sort of outwardly apparent change. *Inbergen* ("enveloping") seems to mean a "holding, carrying, or bearing within," as with a natural quality that is inherent in something. The word *bërgen* also means "to bring (something) to safety," which may imply drawing within or bringing within (to safety, to rest). The connotation of secrecy and hiddenness may also be present, implying that one conceals what is brought within.
28 See Sermon 106a n.37.

Sermon 106d
Aemulor enim vos Dei aemulatione

For I am jealous of you with godly jealousy.[1]

Christendom gathers its children together so that they may give birth to the fruit of God.[2]

Why has God created heaven and earth? Why is it that we pray, we fast? So that God may give birth spiritually to His Son in our souls.[3]

And this birth in his mother was more pleasing to God than when he was physically born from her.

And wherever the birth happens today in a pure soul, it is more delightful for God than when He created heaven and earth.[4]

The masters say that the soul is wider than the heavens,[5] and even though angels and saints fill the heavens, they cannot do that with the soul. If God were to go to earth in a bodily way and give Himself to the soul in time, it would not satisfy[6] her.

---

1 2 Cor 11:2.

2 See Sermon 106a n.10.

3 See Sermon 106a n.11.

4 See Sermon 106a n.13.

5 See Sermon 106a n.14.

6 The word *enkleckete* ("not satisfy") is unusual for Eckhart. The verb *klecken* can mean "to satisfy or help" (in French, Eric Mangin opted for the latter), but also "to arouse or awaken," as one wakes a person from sleep with a loud sound (*klecken* also means "to ring out or resonate").

Augustine said: just as there is a marriage between woman and man, there is also a marriage in the soul.[7] The higher power is the man.[8] And the lower power is the woman.

That's why men go with their heads naked. The higher power nakedly touches and stands before God, free of all things and desiring God alone. And it is the spark of the soul that no one can satisfy[9] or extinguish other than God alone, with Himself and otherwise nothing.

The other power is covered. That is why women go with their heads covered. For they are of a more tender air and move among light things.[10] So they must be caught by and submissive to their husbands[11] in obedience to the higher power, which they should watch and attend to, and not the higher power to the lower, else that would not be right for him.

At all times, nature inherently wants to give birth like the Father does. And if she were not hindered by eternal providence, at all times only a son would be born and never a daughter.

The soul is so eager and so expansively[12] greedy that she wants God according to all His power and perfection,[13] as He is in eternal majesty. Nothing else can satisfy her.

---

7 See Sermon 106a n.21.

8 See Sermon 106a n.22.

9 Here, the soul can only be satisfied (*ersatten*) by being filled (*satten*) by God.

10 The statement that women are of a "tender air" and "move among light things" includes several metaphors of note. First, *luft* refers to "air" and *weicher* means "tender," "gentle," or "soft." The "light" (*lîhten*) things are light in the sense of being easy, frail, or simple. The metaphorics here points to an image like a leaf blowing whimsically in the wind. Finally, the action of moving (*erwegen*) refers to being stirred to move. The metaphors of being airy and lightweight are not common for Eckhart. They simply add additional color to the more common idea of the lower power (symbolized by the woman) of the soul being excited by and motivated to move among lower things. The line that follows about submission and having a wife "trapped" or "ensnared" by her husband may seem superficially offensive, but the idea of the lower and more animal appetite needing to be subdued by the higher faculty of reason is a straightforwardly Platonic one. For all instances of these metaphors, we should not jump to the conclusion that Eckhart was misogynistic. As with Plato, Eckhart's mind is always on the divine. He merely makes use of a metaphor that he knew his audience would understand.

11 Eph 5:22.

12 Eckhart says that the soul is "expansively" (*wîte*) greedy so as to take in God's magnificence. The metaphor of a soul being "wide" or "expansive" is one we encounter in Sermon 100, where we are told that the soul becomes more expansive the more she receives, and as such, can never be filled (Sermon 100, DW IV.1, 272.26–30). We might think here that the soul avariciously "swells" to receive more of God.

13 See Sermon 106a n.31.

Therefore, Philip says: "Show us the Father and that will satisfy us."[14]

Let God Himself help us so that we are not satisfied with anything other than God.

Amen.

---

14 Jn 14:8.

Sermon 107
Qui vult venire post me

Qui vult venire post me, abneget semetipsum et tollat crucem suam et sequatur me. Our Lord said: "Whoever wants to come along with me, let him take up his cross" with consent to martyrdom[1] "and let him renounce himself and follow me."[2]

All things by nature want to move toward God, each in their way: fire strives upward and ... earth falls, and likewise each creature seeks its place, as God ordained them.[3] On this, Origen said: Man renounces himself by struggling to leave the sinful things he is used to and renouncing that part of himself that makes him fragile.[4] He then carries his cross by consenting to his pain and practices virtuous works.[5] These words further correspond with what Saint Basil said: whenever any man leaves the things that are behind him and beneath him and which are not God, such a man has left himself.[6] Saint Augustine said something about this in a book when he said of the soul that she is nobler, stronger, and greater than all creatures, and that

---

1 Cf. Sermon 8; Sermon 25; Sermon 49; Sermon 66; *Counsels on Discernment*, §16; *In Ioh.*, no. 173; *Book of Divine Consolation*, 59.9–11.

2 Mt 16:24; Cf. Sermon XLV, n. 460–68; *Book of Divine Consolation*, 45.13–46.9; *Counsels on Discernment*, §3; Sermon 49; Sermon 59; Sermon 76.

3 Cf. Sermon 23; Sermon 60; *Book of Divine Consolation*, 39.1–7; *In Ioh.* ns.225, 583.

4 The phrase *dâ er ane vellic ist* means "that makes him fragile," since *anevellic* (modern German *anfällig*) means "fragile," "delicate," or "susceptible." However, *vallic* (modern German *fällig*) means "falling" or "tending downward," which is consonant with Eckhart's metaphorics. The soul is encouraged to renounce the part of her that tends downward instead of rising to God. Cf. Thomas Aquinas, *Catena Aurea In Lucam*, 9:23.

5 Thomas Aquinas, *Catena Aurea in Lucam*, 9:23.

6 Cf. Sermon 10.

she is more like God than all things.[7] Only the angels are nobler by nature because they burst forth from and poured out of the divine spirit, though they have a resting place in it.[8] The soul does not have this: she has to pour herself into the body.[9]

On this, some people[10] are inclined to wisely say:[11] since God is entirely one and simple, why did he not make all things entirely one[12] like the angels? This cannot be, the masters say.[13] Any one creature cannot reveal God more than a little.[14] Therefore, God created various creatures so that each might reveal Him in its own way. And they cannot reveal Him any more than a drop of water can reveal the sea.[15] Nevertheless, a drop of water better reveals the sea and all the universe than all creatures can reveal God, for one can make a sea from a drop of water, but with the help of all creatures one cannot come to comprehend God.[16] That's why Saint Gregory said:[17] for the soul in which God shines, so that she may recognize something of him, all creatures become slight[18] or entirely nothing.

---

7 Augustine, *The Greatness of the Soul*, 5.9. Cf. Sermon XLVIII.1, n.501; *In Sap.* n.131; Augustine, *De quantitate animae*, c.5 n.9, c.34, n.77; Sermon 106.

8 The word *enthalt* here means a residence or place where one abides. The important sense for Eckhart is that the spirit is the still point of rest out of which divine activity flows. In that sense, the angels are active insofar as they flowed from the spirit, but yet they still have a resting place, a quiet home within it. Cf. Sermon XXXVI.1, n.365; Sermon 8; Sermon 17; Sermon 18; Sermon 47; Sermon 71; Thomas Aquinas, *I Sent.*, d.3 q.3, *In Ioh.* n.283; *Prol. In opus prop.* n.11; *In Sap.* n.260; *Counsels on Discernment*, §19.

9 Cf. Sermon 57.

10 Avicenna, Maimonides, and possibly Siger of Brabant.

11 Cf. *In Gen. I* n.10–11, 21; *In Sap.* n.36; Sermon XXVIII.2, n.284, 287.

12 The idea expressed here is somewhat foreign to us. It was common in Eckhart's time to speak of the angels as being many but without number. Matter is the principle of division and multiplicity. This resulted in some arguments on distinguishing angels from one another and counting them, such as those we see in Thomas Aquinas, that look strange to us today.

13 Cf. Thomas Aquinas, *Summa Theologiae*, I.47.1, *In Ex.* n.111; Sermon 91.

14 What creatures do here is *bewîsen*, a word that Eckhart uses in various ways, essentially meaning to point to something to demonstrate or explain it like a teacher does.

15 Cf. Sermon 73, Sermon 80; Wis 11:23, Eccl 18:8.

16 Cf. Sermon 95b.

17 Cf. Sermon 73.

18 The word translated as "slight" here is *enge*. Though this means "narrow" in Middle High German and in modern German (*eng*), the sense Eckhart seems to be targeting is the narrowing of something so that it becomes thin and slight before disappearing entirely. In English, we do not often say that something is "narrow" when we mean that it is shrinking and thinning before wasting away or disappearing entirely.

Thirdly, these words altogether match with what Chrysostom[19] said: the man who would suffer martyrdom until bringing death to himself has renounced himself.[20] Our Lord said to Moses: "No one may come to me and live."[21] That's why Chrysostom said: If I am to become other than what I am, I must let go of what I am.[22] That must be created from humility, for as Saint Gregory said, nothing nullifies man so much as humility.[23] This was nicely illustrated by Moses,[24] when he led his flock of sheep into the valley for them to rest. There, he saw the bush burning but not consumed, and he said: "I will go and see the wonder." Then Our Lord spoke to him: "Stay there Moses and go no further. Take your shoes off of your feet." The feet represent the desires of the soul.[25] They should be naked and stripped of all transitory and mortal things so that the soul may offer herself entirely to Our Lord. A saint said:[26] if an impure soul raises herself up and wants to offer herself to God, she would again be crestfallen and fall through base things.[27] Just as

---

19 Cf. Thomas Aquinas, *Catena Aurea in Lucam*, 9,23.

20 *In Ioh.* n.68.

21 This is a stronger form of Ex 33:20, where God says, "Thou canst not see my face: for there shall no man see me, and live" (KJV).

22 We should notice how Eckhart uses one of his favorite techniques and pushes the connotation of denial and renunciation in the direction of detachment. Eckhart cites Chrysostom, ultimately pointing to Matthew 16:24, "If any man will come after me, let him deny himself, and take up his cross, and follow me." (Si quis vult post me venire, abneget semetipsum, et tollat crucem suam, et sequatur me.) The word for "deny" here is *abneget*, which means "renounce" or "deny." While both *abnegat* in Latin and *verliesen* (*verlazen*) in Middle High German can mean "to renounce," Eckhart's term means what *loslassen* does in modern German: "to let go of" or "release" something. In Sermon 5a (*vernûthait*, DW I, 82.13), Sermon 74 (*vernichtigkeit*, DW III, 275.6–8) and *Counsels on Discernment*, §23 (*vernihten sîn selbes*, DW V, 405.3. Cf. DW V, 292.6–11), Eckhart speaks of humility in the context of self-negation, which is closer to denying or renouncing than what we see here in this line. The next line, however, wherein Eckhart cites Saint Gregory, does include *vernihte*, which further motivates translating *verliesen* to distinguish it from *vernihte*.

23 As mentioned above, this idea of the "annihilation of self" (*vernihten sîn selbes*) occurs elsewhere in Eckhart's works. The word for annihilate (*vernihten*) is the same one that appears here with "man" instead of "self." Though annihilate and nullify both have *nihil* or *nulla* as roots, we typically do not hear of "annihilating man." Further, the subject in this clause is "nothing" (*niht*), which might result in a rendering like so: "Nothing reduces man so well to nothing as humility."

24 Cf. Ex. 3:1–5, 33:20; Sermon 45, Sermon 70, Sermon LXXV.

25 Cf. *In Ioh.* n.95; Sermon 108.

26 Cf. Sermon 57, Sermon 97.

27 Several words here do not have easy English equivalents. First, the soul will again be *niderslagen* (modern German: *niederschlagen*), which means "despondent"—literally, "to feel beaten down." She will *vellen* (modern German: *fällen*), which is "to be cut down" or "corrupted." The relevant meaning here is that the soul "falls" from heaven in the sense of the fall from grace, a

a sick eye that impudently wants to look at the sun, it becomes blinder and still sicker. . . .[28]

---

falling away from God and into the temporal world of corruptible things. Finally, the soul falls through *bœsiu* things, a word which differs in Middle High German from the modern German cognate *böse* in that it means "base," "worthless," or "vulgar" (as opposed to divine, eternal, and worthy before God), but not straightforwardly bad or evil. Thus, the overall sense of the sentence seems to be that the impure soul will fall away from God by its attachment to things of this world and thus feel dejected.

28 Cf. *In Ex.* n.237.

Sermon 108
Si non lavero te, non habebis partem mecum

"If I do not wash you, you will have no part with me."
Our Lord said these words to Saint Peter as he wanted to wash the feet of his disciples. Saint Peter was scared of the fact that our Lord wanted to accomplish so great a work, and he said to him: "Lord, you will never wash my feet."[1] He also wanted to show his humility to our Lord.

About this, Saint Augustine said: if our Lord had first come to all the apostles, they would have shown him humility.[2] Another saint said that our Lord had washed the feet of all the disciples before he arrived at Saint Peter.[3] Peter kept silent from simplicity and depth of wisdom to ensure that that they would no longer want to ask him any questions. They knew well that our Lord was so wise that he accomplished all his work in the best way.[4] That is why certain spiritual people start by washing the feet of those who are younger, and then the elders. Bede says as well that our Lord first came to Saint Peter. But Judas, in his pride, sat down first.[5] His feet were washed first. He was so prideful, he understood nothing of this. And through this twofold teaching, some spiritual people start by washing the feet of their elders.

The evangelist spoke again a few words: "As our Lord had loved his own, he loved them until the end."[6] Ultimately, three things are shown by these

---

1 Jn 13:8–9.

2 Augustine, *Homilies on John*, 56 c.1.

3 Jn 13:5–6. Origen, *Commentary on John* 32, Thomas Aquinas, *Catena Aurea in Iohannem*, 13,6.

4 Cf. Sermon 4, *Counsels on Discernment*, §22.

5 In the *Commentary on John*, Aquinas attributes this to Chrysostom.

6 Jn 13:1.

words: first, the perfection of love; second, the usefulness of the gift; third, how people must conduct themselves, in whom God works these things.

First, we consider love. A saint[7] says: the soul which has love for God and which is inflamed with burning desire seeks God eagerly. All that which is not God becomes bitter and distasteful and entirely appalling. It runs around in all creatures and can find no rest.[8] To the extent that it finds itself among creatures, it is appalled by them. The burning desire of the soul must necessarily follow God, as fire must follow its own nature, devouring and transforming all that it grasps.[9]

That's why Saint Augustine said: Lord, if you take yourself away from us, give us another in your place.[10] This means: our souls can have no life without you. Wherever you go, they will follow you. They cannot be without you. It's the perfection of love of our Lord God: "he loves us until the end." He took us into his care by his suffering and dying. Then he gave us another in his place through the sacrament without suffering and without dying, completely free of all that he suffered and of all that can ever die. So "he wanted to remain with us until the end of the world" as he said himself.[11]

The second point is the use or the greatness of the gift. Now, God cannot give a greater gift than when he gives himself.[12] It is written that there are twelve uses or fruits of the body of our Lord and one could still write of more.[13] I want to gather them all together by saying one thing: all grace and blessedness which lies in all good works and in all virtues and in all moral behavior,[14] and all of the blessedness that the saints have possessed in the kingdom of heaven, and all the blessedness that the only-begotten Son of the Heavenly Father has possessed—the soul receives it all through the body of Christ.

---

7 Augustine, *Conf.*, XIII.8.9. Cf. Sermon VIII, n.84; *In Ioh.* n.706; Sermon 56.

8 Augustine, *Conf.*, I.1.1. Cf. Sermon 18; Sermon 81; Sermon 69; *Book of Divine Consolation*, 26.16–27; *On the Nobleman*, 112.10–12.

9 Cf. Sermon 6, Sermon 84, Sermon LXXV.

10 Augustine, *Conf.*, XIII.8.9. Cf. Sermon 20a, Sermon 20b; *Book of Divine Consolation*, 18.3–9.

11 Mt 28:20.

12 Cf. *Counsels on Discernment*, §21.

13 Eckhart may have in mind Guiard von Laon's "Twelve Fruits of the Eucharist."

14 Cf. Sermon 60.

It receives the being of all things,[15] which is so delightful that the soul doesn't ever want to be deprived of it by any means. It only wants to have the being of God.

Secondly, it receives the movement of all things from God. He moves them with his power and joyfully works his own likeness in all good things.[16]

Thirdly, it receives the end of all things from which all things burst forth and to which all things come to an end again. What greater thing can a man desire than to receive the body of our Lord? For through that, he receives the satisfaction and perfection of all things.[17]

If a cabbage knew it could be stripped of its lower nature and transformed into a nature and life as noble as that of man, it would desire by the nature of all its power to become food for man, as all food that man receives which is most fitting for him becomes transformed into flesh and blood,[18] becoming one life with him. But if the food is impure or unrefined, uncooked or raw, then it does not unite with man. It creeps in between the skin and flesh and swells up outside of the body. From this, all kinds of illnesses and afflictions arise.

It is the same with the body of our Lord. Whoever receives it when he is not yet cleansed and purified of sin cannot unite with it, but the sacrament will firmly guide him. That's why the soul must be purified and cleansed. It should desire with all its powers, body and soul[19] to unite with God. Then it becomes by grace with God all that God is in himself by nature.[20]

Were it so bare and abstracted from all things, as God is bare and abstracted from all things and is a pure being over all things, so it would be purely God with God, as far as a creature can.[21] Our Lord Jesus Christ gave this unity to us all: "Father, I want all of them to be one with us, as you and I are one."[22]

The third point is: how must people be in whom this thing should come to pass? It was about this that our Lord said to Saint Peter: "If I do not wash

---

15 Cf. Sermon 47, Sermon 84.
16 Cf. Sermon 82.
17 Cf. Sermon 22.
18 Cf. Sermon 96.
19 Cf. Sermon 67; *Book of Divine Consolation*, 59.24; *Counsels on Discernment*, §20.
20 Cf. Sermon 66; 105; *On Detachment*, 400.2–401.4.
21 Cf. Sermon 20a; Sermon 20b; Sermon 32; Sermon 38; Sermon 40; *Book of Divine Consolation*, 32.8–11.
22 Jn 17:20–23.

you, you will have no part with me." And Peter said to him: "Lord, do not wash only my feet, but also my hands and my head."[23] These indicate three types of purification.[24]

The first purification must be at the level of the highest powers of the soul. As I have often said,[25] it is necessary that "man's head be bare" and "woman's covered," which signifies that the highest powers must be naked and undisturbed[26] so that the soul can offer herself entirely to God in the highest. Thus it can receive from God all that God can give, and become entirely united with him. That the head of women must be covered signifies that the soul with the lowest powers must receive created things with measure[27] and that they must be used with measure with all things. The soul has to suffer and struggle in the lowest part, for there, it is changeable and unstable as a result of things that move in time. With suffering and struggle, it attains divinity. The more it undergoes struggles for God, the more the soul draws near him.[28]

The second purification, that of the hands, signifies that man must have a pure and ordered life, that his works should be done wisely so that they would trouble no one. On the contrary, he would be a light for men and a sign toward God.[29] "If anyone wants to be troublesome, it is not our custom," Saint Paul said.[30]

The third purification at the level of the feet signifies that man must be humble in his desire. I say this absolutely: if man was as humble and as useful as Saint Paul, then God would give him grace as great as he gave Saint Paul.[31] I say this precisely: if man could have so great a humility as Mary, the mother of God, he would possess the same blessedness in the kingdom of heaven as she possessed.[32] May God help us so that this happens in us. Amen.

---

23 Jn 13:8–9.

24 Thomas Aquinas, *Super Iohannem*, 13,9.

25 Sermon 11, Sermon 106a; *On the Nobleman*, 113.25–114.5.

26 Cf. 1 Cor 11:3–13.

27 The word translated as "measure" here is *mâʒe*. We have similar expressions in English using this concept. For example, "He had a measured response," indicating moderation, restraint, and that the proper or fitting amount was determined.

28 Cf. *Counsels on Discernment*, §20.

29 Cf. Sermon XXXIV.3, n.349; Sermon 91.

30 1 Cor 11:16.

31 Cf. *In Ioh.* n.95; Sermon 81, Sermon 107.

32 Cf. Sermon 5a, Sermon 5b, Sermon 93; *Responsio Proc. Col. I* n.61.

Sermon XXIV.2
Domus mea domus orationis est[1]

My house is a house of prayer.
Rearrange the words like this: a house of prayer is my house.

"House" means to lack passion.[2] First, note just how far passion is naturally below the soul,[3] as said in the sermon above, "Be compassionate,"[4] and so how shameful it is to be subject to passion. Second, in this [lack of passion], note the soul's rest. The reason for this is because the Word in which and through which and by means of which the Father works by flowing into the soul, is "without noise," according to Augustine, "while silence enveloped everything"—that is to say, all beings, living things, and understandings.[5] Hence, in building the temple, the sound of the hammer was not heard.[6]

"Of prayer." Take note: when we hear and read, God speaks to us. When we pray, we speak to God.[7] Take note: the theologians[8] say that the lower angels want to speak to the higher angels, but they do not illuminate them.[9] But if we properly consider it, all who speak are of that higher and primary

---

1 Lk 19:46. I have translated portions of several of Eckhart's Latin sermons containing mathematical metaphors, most of which appear in earlier chapters of this book, Since this one was complete, it appears with the other translations.

2 Cf. Sermon LV.3, n.545.

3 Cf. *In Sap.* n.9; *In Ioh.* n.524; Sermon XII.2, n.140.

4 Cf. Sermon XII.2, ns.122–45, esp. 140.

5 Augustine, *En. in Ps.* 103, sermo 4, n 9; *De vera rel.*, c.55 n.110; Wis 18:1–15.

6 1 Kgs 6:7.

7 Cf. Augustine *En. In Ps.* 85, n.7.

8 Thomas Aquinas, *Summa Theologiae*, I.107.2.

9 Cf. *In Gen. I* n.65. *In Gen. II* n.146; *In Ioh.* n.396.

order. Therefore, it is clear how much the soul must be elevated if it wants to speak to God.[10] After saying how this—namely, elevation—is, say it comes only to the humble.[11] When projecting a sphere onto a plane, the pole and the center are the same. Say how to pray "in spirit and mind"[12] following the apostle, as you, with the weakness of the whole world, cast before the feet of God, and secondly, you offer to God the merit and light of the mother of God and all the saints, and thirdly, in the way of the Word itself, in that purity, present to and representing the Father, for in that alone are all things pleasing. Luke: "in you I am very pleased."[13]

Note: every going away [from God] is some unlikeness and consequently some discord and impurity. John 4:24: "in the spirit"—namely, the Holy Spirit—"and truth," it is the Son [in whom[14]] "one must pray." "For the Father also seeks." In the same note, he says, "He seeks." What is sought is higher, at least in reason and apprehension. The soul must then get rid of all things, seeking God in his bare nakedness with nothing else in him.

The second principal thing to note, following the Damascene, is in what way prayer is "the ascent of the intellect to God." And so, it does not touch God except by ascending. It ascends moreover to what is higher. Therefore, it is necessary to transcend not only what can be made an image,[15] but also what can be understood. Likewise, as the intellect resolves[16] things into being, it must surpass being too. For indeed, being is not the cause of being, just as fire is not the cause of fire, but something far higher is, into which it is necessary to ascend.

Furthermore, the intellect receives God unadorned, as he truly is. For that reason, the intellect must ascend, as he says, "in God." Even still, the soul

---

10 Cf. *De elevatione animae*, ns.1, 213, 328, 365, 367.

11 Cf. Sermon XXXVIII, n.38–81.

12 1 Cor 14:15.

13 Cf. Sermon 10.

14 [In whom] since it is "in truth" we must pray.

15 If we render *imaginabilia* as "imaginable," the sentence is not entirely clear or sensible.

16 *Resolutio* is a scholastic term which refers to the "resolving" or "reducing" of specific concepts into the more fundamental and abstract universal concepts of truth, being, goodness, and oneness. Davies's "refer" is unclear for *resolvat*. "Dissolves" is also possible and provides a more interesting physical metaphor insofar as the intellect *dissolves* specificity into generality. In this way, intellect loosens and relaxes the apparent concreteness of sensible things, enabling an understanding that is beyond particular things, which is true to the sense of the passage. See the *Parisian Questions* for more on Eckhart's contention that "understanding is superior to existence" and that existence follows from the Word since a "principle is never the same as that which follows from a principle" (q.1; Maurer, *Parisian Questions and Prologues*, 45, 48).

must pass beyond God himself under this name, for the soul must surpass all names.

In the third place, just as when the intellect by its name proceeds from outward to inward, out of the conversion[17] of the will, and following its nature it abstracts from all outside things as well, its ascension is the entrance into the principal root of all purity, which is in the Word. Note therefore: "ascent of the intellect." Wisdom 1:5 says that the Holy Spirit "withholds itself from thoughts that are without understanding." Thinking has motion[18] and runs about. Likewise, thinking without understanding is thinking in images[19] and has the nature of corporeal things, namely shapes and such. [It says] the "ascent of the intellect" because, properly, God dwells in the substance of the soul. This, therefore, is higher than the intellect. The highest is to have the capacity for God and to take on God: "Israel, how great is the house of God," et cetera.

My house. First note that the house of God is in itself the essence of the soul, in which God may only descend in his nakedness. Note here too how God is enticed to descend into and penetrate the soul once it is first purified of the sensible passions. And next, Avicenna certainty believed otherwise. Tell them how.

Second, note in what way the superior reason is the house of God. That is why he cast out the "buyers and sellers."[20] First, because the work of virtue and greatest love do not concern what is mercantile. Second, because there it is quiet and silent, where the Father speaks the word "without noise." Temporal things, truly, which are with motion, pertain to inferior reason.[21]

Third, note the way in which the intellect grasps God to a greater extent, more truly and more nobly than all the corporeal world, and yet, in God's receiving the other, He dwells in and remains in all creatures, for indeed all creatures seek to become like him. Explain that this is especially true of heaven.

Fourth, note the way in which Plato argues for the immortality of the soul since it has the capacity for wisdom. How much greater the soul is than

---

17 *Converso* means "I turn around," as in religious "conversion." Davies's "contrary to" does not wholly fit the context and may not adequately capture Eckhart's meaning.
18 Richard of St. Victor speaks of thought as having motion (LW IV, 227n5).
19 Again, Eckhart's *imaginaria* seems to refer directly to the way that created things are images (cf. Sermon 2).
20 Cf. Sermon 1.
21 For the idea that motion is inferior, see LW IV, 227.5–6.

even that, for it has the capacity for God. And so all cognitive power from the intellective family is beyond passion and thus is after itself and from itself immortal.

Concordance

The following is a concordance of the modern English translations of Eckhart's works. In addition to the abbreviations defined before the biblography on page 207 (DW, LW, EE, TP) the abbreviations used correspond to the following books:

- **F** Fox, Matthew. *Breakthrough: Meister Eckhart's Creation Spirituality in New Translation.* New York: Doubleday, 1991.
- **W** Walshe, Maurice O'Connell. 2010. *The Complete Mystical Works of Meister Eckhart.* New York: Crossroad, 2009.
- **S** Schürmann, Reiner. *Wandering Joy: Meister Eckhart's Mystical Philosophy.* Hudson, N.Y.: Lindisfarne, 2001.
- **M** Maurer, Armand A., trans. *Parisian Questions and Prologues.* Toronto: Pontifical Institute of Mediaeval Studies, 1974.
- **OD** Davies, Oliver. *Meister Eckhart: Selected Writings.* London: Penguin, 1994.
- **CJ** My translations in the present volume

    I included the sermon names and indexed by the numbering in the critical editions. Pfeiffer (Pf) was the primary source in the nineteenth century. The *Paradisus anime intelligentis* (PA) is a late medieval compendium of sermons, about half of which are Eckhart's. Translations from Evans (1924, 1931) and Blakney (1941) are not included because they were done before the critical editions (DW and LW) were available. Translations by Clark (1957) and Clark and Skinner (1958) are also not included for the vernacular sermons since more modern translations have been produced to replace all of their translations. The numbers in each column for the translations are page numbers. Horizontal breaks indicate different volumes of the critical edition. The last folio of DW IV.2 that includes Sermons 110–117 was not available in time for this book.

VERNACULAR SERMONS

#	Name	Pf	PA	EE	TP	F	W	S	OD	CJ
		DW I								
1	Intravit Iesus in templum	6			239	450	66		152	
2	Intravit Iesus in quoddam castellum	8		177		273	77	3	158	295
3	Nunc scio vere	25			244		165			
4	Omne datum optimum	40			247	397	224			
5a	In hoc apparuit charitas	13					104		188	
5b	In hoc apparuit caritas			181		199	108			
6	Iusti autem vivent in aeternum	65		185			328			
7	Populi eius	72			252	440	367			
8	In occisione gladii	82				83	403		164	
9	Quasi stella matutina	84			255		341			
10	In diebus suis placuit deo	83			261		334		168	
11	Impletum est tempus Elizabeth	90					347			
12	Qui audit me	96			267		295		175	
13	Vidi supra montem Syon						159			
13a	Sant Johannes sach in einer gesichtte	24					163			
14	Surge illuminare iherusalem				271		266			
15	Homo quidam nobilis			189		166	270			
16a	Een meester sprect ware alle middel af						112		192	
16b	Quasi vas auri solidum	14			275		114	96		
17	Qui odit animam suam	21					148	46		
18	Adolescens, tibi dico: surge	36					211			

CONCORDANCE

#	Name	Pf	PA	EE	TP	F	W	S	OD	CJ
19	Sta in porta domus domini	35					207			
20a	Homo quidam fecit cenam magnam	32					191			
20b	Homo quidam fecit cenam magnam						196			
21	Unus deus et pater omnium	100			280	188	466		180	
22	Ave, gratia plena	88		192			279			
23	Compulit Jesus discipulos ascendere in naviculum						285			
24	Induimini dominum Iesum Christum	94			284	102	448			304

		DW II								
25	Moyses orabat dominum	10					226	91		
26	Mulier, venit hora	11					95	53		
27	Hoc est praeceptum meum	12					313	99		
28	Ego elegi vos	81					129		118	
29	Convescens praecepit eis	74			287	354	124			
30	Praedica verbum	66			292	65	133	178	122	
31	Ecce ego mitto angelum meum	48					258			
32	Consideravit semitas domus suae	52					275			
33	Sancti per fidem vicerunt regna		49				401	111		
34	Gaudete in domino	27					172			
35	Si consurrexistis cum Christo	33					200			
36a	Stetis Jesus in medio discipulorum	38					218			

#	Name	Pf	PA	EE	TP	F	W	S	OD	CJ
36b	Venit Jesus et stetit in medio						221			
37	Vir meus servus tuus mortus est	31					187			
38	In illo tempore missus est angelus	29	4				177		112	
39	Iustus in perpetuum vivet	59		296	464		305		144	
40	Manete in me	63		300			318		148	309
41	Qui sequitur iustitiam	43					238		139	
42	Adolescens, tibi dico surge	80				126	398		184	
43	Adolescens, tibi dico surge	79					394			
44	Postquam completi erant dies	20					143			
45	Beatus es, Simon Bar Iona	30					183			
46	Haec est vita aeterna	47			304		255			
47	Spiritus domini replevit orbem terrarum	23				114	155			
48	Ein meister sprichet, alliu glîchiu	60		197			309		133	
49	Beatus venter, qui te portavit	89				338	432			
50	Eratis enim aliquando in tenebris	95					452		136	
51	Hec dicit dominus, honora patrem tuum	102					407			
52	Beati pauperes spiritu	87		199		213	420	210	202	
52	Beati pauperes spiritu (Flasch 1998)	87								283
53	Misit dominus manum suam	22		203		57	152		127	
54a	Unser herre underhuop									314
54b	Haec est vita aeterna, ut cognoscant	46					250			

#	Name	Pf	PA	EE	TP	F	W	S	OD	CJ
55	Maria Magdalena venit ad monumentum	34					203			
56	Mâriâ stuont ze dem grabe und weinete		26				418			
57	Vidi civitatem sanctam Ierusalem novam		61				168			
58	Qui mihi ministrat						243		130	
59	Et nunc sequimur te in toto corde				307		362			
		DW III								
60	In omnibus requiem quaesivi	45				380	246			
61	Misericordia domini plena est terra						384			
62	Got hât die armen gemachet durch die rîchen	55					289			
63	Man liset hütt da haimē in der epistel						388			
64	Die sele die wirt ain mit gotte vnd nit veraint						392			319
65	Deus caritas est	5					62			
66	Euge bone serbe et fidelis	58					300			
67	Got ist diu minne					388	357			
68	Scitote quia prope est regnum dei	69				137	352			
69	Modicum et iam non videbitis me	42			311		233		209	
70	Modicum et non videbitis me	41	28		316		229			
71	Surrexit autem Saulus de terra	19			320		137	119		

#	Name	Pf	PA	EE	TP	F	W	S	OD	CJ
72	Videns Iesus turbas ascendit in montem	98					458			
73	Dilectus deo et hominibus	73					370			
74	Dilectus deo et hominibus	86					374			
75	Mandatum novum do vobis	85				91	427			
76	Videte qualem caritatem dedit nobis pater	7		327	325		72		129	
77	Ecce mitto angelum meum	49					262			
78	Missus est Gabriel angelus	28					175			
79	Laudate caeli et exultet terra	91				151	445			
80	Homo quidam erat dives	97			332		455			
81	Fluminis impetus laetificat civitatem Dei	64				363	322			
82	Quis putas puer iste erit?	62	48				314			
83	Renovamini spiritu	99		206		177	462		235	
84	Puella surge		57		335		413			
85	Pvella surge		58			266	416		230	
86	Intravit Iesus in quoddam castellum	9			338	478	83		193	

		DW IV.1								
87	Ecce, dies veniunt, dicit dominus	1								322
88	Post dies octo vocatum est nomen eius Iesus	8								328
89	Angelus domini apparuit	10								333
90	Sedebat Iesus docens in templo	15								337
91	Voca operarios, et redde illis mercedem suam	16								348

CONCORDANCE

#	Name	Pf	PA	EE	TP	F	W	S	OD	CJ
92	Cum sero factum esset		27							357
93	Quae est ista, quae ascendit quasi aurora		37							362
94	Non sunt condignae passiones huius temporis		42							370
95	Os suum aperuit sapientiae		46							377
96	Elisabeth pariet tibi filium		47							393
97	Qui manet in me		50							398
98	Nisi granum frumenti cadens in terram mortuum fuerit		55							404
99	Laetare sterilis quae non paris						576			
100	Et quaerebat videre Iesum, quis esset		51							410
101	Dum medium silentium tenerent omnia		1			293	29			
102	Ubi est qui natus est rex Iudaeorum		2			251	39		215	
103	Cum factus esset Iesus annorum duodecim		4			238	55		222	
104	In his quae patris mei sunt oportet me esse		3				46			
105	Ich hân gesprochen in einer predige		15				119			

		DW IV.2								
106	Aemulor enim vos Dei aemulatione		26							417
107	Qui vult venire post me		53							436
108	Si non lavero te, non habebis partem mecum		108							442

#	Name	Pf	PA	EE	TP	F	W	S	OD	CJ
109	Nolite timere eos	56				75	292		232	
110	In omnibus requiem quaesivi	44								
111	Sublevatis oculis Iesus dixit	109								
112	Omnis turba quaerebant eum tangere									
113	Adolescens, tibi dico surge									
114	Nû market driu stücke (Auferte ista hinc)									
115	Von dreîerleir liehte		56							
116	Domine rex omnipotens		60							
117	Ze dem êrsten suochet daz riche gotes (Reich Gottes-Predigt)								241*	

* Oliver Davies' translation of Sermon 117 was done before the critical edition was available.

VERNACULAR TREATISES

			Translations						
Name	Pf	PA	EE	TP	F	W	S	OD	CJ
Book of Divine Consolation			209			524		53	
Talks of Instruction			247			486		1	
On the Nobleman			240		510	557		97	
On Detachment			285			566			

LATIN SERMONS

				Translations			
Sermon #	Name	TP	F	CS	M	OD	CJ
I	Caritas dei diffusa est (Rom 5:5)						
II,1	Deus pacis et dilectionis (2 Cor 13:11)			161			
II,2	Gratia domini nostri Iesu Christi (2 Cor 13:13)						
III	Terrena dixi vobis (Joh 3:12)						
IV,1	Ex ipso, per ipsum, et in ipso sunt omnia (Rom 11:36)	207					
IV,2	Ex ipso, per ipsum, et in ipso sunt omnia (Rom 11:36)	210					
V,1	Caro mea vere est cibus (Jn 6:56)						
V,2	Hic est panis (Jn 6:50)						
VI,1	Deus caritas est (1 Jn 4:8)	212					
VI,2	In hoc apparuit gratia (1 Jn 4:9)	214					
VI,3	Qui manet in caritate (1 Jn 4:16)						
VI,4	Timor non est in caritate (1 Jn 4:18)						
VII	Homo quidam erat dives (Lk 16:19)						
VIII	Homo quidam fecit cenam magnam (Lk 14:16)						
IX	Deus omnis gratiae (1 Pt 5:10)						
X	Erant appropinquantes ad Iesum (Lk 15:1)						
XI,1	Non sunt condignae passiones (Rom 8:18)						
XI,2	Existimo quod non sunt condignae passiones (Rom 8:18)			165			
XII,1	Estote misericordes (Lk 6:36)		417				
XII,2	Estote misericordes, et infra: mensuram bonam (Lk 6:36, 38)						
XIII	Omnes unanimes in oratione estote (1 Pt 3:8)						

Sermon #	Name	TP	F	CS	M	OD	CJ
XIV,1	Ascendens Iesus in unam navim (Lk 5:3)						
XIV,2	Subductis ad terram navibus (Lk 5:11)						
XV,1	In novitate vitae ambulemus (Rom 6:4)						
XV,2	In novitate vitae ambulemus (Rom 6:4)						
XVI	Omnis qui irascitur fratri suo (Mt 5:22)						
XVII,1	Nunc vero liberati a peccato (Rom 6:22)						
XVII,2	Nunc vero liberati a peccato (Rom 6:22)						
XVII,3	Stipendia peccati mors (Rom 6:23)						
XVII,4	Stipendia peccati mors (Rom 6:23)						
XVII,5	Gratia dei vita aeterna (Rom 6:23)						
XVII,6	Gratia dei vita aeterna (Rom 6:23)						
XVIII	Misereor super turbam (Mk 8:2)						
XIX	Debitoress sumus (Rom 8:12)						
XX	Attendite a falsis prophetis (Mt 7:15)						
XXI	Non simus concupiscentes malorum (1 Cor 10:6)			169			
XXII	Homo quidam erat dives (Lk 16:1)			171			
XXIII	Nemo potest dicere: dominus Iesus (1 Cor 12:3)						
XXIV,1	Scriptum est: quia domus mea domus orationis est (Lk 19:46)						
XXIV,2	Domus mea domus orationis est (Lk 19:46)					255	448
XXV,1	Gratia dei sum id quod sum (1 Cor 15:10)	216					
XXV,2	Gratia dei sum id quod sum (2 Cor 15:10)	219					

CONCORDANCE

Sermon #	Name	TP	F	CS	M	OD	CJ
XXVI	Duo homines ascenderunt (Lk 18:10)						
XXVII,1	Sufficientia nostra ex deo est (2 Cor 3:5)						
XXVII,2	Idoneos nos fecit ministros (2 Cor 3:6)						
XXVII,3	Ministratio spiritus erit in gloria (2 Cor 3:8)						
XXVIII,1	Bene omnia fecit (Mk 7:37)						
XXVIII,2	Bene omnia fecit: surdos fecit audire et mutos loqui (Mk 7:37)						
XXIX	Deus unum est (Gal 3:20, Dt 6:4)	223		179		258	
XXX,1	Diliges dominum deum tuum (Lk 10:27)		531	184			
XXX,2	Ex toto corde tuo (Lk 10:27)		535	188			
XXXI	Spiritu ambulate (Gal 5:16)						
XXXII	Surge, vade. Fides tua te salvum fecit (Lk 17:19)						
XXXIII	Si spiritu vivimus, spiritu et ambulemus (Gal 5:25)						
XXXIV,1	Nemo potest duobus dominis servire (Mt 6:24)						
XXXIV,2	Nemo potest duobus dominis servire (Mt 6:24)						
XXXIV,3	Quaerite ergo primum regnum dei (Mt 6:33)						
XXXIV,4	Quaerite ergo primum regnum dei (Mt 6:33)						
XXXV	Flecto genua mea (Eph 3:14)						
XXXVI,1	Ibat Iesus in civitatem quae vocatur Naim (Lk 7:11)						
XXXVII	Unus deus et pater omnium (Eph 4:6)						
XXXVIII	Amice, ascende superius (Lk 14:10)						
XXXIX	Gratias ago deo meo pro omnibus vobis (1 Cor 1:4)						

Sermon #	Name	TP	F	CS	M	OD	CJ
XL,1	Diliges dominum deum tuum (Mt 22:37)						
XL,2	Diliges proximum tuum sicut te ipsum (Mt 22:39)						
XL,3	Quid vobis videtur de Christo?					263	
XLI,1	Induite novum hominem (Eph 4:24)						
XLI,2	Sol non occidat super iracundiam vestram (Eph 4:26)						
XLII,1	Fili, remittuntur tibi peccata tua (Mt 9:2)						
XLII,2	Fili, remittuntur tibi peccata (Mt 9:2)						
XLIII,1	Videte quomodo caute ambuletis (Eph 5:15)						
XLIII,2	Dies mali sunt (Eph 5:16)						
XLIII,3	Gratias agentes semper pro omnibus (Eph 5:20)						
XLIII,4	Subiecti invicem in timore dei (Eph 5:21)						
XLIV,1	Simile factum est regnum caelorum homini regi (Mt 22:2)						
XLIV,2	Omnia parata. Venite ad nuptias (Mt 22:4)						
XLIV,3	Multi sunt vocati, pauci vero electi (Mt 22:14)						
XLV,1	Accipite armaturam dei (Eph 6:13)	227					
XLVI	Domine, descende, prius quam moriatur filius meus (Jn 4:49)						
XLVII,1	Confidimus in dominus Iesu (Phil 1:6)						
XLVII,2	Hoc oro, ut caritas vestra magis ac magis abundet (Phil 1:9)					264	
XLVII,3	Hoc oro, ut caritas vestra magis ac magis abundet (Phil 1:9)						
XLVIII,1	Nostra conversatio in caelis est (Phil 3:20)						

Sermon #	Name	TP	F	CS	M	OD	CJ
XLVIII,2	Multi ambulant, qui terrena sapiunt (Phil 3:18–20)						
XLIX,1	Cuius est imago haec et superscriptio? (Mt 22:20)	234					
XLIX,2	Cuius est image haec? (Mt 22:20)	236					
XLIX,3	Imago	236					
L	Non cessamus pro vobis orantes (Col 1:9)						
LI	Ecce dies veniunt, dicit dominus (Jeremiah 23:5–8)						
LII	Induimini dominum Iesum Christum (Rom 13:14)			192			
LIII	Reliquimus omnia et secuti sumum te (Mt 19:27)						
LIV,1	Qui timet deum, faciet bona (Eccl 15:1)						
LIV,2	Implevit eum dominus (Eccl 15:5)						
LV,1	Beatus vir, qui in sapientia morabitur (Eccl 14:22)						
LV,2	Nisi granum frumenti (Jn 12:24)						
LV,3	Si quis vult venire post me (Mt 16:24)						
LV,4	Qui odit anumam suam in hoc mundo (Jn 12:25)						
LVI	Sancti per fidem vicerunt regna (Heb 11:33)						
LW V, p. 89	Sermo die B. Augustini Parisius Habitus: Vas auri solidum ornatum omni lapide pretioso						
LW V, p. 109	Tractatus super oratione dominica						495
LW V, p.131	Sermo Paschalis A. 1294 Parisius Habitus						

LATIN TREATISES

	EE	TP	CS	M
Parisian Questions				43
General Prologue to the Three-Part Work				79
Prologue to the Work of Propositions				93
Prologue to the Work of Commentaries				104
Commentary on Exodus		41 (complete)	197	107
Commentary on the Book of Wisdom		147 no.19–40, 96–120, 144–157, 279–285		
Commentary on Genesis	82 (no.1–28)			
Book of the Parables of Genesis	92 (no.1–40, 135–165)			
Sermons and Lectures on Ecclesiasticus		174 (no.42–61)		
Commentary on John	122 (no.1–131)	182 (no.546–576)	202, 149–160 (no.226–248)	
Commentary on Song of Songs				
Responsio ad Articulos (Eckhart's Defense)	71 (partial from Théry, before LW V)			
In agro dominico	77			
Acta Echardiana				

No English translations have been made for: the *Commentary on the Book of Wisdom* nos. 1–18, 41–95, 121–143, 158–278, 286–300; *Commentary on Genesis* nos. 29-304; *Book of the Parables of Genesis* nos. 41–134, 166–222; *Sermons and Lectures on Ecclesiasticus* nos. 1–41, 62–70; *Commentary on John* nos. 132–225, 249–545, 577–745; and the *Commentary on the Song of Songs*.

Index

active intellect, 42, 45, 57
activity/work, 78, 80, 80n21, 90n13, 149–52, 156, 164, 227n3 [Pr.52], 229–32 [Pr.52], 229n10 [Pr.52], 230n19 [Pr.52], 232n24 [Pr.52], 233 [Pr.2], 234n6 [Pr.2], 240 [Pr.24], 245 [Pr.40], 257 [Pr.88], 257n3 [Pr.88], 258n11 [Pr.88], 263 [Pr.90a], 267 [Pr.90b], 277n3 [Pr.92], 278 [Pr.92], 287 [Pr.94], 297 [Pr.95b], 304 [Pr.96], 333n8 [Pr.107], 338 [Pr.108]
  spontaneous action, 13, 14, 48n137, 55
  vita activa/vita contemplativa, 13, 28–29, 55, 127–34, 257n3 [Pr.88]
Adams, Douglas, 85
adverb (*biwort*), 89n4, 315n5 [Pr.100]
adequatio intellectus ad rem, 41, 45, 56, 56, 90, 175
aesthetics, 72, 82, 201, 201n19, 203, 204. *See also* Plato
Albert the Great, 10, 41, 46, 53, 176, 228n8 [Pr.52], 263 [Pr.90a], 267 [Pr.90b]
allegory, 24, 49, 85, 284 [Pr.93]
Ambrose, 307–8 [Pr.97]
anagogical interpretation, 31
analogy, 20, 43, 89n4, 94, 103, 119–21, 128, 131, 136, 154, 155, 157, 173
anxiety, 15–16, 15n15, 203
apocalyptic writing, 24
apokatastasis, 27, 37

apophatic theology. *See* negative theology
approximate. *See* knowledge
Aquinas, Saint Thomas, 10, 11, 22, 27, 28, 38, 41, 42–43, 45, 47, 48, 48n138, 53, 54, 59, 71, 78, 110n103, 128, 130, 173, 264 [Pr.90a], 269 [Pr.90b], 333n12 [Pr.107]
archetype, 16, 17, 17n16, 18, 19, 24, 25, 26, 27, 127, 199, 201
Arian controversy, 17n20
Aristotle, 5, 22, 23, 26, 27, 38, 44, 55, 56–57, 85n35, 100n59, 104, 122n41, 127, 156, 178–79, 178n34, 199, 201n20, 229n11 [Pr.52], 239n3 [Pr.24], 258n11 [Pr.88], 278n5 [Pr.92], 287 [Pr.94], 291n2 [Pr.95a]
art, 150–51, 150n124, 183, 189. *See also* aesthetics; creation; creativity
attachment, 53, 57, 76, 119n33, 124, 128, 141–42, 144–45, 163, 167n212, 172n5, 177, 186, 227 [Pr.52], 227n2 [Pr.52], 233 [Pr.2], 233n3 [Pr.2], 231 [Pr.52], 233–35 [Pr.2], 238 [Pr.2], 243n2 [Pr.40], 261n19 [Pr.89], 328 [Pr.106c], 328n27 [Pr.106c], 334n27 [Pr.107]
Augustine, Saint, 2n2, 2n3, 3, 21, 27, 31, 32–36, 39, 43, 48, 48n138, 51, 58, 59, 64, 71, 87, 89, 89n4, 90, 94, 96, 98, 106–7, 109, 118, 118n24, 147–48, 175, 181–83, 190, 245 [Pr.40], 247 [Pr.54a], 250 [Pr.54a], 253n5 [Pr.87], 260 [Pr.89], 270 [Pr.90b], 278n8

[Pr.92], 282–83 [Pr.93], 285 [Pr.93], 286 [Pr.94], 292 [Pr.95a], 293 [Pr.95a], 297 [Pr.95b], 299 [Pr.95b], 312 [Pr.98], 316n10 [Pr.100], 317–18 [Pr.100], 320 [Pr.106a], 324 [Pr.106b], 327 [Pr.106c], 330 [Pr.106d], 332 [Pr.107]
  Confessions, 21, 32, 33–36, 74, 95, 111, 257n5 [Pr.88], 272 [Pr.91], 283n31 [Pr.93], 283n32 [Pr.93], 337 [Pr.108]

Aureole, Peter, 45

authority, 25, 40n112, 46, 55, 58–59, 99, 195. *See also* pseudonymity

Averroes, 47

Avicenna, 92, 342 [XXIV,2]

Bacon, Francis, 14

Bacon, Roger, 41, 57

beatific vision, 168, 168n220

beatitude, 41

Beatrijs of Nazareth, 178n32

Beauty (Platonic Form). *See* aesthetics; Plato

Bede, 336 [Pr.108]

Beguines and Beghards, 11, 47, 178n32

belief. *See* faith

Benedict XII, Pope. *See* Fournier, Jacques

Bernard of Clairvaux, Saint, 49, 265 [Pr.90a], 269 [Pr.90b], 281 [Pr.93], 284 [Pr.93], 308 [Pr.97]

biwort. See adverb

blessedness. *See* metaphor

Blumenberg, Hans, 4, 5, 6, 13, 15, 15n15, 56, 57, 63, 71–73, 73n7, 75, 76n12, 77n14, 82, 108, 134, 172, 190n1, 201n20, 205n26

Boethius, 37, 51

"boiling over" (*ebullitio*). *See* metaphor: *ebullitio*

boldly (approach God), 255 [Pr.87], 255n15 [Pr.87]

Bonaventure, Saint, 44, 48, 48n138

Book of Causes (*Liber de Causis*), 38, 51, 55

Book of the Twenty-Four Philosophers, 137, 258n11 [Pr.88]

boulesis, 22

Brabant, Hadewijch of. *See* Hadewijch of Brabant

Bradwardine, Thomas, 45

breakthrough. *See* metaphor

bricoleur/bricolage (Lévi-Strauss), 15, 78, 149

Bruno, Giordano, 15

Buddhism, 3, 12n10, 130, 200; Zen, 81n22, 83, 84, 145n89, 206, 318n33 [Pr.100]

Burke, Edmund, 85n36

Campbell, Joseph, 17n16, 204

cause/causality, 37, 174, 202, 228 [Pr.52], 265 [Pr.90a], 269 [Pr.90b]

chiasmus, 107, 113, 129, 169, 276 [Pr.91], 322 [Pr.106a]

Christ: historical and ceaseless birth, 1, 2, 156–58, 181, 183–85, 195, 199, 201, 235 [Pr.2], 244–45 [Pr.40], 323–24 [Pr.106b], 326 [Pr.106c], *see also* metaphor; paradoxical dual nature, 3, 17n20, 32, 77, 90, 160, 163, 201, 241 [Pr.24], 245 [Pr.40]

Christmas sermons, 1, 156–58, 181

Chrysostom, John, 334 [Pr.107], 334n22 [Pr.107]

Cicero, 57, 172

Cioran, E. M., 196–97

Clairvaux, Bernard of. *See* Bernard of Clairvaux, Saint

Claus, David, 17

co-creator (*mitewürker*). *See* individual

coincidentia oppositorum, 16, 76, 110n106, 161, 203

INDEX 363

Colledge, Edmund, 227n2 [Pr.52], 234n6 [Pr.2], 236n10 [Pr.2], 237n14 [Pr.2], 239n4 [Pr.24]

compassion, 130n13, 161, 248 [Pr.54a], 284 [Pr.93], 340 [XXIV,2]

compression (of the ontological hierarchy), 16, 44, 50, 52, 55, 58, 58n180, 127, 171–73

connoisseurship, 62, 81–83, 134

Connolly, John, 178n32

contemplata aliis tradere, 84–85

contemplation (as part of *vita contemplativa*), 28, 29, 48n137, 127, 129, 193, 249 [Pr.54a]. *See also* activity/work; passivity/receptivity

conversion, 32, 34–36, 47, 95, 253 [Pr.87], 257n3 [Pr.88], 272 [Pr.91], 282n26 [Pr.93], 340 [XXIV,2], 342 [XXIV,2]

cosmology, 91, 101, 172–74, 181, 239 [Pr.24], 248–49 [Pr.54a], 284 [Pr.93]

Councils on Discernment, 10

creativity, 13, 14, 56–58, 149–50, 171, 202n22

cura monialem, 178n32

curiosity, 1, 56, 57, 175–76

Cusa, Nicholas of (Cusanus), 9, 15, 56, 57, 80n20, 94n25, 110n106, 158n172, 269n9 [Pr.90b]

Davies, Oliver, 96n45, 140n61, 145n88, 227n2 [Pr.52], 229n9 [Pr.52], 341 [XXIV,2]

delight. *See* metaphor: joy/blessedness

Descartes, Rene, 45, 71

desire. *See* eros

detachment, 53, 90, 116, 136, 141–44, 150, 161–62, 176, 177, 185, 187, 194–95, 202n22, 244 [Pr.40], 244n4 [Pr.40], 247 [Pr.54a], 250 [Pr.54a], 334n22 [Pr.107]; forsaking, 154, 156, 166

dialectic, 40, 61n2, 78, 90n13, 101, 107–8, 119n33, 159, 191, 313n32 [Pr.98], 315n5 [Pr.100], 328n27 [Pr.106c]

Dietrich of Freiburg, 10, 49, 49n149

Dionysius, 3, 10n6, 29, 37, 38, 41, 55, 59, 71, 134n29, 163, 264 [Pr.90a], 265n15 [Pr.90a], 268 [Pr.90b], 270n13 [Pr.90b], 293 [Pr.95a], 299 [Pr.95b]

disharmony (phenomenology), 14, 15, 74, 77

Dominican order, 9, 10, 11, 47, 54, 65, 84, 92, 199, 228n5 [Pr.52]

Duclow, Donald, 98

Duns Scotus, 43, 44, 45, 53

Durandus of Saint-Pourçain, 69

ebullitio. *See* metaphor: *ebullitio*

Eckhart: appearing medieval, 2, 5, 72, 171–73, 175; current appeal of, 3, 5, 189, 191–92, 195–96, 200; defense, 10, 13, 32, 46, 64–68, 84, 241n10 [Pr.24]; negative theology, 37, 75; as philosopher, 62–63, 83n26, 84, 190, 197, 199; on philosophical speculation, 175; provoking or catalyzing interest, 1, 3

enthusiasmos. *See* possession

Epictetus, 23

Eriugena, John Scotus, 38–39, 46, 48, 51, 156

eros, 20, 25, 29, 38, 115, 121, 160, 188, 189, 191, 231 [Pr.52], 243 [Pr.40], 245 [Pr.40], 251 [Pr.64], 281 [Pr.93], 298 [Pr.95b], 316 [Pr.100], 318 [Pr.100], 334 [Pr.107], 340 [XXIV,2]. *See also* Plato: eros

esse formale, 103, 174, 174n13

essence, 27, 48, 54, 128

esse virtualiter, 174

Evagrius Ponticus, 29

Evans, C. de B., 225, 345

exegesis, 3, 23–24, 31, 88, 98, 165

expectation, 1, 116

experience, 12, 16, 24, 62, 64, 73, 74, 83–85, 88, 90, 99–100, 107, 121, 133, 157, 177, 189, 190, 194, 195, 202, 203, 205, 258n11 [Pr.88], 259n15 [Pr.88], 287 [Pr.94], 296n2 [Pr.95b], 303n2 [Pr.96]; immediate, 4, 71, 78, 80, 86, 193–94, 203, 205n26

expertise. *See* connoisseurship

external practices (works), 177, 179, 227 [Pr.52], 230n19 [Pr.52], 234 [Pr.2], 337 [Pr.108]

faith, 35–37, 41, 43, 177, 189, 192, 194–99, 300 [Pr.95b]

familiar, 1, 13, 14, 15, 96–98, 100, 114, 116, 117, 120–21, 133, 139–43, 187, 190, 193, 195, 197, 200, 239 [Pr.24], 239n2 [Pr.24], 240 [Pr.24], 247 [Pr.54a], 253 [Pr.87], 292 [Pr.95a], 297 [Pr.95b]

feeling, 3, 72, 83, 107, 201n20, 202

fire. *See* metaphor: fire/burning/heat

fit (of a story, theory, or metaphor), 4, 72, 74, 86, 94

Flasch, Kurt, 62, 225, 226 [Pr.52], 230n18 [Pr.52], 231n21 [Pr.52], 232n23

Fleming, Ursula, 66

Forman, Robert K. C., 61, 73, 76, 77n13, 92

Fournier, Jacques, 66

Fox, Matthew, 134n29, 163, 184n63

Franciscan order, 228n5 [Pr.52]

Free Spirit, 47, 157, 186, 186n70

free will, 55, 186, 228 [Pr.52]

Freiburg, Dietrich of. *See* Dietrich of Freiburg

frontier, 79

Galileo, 172

Ghent, Henry of, 43, 53

God:
  being, 2, 28, 50, 52, 52n164, 54, 95–96, 103, 104, 127, 140, 168, 169, 188, 201, 230 [Pr.52], 250 [Pr.54a], 268–69 [Pr.90b], 273 [Pr.91], 289 [Pr.94], 338 [Pr.108]
  as *deus absconditus* (hiddenness), 44, 56, 96, 202
  as eros/desire/lust, 29, 96
  fear of, 97, 117, 119n31, 124, 156, 254–55 [Pr.87], 262 [Pr.89]
  goodness, 48, 52, 89n7, 104, 116–17, 120, 127, 143–44, 173–74, 178–79, 191, 240 [Pr.24], 243–44 [Pr.40], 244n4 [Pr.40], 248 [Pr.54a], 251n5 [Pr.64], 282 [Pr.93], 284 [Pr.93], 293 [Pr.95a], 308 [Pr.97], 310 [Pr.97], 321 [Pr.106a], 341n16 [XXIV,2]
  ground. *See* metaphor: ground
  hurrying, 95
  immanence in creation, 28, 51, 54
  joy, 96, 124–25, 154, 235 [Pr.2], 261 [Pr.89], 278 [Pr.92], 320 [Pr.106a], 326–27 [Pr.106c], 329 [Pr.106d], 338 [Pr.108]. *See also* metaphor: joy
  love, 27, 96, 112, 148, 187, 188, 199, 271 [Pr.91], 275 [Pr.91]. *See also* love
  lured or drawn back to, 5, 94, 96, 180, 199, 254 [Pr.87], 271–72 [Pr.91], 275 [Pr.91], 287 [Pr.94]
  return to (*reditus*), 4, 26, 27, 78, 100, 100n59, 141, 181–82, 190, 191, 194, 247 [Pr.54a], 271 [Pr.91]
  speech/Word. *See* Word
  unity of, 26, 37, 144, 151, 181, 191, 200, 205, 333 [Pr.107]. *See also* oneness
  will, 23, 33, 36, 45, 55, 152, 186, 187, 227 [Pr.52], 228n8 [Pr.52], 230–32 [Pr.52], 268 [Pr.90b], 303 [Pr.96]

gods (Ancient Greek), 16n16, 17n16, 18, 20, 21, 38, 137, 137n47, 163, 313n30 [Pr.98]

INDEX 365

Good (Platonic Form). *See* Plato: Form of the Good

Gorgias, 18

grace, 33, 100, 137n44, 150, 159, 165, 182, 186, 231 [Pr.52], 241 [Pr.24], 294 [Pr.95a], 304 [Pr.96], 305 [Pr.96], 337–38 [Pr.108]

greenness. *See* metaphor: greenness

Greer, Rowan, 25, 28, 29, 31

Gregory of Nyssa. *See* Nyssa, Gregory of

ground (*grunt*). *See* metaphor: ground

habit, 4, 33–34, 53, 76–77, 81, 86, 93, 96–97, 97n45, 99, 110, 177, 190, 194

Hadewijch of Brabant, 178n32

harmony (phenomenology). *See* disharmony

Hebrews, 19, 23

hegemonikon, 22

Heimsoeth, Heinz, 205n26

hekousion, 22

hell, 36, 97, 146, 275 [Pr.91], 317 [Pr.100], 317n24 [Pr.100]

Heraclitus, 16

heresy, 9n2, 10, 11, 13, 47, 65–68, 186n70, 252 [Pr.64]

hierarchy, ontological. *See* Plato: ontological hierarchy

higher powers of the soul. *See* powers

Hildegard of Bingen, 48, 155n154, 319n4 [Pr.106a]

hinderance (ineluctable attraction), 95, 103, 129, 130, 133, 139, 148, 152, 176, 177, 181, 233–34 [Pr.2], 237 [Pr.2], 248 [Pr.54a], 261 [Pr.89], 292 [Pr.95a], 297 [Pr.95b], 318n33 [Pr.100], 321 [Pr.106a], 327 [Pr.106c], 330 [Pr.106d]

Hippolytus, 156

history, cyclic and linear accounts of. *See* time

Homer, 17, 18

hope, 1, 262 [Pr.89]

hubris, 14, 18

humility, 55, 111–12, 133, 144, 188, 247–48 [Pr.54a], 263 [Pr.90a], 267 [Pr.90b], 284 [Pr.93], 292 [Pr.95a], 297 [Pr.95b], 300 [Pr.95b], 316 [Pr.100], 334 [Pr.107], 334n22 [Pr.107], 336 [Pr.108], 339 [Pr.108], 341 [XXIV,2]

Husserl, Edmund, 64, 71, 77n14

Huxley, Aldous, 73

I (pronoun), 104, 169

Iamblichus, 37

ignorance (learned), 40

image: Eckhart's, 53, 78, 93, 101, 103, 128, 134, 135, 136, 142–43, 176, 200, 227n3 [Pr.52], 239 [Pr.24], 240 [Pr.24], 244–45 [Pr.40], 245n11 [Pr.40], 247 [Pr.54a], 252 [Pr.64], 264 [Pr.90a], 268–70 [Pr.90b], 312 [Pr.98], 312n18 [Pr.98], 313 [Pr.98], 341–42 [XXIV,2], 342n19 [XXIV,2]; "image of," 27, 103, 151, 154, 176, *see also* Plato: images; *imago dei*, 20, 29, 32, 40, 54, 77, 78, 103, 107, 163, 260 [Pr.89]

imaginative horizon, 4, 64, 72, 81, 82, 86

Immaculate Conception, 182

immediate experience. *See* experience

imperfection. *See* perfection

impermanence, 273n206

In Agro Dominico. *See* Eckhart: defense

Incarnation, 1, 4, 21, 23, 78, 128, 156, 158, 182–85, 199, 201

individual, 43, 44, 45, 51, 106, 127, 138, 172, 187

annihilation of, 16, 17, 62, 128, 138, 186, 334n22 [Pr.107], 334n23 [Pr.107]

being, 37, 317 [Pr.100]

changing conception of, 2, 4, 11–24, 42, 55, 57, 71, 74, 156, 174, 201 as created nothing, 52, 55, 291–92 [Pr.95a], 296 [Pr.95b], 318n32 [Pr.100], 333 [Pr.107]

as creator/co-creator (*mitewürker*), 55–56, 159, 159n176, 231 [Pr.52], 244 [Pr.40], 257n3 [Pr.88], 271 [Pr.91], 289 [Pr.94], 308 [Pr.97], 319 [Pr.106a], 323 [Pr.106b], 326 [Pr.106c], 329 [Pr.106d]

as divine, 5, 23, 52, 54, 56, 60, 128, 139, 151–52, 158, 163, 177, 199, 260–61 [Pr.89]

giving birth to God. *See* metaphor: birth of the Word in the soul

as paradoxical (temporal/eternal, unity/multiplicity, universal/particular), 14, 17, 17n16, 20, 21, 52, 89, 164, 166–67, 199–200

as Son of God, 1, 2, 30, 95, 98, 101, 103, 57–158, 165, 167, 169

will, 20, 22, 23, 33–36, 95, 98, 128, 129, 142, 144, 160, 169, 188, 193, 227–28 [Pr.52], 228n5 [Pr.52], 232 [Pr.52], 257 [Pr.88], 278 [Pr.92], 294 [Pr.95a], 304 [Pr.96], 342 [XXIV,2]

ineffable, 62, 64, 87, 89, 90; as a "veil," 32, 89, 89n8, 174n16, 192, 204, 275n33 [Pr.91], 286n6 [Pr.94], 311–12 [Pr.98], 318 [Pr.100]

infinity, 50, 109–10, 117, 120, 137, 264 [Pr.90a]; infinite sphere, *see* metaphor: infinite sphere; intensive, 28, 54, 57, 112–13, 128, 130, 173n10, 175, 183, 201, 203

inflation (ontological, of the individual), 12–14, 14n12, 16, 23, 36, 139, 199

in illo tempore (Mircea Eliade), 17

in quantum (insofar as), 52, 67, 99–100, 127, 167–69, 168n219, 173, 228n7 [Pr.52], 238 [Pr.2], 238n16 [Pr.2], 245–46 [Pr.40], 245n9 [Pr.40]

Inquisition. *See* Eckhart: defense

intellect, 22–23, 39, 43, 49n149, 88, 100, 102–3, 102n70, 122, 127, 137, 141–43, 147, 152, 164, 167n212, 173, 249 [Pr.54a], 264–65 [Pr.90a], 269–70 [Pr.90b], 316n6 [Pr.100], 341–43 [XXIV,2]

James, William, 4, 83, 99n57, 105, 190, 204

John, Saint, 320 [Pr.106a], 324 [Pr.106b]

John XXII, Pope, 47, 65

Johnson, Mark. *See* Lakoff, George and Mark Johnson

joy. *See* metaphor: joy/blessedness

Jung, Carl, 19n24

kairos (rhetorical exigency), 46, 46n134, 64, 71, 193–94

Kant, Immanuel, 71, 73, 73n7

Katz, Steven, 63, 73

Kelley, C. F., 41, 91, 101, 199

kenosis, 164, 187, 193–94, 193n3, 287n9 [Pr.94], 306 [Pr.96]. *See also* metaphor: emptiness; metaphor: forgetting/forgoing

Kierkegaard, 59, 74, 205

Kivavia (Lévy-Bruhl), 17

knowledge and understanding, 5, 19, 21, 22, 35–37, 40–45, 54, 56, 57, 82, 118n25, 134–35, 162, 163, 165, 167, 175–79, 187, 194, 196, 228n5 [Pr.52], 229 [Pr.52], 244 [Pr.40], 250 [Pr.54a], 264 [Pr.90a], 268–69 [Pr.90b], 289 [Pr.94], 300 [Pr.95b], 309–10 [Pr.97], 317 [Pr.100]; approximate, 15–16, 15n15, 56–57, 101, 173, 175. *See also* unknowing

Koch, Josef, 10

Kohàk, Erazim, 4, 202

Lakoff, George and Mark Johnson, 4, 82, 91, 105–6

lebemeister/lesemeister, 178

Leff, Gordan, 46

INDEX

Leibniz, 55
Lévi-Strauss, Claude, 14
Lévy-Bruhl, Lucien, 16–17, 19n24
likeness, 20, 22, 27, 75, 85n35, 93, 100–101, 109, 116–17, 131–35, 151, 154, 157n168, 167, 181, 194, 197, 226 [Pr.52], 228n9 [Pr.52], 234–36 [Pr.2], 239 [Pr.24], 245 [Pr.40], 249 [Pr.54a], 253 [Pr.87], 258n11 [Pr.88], 261 [Pr.89], 271–72 [Pr.91], 276 [Pr.91], 283 [Pr.93], 295 [Pr.95a], 298–301 [Pr.95b], 299n27 [Pr.95b], 303–5 [Pr.96], 309 [Pr.97], 321 [Pr.106a], 324–25 [Pr.106b], 327 [Pr.106c], 333 [Pr.107], 338 [Pr.108], 341 [XXIV,2]. *See also* truthlikeness
literal, 49, 59
living without a why, 5, 16, 78, 178–79, 178n32, 201–2, 202n22, 203
logos (world-ordering principle), 21, 23, 40, 48. *See also* metaphor: ordering
love, 36, 116, 118, 118n25, 131, 161–62, 167, 179, 183, 228n5 [Pr.52], 248 [Pr.54a], 255 [Pr.87], 265 [Pr.90a], 269–70 [Pr.90b], 272 [Pr.91], 278 [Pr.92], 282–83 [Pr.93], 286 [Pr.94], 294 [Pr.95a], 300 [Pr.95b], 308 [Pr.97], 316 [Pr.100], 337 [Pr.108]. *See also* eros; God: as eros/desire/lust
lower powers of the soul. *See* powers
Löwith, Karl, 15
Luther, Martin, 9

Magdeburg, Mechthild of. *See* Mechthild of Magdeburg
Maimonides, 41
Mangin, Eric, 95n37
Mary and Martha (*vita activa/vita contemplativa*). *See* activity/work; passivity/receptivity
mathematics. *See* metaphor: mathematics
Maurer, Armand, 41

Maximus the Confessor, 10n6, 156
McGinn, Bernard, 19n22, 46, 47, 58, 63, 64, 100n61
meaning (in life), 15, 16, 18, 74, 81, 84, 130, 200–203
Mechthild of Magdeburg, 11
meditation, 81, 133, 148, 195n7
Meno's paradox (Sophistic paradox), 194, 196, 198
metaphor, 3, 5, 6, 11, 71–72, 76–77, 82, 86, 87, 87n1, 106, 107, 225
baking/cooked/raw, 94, 338 [Pr.108]
birth of the Word in the soul, 3, 40, 48n137, 96, 98, 116, 119, 146, 152, 156–59, 157n168, 185, 199, 201, 231n21 [Pr.52], 234–37 [Pr.2], 257n5 [Pr.88], 313 [Pr.98], 320–21 [Pr.106a], 324 [Pr.106b], 326 [Pr.106c], 329–30 [Pr.106d]
breaking through (*durchbrechen*), 107, 163, 164, 202, 232 [Pr.52], 308 [Pr.97], 316 [Pr.100]
clothing and nakedness, 116, 139–44, 142n69, 165, 237 [Pr.2], 239 [Pr.24], 240–41 [Pr.24], 244–46 [Pr.40], 244n4 [Pr.40], 244n8 [Pr.40], 248–50 [Pr.54a], 273 [Pr.91], 287–90 [Pr.94], 288n20 [Pr.94], 316n6 [Pr.100], 321 [Pr.106a], 330 [Pr.106d], 334 [Pr.107], 338–39 [Pr.108], 341–42 [XXIV,2]
container/vessel/capacity, enlarging/expanding/inflation, emptiness 111–12, 136–42, 142n69, 151, 158, 167, 172, 174–75, 187, 203, 230n14 [Pr.52], 232 [Pr.52], 251 [Pr.64], 258 [Pr.88], 258n11 [Pr.88], 262 [Pr.89], 265 [Pr.90a], 269 [Pr.90b], 273 [Pr.91], 276 [Pr.91], 283 [Pr.93], 285 [Pr.93], 295 [Pr.95a], 301 [Pr.95b], 301n45 [Pr.95b], 309 [Pr.97], 309n22 [Pr.97], 316–17 [Pr.100], 320 [Pr.106a], 326 [Pr.106c], 329–30 [Pr.106d],

330n12 [Pr.106d], 342–43 [XXIV,2]

dazzle, 271n3 [Pr.91]

desert/wilderness, 49–50, 154

ebullitio (boiling over, overflowing), 42, 48n137, 48n138, 125, 130, 146–47, 169, 203, 259n13 [Pr.88], 271n3 [Pr.91], 300 [Pr.95b], 300n31 [Pr.95b], 322n33 [Pr.106a]

explosive, 75, 76, 76n12, 90, 101, 106, 107, 108, 121, 134, 137, 151, 184, 196, 258n11 [Pr.88]

fire/burning/heat, 90–91, 95, 132–33, 151, 153n138, 154, 157, 160, 236 [Pr.2], 238 [Pr.2], 253n5 [Pr.87], 258 [Pr.88], 258n11 [Pr.88], 278 [Pr.92], 278n10 [Pr.92], 286 [Pr.94], 294 [Pr.95a], 301 [Pr.95b], 304 [Pr.96], 307 [Pr.97], 310n32 [Pr.97], 337 [Pr.108], 341 [XXIV,2]

flow and pouring (emanation), 50, 53, 93, 98, 100n61, 123, 150, 161, 169, 176, 193n3, 202, 203, 232 [Pr.52], 236 [Pr.2], 240 [Pr.24], 243 [Pr.40], 247–49 [Pr.54a], 252 [Pr.64], 260 [Pr.89], 264–65 [Pr.90a], 273 [Pr.91], 276 [Pr.91], 276n39 [Pr.91], 285 [Pr.93], 289 [Pr.94], 294 [Pr.95a], 297 [Pr.95b], 304 [Pr.96], 307 [Pr.97], 322 [Pr.106a], 325 [Pr.106b], 328 [Pr.106c], 328n27 [Pr.106c], 333 [Pr.107], 333n8 [Pr.107], 338 [Pr.108], 340 [XXIV,2]

foreignness/strangeness. *See* familiar

forgetting/forgoing, 119n31, 154–55, 154n146, 174–75, 252 [Pr.64], 271–72 [Pr.91]

greenness (sprout, blossom, verdant), 48, 147, 153, 153n135, 153n137, 155, 155n154, 235 [Pr.2], 237 [Pr.2], 240 [Pr.24], 250 [Pr.54a], 275 [Pr.91], 275n31 [Pr.91], 310 [Pr.97], 319n4 [Pr.106a], 321–22 [Pr.106a], 325 [Pr.106b], 328 [Pr.106c], 319 [Pr.106a], 319n4 [Pr.106a], 323 [Pr.106b], 326–28 [Pr.106c]

ground, 90, 103, 149, 160, 163, 164, 184, 192, 196, 199, 240 [Pr.24], 247–48 [Pr.54a], 314 [Pr.98]; of being, 3, 89n7, 241 [Pr.24], 249 [Pr.54a], 313 [Pr.98]; groundless ground, 167, 226 [Pr.52]; of thought, 12

hinge, 75, 131, 144–45, 258 [Pr.88], 258n8 [Pr.88]

infinite sphere, 102n66, 137, 258n11 [Pr.88]

inner man/outer man, 161, 167, 168, 247 [Pr.54a], 265 [Pr.90a], 270 [Pr.90b]

joy/blessedness, 95–96, 96n41, 124–25, 125n63, 148, 184, 191, 229 [Pr.52], 236 [Pr.2], 246 [Pr.40], 253 [Pr.87], 253n5 [Pr.87], 254 [Pr.87], 256 [Pr.87], 256n111 [Pr.87], 259n15 [Pr.88], 260 [Pr.89], 262 [Pr.89], 272 [Pr.91], 274 [Pr.91], 276 [Pr.91], 282 [Pr.93], 282n26 [Pr.93], 285 [Pr.93], 285n40 [Pr.93], 287 [Pr.94], 287n9 [Pr.94], 288 [Pr.94], 293 [Pr.95a], 295 [Pr.95a], 296–97 [Pr.95b], 301 [Pr.95b], 310 [Pr.97], 317 [Pr.100], 320 [Pr.106a], 324 [Pr.106b]. *See also* God: joy

light/sun/heat, 100–101, 132–33, 141, 147–48, 153, 157, 161, 174, 174n13, 174n13, 235–37 [Pr.2], 240 [Pr.24], 248–49 [Pr.54a], 253 [Pr.87], 253n5 [Pr.87], 254 [Pr.87], 258 [Pr.88], 261 [Pr.89], 261n19 [Pr.89], 263–64 [Pr.90a], 267–69 [Pr.90b], 272–73 [Pr.91], 277 [Pr.92], 277n3 [Pr.92], 281 [Pr.93], 284–85 [Pr.93], 293 [Pr.95a], 295 [Pr.95a], 296 [Pr.95b], 297 [Pr.95b], 299–300 [Pr.95b], 301 [Pr.95b], 303 [Pr.96], 303n2 [Pr.96], 310 [Pr.97], 318 [Pr.100], 333 [Pr.107], 335 [Pr.107], 340–41 [XXIV,2]

INDEX

mathematics, 44, 58, 73, 75, 76n12, 80, 89, 108–13, 108n94, 120, 131, 144–45, 172, 249–50 [Pr.54a], 258n8 [Pr.88], 274 [Pr.91], 291 [Pr.95a], 291n5 [Pr.95a], 299 [Pr.95b], 317n16 [Pr.100], 340 [XXIV,2]

melting, 147, 248 [Pr.54a], 259 [Pr.88], 259n13 [Pr.88], 275 [Pr.91], 310n32 [Pr.97], 328 [Pr.106c], 328n27 [Pr.106c]. *See also* metaphor: *ebullitio*

mirror/reflection, 22, 38, 128, 176, 255 [Pr.87], 261 [Pr.89], 283 [Pr.93]

nobility, 273n22 [Pr.91]

ordering (of the soul), 161–62, 185, 248 [Pr.54a], 262 [Pr.89], 265 [Pr.90a], 269 [Pr.90b], 278n8 [Pr.92], 279 [Pr.92], 285n38 [Pr.93], 291 [Pr.95a], 298 [Pr.95b], 302 [Pr.95b], 308 [Pr.97], 312 [Pr.98], 312n13 [Pr.98], 315n4 [Pr.100], 339 [Pr.108]

poverty, 76, 142, 142n69, 226–32 [Pr.52], 292 [Pr.95a], 297 [Pr.95b], 315 [Pr.100]

proper (*eigen*)/right (*reht*), 230–31 [Pr.52], 260 [Pr.89], 261n17 [Pr.89], 266 [Pr.90a], 278n5 [Pr.92], 291n2 [Pr.95a], 313 [Pr.98]

property and ownership, 119, 129, 160, 246 [Pr.40]

rest/indwelling/abiding/peace/stillness/home/ease, 102n67, 135, 137, 143–49, 149n114, 162, 166–67, 179, 228n8 [Pr.52], 236 [Pr.2], 241 [Pr.24], 243–46 [Pr.40], 249 [Pr.54a], 253 [Pr.87], 253n5 [Pr.87], 258 [Pr.88], 258n12 [Pr.88], 261n19 [Pr.89], 262 [Pr.89], 262n22 [Pr.89], 263 [Pr.90a], 267 [Pr.90b], 272 [Pr.91], 277n3 [Pr.92], 278–79 [Pr.92], 281 [Pr.93], 283 [Pr.93], 285n38 [Pr.93], 297 [Pr.95b], 301n45 [Pr.95b], 307–9 [Pr.97], 311 [Pr.98], 313n31 [Pr.98], 317n24 [Pr.100], 318n33 [Pr.100], 321 [Pr.106a], 327–28 [Pr.106c], 328 [Pr.106c], 328n27 [Pr.106c], 333–34 [Pr.107], 333n8 [Pr.107], 337 [Pr.108], 340 [XXIV,2], 342 [XXIV,2]

root/taking root/penetration, 132, 147, 153, 250 [Pr.54a], 253n5 [Pr.87], 294 [Pr.95a], 310 [Pr.97], 310n28 [Pr.97], 325 [Pr.106b], 328 [Pr.106c], 328n27 [Pr.106c], 342 [XXIV,2]

satisfaction, 104, 123, 228n8 [Pr.52], 254 [Pr.87], 254n12 [Pr.87], 273 [Pr.91], 282–83 [Pr.93], 305 [Pr.96], 317 [Pr.100], 329–31 [Pr.106d], 329n6 [Pr.106d], 338 [Pr.108]

secret/hidden, 248–49 [Pr.54a], 261 [Pr.89], 265 [Pr.90a], 269–70 [Pr.90b], 288 [Pr.94], 293 [Pr.95a], 307 [Pr.97], 310 [Pr.97], 328n27 [Pr.106c]. *See also* God: as *deus absconditus*

seed/implanting, 155–56, 253 [Pr.87], 254 [Pr.87], 288 [Pr.94], 303 [Pr.96], 324 [Pr.106b]

shell (breaking), 172–73

silence, 81, 82n23, 146–47, 226 [Pr.52], 241 [Pr.24], 253n5 [Pr.87], 263 [Pr.90a], 267 [Pr.90b], 275 [Pr.91], 292 [Pr.95a], 297 [Pr.95b], 333n8 [Pr.107], 340 [XXIV,2], 342 [XXIV,2]

smell/scent, 121–22, 193, 286 [Pr.94], 291 [Pr.95a], 293–94 [Pr.95a], 300 [Pr.95b]

space, 91–92, 113

spark (*scintilla, vünkelîn*), 43, 102, 128, 141, 152–55, 153n138, 166, 172n4, 229n12 [Pr.52], 237 [Pr.2], 237n13 [Pr.2], 313n31 [Pr.98], 330 [Pr.106d]

speech, 149, 257 [Pr.88], 257n3 [Pr.88], 320 [Pr.106a], 324

[Pr.106b], 327 [Pr.106c]. *See also* Word

stamp/imprint, 134–35, 135n37, 135–36, 150, 153, 177, 232 [Pr.52], 232n24 [Pr.52], 264 [Pr.90a], 268 [Pr.90b], 303 [Pr.96], 305 [Pr.96], 328 [Pr.106c], 328n27 [Pr.106c]

taste/savor, 109, 116, 121–24, 228 [Pr.52], 249 [Pr.54a], 259 [Pr.88], 259n15 [Pr.88], 264 [Pr.90a], 269 [Pr.90b], 273 [Pr.91], 273n22 [Pr.91], 279n15 [Pr.92], 294–95 [Pr.95a], 296n2 [Pr.95b], 298 [Pr.95b], 300–302 [Pr.95b], 307–8 [Pr.97], 310 [Pr.97], 310n25 [Pr.97], 316 [Pr.100], 337 [Pr.108]

water/wine, 160, 185, 248 [Pr.54a], 251 [Pr.64], 255–56 [Pr.87], 295 [Pr.95a], 303 [Pr.96], 333 [Pr.107]

wood (including wood/eye from Pr.48), 27, 120–21, 125, 150, 151, 154, 173, 251 [Pr.64]

metaphorology. *See* Blumenberg, Hans

Middleton, Richard of, 43

Milem, Bruce, 94n29, 165n199, 169, 202n22, 226 [Pr.52], 234n6 [Pr.2], 236n10 [Pr.2], 237n14 [Pr.2]

miracles (wonders), 41, 100, 142n69, 202, 248 [Pr.54a], 272 [Pr.91], 300 [Pr.95b]

Moerbeke, William, 10n6, 38, 47

Mojsisch, Burkhardt, 62n3, 89n7, 128n1

monotheism, 19, 24

Moses, 21, 94, 334 [Pr.107]

motion (spiritual), 1, 2n2, 4, 12, 39, 71, 74, 77, 77n14, 88, 93, 96, 101, 115–16, 124, 131, 144–49, 145n88, 162, 174–75, 180, 189, 191, 193–94, 197–98, 200, 201n20, 258 [Pr.88], 258n11 [Pr.88], 330n10 [Pr.106d]. *See also* "running about"

multiplicity, 13, 16, 34n84, 333n12 [Pr.107]

mystery, 4, 77–79, 81, 164, 192

mystery religions, 24

mysticism, 3, 12, 16, 19, 21, 23, 46, 49, 53, 57, 60–63, 68, 72, 73, 76, 83, 83n26, 84, 92, 138, 163, 192, 196–200, 203, 205

Nazareth, Beatrijs. *See* Beatrijs of Nazareth

Nazianzus, Gregory, 31

necessity/where God must act, 186–88, 202n22, 233–34 [Pr.2], 238 [Pr.2], 246 [Pr.40], 252 [Pr.64], 254–55 [Pr.87], 272 [Pr.91], 283 [Pr.93], 298 [Pr.95b], 316–17 [Pr.100]

negatio negationis. 37, 89n7, 201

negative theology, 3, 4, 22, 37, 50, 201, 293 [Pr.95a], 299 [Pr.95b]

Neoplatonism, 21, 25–27, 36–38, 46, 47, 50, 55, 100n61, 141, 144, 163, 182, 182n58, 192, 200, 313n31 [Pr.98]

new and unusual (*nova et rara*). *See* rhetoric: "new and unusual"

Nicholas of Cusa. *See* Cusa, Nicholas of (Cusanus)

Nietzsche, Friedrich, 16, 71, 74, 77, 204

nihilism, 16, 198, 200, 203

nominalism, 171. *See also* Ockham, William of

nonconceptuality, 4, 64, 72, 74, 75, 80, 82, 84, 86

novelty: in rhetoric, 2, 2n5, 4, 12, 71, 85, 86, 97–98; in science, 15

Nyssa, Gregory of, 31, 49

obedience, 55

Ockham, William of, 44–45, 55, 58, 69

Olivi, Peter, 41

oneness, 3, 13, 16, 19n23, 39n108, 61, 73, 83, 83n26, 89, 93, 100, 102, 102n67, 105, 109, 139, 144, 154, 155, 159, 164–65, 172n5, 176n26, 181, 187, 191–93, 200, 204, 228n9 [Pr.52], 234 [Pr.2], 241 [Pr.24], 245 [Pr.40], 246 [Pr.40], 250 [Pr.54a], 251–52 [Pr.64],

259 [Pr.88], 265 [Pr.90a], 269 [Pr.90b], 301 [Pr.95b], 314 [Pr.98]

Opus Tripartitum (Three-Part Work), 11

Origen, 2n2, 2n3, 25–36, 37, 71, 95, 145n86, 156, 332 [Pr.107]

Paradisus anime intelligentis, 11, 345

paradox, 3, 4 17, 54, 74–81, 102, 113–14, 141, 159, 167, 191, 196, 201, 203, 257n2 [Pr.88]; as feeling, 3; Eckhart insisting upon, 4, 62, 76, 76n12, 159, 190; created and uncreated, 40

Paris, 9, 10, 11

Parisian Questions, 10, 341n16 [XXIV,2]

Parmenides, 16, 37n96, 200

participation mystique, 19–20

passivity/receptivity, 13, 48n137, 80, 80n21, 93, 110, 127, 131–33, 136, 138, 138n48, 140, 158, 161–65, 228n8 [Pr.52], 229n10 [Pr.52], 230n19 [Pr.52], 231 [Pr.52], 232n24 [Pr.52], 233–37 [Pr.2], 233n2 [Pr.2], 234n6 [Pr.2], 238 [Pr.2], 240 [Pr.24], 245 [Pr.40], 253n5 [Pr.87], 261 [Pr.89], 261n17 [Pr.89], 276n225 [Pr.91], 277n3 [Pr.92], 279n14 [Pr.92], 284 [Pr.93], 287 [Pr.94], 287n10 [Pr.94], 288 [Pr.94], 293–94 [Pr.95a], 300 [Pr.95b], 304 [Pr.96], 304n14 [Pr.96], 310 [Pr.97], 310n29 [Pr.97], 311 [Pr.98], 337–39 [Pr.108], 342 [XXIV,2]

Paul, Saint, 30, 34, 39, 45, 231 [Pr.52], 235 [Pr.2], 241 [Pr.24], 254 [Pr.87], 265 [Pr.90a], 272 [Pr.91], 282 [Pr.93], 290 [Pr.94], 307 [Pr.97], 319 [Pr.106a], 323 [Pr.106b]

Pelagianism, 26

perfection/imperfection, 20n28, 26, 29–30, 50, 52, 54, 62–63, 90, 100, 104, 109, 109n99, 124, 127, 129, 130, 133, 150–51, 156, 157n168, 167, 175, 181, 185, 186n70, 192, 199, 187, 230–31 [Pr.52], 237 [Pr.2], 260–61 [Pr.89], 271 [Pr.91], 276 [Pr.91], 281–85 [Pr.93], 301 [Pr.95b], 304–5 [Pr.96], 309 [Pr.97], 319 [Pr.106a], 323 [Pr.106b], 326 [Pr.106c], 330 [Pr.106d], 337–38 [Pr.108]

Peter, Saint, 316 [Pr.100], 336 [Pr.108]

phenomenology, 71, 73, 191. *See also* disharmony

Philip, Saint, 288 [Pr.94], 322 [Pr.106a], 325 [Pr.106b], 253n5 [Pr.87] 328 [Pr.106c], 331 [Pr.106d], 334n27 [Pr.107]

Philo of Alexandria, 25

physics, 50, 181

Plato, 12, 13, 17, 19, 26, 30, 35, 43, 57, 59, 75, 76, 93, 100n59, 110, 129, 143, 163, 182, 190–91, 199, 253n5 [Pr.87], 303n2 [Pr.96], 330n10 [Pr.106d]

    Beauty, 20, 82, 93, 190, 192–93, 199, 201n19, 204, 253 [Pr.87], 271 [Pr.91], 273n17 [Pr.91]. *See also* aesthetics

    children of the Good, 138, 192

    divided line, 44, 117, 175, 253–54n5 [Pr.87]

    eros, 29, 38. *See also* eros; love

    evil (privation), 33, 52, 129, 146, 161, 192, 253n5 [Pr.87]

    Form of the Good, 19–23, 36, 41, 44, 143–44, 146, 166n206, 192, 201, 244 [Pr.40], 253n5 [Pr.87], 273n17 [Pr.91], 279n12 [Pr.92]

    Forms, 19, 20, 22, 52, 89

    individual participation in the Forms, 19, 21, 41, 137, 137n47

    image/imitation/manifestation, 22, 151, 163, 192, 303 [Pr.96]

    mania, 20–21, 28

    ontological hierarchy 16, 18–19, 36, 44, 51–53, 55, 116, 127, 140, 146, 150, 166, 175, 177, 192–93, 240 [Pr.24], 249 [Pr.54a], 253n5 [Pr.87], 278n10 [Pr.92]

Phaedrus, 19, 20, 77n14, 162n188, 201n19, 278n8 [Pr.92], 258n11 [Pr.88], 315n4 [Pr.100]

Republic, 13, 20, 37n96, 117, 175, 254n5 [Pr.87], 278n8 [Pr.92], 315n4 [Pr.100]

Seventh Letter, 19

Symposium, 19, 201n19

Thaetetus, 20, 239n3 [Pr.24]

theoria, 19, 24

Timaeus ("likely story," verisimilitude and truthlikeness). *See* truthlikeness

play, 85, 261 [Pr.89]

Plotinus, 20, 36, 151, 181, 253n5 [Pr.87]

Poison Arrow, Parable of, 87, 202n21

Porete, Marguerite, 11, 47, 178n32

Porphyry, 37

possession (divine), 13, 17–18, 20, 58–59, 150n124

potential/potency, 139, 258n11 [Pr.88], 269 [Pr.90b], 269n9 [Pr.90b]. *See also* Aristotle; Cusa, Nicholas of

powers (lower and higher powers of the soul), 101n65, 139–41, 152, 157–62, 166, 175, 229 [Pr.52], 235–38 [Pr.2], 246 [Pr.40], 277–78 [Pr.92], 289 [Pr.94], 291 [Pr.95a], 293 [Pr.95a], 297–98 [Pr.95b], 309 [Pr.97], 320–21 [Pr.106a], 324 [Pr.106b], 327 [Pr.106c], 330 [Pr.106d], 330n10 [Pr.106d], 339 [Pr.108]; attunement of, 161–63, 258 [Pr.88], 258n11 [Pr.88], *see also* metaphor: ordering

pragmatic/practical, 87–88, 90, 92, 176, 178–82, 190, 194–97, 203, 260–61 [Pr.89], 337 [Pr.108], 339 [Pr.108]

pratfall effect, 99

Proclus, 10n6, 37, 38, 46, 47, 55

prohairesis, 22, 23

Prometheus, 313 [Pr.98], 313n30 [Pr.98]

pseudonymity, 25, 58–59

purpose. *See* meaning

Pythagoreans, 18, 200

Quine, Willard Van Orman, 45

Quint, Josef, 241n10 [Pr.24], 244n8 [Pr.40]

Radcliffe, Timothy, 66

Raft, Parable of the, 180, 191

Ramelli, Ilaria, 158n169, 290n327 [Pr.94]

resurrection, 25, 26

renunciation/denial/forsaking, 95, 168, 243 [Pr.40], 294 [Pr.95a], 300 [Pr.95b], 332 [Pr.107], 334 [Pr.107], 334n22 [Pr.107], 341 [XXIV,2]

rhetoric, 51, 55, 59, 61, 64, 75–76, 92, 105, 108, 113, 187, 199, 232n26 [Pr.52], 303n2 [Pr.96]

of this book, 2, 64

dangerous, 118

devices, 5, 106–7

of the individual, 46, 163–64

"new and unusual" (*nova et rara*), 3, 5, 5n7, 6, 25, 120, 188, 239 [Pr.24]

omission, 56, 75, 91, 97

rash, 99

repetition, 90, 91, 97, 123n53, 190, 225, 239 [Pr.24], 240n7 [Pr.24], 256n26 [Pr.87]

shocking, 1, 3, 4, 96n45, 99, 121, 164

in vernacular works, 13

Richard of Middleton. *See* Middleton, Richard of

Richard of St. Victor, 53n166

Ruh, Kurt, 46

"running about" (motion of the mind), 148, 342 [XXIV,2], 342n18 [XXIV,2]. *See also* motion

"rushing ahead" (faith and knowledge), 35, 77, 88, 93, 93n20, 177, 194, 196–97, 203, 316n6 [Pr.100]

Saint-Pourçain, Durandus of. *See* Durandus of Saint-Pourçain

sapere aude, 194

Schopenhauer, Arthur, 80n20, 193, 197, 204

Schürmann, Reiner, 156, 227n2 [Pr.52], 234n6 [Pr.2], 236n10 [Pr.2], 237n14 [Pr.2]

self. *See* individual

Senner, Walter, 67

shock. *See* rhetoric

sin, 33, 34, 34n85, 36, 47, 124, 157n168, 162–63, 186–87, 186n70, 253 [Pr.87], 253n5 [Pr.87], 256 [Pr.87], 261 [Pr.89], 272 [Pr.91], 274 [Pr.91], 277 [Pr.92], 281–82 [Pr.93], 304–5 [Pr.96], 310 [Pr.97], 332 [Pr.107], 338 [Pr.108]

Smith, Cyprian, 78–79, 81–82, 82n23, 96n45, 158n169, 195, 197, 198

Smith, Huston, 1, 195, 204, 205–6

Socrates. *See* Plato

"something" (*etwaz*) in the soul, 102n70, 104, 201, 229 [Pr.52], 229n13 [Pr.52], 237 [Pr.2], 237n13 [Pr.2], 240 [Pr.24], 240n5 [Pr.24], 275n32 [Pr.91], 290 [Pr.94], 290n40 [Pr.94], 317 [Pr.100], 317n18 [Pr.100], 317n24 [Pr.100]

Song of Songs, 25, 29

soul: immortality of, 18, 137, 163, 342 [XXIV,2]; as uncreated, 164

sound, 80–82, 106, 134, 204

Stoicism, 22

Sturlese, Loris, 47

surprise, 1, 2, 3, 69–71, 75, 96, 99–100, 102, 191

Suso, Henry, 9, 9n2

Suzuki, Daisetz, 83, 84, 84n28

synderesis (striving, thirst for God), 22, 34–35, 38, 96, 116, 146, 150, 174, 193, 228 [Pr.52], 258n11 [Pr.88], 321 [Pr.106a], 332 [Pr.107]

synkatathesis, 22

Talks of Instruction. *See Councils on Discernment*

Tauler, Johannes, 9, 199

teleology, 5, 16, 178–79, 201n20

Tempier, Étienne (Stephen), 9, 47; condemnation of 1277, 9–10

Thales, 18

Theologia Germanica (*Theologia Deutsch*), 9

theophany, 38–40

theurgy, 37

Thierry, William of, Saint, 49

"this or that" (*hoc et hoc*), "neither this nor that" (*noch diz noch daz*), 230n15 [Pr.52], 237 [Pr.2], 237n12 [Pr.2], 238 [Pr.2], 240 [Pr.24]

time, 109, 111, 184–85, 241 [Pr.24], 249 [Pr.54a], 322 [Pr.106a], 327–28 [Pr.106c]; cyclic conception of 16, 18, 24, 25; linear conception of, 24, 199

Tobin, Frank, 178n32, 245n9 [Pr.40]

"total understanding" (Lévi-Strauss), 14, 15, 204

transcendence, 28, 197, 202

transcendentals, 20, 29, 89, 89n7, 104n75, 120, 143, 173, 174, 181

Trinity, 4

truth, 12, 22, 28–32, 39, 44, 57, 64, 67, 71, 73, 74, 89, 89n7, 90, 94, 100, 101, 107, 122, 134, 143, 173, 181, 189, 190–91, 197, 199, 200, 205, 227–28 [Pr.52], 250 [Pr.54a], 270 [Pr.90b], 277 [Pr.92], 281 [Pr.93], 292 [Pr.95a], 313 [Pr.98]

truthlikeness, 21–22, 44, 64, 149, 151, 194

undergoing. *See* passivity/receptivity

understanding. *See* knowledge

unfamiliar. *See* familiar

union/unity. *See* oneness

univocity, 102–4

unknowing, 96, 134, 134n29, 138, 140, 142, 176, 229–30 [Pr.52], 232n25 [Pr.52], 310 [Pr.97], 317 [Pr.100]

unusual (rhetoric). *See* rhetoric

verisimilitude. *See* truthlikeness

viriditas. *See* metaphor: greenness

vita activa. *See* activity/work

vita contemplativa. *See* passivity/receptivity

voluntas, 22

Walshe, Maurice O'Connell, 105n80, 239n4 [Pr.24], 241n8 [Pr.24], 243n2 [Pr.40], 244 [Pr.40], 245n9 [Pr.40], 247n1 [Pr.54a], 251n5 [Pr.64]

Ware, William of, 43n123

Weigel, Valentin, 55

Wetz, Franz Josef, 72–73

"Wild One," 9

will. *See* free will; God: will; individual: will

William of Ockham. *See* Ockham, William of

wonder/awe, 239 [Pr.24], 239n3 [Pr.24], 293 [Pr.95a]

Word, 41, 80, 100, 147, 156, 187, 341 [XXIV,2]; birth of the Word in the soul, *see* metaphor: birth of the Word in the soul; as image of the Father, 26; made flesh, 1, 183; why, *see* living without a why; meaning

Zen. *See* Buddhism

www.ingramcontent.com/pod-product-compliance
Lightning Source LLC
Chambersburg PA
CBHW070247010526
44107CB00056B/2367